D1521318

# The Tanner Lectures on Human Values

# THE TANNER LECTURES

# ON HUMAN VALUES

23

2002

Richardson, Kentridge, Hrdy, Raz,
Pinsky, Nehamas, Appiah, Allison

Grethe B. Peterson, *Editor*

THE UNIVERSITY OF UTAH PRESS
Salt Lake City

THE TANNER LECTURES ON HUMAN VALUES
was set in Garamond by The Typeworks, Vancouver, BC, Canada

# THE TANNER LECTURES ON HUMAN VALUES

The purpose of the Tanner Lectures is to advance and reflect upon scholarly and scientific learning that relates to human values.

To receive an appointment as a Tanner lecturer is a recognition of uncommon capabilities and outstanding scholarly or leadership achievement in the field of human values. The lecturers may be drawn from philosophy, religion, the humanities and sciences, the creative arts and learned professions, or from leadership in public or private affairs. The lectureships are international and intercultural and transcend ethnic, national, religious, or ideological distinctions.

The Tanner Lectures were formally founded on July 1, 1978, at Clare Hall, Cambridge University. They were established by the American scholar, industrialist, and philanthropist, Obert Clark Tanner. In creating the lectureships, Professor Tanner said, "I hope these lectures will contribute to the intellectual and moral life of mankind. I see them simply as a search for a better understanding of human behavior and human values. This understanding may be pursued for its own intrinsic worth, but it may also eventually have practical consequences for the quality of personal and social life."

Permanent Tanner lectureships, with lectures given annually, are established at nine institutions: Clare Hall, Cambridge University; Harvard University; Brasenose College, Oxford University; Princeton University; Stanford University; the University of California; the University of Michigan; the University of Utah; and Yale University. Other international lectureships occasionally take place. The institutions are selected by the Trustees.

The sponsoring institutions have full autonomy in the appointment of their lecturers. A major part of the lecture program is the publication and distribution of the Lectures in an annual volume.

The Tanner Lectures on Human Values is a nonprofit corporation administered at the University of Utah under the direction of a self-perpetuating, international Board of Trustees. The Trustees meet annually to enact policies that will ensure the quality of the lectureships.

The entire lecture program, including the costs of administration, is fully and generously funded in perpetuity by an endowment to the University of Utah by Professor Tanner and Mrs. Grace Adams Tanner.

Obert C. Tanner was born in Farmington, Utah, in 1904. He was educated at the University of Utah, Harvard University, and Stanford University. He served on the faculty at Stanford University and was a professor of philosophy at the University of Utah for twenty-eight years. Mr. Tanner was also the founder and chairman of the O. C. Tanner Company, the world's largest manufacturer of recognition award products.

Harvard University's former president Derek Bok once spoke of Obert Tanner as a "Renaissance Man," citing his remarkable achievements in three of life's major pursuits: business, education, and public service.

Obert C. Tanner died in Palm Springs, California, on October 14, 1993, at the age of eighty-nine.

GRETHE B. PETERSON
*University of Utah*

# CONTENTS

# PREFACE TO VOLUME 23

Volume 23 of the Tanner Lectures on Human Values includes lectures delivered during the academic year 2000–2001.

The Tanner Lectures are published in an annual volume.

In addition to the Lectures on Human Values, the Trustees of the Tanner Lectures have funded special international lectureships at selected colleges and universities which are administered independently of the permanent lectures.

# Reconceiving Health Care To Improve Quality

*WILLIAM C. RICHARDSON*

THE TANNER LECTURES ON HUMAN VALUES

Delivered at

University of California, Santa Barbara
January 29, 2001

WILLIAM C. RICHARDSON is president and chief executive officer of the W. K. Kellogg Foundation. He is also professor and president emeritus of the Johns Hopkins University. He was educated at Trinity College, Connecticut, and at the University of Chicago, where he received his Ph.D. He was executive vice president and provost of the Pennsylvania State University, and was dean of the Graduate School and vice provost for research of the University of Washington. He is a member of the Institute of Medicine of the National Academy of Sciences and a fellow of the American Academy of Arts and Sciences and the American Public Health Association. He has served in many capacities in the U. S. Department of Health, Education and Welfare, and the U. S. Department of Health and Human Services; on advisory committees for the Robert Wood Johnson Foundation, the Rockefeller Foundation, and the Pew Charitable Trusts; and on the board of trustees of the Henry J. Kaiser Family Foundation and the Glenmede Trust Company. He is currently serving on the board of the Council of Michigan Foundations and as chairman of the board of trustees of the Council on Foundations. He is the author of numerous articles, monographs, and reports on issues related to public health.

Good evening and thank you for the warm welcome.

Our society and economy have been undergoing some marked changes over the past twenty years. My topic this evening is envisioning a new set of relationships in health care and a degree of professional and organizational rearrangement that reflect these changes and that will, in the process, materially improve health care quality (Institute of Medicine 2000).

Let me begin with the basic premise of any encounter or relationship with a health care provider. We expect—at the very least—to be the better for it, and certainly no worse off. Since the days of ancient Greece, "First, do no harm" has been the first principle of medicine.

A little over a year ago, however, the Institute of Medicine of the National Academy of Sciences (which I will refer to as the IOM) released a groundbreaking report on medical errors that suggested we *are* doing harm (Institute of Medicine 2000). Although we have, in many ways, the world's finest health care system, the report found a surprisingly high level of medical errors. And, although Americans are healthier and are living longer than ever, our over-stressed health care establishment too often fails to insure the basic safety of its patients.

The report received extraordinary media attention—two days of near-saturation coverage on the national networks and a great deal of local media coverage as well. Further, the story turned out to have what some refer to as "legs." I don't think there has been a week in the last year that there wasn't some national coverage of the medical errors issue, except maybe the second week of November.

Naturally, much of the media's attention focused on the statistics and personal stories related to medical errors. And these are certainly a vital aspect of the quality problem. But this evening I'd like to offer something of a sequel to the medical errors report. A range of pertinent demographic trends; technical, scientific, and societal developments; and changes in health care have been discussed by members of the IOM Committee that was responsible for the errors report. Based on these

This lecture draws heavily on the deliberations and contributions of members of the Committee on the Quality of Health Care in America, which I chair. The first report of this Institute of Medicine Committee is a key source, as are sections of our committee's second report, available in the spring of 2001.

discussions, I will provide an overview of what a safer and more patient-centered health care system might look like. I think the ideas that are emerging can reduce medical errors but also lead to a much more effective and productive health care enterprise. Our report on these broader considerations should be out in early spring 2001 (Institute of Medicine 2001).

But first let me provide a brief recap.

In December 1999, along with several health care leaders, I joined President Clinton at the White House to discuss the implications of the medical errors report. As I said, the report had made headline news across the country, but as important to me was the groundswell of public interest that was prompted by its release. For weeks afterward the Institute of Medicine was flooded with calls from hundreds of people who had questions or personal stories to share. (The number I received personally was startling.) The report clearly touched a nerve with the American people. While health policy can be highly technical and obscure, everyone can relate to the tragedy of a serious medical mistake.

Local and national and private and public sector leaders have all taken notice. Many professional groups (such as the American Medical Association, American Nurses Association, American Hospital Association, American College of Physicians/American Society of Internal Medicine, American College of Surgeons, American Board of Medical Specialties, and the Accreditation Council for Graduate Medical Education, to name but a few) are taking action, including institutional practices, a careful examination of the roles of board certification and recertification, and undergraduate, graduate, and continuing health professions education in improving safety. The business community, including the Business Roundtable and the National Business Coalition on Health, has announced purchasing initiatives to promote patient safety. Last November the so-called Leapfrog Group unveiled a market-based strategy to improve safety and quality, including encouraging the use of computerized physician-order entry, evidence-based hospital referrals, and the use of intensive care units staffed by physicians credentialed in critical care medicine.

The Clinton administration and the Congress have also been active. The Senate held its first hearings on the issue within a few weeks of the report's release, and additional hearings were conducted by committees of both the House and the Senate. The administration launched an ambitious plan of federal action to reduce medical errors. In general, then, there is broad bipartisan support for taking action, and I would be surprised if quality of health care were not a significant issue for the Bush administration.

What the report found, after an exhaustive review of the literature, was a staggering number of medical errors. Based on the findings of one major study, about 44,000 patients die each year from medical errors in hospitals alone (Thomas et al. 2000). Another study puts that figure even higher, at 98,000 patients a year (Leape et al. 1991). Even if we use the 44,000 patient figure, medical mistakes in hospitals rank eighth in the United States among the leading causes of death. More people die each year in the United States from medical errors, for example, than from traffic accidents, breast cancer, or AIDS.

Within a short time of the report's release, some began to question the numbers. "Could the problem really be this serious?" they asked. We will never know the exact number of medical errors, but there is little doubt that the evidence is strong and consistent. Let me take a moment to point out several things about the nature of the evidence base. First, the conclusions of the IOM Committee were not based on just these two studies. There are two large studies—the Harvard Medical Practice Study using about 30,000 medical records and a study in Colorado and Utah (Thomas et al. 2000; Leape et al. 1991) based on about 15,000 records—and more than thirty others (chapter 2 in Institute of Medicine 2000) in leading peer-reviewed journals in the last ten years.

Second, in some ways, we have really only looked "under the lamp post" for errors. Nearly all studies focus on hospital settings, yet most care is delivered in doctors' offices, ambulatory surgery centers, clinics, patients' homes, and nursing homes. Granted, most would concur that the hospital is a higher-risk environment for errors, because patients in hospitals are generally receiving more medical interventions and more drugs, sometimes under hurried or critical circumstances. But we have seen a steady migration of many procedures such as some laparoscopic surgery to ambulatory settings. One study has found that some 7,000 patients die each year just from medication errors that occur both in and out of hospitals (Phillips et al. 1998).

Third, most studies identify errors from information that is documented in handwritten medical records. It is likely that many errors never get documented in medical records. Providers are acutely aware of liability concerns. In addition, some errors are not recognized or noticed by clinicians. Studies that rely on "automated signals" to detect errors (such as abnormal or unexpected laboratory test results) reveal higher rates of errors than do studies that rely on the documentation or reporting of errors by clinicians (Classen et al. 1991).

At this point, anyone who is not familiar with the report might gather that it is an indictment of health professionals. But this is not at all the case. Indeed, a main conclusion of the report is that no particular group or entity is to blame. A fundamental conclusion is that this is not a "bad apple" problem. And indeed that pinpointing and placing blame is actually a counterproductive exercise. To reduce medical errors and improve patient safety we need to recognize this as a systems problem.

The comprehensive strategy put forth by the IOM report calls for action by government, industry, consumers, and health care providers. The report notes that it may be human to err, but it's also human to create solutions, find better alternatives, and devise new approaches for the challenges ahead. In order to meet these challenges, however, we must first face facts. Our health care system is a decade or more behind other high-risk industries in its attention to ensuring basic safety. The ordinary risk of dying in a domestic airline flight or at the workplace has declined dramatically in recent decades. That is due in part to increased attention by industry efforts, and in part because federal agencies were created to improve safety. Drawing on these models, my colleagues and I urge several courses of action, which are detailed in the report. Let me just quickly summarize them here before moving on to the topic of quality of health care more broadly defined.

First, we urged Congress to create a national center to set national safety goals, track progress in meeting them, and support research to learn more about preventing errors. It would also act as a clearinghouse—an objective source of the latest information on patient safety for the nation. I am pleased to say that prompt action has been taken.

We also recommend that a nationwide, mandatory public reporting system be established by the states. Currently, only about one-third of the states have reporting requirements. And yet, this information is critical if we are to learn, in any systematic way, about practices that lead to serious injury or death. It's not unlike our being required to report serious traffic accidents or deaths from workplace accidents. During the last year, the National Academy for State Health Policy has convened leaders from both the legislative and executive branches of the states to discuss approaches to improving safety and with the support of private foundations has recently completed an inventory of current state reporting initiatives (National Academy for State Health Policy, forthcoming).

At the same time, we also recommend federal legislation to protect the confidentiality of certain information. This protection would cover medical mistakes that do not result in harm—so-called near misses— where information is collected and analyzed solely to improve safety and quality. Such legislation would encourage the growth of voluntary, confidential reporting systems so that practitioners and health organizations can correct problems before serious harm occurs. Without such legislation, a doctor or hospital may be afraid to gather such information, for fear that it would be subpoenaed and used to establish a pattern of error in a subsequent lawsuit.

Again, the majority of errors in hospitals do not result from impaired professionals or recklessness. Most mistakes occur because of basic flaws in how elements of the health system are designed and organized. For example, equipment controls that vary from one manufacturer to another, or from year to year, can contribute to errors. Stocking patient care units with drugs that are potentially lethal unless they're diluted has led to deadly overdoses. And, because of illegible handwriting in medical records, patients have been given drugs in wrong doses or given drugs to which they have a known allergy.

There is no single solution sufficient to bring about the degree of needed change. Rather, we should think and act systemically, to create an environment where safety will become a top priority for health care organizations and providers. The goal here is not to blame individuals or to seek retribution. Instead, we want to design new systems that prevent, detect, and minimize hazards and the likelihood of error. In short, we want to create a new culture of safety in the American health care system. We want a system in which it is hard to make a mistake.

We are not, however, calling for a nationwide master plan to solve the problem of patient safety. The American health system doesn't work that way. There are too many markets and too many variables. What works well for the Henry Ford Health System in Detroit may not be applicable in Santa Barbara—much less in Maine.

While the findings on medical errors are sobering, perhaps more sobering is the realization that medical errors are but one manifestation of an even larger problem. Medical errors, the failure to execute a care plan as intended, are not the only type of "system weakness." There is ample and growing evidence that much of health care is not strongly science-based (Schuster et al. 2001). In many instances, patients don't receive effective care. That is, many people receive services for which the potential risks exceed potential benefits—some call this "overuse." Others do not receive services from which they would likely benefit—generally called "underuse."

The most extensive reviews of the literature on quality have been conducted by colleagues at RAND (Schuster et al. 1998). The RAND review now includes over 100 publications in leading peer-reviewed journals documenting overuse, underuse, and errors (Schuster et al. 2001). Overuse of health services is common. Examples include performance of surgery for hysterectomy, coronary artery bypass graft, and other procedures without appropriate reasons; provision of antibiotics for the common cold and other viral upper respiratory tract infections for which they are ineffective; and insertion of tubes in children's ears in the absence of clinically appropriate indications.

Underuse is also a serious concern for all types of clinical conditions. In a study of approximately 3,700 Medicare patients with a diagnosis of heart attack and eligible for treatment with beta blockers, only 21 percent received beta blockers within 90 days of discharge. The adjusted mortality rate for patients with treatment was 43 percent less than that of patients without treatment (Soumerai et al. 1997). Another study found that an estimated 18,000 people die each year from heart attacks because they do not receive effective interventions (Chassin 1997).

Overall, it is not an overstatement to say that the health care delivery system is unable to provide consistently high-quality care. Or said another way, many people simply do not benefit from what medicine has to offer. There is a large "quality gap." Several expert panels in recent years have come to this conclusion (President's Advisory Commission 1998; Chassin et al. 1998). One example would be the IOM National Cancer Policy Board. Its report *Ensuring Quality Cancer Care* (Institute of Medicine 1999) examined the quality of cancer care in depth and concluded that there is a large gap between what care should be and the care that many patients actually experience.

The significance of the report *To Err Is Human* (Institute of Medicine 2000) was not that it reinforced the messages of these other reports, but that it focused on one readily understandable aspect of quality—medical errors—and it communicated this problem effectively to a very broad audience, including the lay public.

These panels, of course, are not the only groups that have been raising issues about quality. The Institute for Healthcare Improvement, the National Committee for Quality Assurance, the Foundation for Accountability, many local institutions (such as the Institute for Clinical Systems Improvement in Minnesota), and others have been calling for action to address quality concerns for some time.

All of these efforts have contributed to what I think is a "sea change" in the way health care leaders, policymakers, purchasers, physicians, nurses, and, increasingly, consumers view quality. This range of activity has achieved widespread recognition that quality in health care is not what it should be and that this is a problem that must be dealt with. We have in many ways turned a corner, with much change now possible that wasn't possible just a few years ago.

Not only is there increased recognition that we have a serious problem, but there is also recognition that we cannot address it successfully by simply tweaking today's health care system. Telling providers to work harder on coming up with more quality measurement tools just isn't going to be enough. Fundamental change is needed in how we organize and deliver health care; and for this to happen, we need far-reaching changes in the culture of medicine and in the environment in which health care is provided.

As we chart a course for the redesign of health care, it is helpful to understand some of the major technological and demographic forces that are currently shaping it and will continue to do so in the future. There are three that I would like to highlight—the rapidly expanding knowledge base; demographic changes, leading most notably to the prevalence of chronic disease in the population; and information technology.

The quality gap is attributable in part to the extraordinary increase in medical knowledge and technology in recent decades. Starting in the mid-1960s and continuing to this day, investment in biomedical research, public and private, has increased in inflation-adjusted dollars (National Institutes of Health 2000). These investments have clearly paid off in terms of new knowledge, procedures, drugs, and medical devices. For example, laparoscopic surgery has dramatically changed the functional impact of many procedures, such as cholescystectomy; and thrombolytic therapy has had a major influence on the treatment of persons with heart attacks.

These innovations in medicine have significantly, and positively, affected the health of the population. Yet they also pose a challenge for health care practitioners who want to keep their skills up to date. Just reading about advances—let alone active training in or experience with new techniques—is a daunting task. For instance, the number of citations reporting on randomized controlled trials has increased from an average of 509 annually in the 1970s to over 10,000 annually today (Chassin 1998). Although no practitioner needs to follow advances across all areas of medicine and surgery, rapid expansion of knowledge is occurring even within specific areas. I have been told that the number of randomized controlled trials published on diabetes in these same periods, the 1970s to the 1990s, increased from a few (less than ten) per year to well over 150 per year.

The process of diffusing knowledge and new tools is also quite slow. The lag between discovery of more efficacious forms of treatment and their incorporation into routine patient care is in the fifteen- to twenty-year range (Balas and Boren 2000). And if we can't keep up now, how will we respond to the extraordinary advances that will emerge during this new century?

Another consequence of advances in medical science, technology, and health care delivery is that people are now living longer. Although health care is by no means the only factor that affects morbidity and mortality, innovations in medical science and technology have contributed greatly to the increase in life expectancy. As a result of changing mortality patterns, those age sixty-five and over constitute an increasingly large number and proportion of the U.S. population. In 1994 this age group accounted for approximately one in eight persons, or 13 percent of the population (National Center for Health Statistics 1999). In 2030, when the large baby boom cohorts have become elders, one person in five, or 20 percent, is expected to be in the sixty-five and over age group. The very old, of course, are also growing in numbers and as a proportion of the population.

The increasing likelihood of survival due to scientific and technologic advances will continue to result in larger proportions of people with continuing morbidity and disability. Chronic conditions are now the leading cause of illness, disability, and death and account for about 70 percent of care (Hoffman et al. 1996). Almost 100 million people in the United States have one or more chronic conditions (Robert Wood Johnson Foundation 1996).

These demographic changes have very important implications for the organization of the health care delivery system, but we have yet to address them in any significant way. In many cases we are organized for and oriented to acute care, while the majority of health care resources are now being devoted to the treatment of chronic disease. There is a dearth of clinical programs with the infrastructure to provide the full complement of services needed by people with heart disease, diabetes, asthma, or other common chronic conditions. Most people with these conditions require care from multiple providers and across multiple settings over long periods. Effective and efficient care of this population necessitates a well-organized program, which would include:

- an interdisciplinary team,
- mechanisms for ongoing communication and coordination of services across providers and settings,
- education programs and communication mechanisms directed at patients, their families, and other informal caregivers,
- a formally organized care process designed to achieve best practice, and
- the ability to measure both medical care process and patient outcomes for purposes of quality improvement.

And providing state-of-the-art health care to a mostly chronically ill population is further complicated by the fact that many have co-morbid conditions. About 44 percent of those with a chronic condition have more than one condition (Robert Wood Johnson Foundation 1996).

Our challenge, then, is to move from the highly decentralized, often cottage industry that we have now to one that can provide excellent tertiary intervention and care, both primary and preventive care, and, increasingly, the necessary "packages" of services that are needed for care of the chronically ill. We fall particularly short in this last category.

It is true that the health care sector is more complex than other industries. I think it is probably the most complex industry. There are large number of conditions and ailments, and in some important respects each patient is unique.

But I would suggest that the heavy focus in health care on the clinical needs of individual patients has in some ways blinded us to some of the principles that have guided the development of better systems in other industries. The so-called 80/20 rule should apply to health care.

For example, a study at one health maintenance organization found that 78 percent of direct medical costs were attributable to just twenty-five acute and chronic conditions and that three cardiovascular conditions (ischemic heart disease, hypertension, and congestive heart failure) accounted for 17 percent of these costs (Ray et al. 2000).

The Agency for Health Care Research and Quality in its work on the Medical Expenditure Panel Survey identifies a limited number of "priority conditions" (Medical Expenditure Panel Survey 2000). These conditions account for a sizable proportion of the national health burden. They include cancer, diabetes, emphysema, and hypertension. If we were to make it a *priority* to develop well-organized care programs based on "best practices" for this limited number of conditions, we would be well on our way to addressing many quality problems.

In following the 80/20 approach, we determine what work is routine and design a simple, standard, and low-cost process to perform this work efficiently and reliably. This not only results in safer, higher-quality, and more reliable health care for common conditions but frees up resources and the time of highly skilled clinicians to focus on the more unusual, complex cases. Standardizing care processes doesn't mean "one size fits all." As I said a moment ago, patients are not the same. They have a range of preferences, and some have special needs. In other industries, we use what is called mass customization to standardize common services needed by many patients, while customizing or tailoring other aspects of services to respond to particular preferences and needs.

As we struggle to address this challenge, we must also keep in mind that the health care industry is changing at an extraordinary rate. Our efforts to narrow the quality gap will be far more successful if they are congruent with the ways in which the industry is being transformed by information technology and consumerism. As the saying goes, it is easier to ride a horse in the direction it is going.

The Internet places us on the threshold of a change that is reshaping virtually all aspects of society, including health care delivery. The Internet supports rising consumerism, with greater demands for information and convenience in all areas of commerce. The effect of these trends on health care will likely be a fundamental transformation in how services are organized and delivered and how doctors and patients interact with each other.

To better understand how information technology can contribute to quality improvement, our IOM Committee convened a special workshop. The participants identified five key areas where information technology can make a difference.

The first area is translating science into practice. Through more effective use of the Internet, we can help providers gain better access to the medical science base. The Internet has opened up many new opportunities to make evidence, both primary publications and secondary analyses, more accessible to clinicians. The efforts of the National Library of Medicine, through Medline, are particularly promising. Medline contains more than 9 million citations and abstracts to articles drawn mainly from professional journals (Miller et al. 2000). In June 1997 the Library of Medicine made Medline on the Web available free of charge. Usage jumped about ten-fold, to 75 million searches annually (Lindberg and Humphreys 1998).

Second, information technology also facilitates consumer access to health information. Patients and their families will be far more effective caregivers (and team members) if they are knowledgeable about their health conditions, options for treatment, and expected outcomes. Some 77 million Americans retrieve health-related information annually (Morrison 1999), but the volume of health-related information can be overwhelming. There are some 61,000 web sites that contain information on breast cancer and about 40,000 for diabetes (Boodman 1999; National Research Council 2000). This information is of varying quality—some is incorrect and some is misleading. In 1998 the Library of Medicine started Medline Plus, a web site for consumers. Medline Plus includes information on more than 300 health topics and also contains links to reputable web sites maintained by professional associations and other government agencies.

The third area is the collection and sharing of clinical information. Perhaps the single most important contribution of information technology will be to supplement paper medical records, which are so often illegible or incomplete. Handwritten orders are a major source of medical errors. Paper records are often unavailable, which contributes to many unnecessary services, especially repeat laboratory and radiology services. I realize there are important confidentiality and data security issues to be resolved, but we can and must work our way through them. We shouldn't deny patients the very important benefits of automated clinical information, which include improved quality, safety, convenience, and efficiency.

Fourth, information technology can help reduce errors by standardizing and automating certain decisions and by identifying errors before they occur—errors such as adverse drug interactions. Computerized drug prescribing has great potential to have a positive impact on dosing calculations and scheduling, drug selection, screening for interactions, monitoring and documenting adverse side effects, and other areas. Yet comprehensive medication order entry systems have been implemented in only a limited number of health care settings.

Fifth, information technology can change the way individuals receive care and interact with their providers. Instead of a $65 office visit and a half-day off work, a ten-minute e-mail communication could meet the patient's needs. Similarly, patients will be able to go online to get test results, inform their physicians about how they are doing, participate in interactive disease management services, and receive after-care instructions. Touch and face-to-face interaction will always be important. The essence of high-quality health care is a "healing relationship." But in many instances face-to-face encounters are neither needed nor wanted by the patient or clinician.

Of course, there are challenges we must confront to take advantage of the many beneficial applications that information technology (IT) has to offer. First and foremost are privacy considerations. The public have been given little information to help them evaluate the many benefits of IT, while at the same time they have heard potential horror stories that can come from automated personal health information. There is a very real need to open the dialogue and inform public debate in this area. For an interesting example of how public concerns about privacy can halt efforts to advance our use of IT, we need only look back two years, when the Department of Health and Human Services halted plans to establish a unique patient identifier in response to public outcry over potential violations of medical privacy (Goldman 1998).

Second, the lack of national standards for the collection, coding, and sharing of data is also viewed by many as an impediment to moving forward. The efforts of the National Committee for Vital and Health Statistics are very important in moving us forward in this area. Progress has been slow.

Third, significant financial investments in IT will be needed—far greater than the current investments being made by most health care organizations. Capital will be required to purchase and install new technology. The installation of new computerized systems often produces temporary disruptions in the delivery of patient care. Considerable specialized training and education will be needed to help the workforce adapt to a new environment. These capital decisions must be made in an environment where benefits are hard to quantify. Unlike capital investments in new medical technology, which immediately generate revenues under our predominantly fee-for-service system of payment, IT investments to automate clinical data have only an indirect effect on the bottom line.

Lastly, not all patients will take advantage of the opportunities afforded by information technology. There will be a need to operate the "old" and the "new" delivery systems in parallel.

It is not possible to foresee all the new organizations, forces, technologies, needs, and relationships that will develop in the health care system over the coming decade. The IOM Committee is attempting to specify some general *aims* that the system should try to achieve and what might be called some rules for the road. Our framework is based on an understanding of systems that can self-organize to achieve a shared purpose and improve by adhering to well-thought-out general rules.

Our report on twenty-first-century health care will be released early this spring, so this is still a work in progress; but I can share with you some of our thinking. First, let me again emphasize that fundamental change is needed. The American people should get a much higher return on their investment in health care than they currently do.

The IOM Committee has identified six Aims for Improvement—six dimensions of quality where, we believe, today's health system functions at far lower levels than it should. Health care should be:

- Safe: avoiding injuries to patients from the care that is intended to help them.
- Effective: providing services based on scientific knowledge to all who could benefit and refraining from providing services not likely to benefit (avoiding overuse and underuse).
- Patient-centered: providing care that is respectful and responsive to individual patient preferences, needs, and values; and assuring that patient values guide all clinical decisions.
- Timely: reducing waits and sometimes harmful delays for both those who receive care and those who give care.
- Efficient: avoiding waste, including waste of equipment, supplies, ideas, and energy; and

- Equitable: providing care that does not vary in quality because
  of personal characteristics such as gender, ethnicity, geographic
  location, or socioeconomic status.

A health care system that achieves major gains in these six dimensions would be a great benefit for patients.

The culture of medicine and the roles of physicians, nurses, and other clinicians and the clinician/patient relationship are all likely to change substantially over the coming decade.

To help guide this transition, we have been formulating ten "simple" rules in our IOM Committee work.

First, care should be based on continuous healing relationships. In today's health system the product of health care is the visit or hospital episode. In the future the product of the health care field will be the "healing relationship." In the current framework of health care delivery, interaction and relationship are regarded more as a toll on health care than as one of its goals or products. The system today often acts as if interactions and relationships were an added burden for the real care process. In the twenty-first-century health system, interaction is not the price of care, it is care. In practical terms, care based on continuous healing relationships means that the health care system should be responsive at all times. It also means that care should be provided in many forms, including over the Internet and by telephone, not just through face-to-face visits.

Second is customization based on patient needs and values. I've already mentioned the concept of "mass customization" in other industries. In health care, customization means that the system of care should be designed to meet the most common types of needs but have the capability to respond to individual patient preferences and choices.

Third is the patient as the source of control. Patients should be given the necessary information and opportunity to exercise the degree of control they choose over health care decisions affecting them. Throughout most of the twentieth century the physician has served as the principal care provider, exercising a great deal of authority and autonomy. In the twenty-first century the role of the physician, in addition to providing highly technical services, will more likely be that of a "care partner" and coach. The notion is sometimes called "patient-centered care," and it means that control over care and choices resides more in the patient. To be sure, it takes time for patients to be included as partners in care, and they'll often need to be coached in this new role. However, in settings where this has occurred, its value has been shown by medical research. In sixteen of twenty-one studies published in recent years, patients who partnered with physicians were more likely to follow treatment advice (Stewart 1995). This held true for a range of health problems, including breast cancer, diabetes, hypertension, headaches, and gastrointestinal disease. This rule is not intended to imply that patients should be forced to share decision-making, only that it should be possible for them to exercise the degree of control they wish.

Fourth is shared knowledge and the free flow of information. Patients should have unfettered access to their own medical information and to clinical knowledge. This rule goes hand in hand with the preceding ones. It recognizes that information is the key to the patient-clinician relationship and that in most instances the exchange of information is the essence of the healing relationship.

Fifth is evidence-based decision-making. Patients should receive care based on the best available scientific knowledge. I've already discussed the importance of moving toward science-based practice. Another general rule is best practice based on systematically acquired evidence. In the twentieth century a commitment to autonomy of clinical decision-making has been a fundamental health care value. In the future a commitment to excellence—standardization to the best-known method, given the patient's circumstances—should be preeminent.

Sixth is safety as a system property. Threats to patient safety are the end result of complex causes such as faulty equipment, system design, and the interplay of human factors such as fatigue, limitations on memory, and distraction. The way to improve safety is to learn about causes of error and to use this knowledge to design systems of care to prevent error when possible, to make visible those errors that do occur (so that they can be intercepted), and to mitigate the harm done when an error does reach the patient.

Seventh, transparency is necessary. The health care system should make information available to patients and their families that allows them to make informed decisions when selecting a health plan, hospital, or clinical practice or choosing between alternative treatments.

Eighth is anticipation of needs. The health system should anticipate patient needs, rather than simply reacting to events. Our current health care system works largely in a reactive mode. The twenty-first-century system should organize health care to predict and anticipate need based on knowledge of patients, local conditions, and the natural history of illness.

Ninth, waste should be continuously reduced. The health system should not waste resources or patient time. Members of the committee do not believe that increased value will come by stressing the current system—that is, by asking people to work harder, faster, and longer. Rather, increased value will come from systematically developed strategies that focus on the six Aims for Improvement of the health care system.

Tenth is cooperation among clinicians. Clinicians and institutions should actively collaborate and communicate to assure appropriate exchange of information and coordination of care. The current system shows too little cooperation and teamwork. Each discipline and type of organization tends to defend its authority at the expense of the total system's function—a problem known as suboptimization. Patients suffer through lost continuity, redundancy, excess costs, and miscommunication. The new rule asserts that cooperation in patient care is more important than professional prerogatives and roles.

Although I have used the term "simple rules" to refer to the guiding principles, our committee recognizes that adhering to these rules will be very challenging. Some of these rules bump up against professional norms and behaviors, while others will require major cultural changes in health care organizations. And there are environmental barriers that must be overcome as well. Legal liability, payment policies, regulatory systems, and other external forces that influence health care must be changed to encourage the types of behavior consistent with quality improvement.

How do we get from here to there? Changes will be needed at two levels: the care delivery and the environmental level.

Although we cannot foresee the range of new organizations, relationships, and technologies that will emerge over the coming decade, there are certain functions that organizational structures—whether virtual or bricks and mortar—will need to perform. Quality health care cannot be delivered through a cottage industry any longer. Well-designed care processes that are based on sound clinical and engineering principles and make the best use of information technology and human resources are essential.

Health care today is more and more an interaction between the system and a person who needs help from that system. To be sure, the physician plays a critical role, but his/her effectiveness is increasingly determined by the characteristics of the system within which practice takes place.

Changes will also be needed in the environment of care. Current payment policies do not adequately encourage or support the provision of quality health care. Although payment is not the only factor that influences provider and patient behavior, it is a very important one. Too little attention has been paid to the careful analysis and alignment of payment incentives with quality improvement. The current health care environment is replete with examples of payment policies that work against the efforts of clinicians, health care executives, and others to improve quality. For example, a safety improvement initiative that reduces adverse drug events may also reduce payments for physician visits or shift hospital patients into Diagnosis Related Group categories that are less complicated and generate less revenue. Similarly, under current visit-based payment systems, clinicians have little incentive to communicate with patients through e-mail.

There will also need to be changes in health professional education and training programs. The traditional emphasis in clinical education, particularly medical education, has been on teaching a "core of knowledge," much of it focusing on the basic mechanisms of disease and patho-physiologic principles. Given the expansiveness and dynamic nature of the science-base in health care, this approach should be expanded to include knowledge management as a means to support clinical decision-making. Similarly, as more care is provided in teams, more opportunities for interdisciplinary training should take place.

In order for innovative programs to flourish, our regulatory environments will also need to adapt. In general, regulation in this country can be characterized as a dense patchwork of federal and state requirements that are slow to change. One of the key regulatory issues affecting the workforce and how it is used is licensure and scope of practice acts, implemented at the state level. One effect of these acts is to define how the health care workforce is deployed. Although scope of practice acts are motivated by the desire to establish minimum standards to ensure the safety of patients, they also can make it difficult to use alternative approaches to care delivery, such as telemedicine, e-visits, nonphysician providers, and multidisciplinary teams.

These are but a few examples of some of the far-reaching changes that will be necessary. In short, the need for leadership has never been greater—organizational leadership, physician/clinician leadership, and community participation. The transformation of the health care system will not be an easy process. But the potential benefits are tremendous.

This field has changed over time as the society has changed and as its capabilities have developed. It was only a century ago that care got complex enough, capital-intensive enough, and successful enough to warrant the middle class even wanting to be in a hospital. Physicians who volunteered in indigent clinics at hospitals applied for privileges. What was the privilege? To admit their private patients to the hospital and provide them care.

Today we're at the dawn of a new era of complexity, capital requirements, and potential effectiveness. The privilege for us in this new era will be to support development of new sets of organizational and financial capacities, just as we did during the last century, to make the most of these opportunities for all of our people.

### REFERENCES

Balas, E. Andrew, and Suzanne A. Boren. 2000. Managing Clinical Knowledge for Health Care Improvement. In *Yearbook of Medical Informatics,* pp. 65–70. Bethesda, Md.: National Library of Medicine.

Boodman, Sandra G. 1999. Medical Web Sites Can Steer You Wrong: Study Finds Erroneous and Misleading Information on Many Pages Dedicated to a Rare Cancer. *Washington Post,* August 10, Health-Z07.

Chassin, Mark R. 1997. Assessing Strategies for Quality Improvement. *Health Affairs* 16, no. 3: 151–61.

————. 1998. Is Health Care Ready for Six Sigma Quality? *Milbank Quarterly* 76, no. 4: 575–91.

Chassin, Mark R., Robert W. Galvin, and the National Roundtable on Health Care Quality. 1998. The Urgent Need to Improve Health Care Quality. *Journal of the American Medical Association (JAMA)* 280, no. 11: 1000–1005.

Classen, David C., Stanley L. Pestonik, Scott Evans, and John P. Burke. 1991. Computerized Surveillance of Adverse Drug Events in Hospital Patients. *JAMA* 266, no. 20: 2847–51.

Goldman, Janlori. 1998. Protecting Privacy to Improve Health Care. *Health Affairs* 17, no. 6: 47–60.

Hoffman, Catherine, Dorothy P. Rice, and Hai-Yen Sung. 1996. Persons with Chronic Conditions: Their Prevalence and Costs. *JAMA* 276, no. 18: 1473–79.

Institute of Medicine. 1999. *Ensuring Quality Cancer Care.* Ed. Maria Hewitt and Joseph V. Simone. Washington, D.C.: National Academy Press.

———. 2000. *To Err Is Human: Building a Safer Health System.* Ed. Linda T. Kohn, Janet M. Corrigan, and Molla S. Donaldson. Washington, D.C: National Academy Press.

———. 2001. *Crossing the Quality Chasm: A New Health System for the Twenty-first Century.* Washington, D.C.: National Academy Press.

Leape, Lucian L., Troyen A. Brennan, Nan M. Laird, et al. 1991. The Nature of Adverse Events in Hospitalized Patients: Results of the Harvard Medical Practice Study II. *JAMA* 324, no. 6: 377–84.

Lindberg, Donald A. B., and Betsy L. Humphreys. 1998. Updates Linking Evidence and Experience—Medicine and Health on the Internet: The Good, the Bad, and the Ugly. *JAMA* 280, no. 15: 1303–4.

Medical Expenditure Panel Survey. 2000. MEPS HC-006R: 1996 Medical Conditions. Online. Available at http://www.meps.ahrq.gov/catlist.htm (accessed December 7, 2000).

Miller, Naomi, Eve-Marie Lacroix, and Joyce E. B. Backus. 2000. MEDLINE-plus: Building and Maintaining the National Library of Medicine's Consumer Health Web Service. *JAMA* 88, no. 1: 11–17.

Morrison, J. Ian. Healthcare in the New Millennium: The Promise of the Internet. 1999. New York: Presentation at Internet Health Care II: Health Care in Transition—Preparing for an Interactive Future, October 12.

National Academy for State Health Policy. Forthcoming. *State Systems to Track Adverse Events.* Portland, Maine: National Academy for State Health Policy.

National Center for Health Statistics. 1999. *Health, United States, 1999: With Health and Aging Chartbook.* Hyattsville, Md.: U.S. Government Printing Office.

National Institutes of Health. 2000. An Overview. Online. Available at http://www.nih.gov/about/NIHoverview.html (accessed August 11, 2000).

National Research Council. 2000. *Networking Health: Prescriptions for the Internet.* Washington D.C.: National Academy Press.

Phillips, David P., Nicholas Christenfeld, and Laura M. Glynn. 1998. Increase in U.S. Medication-Error Deaths between 1983 and 1993. *Lancet* 351: 643–44.

President's Advisory Commission on Consumer Protection and Quality in the Health Care Industry. 1998. Quality First: Better Health Care for All Americans. Online. Available at http://www.hcqualitycommission.gov/final/ (accessed September 9, 2000).

Ray, G. Thomas, Tracy Lieu, Bruce Fireman, et al. 2000. The Cost of Health Conditions in a Health Maintenance Organization. *Medical Care Research and Review* 57, no. 1: 92–109.

Robert Wood Johnson Foundation. *Chronic Care in America: A Twenty-first Century Challenge.* Princeton, N.J.: Robert Wood Johnson Foundation, 1996. Available at http://www.rwjf.org/library/chrcare/.

Schuster, Mark A., Elizabeth A. McGlynn, and Robert H. Brook. 1998. How Good Is the Quality of Health Care in the United States? *Milbank Quarterly* 76, no. 4: 517–63.

Schuster, Mark A., Elizabeth A. McGlynn, Cung B. Pham, Myles D. Spar, and Robert H. Brook. 2001. Appendix A: The Quality of Health Care in the United States: A Review of Articles since 1987. In Institute of Medicine, *Crossing the Quality Chasm: A New Health System for the Twenty-first Century.* Washington, D.C.: National Academy Press.

Soumerai, S. B., T. D. McLaughlin, E. Hertzmark, G. Thibault, and L. Goldman. 1997. Adverse Outcomes of Underuse of Beta-Blockers in Elderly Survivors of Acute Myocardial Infarction. *JAMA* 277: 115–21.

Stewart, Moira A. 1995. Effective Physician-Patient Communication and Health Outcomes: A Review. *Canadian Medical Association Journal* 152, no. 9: 1423–33.

Thomas, Eric J., David M. Studdert, Helen R. Berstin, et al. 2000. Incidence and Types of Adverse Events and Negligent Care in Utah and Colorado. *Medical Care* 38, no. 3: 261–71.

# Human Rights: A Sense of Proportion

*SIR SYDNEY KENTRIDGE Q.C.*

THE TANNER LECTURES ON HUMAN VALUES

Delivered at

Brasenose College, Oxford
February 26 and 27, 2001

SIR SYDNEY KENTRIDGE Q.C. was educated at the University of Witwatersrand and at Oxford University, where he took an honors degree in jurisprudence. He was called to the Bar in South Africa in 1949 and practiced there as an advocate for more than thirty years. In the early 1960s he acted for Nelson Mandela in the first of his treason trials and acted for the family of Steven Biko at the inquest into the events surrounding his death. Since the early 1980s he has practiced as a barrister in London, where he was appointed a Queen's Counsel in 1984. In 1995 and 1996 he sat as a judge of the new Constitutional Court of South Africa. He has also acted as counsel in cases in the European Court of Human Rights in Strasbourg. He is an honorary fellow of Exeter College, Oxford, a fellow of the Institute of Advanced Legal Studies, and an honorary fellow of the American College of Trial Lawyers. He was knighted by the Queen in 1999 for "services to international law and justice."

# I. THE STORY SO FAR

The Tanner Lectures are, by their founder's desire, devoted to Human Values. Many, perhaps most, of the Tanner lecturers have approached this broad concept as philosophers, theologians, moralists, historians, or poets. I speak only as an English legal practitioner, and my subject is a narrower one—a single statute of the United Kingdom Parliament[1]—which has incorporated into the law of the United Kingdom the rights and fundamental freedoms set out in the European Convention on Human Rights. My concern will be the effect that this statute has already had on the law of the United Kingdom and its likely future effect. These lectures will have little, if anything, in them that could be called philosophy, even legal philosophy.[2] I shall, indeed, scarcely pause to consider what it is that makes some rights "fundamental." The rights and freedoms set out in the Convention are fundamental because the Convention itself and the United Kingdom Parliament have described them as fundamental. So I shall be speaking about what is sometimes called positive law. Yet the human values involved should be self-evident.

Some years ago I had the privilege of appearing in the House of Lords in a case in which my client was seeking to cite the Home Secretary for contempt of court. Sir William Wade had described that case as the most important constitutional case to come before English courts in over 200 years. Some three weeks later I appeared in a divisional court on behalf of the Foreign Secretary in order to defend the constitutionality of the United Kingdom's adherence to the Maastricht Treaty. My opponent told the Court that that was the most important constitutional case for 300 years.[3] My comment was that it was at least the most important constitutional case for three weeks. In consequence of that exchange, I am

[1] The Human Rights Act, 1998, which came into full operation in England and Wales on October 2, 2000. It had come into operation in Scotland much earlier, in terms of the Scotland Act, 1998.

[2] There are innumerable writings on the philosophical underpinnings of "human rights." Among the modern ones Ronald Dworkin, *Taking Rights Seriously* (7th impression, Oxford University Press, 1994), remains preeminent. For a bracingly sceptical view of the dominance of human rights in legal and political discourse, see Mary Ann Glendon, *Rights Talk* (Macmillan, 1991).

[3] The two cases were *M. v. The Home Office* [1994] 1 AC 377, and *R. v. Secretary of State for Foreign and Commonwealth Affairs ex parte Rees-Mogg* [1994] QB 552.

too cautious to say what I would otherwise have been tempted to say, namely that the Human Rights Act, 1998, is the most remarkable development in British constitutional law since the Bill of Rights of 1689. In incorporating the European Convention on Human Rights into domestic law Parliament has not so much created for us hitherto unknown rights, but has rather given to certain individual rights a special status that they had not previously been accorded. Now, any infringement of such rights by any public authority inferior to the United Kingdom Parliament itself may be held to be *per se* unlawful and nullified by the courts of the United Kingdom. What is still more remarkable in a country in which parliamentary supremacy is a legal and constitutional axiom, even acts of Parliament are now subject to the scrutiny and judgment of British courts, applying the norms of the European Convention.

The history of the incorporation of the Convention is too recent to need recapitulation. So are the debates and the issues that surrounded it. For example, would incorporation politicise the English and Scottish judiciaries? Would it have been better to wait until we had a home-grown British Bill of Rights instead of incorporating a fifty-year-old international convention? Would the inescapable doctrine of the supremacy of Parliament make the Act no more than the shadow of a real Bill of Rights? These are still legitimate questions (although I would answer "no" to all of them). But they will now fall to be answered in the light of experience and not, or not entirely, speculatively. How they will be answered depends to a large extent on the performance of our profession (in which I include the judicial, the practising, and the academic branches).

In relation to the supremacy of Parliament I must say a little more about the relationship between the courts and Parliament under the Human Rights Act. A few moments ago I said, speaking with considerable care, that the courts could now scrutinise and pass judgment on acts of Parliament. It is well-known that under the Human Rights Act the courts of this country (unlike those in, e.g., the USA, Canada, South Africa, and Germany) do not have the power to strike down and invalidate acts of Parliaments. A court may do no more than declare that a provision of an act of Parliament is not compatible with a Convention right.[4] But the Human Rights Act nonetheless contains a sophisticated mechanism that will, I believe, effectively outflank the obstacle of par-

---

[4] Section 4 of the Act.

liamentary supremacy. Section 19, which came into operation at an earlier stage than the rest of the Act, requires Ministers in charge of a bill coming before either House of Parliament to make one of two statements: either that in their opinion the provisions of the bill are compatible with the Convention or that they are unable to express that opinion but nevertheless wish the bill to go forward. I surmise that there will be few occasions on which a government will be willing to justify the second type of statement. As to the former type of statement, to have it contradicted by a judicial declaration of incompatibility would be embarrassing and could be costly in political terms. The Act also provides a fast-track procedure enabling Parliament rapidly to repair an act held to be incompatible with the Convention.[5] That provision was surely intended to be used, and I do not doubt that it will be used. Further, under Section 3 of the Act legislation must now, as far as possible, be read and given effect in a way compatible with Convention rights—a way that may be very different from its ordinary meaning. So we shall in future have the pleasure of hearing Treasury counsel, rather than risk a declaration of incompatibility, argue strenuously that a statutory provision before the court must be interpreted in the way most favourable to the other party in the case.

In the United States the written Constitution, including the Bill of Rights, has been referred to as "the Silent Sentinel," meaning that the very existence of the Constitution induces legislators (and drafters of legislation) and administrators to respect and give effect to the rights embodied in it—well before any question of judicial review arises. I believe that the Human Rights Act both before and after it came into force in October of last year has been just such a silent sentinel. There is already much evidence that ministries and both Houses of Parliament are sensitive to the requirements of the Act. One piece of evidence is that Professor David Feldman has been appointed to be Special Adviser to the joint committee on Human Rights of both Houses of Parliament. Another is the unexpected (and some would say over-cautious) promotion of all assistant-recorders to the rank of full recorder,[6] to ensure that

---

[5] Section 10.

[6] A recorder is a part-time judge, exercising limited criminal jurisdiction, usually appointed from the ranks of practising barristers or solicitors. The (rough) Scottish equivalent of an assistant-recorder was a temporary sheriff. A Scottish court had held that temporary sheriffs were not "independent," because their tenure was at the pleasure of the executive—*Starrs* v. *Procurator Fiscal, Linlithgow, The Times* (London), November 17, 1999.

their independence cannot be questioned under Article 6 of the Convention.[7] The Bill of Rights is no mere shadow.

I have already said that the Human Rights Act is revolutionary in the context of our constitutional law. But it is necessary to consider the extent of that revolution. What changes can we expect it to bring? Or, to put the same question in another way, how are the courts going to read it and apply it? The canon of interpretation most frequently cited in the Privy Council in appeals concerning Commonwealth constitutions is that stated by Lord Wilberforce in *Minister of Home Affairs Bermuda* v. *Fisher* in 1980,[8] namely, that a constitutional instrument calls for "a generous interpretation avoiding what has been called 'the austerity of tabulated legalism,' suitable to give to individuals the full measure of the fundamental rights and freedoms referred to."[9]

It remains to be seen whether this will be the approach of British courts to the Convention. Of course, as Lord Wilberforce himself emphasised, a constitution is a written instrument. Its language cannot be ignored. The Privy Council has recently cited with approval a statement in a judgment of the South African Constitutional Court: "If the language used by the law giver is ignored in favour of a general resort to values the result is not interpretation but divination."[10]

So the hard judicial process of interpretation must continue. Section 2 of the Act directs our courts to take into account the judgments of the European Court of Human Rights and the judgments of the now defunct European Commission of Human Rights. But those decisions will not be binding. One may expect our courts to reconsider some of them and to have regard to the judgments of foreign courts. Human rights will be a great field for the comparative lawyer.

In 1993 in an appeal from Hong Kong involving the then colony's Bill of Rights Lord Woolf in the Privy Council said that issues involving the Bill of Rights "should be approached with realism and good sense, and kept in proportion. If this is not done the Bill will become a

---

[7] Article 6 requires judges to be "independent" as well as impartial.

[8] [1980] AC 319.

[9] At pages 328–29. (I have not been able to trace the original source of Lord Wilberforce's reference to "the austerity of tabulated legalism," nor, indeed, to do more than guess what it means.)

[10] *State* v. *Zuma* 1995 (4) BCLR 401, para. 18, cited in *Matadeen* v. *Pointu* [1999] 1 AC 98 at page 108. (BCLR refers to Butterworths Constitutional Law Reports, published by Butterworths, Durban, South Africa.)

source of injustice rather than justice and it will be debased in the eyes of the public."[11]

That must be equally true of this country. Few of the litigants who invoke their Convention Rights will be village-Hampdens confronting with dauntless breast some executive tyrant. Many "victims," as the Act calls them, will be distinctly unappealing, and the courts in applying the Act will have to make some decisions that will not be generally popular. Undoubtedly, in the long run the survival of any bill of rights depends on public confidence in the fairness and reasonableness with which the courts apply it. But the courts cannot and will not bow to public opinion, still less to party political opinion, and least of all to the manufactured indignation of sensational journalism. What realism and good sense demand will not always be self-evident.

If I may return to Lord Wilberforce, in the judgment from which I quoted he said that respect must be paid not only to the language that has been used in a written constitution but also "to the traditions and usages which have given meaning to that language."[12]

Similarly, in the Canadian Supreme Court the great expounder of the Canadian Charter of Rights and Freedoms, Sir Brian Dickson, said that the meaning of a right or freedom guaranteed by the Charter must be ascertained by analysis of the purpose of such guarantee: and that the purpose is to be sought by reference, *inter alia,* to "the historical origins of the concept enshrined."[13] Although the Convention is an international treaty, the British contribution to its drafting is well known, and it is now part of a British statute. Many of the concepts in the Convention have their origin in this island. So courts can legitimately consider the history in this country of the rights in the Convention. In our expectations of the changes that the Human Rights Act will bring us we must remember the peculiarly British background to the Act.

This background is very different from that of some other twentieth-century constitutional bills of rights. To make two obvious comparisons, the postwar German Constitution can be seen as a direct and radical reaction against the savage and immoral laws of the Nazi dictatorship. The South African Interim Constitution of 1993 and the final

[11] *Attorney-General of Hong Kong* v. *Lee Kwong-Kut* [1993] AC 951 at page 975.

[12] At page 329.

[13] *R.* v. *Big M Drug Mart Limited* (1985) 18 DLR (4th) 321 at pages 395–96.

Constitution of 1996 explicitly set out to redress the wrongs of the apartheid era and, indeed, of the decades of white supremacy and black subjection that had preceded it. To bolster the authoritarian regime criminal procedures originally taken over from England had been systematically subverted. Capital punishment had been extended beyond cases of murder. (In the heyday of apartheid there were more persons executed each year in South Africa than in the whole of the United States.) Suspected subversives could be detained indefinitely with no right of *habeas corpus* and indeed no right to see a lawyer. In criminal cases there was no "equality of arms": the whole of the prosecution docket was regarded as absolutely privileged. The Attorney-General had the overriding power to deny bail to persons awaiting trial. In numerous criminal statutes heavy burdens of proof were placed on the accused, including the burden of proving that a signed confession was *not* voluntary. It was not surprising therefore that judges exercising their powers under the new Bill of Rights felt called on to slash and burn parts of the statute book in order to restore the rule of law.

Our new bill of rights emerges from a very different background, the background of a society in which in our day individual rights have on the whole been respected. The abolition of the death penalty for murder, the measures designed to achieve equality of arms in criminal cases, the measures outlawing sex and race discrimination in employment—none of these had to await the Human Rights Act. What is more, the language of individual rights with the corresponding limitation of executive power has been the staple of English legal discourse at least since Magna Carta. The Bill of Rights of 1689 is the ancestor in content as well as title of the innumerable national and international bills of rights of our time. Sir William Blackstone, in his *Commentaries,* stated that the "principal aim of society" in England was to protect individuals in the enjoyment of what he called the absolute rights of life, liberty, and property.[14] He also described England as perhaps the only land in the universe in which political and civil liberty was the very end and scope of the constitution and contrasted it with other states on the continent of Europe, which, he said, vested an arbitrary and despotic power in the prince or in a few grandees.[15] All this was doubtless over-enthusiastic for Blackstone's time and for other times too.

---

[14] *Commentaries on the Law of England,* vol. 1, 124.

[15] Ibid., vol. 1, 127.

It is almost unnecessary to acknowledge that there was no period when Blackstone's absolute rights were absolutely respected. Magna Carta and the Bill of Rights probably helped only a small section of the population and were in any event at the mercy of Parliament. Against the Bill of Rights one can place the Black Acts. Against Lord Mansfield one can set Lord Braxfield. Against *Entick* v. *Carrington*[16] one can set *Liversidge* v. *Anderson.*[17] Certainly in the first half of the twentieth century the contribution of the English judiciary to the protection of the individual against executive power was modest indeed. Sir William Wade has called the public law cases of that era "a dreary catalogue of abdication and error."[18] In a recent book Professor K. D. Ewing and Professor Conor Gearty have exposed the judicial failures of the period.[19] Yet the language of individual rights persisted, even if mainly in the resounding statements of Lord Atkin.[20] But, as every student of administrative law knows, all this changed in the 1960s when the boundaries of judicial review were extended by such cases as *Ridge* v. *Baldwin,*[21] *Anisminic,*[22] and *Padfield.*[23] In the last decade of the last century the courts exercised their powers of review ever more boldly. The concept of a fundamental human right was recognised by courts at the highest level with the corollary that such a right could not be overridden save by a clear enactment of Parliament—all this before the commencement of the Human Rights Act.[24] Lord Hoffmann, still before the commencement of the Act, said in the House of Lords (perhaps with a touch of Blackstonian enthusiasm) that "the courts of the United Kingdom, though acknowledging the sovereignty of Parliament, apply principles of constitutionality little different from those which exist in countries

[16] (1765) 19 St. Tr. 1030, in which it was held that, absent statutory authority, a Secretary of State had no authority to issue a search warrant.

[17] [1942] AC 206, a wartime case in which the majority of the House of Lords (Lord Atkin dissenting) gave an unduly broad interpretation to the Home Secretary's statutory powers of detention.

[18] H. W. R. Wade and C. F. Forsyth, *Administrative Law* (8th ed., Oxford University Press, 2000), at page 16.

[19] K. D. Ewing and C. A. Gearty, *The Struggle for Civil Liberties: Political Freedom and the Rule of Law in Britain, 1914–1945* (Oxford University Press, 2000).

[20] E.g., in *Eshugbayi Eleko* v. *Officer Administering the Government* [1931] AC 662 and in *Liversidge* v. *Anderson* [1942] AC 206.

[21] [1964] AC 40.

[22] *Anisminic Ltd.* v. *Foreign Compensation Commission* [1969] 2 AC 147.

[23] *Padfield* v. *Minister of Agriculture* [1968] AC 997.

[24] *R.* v. *Lord Chancellor Ex parte Witham* [1998] QB 575, per Laws, J.

where the power of the legislature is expressly limited by a constitutional document."[25]

Add to this that the United Kingdom has since 1966 accepted the right of individuals to petition the European Court of Human Rights, and one sees that by the time the Act came into force this country already had a lively culture of rights with a panoply of statutory and judicial protections. The revolution, real as it is, has not been an upheaval. The judges here should not feel tempted to slash and burn. That is why I have given these lectures the title "A Sense of Proportion."

To maintain a sense of proportion we must also bear in mind the limits inherent in the European Convention itself. The Convention is now fifty years old. I assume that this audience is generally acquainted with the rights enumerated in the Convention, so you will know what is missing when compared with the constitutions of, for example, Germany, the United States, Canada, and South Africa. Thus, Article 14 of the Convention prohibits discrimination only in respect of the rights and freedoms actually set out in the Convention. There is no general right of equality before the law, no general prohibition of discrimination. There is no reference to human dignity—a right in the forefront of the German and South African constitutions. The right of citizens to enter, leave, or move freely in their own country is not to be found in the Convention. You must go back to Magna Carta for that. So too with the right to reasonable bail. Nor (understandably in a European Convention) is there any mention of trial by jury—as there is in, for example, Section 11(f) of the Charter of Rights and Freedoms in Canada.

In spite of these limitations there have already been important changes in both criminal and civil law. Others are in the offing. Before mentioning some of these changes I must point to an aspect of the format of the Convention, which can be best explained by a comparison with the Canadian Charter of Rights and Freedoms. Section 1 of the Canadian Charter states that the Charter guarantees the rights and freedoms set out in it, but subject "only to such reasonable limits prescribed by law as can be demonstrably justified in a free and democratic society."

There is a corresponding general limitation clause in the South African Constitution. In the Convention (as in the American Bill of Rights) there is no such general clause. There are clauses of limitation

---

[25] R. v. *Secretary of State for the Home Department, Ex parte Simms* [2000] 2 AC 115 at page 131.

within some individual articles of the Convention. Thus, Article 10.1 states that everyone has a right to freedom of expression "without interference by public authority." But Article 10.2 goes on: "The exercise of these freedoms, since it carries with it duties and responsibilities, may be subject to such formalities, conditions, restrictions or penalties as are prescribed by law and are necessary in a democratic society, [and here I summarise] in the interests of national security, for the prevention of disorder or crime, for the protection of the reputation or rights of others, or for maintaining the authority and impartiality of the judiciary."[26]

Other articles with similar limitation clauses are Article 8 (respect for private and family life) and Article 11 (freedom of assembly and association). Other rights have no stated limitations. There is ample authority in the European Court of Human Rights and, already, in the English and Scottish courts that limitations may be read by implication into at least some of the latter rights. Are any of those rights that are stated in absolute terms really absolute? I suggest that only three of them are:

1. the right not to be tortured or subjected to inhuman or degrading treatment or punishment;
2. the right not be held in slavery or servitude; and
3. the right to a fair hearing in the civil or criminal courts.

Surely there can be no exceptions to those three rights. In particular one cannot envisage an argument that some competing interest requires that someone should have a less than fair hearing. This was cogently stated by Lord Bingham of Cornhill in the *Kebilene* case in the Divisional Court,[27] and by the Privy Council in *Brown* v. *Stott (Procurator-Fiscal),*[28] an appeal from the Scottish High Court of Justiciary in which judgment was given last December. In the latter case Lord Hope of Craighead said that "the right to a fair trial is absolute in its terms and the public interest can never be invoked to deny that right to anybody under any circumstances...."[29]

That absolute right to a fair trial is a new right in England. This may

---

[26] I note in passing that this is the only reference in the Convention to "duties and responsibilities."

[27] *R.* v. *Director of Public Prosecutions Ex parte Kebilene* [2000] 2 AC 326.

[28] [2001] 2 WLR 817.

[29] At page 851.

sound heretical, but I do not believe that before the Human Rights Act came into force there was a general right to a fair trial in England. What there was was a right to a trial in accordance with rules and procedures laid down by statute or judicial decision. Those rules and procedures were doubtless aimed at achieving fairness and, at least since extended duties of disclosure have been imposed on or recognised by the prosecution, the great majority of criminal trials in this country have been fair. But that is not the same thing as an overriding general right to a fair trial. Thus, under the present Criminal Appeal Act whatever the irregularities in the trial the Court of Appeal may allow an appeal against a conviction only if it thinks that the conviction is "unsafe."[30] In any other case the appeal must be dismissed. What this has meant is that the Court of Appeal could in effect say: "It does not matter what went wrong with the trial. The conviction is not unsafe because we are sure that the accused would have been convicted even if he had had a fair trial." That approach can no longer stand. Now a defendant who has not had a fair trial has by definition been treated unlawfully and must have a remedy. This was the effect of the decision of the European Court of Human Rights in *Condron* v. *The United Kingdom.*[31]

The appellants had contended in the Court of Appeal in England that their trial had been unfair because the jury had not been given proper directions as to the inferences that could properly be drawn from their silence. Their appeal was dismissed. But they succeeded in the European Court of Human Rights. That court said that

> the Court of Appeal was concerned with the safety of the applicants' conviction, not whether...they had received a fair trial.... The question whether or not the rights...guaranteed to an accused under Article 6 of the Convention were secured cannot be assimilated to a finding that his conviction was safe....[32]

The English Court of Appeal in 2000 endorsed this approach in the case of *The Queen* v. *Togher and Others.*[33] Lord Woolf C.J. quoted the judg-

---

[30] Criminal Appeal Act, 1968, Section 2.

[31] Application No. 35718/97. Judgment given at Strasbourg, May 2, 2000. (Strasbourg is the seat of the European Court of Human Rights.)

[32] Paragraph 65.

[33] *The Times* (London), November 21, 2000, a judgment given within a few weeks of the coming into operation of the Human Rights Act. This judgment has been endorsed by the House of Lords in *R.* v. *Forbes* [2001] 2 WLR 1, paragraph 24.

ment in *Condron* and said that it would be unfortunate if the approach of
the European Court of Human Rights and the approach of the Court of
Appeal were to differ. Section 3 of the Human Rights Act now required
all acts of the United Kingdom Parliament to be read in a way that was
compatible with Convention rights. A broader rather than a narrower
meaning must therefore be given to the word "unsafe" in the Criminal
Appeals Act and, he said, "if a defendant had been denied a fair trial it
would almost be inevitable that the conviction would be regarded as
unsafe." (That "almost" expressed, I suspect, no more than the normal
judicial reluctance to give hostages to fortune.) In my respectful opinion
Lord Woolf's is a seminal judgment, both in its result and in its method
of interpreting the English statute so as to bring it into accord with the
Convention.

There have been two other judgments of great importance in the
field of criminal law about which I cannot be so wholehearted. They are
both judgments of the Privy Council in appeals from Scotland. The
first, *Brown* v. *The Procurator-Fiscal*,[34] concerned a right not expressed in
the Convention but long accepted as a fundamental ingredient of a fair
trial—the right not to be compelled to incriminate oneself. *Brown*'s case
arose under Section 172 of the Road Traffic Act, 1988. This provides
that where the driver of a particular motor car is alleged to be guilty of
any of a range of serious driving offences any person (including a person
suspected of being the driver) must on request give the police any information in his or her power to give as to the identity of the driver. Failure
to comply is an offence. Moreover, although the Road Traffic Act is
silent on the point the courts have held that the answer given to the police was admissible in evidence against the person who gave it notwithstanding that it was (usually) incriminating. The defendant Brown,
who was suspected of driving a particular car after consuming excessive
alcohol, and who had the keys of the car in her possession, was asked by
the police who had been driving the car. She replied: "It was me." She
was prosecuted for driving the car having consumed excessive alcohol.
The High Court of Justiciary in Scotland held that her answer would
not be admissible against her at her trial,[35] because her statement was
made under compulsion, it was incriminating, and to use it against her

---

[34] [2001] 2 WLR 817. (The final court of appeal in respect of Convention issues arising
in criminal cases in Scotland is, for constitutional reasons, the Privy Council and not the
House of Lords.)

[35] 2000 SLT 379.

breached her rights under Article 6 of the Convention. The Scottish court relied particularly on the well-known case of *Ernest Saunders* v. *The United Kingdom,* in which the European Court of Human Rights had held that the right not to incriminate oneself lay at the heart of, and was a basic principle of, the notion of fair procedure, and had stated further that "[t]he public interest cannot be invoked to justify the use of answers compulsorily obtained in non-judicial investigation to incriminate the accused during trial proceedings."[36]

The Privy Council reversed the High Court of Justiciary. It criticised the dictum from the *Saunders* judgment as excessively absolute and did not apply it. It held that the right not to incriminate oneself was not unqualified and that the court's task was to find a fair balance between the rights of the individual and the general interest of the community in the successful prosecution of serious driving offences. The statutory inroad into the rights of the accused was proportionate in the sense that it was not unduly prejudicial or oppressive. Accordingly Brown's statement could be used against her.

I do not find the result of the *Brown* case alarming. I do not think that the privilege against self-incrimination is or should be absolute. Scottish criminal procedure provides other protections for the accused, such as the need for corroboration of the admission. And, while I confess that as the losing counsel in the *Saunders* case I am particularly receptive to criticisms of that judgment, I believe that the Privy Council's reservations about the passage quoted above were justified.[37] It is also worth pointing out that JUSTICE,[38] as *amicus curiae,* had supported the admissibility of Brown's statement. But, with all respect, I find their Lordships' approach to the issue of self-incrimination in many ways disappointing.

One cannot fault the Judicial Committee's finding that the privilege

---

[36] (1996) 23 EHRR 313, paragraph 74.

[37] Section 2 of the Human Rights Act directs all courts to "take account of" the decisions of the European Court of Human Rights and the European Commission on Human Rights. It is to be hoped that these decisions, being of variable quality, will be examined critically rather than simply accepted. A particularly crass example is the unreasoned decision of the Commission on the reverse onus provision in the Dangerous Dogs Act, 1991, in *Bates* v. *United Kingdom* [1996] EHRLR 312. Such a decision justifies the late Dr. F. A. Mann's strictures on the (now defunct) Commission in 1994 LQR at pages 529–30. The case was unfortunately cited without criticism by the House of Lords in the *Kebilene* case cited above and by the Privy Council in the *Brown* case.

[38] JUSTICE is an influential independent organization devoted to improving the administration of justice and to the establishment of human rights norms in England.

against self-incrimination is subject to limitations. Lord Bingham said that a limited qualification of this as of other rights is permissible if directed toward a proper public objective and if the qualification of the right is no greater "than the situation calls for."[39] A balance had to be struck "between the general interests of the community and the personal rights of the individual" in a manner not "unduly prejudicial to the individual." The Road Traffic Act, he held, struck that balance. Lord Steyn said the question was whether the legislative encroachment on the right not to incriminate oneself was "necessary and proportionate" to the aim of effectively prosecuting serious driving offences.[40] He held that it was. Lord Hope said that the question was "whether a fair balance had been struck between the general interest of the community in the realisation of that aim and the protection of the fundamental rights of the individual."[41] Their Lordships all held that the fair balance had been achieved.

All this is very well as far as it goes. But what is missing? First, while there is a passing reference to the privilege against self-incrimination as being deep-rooted in English law, there is no emphasis on the fundamental place of that principle in our concept of fair criminal procedure, a principle rightly described in a Canadian case not indeed as absolute but as overreaching. Second, there is no overt recognition that the maintenance of the privilege is in the interest not only of the particular accused but of society as a whole. The weighing of the general interest in the prosecution of crime is obviously relevant, but it has great dangers unless it is accompanied by the consciousness that if a public interest is permitted to prevail over an individual's fundamental right simply because it is a public interest then the right can hardly be called fundamental.

The approach that I would have hoped for would start with the axiom that an authority seeking to justify a limitation on so fundamental a right has a heavy burden of persuasion. By analogy, the right of free expression under Article 10 of the Convention is subject to restrictions, but only such as are "necessary in a democratic society." "Necessary" does not mean "indispensable," but it does connote the existence of a pressing social need. There is no reason why the right not to incriminate

---

[39] At pages 836–37.

[40] At page 841.

[41] At page 852.

oneself should be vulnerable to any lesser demonstration of need. It is only on the showing of such need that the question of proportionality or "balancing" should arise.

It must be remembered that we have many statutes that compel people to reply to incriminating questions but that provide that the answers cannot be used against them in criminal proceedings.[42] The real question, I suggest, was not whether such evidence was helpful in the prosecution of the crime—it plainly was—but whether in the interests of justice there was a pressing need for answers like Brown's to be used not merely in investigation but against her in court. That question does not seem to have been asked, and there seems to have been no evidence on the issue. (There was evidence of the high rate of serious road accidents, but that is not the same thing.)

It is possible or even probable that a pressing need could have been shown to exist and the consideration of proportionality would then have led to the same result, but the opportunity was missed, I fear, to lay down a proper framework for the consideration of similar questions, which now come daily before the courts. Flexibility is no substitute for analysis.

There is a feature of one of the judgments that I must mention. Lord Clyde said that the Convention

> is not to be applied in ways which run counter to reason and common sense. If the Convention was to be applied by the courts in ways which would seem absurd to ordinary people then the courts would be doing disservice to the aims and purposes of the Convention and the result would simply be to prejudice public respect for an international treaty which seeks to express the basic rights and freedoms of a democratic society.[43]

This illustrates the care that is needed in invoking what Lord Woolf called "realism and good sense" in applying the Convention.[44] There are many rules applied by the courts that to ordinary people may sometimes seem absurd, perhaps even the privilege against self-incrimination itself. The judgment appealed from, a unanimous judgment of the High

[42] E.g., Criminal Justice Act, 1987, Section 2 (Director of Serious Fraud Office may compel suspect to answer questions notwithstanding self-incrimination, but answers not admissible in criminal trial).

[43] At page 859.

[44] See note 11 above.

Court of Justiciary, presided over by the Lord Justice General, Lord
Rodger of Earlsferry, was held by their Lordships to be wrong: but Lord
Clyde could hardly have meant to say that their judgment was absurd.
Even if ordinary people thought so (a doubtful proposition) that is
hardly an adequate basis for cutting down a fundamental right.

The second Privy Council case to which I want to refer is *Her
Majesty's Advocate* v. *McIntosh*.[45] It arose from a confiscation order made
against McIntosh following his conviction for drug trafficking offences.
The legislation providing for confiscation of the assets of convicted deal-
ers contains a number of presumptions that place burdens of proof on
the convicted dealer to establish that his assets are not the proceeds of
drug trafficking. One of the issues in the case was whether these provisions were in conflict with Article 6(2) of the Convention, which states
that everyone charged with a criminal offence shall be presumed innocent until proved guilty according to law. The High Court of Justiciary,
by a majority, had held the presumptions in the legislation to be incompatible with Article 6(2). The Privy Council reversed this decision. In
what was, for technical reasons, an extended *obiter dictum* Lord Bingham
considered reverse onus provisions in light of the general (but conced-
edly not absolute) presumption of innocence. He said:

> In weighing the balance between the general interest of the commu-
> nity and the rights of the individual, it will be relevant to ask...what
> public threat the provision is directed to address, what the prosecu-
> tor must prove to transfer the onus to the defendant and what
> difficulty the defendant may have in discharging the onus laid upon
> him.[46]

He found the balance to be on the side of the general interest in combating drug trafficking.

I respectfully agree with the result reached (which also has the support of the English Court of Appeal in *R.* v. *Benjafield*),[47] but again I
doubt whether this general balancing of interests is sufficiently rigorous
to protect as fundamental a right as the presumption of innocence.

The vice of reverse onus provisions was succinctly stated by Dickson
C.J. in the Canadian Supreme Court: "If an accused bears the burden of

[45] *The Times* (London), February 8, 2001.

[46] Paragraph 31.

[47] Unreported, December 21, 2000.

disproving on a balance of probabilities an essential element of an offence, it would be possible for a conviction to occur despite the existence of a reasonable doubt."[48]

This statement had been endorsed by Lord Bingham himself, sitting in the Divisional Court in *Kebilene* in 1999.[49] If such a conviction can occur there is *prima facie* a serious breach of the presumption of innocence. Reverse onus provisions are a useful prosecutorial resource in combating crime, but again I suggest that justification of the breach of the presumption of innocence must be based on a showing of a real and pressing need for reversing the onus of proof. Such a need could have been, perhaps was, established in the *McIntosh* case. But if so it would have been better had that been expressly stated. Lord Bingham did say that the general interest of the community in suppressing crime would not justify a state in riding roughshod over the rights of a criminal defendant,[50] "as graphically pointed out by Sachs J. in *State* v. *Coetzee*,"[51] in the South African Constitutional Court. What Sachs J. said is relevant to every exception sought to be made to the presumption of innocence:

> There is a paradox at the heart of all criminal procedure in that the more serious the crime and the greater the public interest in securing convictions of the guilty, the more important do constitutional protections of the accused become. The starting point of any balancing enquiry where constitutional rights are concerned must be that the public interest in ensuring that innocent people are not convicted and subjected to ignominy and heavy sentences massively outweighs the public interest in ensuring that a particular criminal is brought to book. Hence the presumption of innocence, which serves not only to protect a particular individual on trial, but to maintain public confidence in the enduring integrity and security of the legal system. Reference to the prevalence and severity of a certain crime therefore does not add anything new or special to the balancing exercise. The perniciousness of the offence is one of the givens, against which the presumption of innocence is pitted from the beginning, not a new element to be put into the scales as part of a justificatory balancing exercise. If this were not so, the ubiquity and ugliness argument could be used in relation to murder, rape, carjacking, housebreaking, drug-smuggling, corruption...the list is

[48] *R.* v. *Oakes* (1986) 26 DLR (4th) 200 at page 222.

[49] See note 27 above.

[50] Paragraph 31.

[51] 1997 (4) BCLR 437.

unfortunately almost endless, and nothing would be left of the presumption of innocence, save, perhaps, for its relic status as a doughty defender of rights in the most trivial of cases.[52]

It would have been reassuring if the words of Justice Sachs had been quoted and endorsed, for the guidance of other courts.[53]

In reading these and other English cases under the Human Rights Act, I have been struck by an odd omission. What has happened to Lord Wilberforce's golden rule, his call for a generous interpretation suitable to give individuals the full measure of their fundamental rights? It is still invoked by the Privy Council in Commonwealth appeals.[54] Is it not appropriate in the home country?

Keeping a sense of proportion about human rights has two sides to it. The one is that few rights are absolute, and that pressing public needs can sometimes justify encroachment on individual rights. The other side is that the Human Rights Act (unlike some Commonwealth constitutions) should not be read as merely safeguarding our existing rights. It may also extend our rights. In a judgment in the South African Constitutional Court it was said: "Constitutional rights conferred without express limitation should not be cut down by reading implicit restrictions into them, so as to bring them into line with the common law."[55]

While our legal traditions explain the origins and purposes of many Convention rights, one should not assume that Convention law is no different from existing English law. Hitherto accepted legal doctrines and practices will have to be reexamined with an open mind. In my next lecture I shall give some encouraging examples of this approach.


## II. HOW WILL IT END?


A fear often expressed when the Human Rights Act was passed was that the courts would be flooded with extravagant claims of infringement of Convention rights. That prophecy has not come true. There has been no

---

[52] Paragraph 220.

[53] Since the date of this lecture Lord Steyn has repaired this omission in *R.* v. *Lambert* [2001] 3 WLR 206.

[54] See, e.g., *Darmalingum* v. *The State* [2000] 1 WLR 2303 at page 2309, an appeal from Mauritius.

[55] *State* v. *Zuma* (see note 10 above) paragraph 15.

flood. There has, however, been a steady stream of cases in which litigants have raised a human rights point. Some of them have been hopeless. There have been attempts to argue that any restriction on the use of
residential property under a town-planning scheme is an infringement
of the right (under the First Protocol to the Convention) to the peaceful
enjoyment of one's possessions. It has been argued, equally unsuccess-
fully, that the right of freedom of expression somehow expanded the
statutory defences to infringements of copyright. One can safely say that
every day an argument under the Human Rights Act is advanced in
some court in this country. It is no bad thing that so many human rights
points are taken, even if many of them are doomed to fail. Even the bad
points will help the courts to define the general boundaries of the
Human Rights Act.

Outside the courts there are also over-optimistic expectations of the
reach of the Act. The actor Sean Connery is reported to have said that a
rule prohibiting donations to British political parties by persons living
abroad would be an infringement of his human rights. Suggestions have
been made in the press that succession to the throne in the male line can
no longer be the rule under the Human Rights Act. In a recent case, the
Court of Appeal was compelled by the clear words of a statute to hold
that a grandchild could not inherit from his grandparents on their in-
testacy while his father was still alive, the father being disqualified from
inheriting because he had murdered the grandparents. After the judgment a solicitor commented that there "must be a remedy" under the
Human Rights Act. Lorry drivers threatened with arrest for obstructing
the highway in the course of their demonstration against fuel prices said
that they were only exercising their right of free speech. They will find
little comfort in the Human Rights Act. This may be disappointing to
many people suffering genuine grievances. But, as Lord Bingham said
in the *Brown* case,[1] the Convention does not "as is sometimes mistakenly
thought offer relief from 'the heart-ache and the thousand natural
shocks that flesh is heir to.'"

In due course the Act will be better understood. I would say again
that it is no bad thing that members of the public are conscious that
they now have rights that may be superior to the ordinary law, even if
they are at present mistaken as to the scope and limits of those rights.

Not all the human rights issues that have come before the courts

[1] Note 28 above.

have been ill founded. Far from it. In my first lecture I spoke of the difference that the Act has already made to the idea of a fair criminal trial. Let me give a striking example of the effect of the Act on civil procedure. Article 6 of the Convention provides that for the determination of civil rights and obligations everyone is entitled to an independent and impartial tribunal. There have been many English cases in which the requisite standards of impartiality in English law have been discussed. In 1994 the House of Lords in a definitive judgment held that a judge's impartiality could be impugned only on a showing that the judge's conduct or relationship with the parties or any other circumstance gave rise to "a real danger" of bias. The House of Lords rejected an argument that a judge ought not to sit if the circumstance gave rise merely to a reasonable apprehension or suspicion of bias.[2]

In 1999 the issue was reconsidered by an especially powerful Court of Appeal, consisting of the then Lord Chief Justice, the then Master of the Rolls, and the then Vice-Chancellor. They endorsed the House of Lords decision, which indeed bound them.[3] Then came the Human Rights Act. Last December another Court of Appeal,[4] presided over by the present Master of the Rolls, Lord Phillips of Worth Matravers, reconsidered the issue in light of the jurisprudence of the European Court of Human Rights and made what Lord Phillips modestly called a modest adjustment to the law, and what I would call a good push in the right direction. The court held that "reasonable apprehension" of bias was now the criterion for recusal of a judge and thus brought our law into line with Strasbourg and, incidentally, with Scotland, Australia, and South Africa. Thus recent and formidable English authority was reconsidered in the light of the Convention, with no presumption that the existing English rule was necessarily consistent with what the Convention required.

Another example of a major change brought about by the Human Rights Act is the recent judgment in which a Divisional Court held that the procedures whereby applications for planning permission were determined under the Town and Country Planning Act, 1990, did not accord to the applicants an independent and impartial tribunal as required by the Convention.[5] The vice of the procedure was that, whatever the

---

[2] *R. v. Gough* [1993] AC 646.

[3] *Locabail (U.K.) Ltd. v. Bayfield Properties Ltd.* [2000] QB 451.

[4] *In re Medicaments (No. 2)* [2001] 1 WLR 700.

[5] *R. v. Secretary of State for the Environment Ex parte Holding & Barnes plc, The Times* (London), January 24, 2001.

recommendations made by the inspector following an admittedly fair public hearing, the final decision was made by the Secretary of State for the Environment. Because the latter's own policy was in issue, he could not be regarded as independent and impartial. As Lord Justice Tuckey put it, under Convention jurisprudence he could not be both policy maker and decision taker. In a significant passage Lord Justice Tuckey said:

> ...the question now was not how article 6 [of the Convention] could best be accommodated in the interests of fairness given the existing statutory scheme, but rather whether the scheme itself complied with article 6.
>
> To accept that the possibility of common law bias was inherent in the system and mandated by Parliament was merely to admit that the system involved structural bias and required determinations to be made by a person who was not impartial.

In the event the court made a declaration of incompatibility. In due course we shall see how the Secretary of State and Parliament respond to this declaration, but it is safe to say that it is likely to have far-reaching effects on many existing administrative tribunals.[6]

All in all, it has been a busy five months for the English and Scottish courts. No one will agree with all their judgments, but what is plain is their readiness to grapple with Convention issues and their familiarity with human rights jurisprudence and the decisions of the European Court of Human Rights.

As to the future, one can already make guesses at some developments; some guesses reasonably safe, others highly speculative. I take this as an occasion where I am privileged to make both sorts of guesses. I shall also say what developments I hope to see and what developments I would fear.

A development I foresee, and welcome, is the reappraisal of the immunities from suits for damages hitherto enjoyed by certain public authorities. This reappraisal must follow the case of *Osman* v. *The United Kingdom* decided by a Grand Chamber of the European Court of Human Rights.[7] The key facts were that over a period school authorities had be-

---

[6] This judgment has now been reversed by the House of Lords—see [2001] 2 WLR 1389—but it has nonetheless led to reforms in the constitutions of administrative tribunals.

[7] (1998) 29 EHRR 245.

come convinced that one of their teachers who seemed to be disturbed posed a serious threat to the physical safety of one of the pupils at the school, Ahmet Osman. There was good reason to believe that this teacher was responsible for criminal damage to the pupil's home and had made threats to harm the boy. The police were kept informed by the school and the parents, but the police provided no special protection to the boy. The teacher thereafter shot and killed the boy's father and wounded the boy.

The boy and his mother instituted proceedings in the English courts against the Metropolitan Police Commissioner on the ground of negligent failure to provide protection to the boy. The Commissioner applied to strike out the claim as disclosing no reasonable cause of action. The Court of Appeal in due course struck out the claim on the grounds that public policy required that the police, in carrying out their duty of crime prevention, should have immunity from claims for negligence.[8] In this they followed binding House of Lords authority. The Osmans took the case to Strasbourg, asserting *inter alia* that this dismissal of their action on the grounds of police immunity amounted to an unlawful restriction on their right of access to a court for the determination of their civil rights, in breach of Article 6(1) of the Convention. The Grand Chamber of the Strasbourg court, consisting of twenty judges including the British judge, unanimously accepted this argument. This decision had repercussions beyond the police forces. A similar immunity had been held to exclude any suit against a local authority for negligence in carrying out its duties of child protection—*X* v. *Bedfordshire County Council*;[9] or for negligence in carrying out its powers to repair highways—*Stovin* v. *Wise*[10]—both decisions of the House of Lords.

The judgment of the European Court of Human Rights in the *Osman* case therefore caused considerable perturbation. Among others, two Law Lords who had respectively given the leading judgments in *X* v. *Bedfordshire County Council* and in *Stovin* v. *Wise* penned vigorous responses.[11] They suggested that the European Court had not understood the English striking out procedure. Nor had it understood that the ruling that

---

[8] *Osman* v. *Ferguson* [1993] 4 All ER 344.

[9] [1995] 2 AC 633.

[10] [1996] AC 923.

[11] Respectively, Lord Browne-Wilkinson in the course of his judgment in *Barrett* v. *Enfield London Borough Council* [1999] 3 WLR 79 at pages 84–85; Lord Hoffmann in (1999) 62 *Modern Law Review* 159.

as a matter of public policy it was not fair, just, and reasonable to impose a liability on a class of defendants, however large, for a range of activities, however broad, was simply an aspect of the English law of tort and did not amount to an immunity. For my part I believe that the Strasbourg court understood the English law and procedure perfectly well and knew an immunity when they saw it.[12] At all events, in a case heard after the Osman judgment (*Barrett* v. *Enfield London Borough Council*),[13] also involving child protection, the House of Lords somehow distinguished *X* v. *Bedfordshire County Council* and refused to strike out the plaintiff's case against the local authority.[14] I believe that many more cases will be similarly "distinguished," if not overruled.

I must add that *X* v. *Bedfordshire County Council* was itself taken to the European Court of Human Rights. The hearing took place nine months ago.[15] At the time of writing judgment has not yet been given. So I may yet be shown to be wrong. In the meantime, however, in a very recent House of Lords case (*Phelps* v. *Hillingdon London Borough Council*),[16] *X* v. *Bedfordshire County Council* was again either distinguished or ignored; and at least one Law Lord referred to the Strasbourg decision in the *Osman* case with apparent approval.

Now, a guess at a possible development of which there is so far no hint in this country, but which I invite criminal lawyers to take note of. Minimum sentences for criminal offences are disliked by judges, but all governments like to be seen as tough on crime, so parliamentary repeal of minimum sentence laws is not on the cards. I would suggest that some minimum sentences may be vulnerable to declarations of incompatibility with the Convention as constituting inhuman punishment. The Supreme Court of Canada has given a lead here. The test that it applies is whether the minimum penalty is so disproportionate as to be cruel when notionally applied to the least culpable circumstances that could trigger the penalty.[17] It will not be overlooked that the mandatory penalty of life imprisonment for murder is a minimum penalty.

---

[12] I respectfully suggest that the Eastern European judges in particular would have had a good understanding of police immunities.

[13] See note 11 above.

[14] See note 9 above.

[15] I.e., in the spring of 2000. The judgment of the European Court of Human Rights was handed down on May 10, 2001, under the heading *Z & Others* v. *the United Kingdom*. The court departed from the reasoning in the *Osman* case but held nonetheless that United Kingdom law did not accord the children concerned an adequate remedy and awarded damages.

[16] [2000] 3 WLR 776.

[17] See, e.g. *R.* v. *Goltz* [1991] 3 SCR 485.

As a final example of what I would consider a desirable if as yet spec-ulative development under the Human Rights Act I must enter a much more controversial area of law. Under the law of the European Commu-nity the European Commission has extensive but rather vaguely defined powers, to be used in furtherance of the objectives of the Treaty of Rome. It has rule-making powers of various kinds and also has the duty and power of policing compliance with European Community legislation. In so doing it may institute proceedings before Community tribunals against individuals in member states and may impose very considerable fines or other penalties for infringements of such legislation. Its mea-sures can be enforced against individuals in their own states.

The European Court of Justice has held that Community law is supreme,[18] in the sense that it renders any conflicting provision of a na-tional law inapplicable.[19] The direct enforceability of Community law in this country is affirmed by Section 2 of the European Communities Act, 1972.

Does this mean that proceedings of the European Commission that lead to fines or other penalties enforceable in the United Kingdom are not subject to scrutiny under the Human Rights Act? My tentative sug-gestion is that they are subject to the Act.

Decisions of the European Court of Justice as well as the Maastricht Treaty itself have recognised fundamental rights including the rights embodied in the European Convention on Human Rights as part of the law of the European Community.[20] What is not, however, clear is to what extent those rights are actually observed in the practices of the European Commission. Nor is it necessarily the case that Community organs, including the European Court of Justice, would interpret Convention rights the same way as an English or Scottish court or the Strasbourg court would do. Section 6(1) of the Human Rights Act states that it is unlawful for a public authority to act in a way that is incompatible with a Convention right. Any authority that takes action to enforce a Com-mission decision in the United Kingdom, whether it be the Commis-sion itself or a U.K. surrogate, will presumably be a public authority, and thus on the face of it amenable to scrutiny under Section 6(1) of the Act. There is surely no warrant for reading into the Act an exception in favour of the organs or servants of the European Commission.

---

[18] This court sits in Luxembourg, not to be confused with the European Court of Hu-man Rights at Strasbourg.

[19] *Costa* v. *ENEL* [1964] ECR 586; *Simmenthal* [1978] ECR 629.

[20] See, e.g., *P.* v. *S.* [1996] All ER 397 (EC): *ERT* v. *DEP* [1994] 4 CMLR 490.

The German Constitutional Court faced a similar question in 1974. In that year the Court held that it had the power to measure provisions of Community law against the fundamental rights entrenched in the German Basic law. It also held that at that time Community law did not adequately protect fundamental rights of Germans. The German court could therefore protect them against Community infringements of those rights.[21] In 1986, however, it decided that protection of basic rights under Community law had developed so that it was substantially equal to that accorded by German law. The Constitutional Court continued to assert its jurisdiction to scrutinize Community measures, but it announced that for the time being it would refrain from exercising that jurisdiction.[22] That, as far as I know, is still its attitude.[23]

The Basic Law is the constitutional foundation of Germany. The Human Rights Act does not have that status, yet it does embody rights that in other countries have constitutional status. In enacting it Parliament gave effect to Article 1 of the Convention, which calls on the High Contracting Parties to secure to everyone within their jurisdiction the rights and freedoms defined in the Convention. Moreover, if our courts have jurisdiction over the acts of a public authority then (unlike the German Constitutional Court) they may not simply refrain from exercising it. In a proper case I would hope to see them exercise that jurisdiction.

Now I propose to turn to what I see as some of the dangers that may flow from an over-enthusiastic application of the Human Rights Act. High on the list I put the continuing attempts to give a predominant weight to the right of freedom of expression, as against other rights and interests. As I reminded you in my first lecture, the right to freedom of expression under Article 10 of the Convention is one of those rights that is subject to express limitations. At this stage it is convenient to state those limitations. Article 10.1 says that everyone has the right to freedom of expression, which includes the freedom to receive and impart information without interference by public authority. Article 10.2 reads:

---

[21] BverfGE 37, 371 (1974), a decision popularly referred to as *Solange I*. There is an English translation in [1974] CMLR 540.

[22] BverfGE 73, 339 (1986), *Solange II*. There is an English translation in [1987] CMLR 225.

[23] For a clear exposition of the German jurisprudence, see Professor Dieter Grimm, "The European Court of Justice and National Courts: The German Constitutional Perspective," 3 *Columbia Journal of European Law* 229 (1997).

The exercise of these freedoms, since it carries with it duties and responsibilities, may be subject to such formalities, conditions, restrictions or penalties as are prescribed by law and are necessary in a democratic society, in the interests of national security, territorial integrity or public safety, for the prevention of disorder or crime, for the protection of health or morals, for the protection of the reputation or rights of others, for preventing the disclosure of information received in confidence, or for maintaining the authority and impartiality of the judiciary.

This is an extensive list of restrictions. It will be seen that it includes restrictions not only in the general interest (national security, prevention of crime) but also in the interest of individuals with competing rights (e.g., the right to reputation). As any restrictions must, however, be prescribed by law, and must be shown to be necessary in a democratic society, there is on the face of it a proper balance between on the one hand free speech, and on the other hand competing public interests and individual rights. Many would say that it is the balance more or less struck in the common law, even if occasionally departed from in some statutes. Nobody denies the vital importance of free speech and a free press to a democratic society. Where then is the danger? In my opinion it lies in the constant and powerful pressure exerted by all branches of the media to extend the boundaries of freedom of expression at the expense of other rights and interests.

An instance of such pressure is to be found in the Human Rights Act itself. No one who followed the debates on the Human Rights Act could be in doubt that Section 12 was inserted into the Act as a response to pressure by the press and other media. The section, in brief, is designed to make it more difficult to obtain injunctions restraining publication of journalistic or literary material. It is right that restraints on publication should be rare. To Milton and to Blackstone freedom from prior restraint was the very essence of freedom of speech. Under the common law injunctions restraining publication are never easy to obtain, and the new section may not make much difference in practice. But the section instructs the court to which application is made for an injunction to have "particular regard" to the importance of the Convention right to freedom of expression and to the extent to which it would be in the public interest for the material to be published. Thus, the section points in one direction only. The court is not instructed to have particular regard to the right to a fair trial, or the right to respect for family life and private life, both of them Convention rights.

We are time and again told by the press that the law of libel bears too hard upon them. They complain that save on occasions that the law recognises as privileged,[24] they have the burden of proving the truth of defamatory allegations. They urge the adoption of the American doctrine stated in *New York Times* v. *Sullivan,*[25] and developed in later cases, under which any public figure, however grossly defamed, has no redress unless he or she can prove not only that the defamatory obligations are false, but that the publisher had no belief in the truth of the defamatory statement. Those who, encouraged by the Human Rights Act, press for the American rule are apparently impervious to its now widely recognised injustices and inconveniences.

More worrying even than the overt pressure to tilt the law of defamation in favour of the publishers is the insidious loosening of restraints on comment and reports on pending criminal trials. This has become ever freer, especially in high-profile cases. In many instances the reports seem clearly likely to impair the fairness of a pending jury trial, to the prejudice of both the accused and the public, as represented by the Crown. Yet prosecutions for contempt of court are rare and when they are instituted are attacked as attempts to stifle free speech.

More than twenty-five years ago in the *Sunday Times* thalidomide case,[26] Lord Reid said that in England there was a strong feeling that trial by newspaper should be prevented. He said: "If we were to ask the ordinary man or even a lawyer...why he has that feeling I suspect that the first reply would be—well look at what happens in some other countries where that is permitted."[27]

That was a judicial and polite way of referring to the United States. We have observed what to many of us, at least, was the repellent spectacle of completely unrestrained public comment on a murder trial in California. This was not journalistic lawlessness. It flowed from the United States Supreme Court's 1941 decision that comment on a pending case was permissible unless it could be shown to create a "clear and present danger" of unfairness in the trial.[28] That decision was fortified by a Supreme Court ruling in 1976, permitting local newspapers, while the

[24] Occasions of considerable scope under the common law as expounded by the House of Lords in *Reynolds* v. *Times Newspapers Ltd.* [1999] 3 WLR 1010.

[25] 376 US 254 (1964)

[26] *Attorney-General* v. *Times Newspapers* [1974] AC 273.

[27] At page 300.

[28] *Bridges* v. *California*, 314 US 252 (1941).

trial of a murder case was pending, to report a disputed confession alleged to have been made by the accused.[29] Chief Justice Warren Burger said that no restraint on publication was justifiable unless alternative measures to enforce fairness, such as change of venue, were shown to be ineffectual. Why it is the accused and not the press that has to bear the burden of proof is not clear to me. The Chief Justice said that freedom of speech from prior restraint "should have particular force as applied to the reporting of criminal proceedings." In the case of pending or current criminal proceedings, that is when I should have thought it ought to have the least force. What we saw in the O. J. Simpson case was the direct result of allowing freedom of speech to trump competing rights, including the right to a fair trial.

Another area in which I believe we should be on guard against media encroachments in the name of free speech is electioneering expenditure. In the United Kingdom we have strict limits on the amounts that parliamentary candidates may spend on their own election. And we do not permit political advertising on radio and television. The object of these restrictions is to achieve fairness and equality in the political process. Again, as we know, they do things differently in the United States. The U.S. Congress in 1971 passed a law that sought to limit to $50,000 the amount that a candidate in a federal election might expend out of his or her own family's monies. The U.S. Supreme Court held that this was an infringement of the First Amendment because it imposed restrictions on communication with the electorate and, as the majority put it, restricted the voices of those with money to spend.[30] Justice Thurgood Marshall, dissenting, considered that the law was justified to ensure that candidacy did not become the exclusive province of the wealthy,[31] but the majority held this to be an inadequate justification for the interference with the freedom of speech. Similarly, in 1992 the High Court of Australia declared invalid an Act of Parliament that prohibited paid advertising on radio or television during an election period on the ground that it infringed the right of communication on matters relevant to political discussion.[32]

Is it entirely unreal to envisage radio and television companies

[29] *Nebraska Press Association* v. *Stuart* 427 US 539 (1976).

[30] *Buckley* v. *Valeo* 424 US 1 (1976) at page 17.

[31] At page 288.

[32] *Australian Capital Television Pty. Ltd.* v. *The Commonwealth of Australia* (1992) 177 CLR 106.

advancing such arguments under Article 10 of the Convention, invoking freedom of expression in order to open the way to lucrative political advertising?

I have always thought of myself as, for the want of a better term, a civil rights lawyer, and I spent a large part of my professional life under a government whose laws and practices, including stringent censorship of publications, grossly violated the right of free speech. It may seem strange that I should view with apprehension the extension of so great a right, one so vital to a free society. But I do not think that it should overbear other rights and interests equally worthy of regard in a free society, including the right to a fair trial, the right to reputation, or the interest in fair and equal electoral procedures.

How is a reasonable balance to be maintained, given the heavy burden of justifying restrictions on the right of free speech as necessary in a democratic society in terms of Article 10.2? I suggest that a purposive construction should be given to Article 10. What are the purposes of freedom of speech as understood in common law countries? This has been comprehensively considered by Professor David Feldman in his book on *Civil Liberties and Human Rights in England and Wales.*[33] I would, by way of a summary, say that the main purposes are individual self-fulfillment, the attainment of truth through free expression of conflicting views, and, perhaps most important, promoting political debate and informing the electorate about the character and deeds of those who govern us or wish to govern us; in short to maintain effective democratic government. It is thus legitimate when judging claims to freedom of expression at the expense of other rights to ask which of those purposes it furthers. Does the liberty to spend unrestricted amounts of money on political advertising or electioneering assist in maintaining effective democratic government? Does free comment on pending trials help in the search for truth? What would be lost by deferring comment until after the trial? What political or social purpose is served by extending the right of the press to make false and defamatory statements of fact about individuals? I respectfully express the hope that the judges will ask these questions when presented with broad claims under Article 10.[34]

I have one more caveat. Courts are sometimes presented with diffi-

---

[33] (Oxford University Press, 1993), pages 547ff.

[34] I dealt more fully with these issues in my F. A. Mann Lecture in 1995. See S. Kentridge, "Freedom of Speech: Is It the Primary Right?" (1996) 45 *International and Comparative Law Quarterly* 253.

cult social or moral problems, which may have little legal content but which come to the courts largely because there is no other authority that can be appealed to. I have in mind such cases as *Gillick* (was a doctor entitled to supply contraceptives to a girl under sixteen years of age without parental consent?),[35] the cases on the turning off of life-support systems,[36] or the recent case of the separation of Siamese twins with the known consequence that one would die. Lord Bridge in *Gillick* warned against courts expressing *ex cathedra* opinions in areas of social and ethical controversy in which they have no claim to speak with authority.[37] My caveat is that judicial determination of these controversies will not be made more authoritative by attempts to fit them into the framework of the Convention on Human Rights. The general rights to life, liberty, security of the person, respect for family life, freedom of conscience— these do not answer the ethical questions posed by cases such as I have mentioned. One can read the judgment of Justice Harry Blackmun in the United States Supreme Court in *Roe* v. *Wade*[38] with some admiration for its humanity and wonder nonetheless whether his and his court's ruling on the regulation of abortions really owed anything to the invocation of the right to personal liberty and due process under the Fourteenth Amendment or to the constitutional right to privacy (a right unstated but said to be implied in the United States Constitution). The European Convention is not adapted to assist the proponents on either side of abortion law reform or to resolve the debate on euthanasia, and I hope it will not be invoked for such purposes in the courts of the United Kingdom.

There are as yet many unsolved conundrums in the Human Rights Act. One that arouses apparently endless controversy is whether, in terms of the Act, Convention rights have horizontal effect (i.e., whether they can be invoked by one individual against another) or whether they have only vertical effect (i.e., whether they are intended only as a protection against governmental power).[39] I have engaged in this controversy myself, on the verticalist side, and I believe that Lord Justice

---

[35] *Gillick* v. *West Norfolk and Wisbech Area Health Authority* [1986] AC 112.

[36] Such as *Airedale NHS Trust* v. *Bland* [1993] AC 789.

[37] At page 194.

[38] 410 US 113 (1973).

[39] See, e.g., Murray Hunt in [1998] *Public Law* 423, Lord Justice Buxton in (2000) 116 *Law Quarterly Review* 48, Sir William Wade in (2000) 116 *Law Quarterly Review* 217, and Nicholas Bamforth in (2001) 117 *Law Quarterly Review* 34.

Buxton's arguments in favour of a vertical interpretation are unanswerable even by Sir William Wade. On this occasion I shall content myself with saying that I now believe that the issue is not of major importance and will be solved by the courts with little difficulty.[40]

I should like to end by returning to a question that I mentioned early in my first lecture: will incorporation of the Convention politicise the judiciary? This has been a serious concern. It was raised by the former Lord Chancellor, Lord Mackay of Clashfern, before the Human Rights Act was passed, and has recently been raised again by Lord Kingsland, the Shadow Lord Chancellor. I call it a serious concern because the incorporation of the Convention had undoubtedly introduced a new element into the work of English and Scottish judges. The weighing of the needs of society against an individual's Convention right and consideration of the proportionality of measures that infringe a Convention right are new tasks, which go well beyond even the extensive powers of judicial review now asserted by the courts. As Lord Mackay put it,[41] the measuring of policy against principles has not hitherto been the role of the judiciary in this country. To that extent the new element in adjudication has political connotations. An Act of Parliament that courts may hold to be incompatible with the Convention may embody not merely a technical point of court procedure, but a policy dear to the heart of the government in power.

Nonetheless, I see little reason to fear that such issues, when they arise, will be decided according to the political predilections of the judges. As we know, in the United States when candidates for judicial appointments at the higher levels of the Federal Courts are considered, the candidate's judicial philosophy, political philosophy, and party affiliation are closely scrutinised. These matters have at least in recent times been irrelevant to judicial appointments in this country. I believe they will remain largely irrelevant. In 1992, after ten years of judicial enforcement of the Canadian Charter, the Hon. Brian Dickson, the for-

[40] This belief is based in part on the South African experience. The Bill of Rights in South Africa's Interim Constitution of 1994 was interpreted as having vertical and not horizontal effect—*du Plessis* v. *de Klerk* 1997 (4) BCLR 562. The final Constitution of 1996 authorises the courts to give horizontal effect to the Bill of Rights where they deem it appropriate. I am aware of no reported case in which any provision of the Bill of Rights has been so applied. Rather, the values embodied in the Bill of Rights have indirectly influenced the development of the common law. I fancy that that is what will happen in the United Kingdom.

[41] In a speech to the Citizenship Foundation on July 8, 1996.

mer Chief Justice of Canada, gave a lecture with the title "Has the Charter Americanized the Canadian Judiciary?"[42] His answer was "no." He
observed that in the United States candidates for the Supreme Court
and other federal courts were put forward to satisfy particular political
constituencies. That did not happen in Canada. He also said that issues
such as abortion and the death penalty did not in Canada arouse the
same ferocious debate as in the United States. All that is equally true of
this country.

This is not to say that the qualifications for the highest judicial offices
must remain unchanged. Experience in public law may now count more
heavily. Sensitivity to social issues and an understanding of the importance of individual rights would be good qualifications if, of course,
there were some way of detecting them. Perhaps a marked absence of
those attributes should be a disqualification. It is, I think, inevitable that
the new political element in the judicial function, although not party
political, will call for some change in the process of appointing judges to
the Court of Appeal and the House of Lords. I see no necessity for appointments to require nomination by a Judicial Services Commission, as
is the case in South Africa. (That system was required for historical reasons peculiar to South Africa.) But public confidence in the new role of
the senior judges would surely be enhanced by a more formal system of
consultation, perhaps with a standing committee, which would include
representatives of all parliamentary parties. However that may be, in the
end we shall have to rely, as we have always done, on the ability, good
sense, and integrity of our judges.

All in all I conclude that the Human Rights Act has given us a real
bill of rights and that it will establish a new principle in our constitutional law. In 1942 Justice Robert Jackson of the United States Supreme
Court said this:[43]

> The very purpose of a bill of rights is to withdraw certain subjects
> from the vicissitudes of political controversy, to place them beyond
> the reach of majorities...and to establish them as legal principles to
> be applied by the Courts. One's...fundamental rights may not be
> submitted to vote, they depend on the outcome of no elections.

The Human Rights Act can and should achieve that purpose.

[42] Published in the *University of British Columbia Law Review,* 1995.
[43] In *West Virginia State Board of Education* v. *Barnett* 319 US 625 (1942) at page 638.

# The Past, Present, and Future

# of the Human Family

*SARAH BLAFFER HRDY*

THE TANNER LECTURES ON HUMAN VALUES

Delivered at

University of Utah
February 27 and 28, 2001

SARAH BLAFFER HRDY is professor emeritus of anthropology at the University of California, Davis. She was educated at Radcliffe College and received her Ph.D. from Harvard University. Hrdy is the recipient of a Guggenheim Fellowship, a member of the National Academy of Sciences and the California Academy of Sciences, and a fellow of the Animal Behavior Society and the American Academy of Arts and Sciences. She is past editor of the book series *The Foundations of Human Behavior* and serves on the editorial boards of *Evolutionary Anthropology* and *Human Nature.* Her work in primate sociobiology has led to a number of publications, including *The Woman that Never Evolved* (1981), a *New York Times* Notable Book; and *Infanticide: Comparative and Evolutionary Perspectives* (1984, co-edited with Glen Hausfater), a *Choice* Outstanding Academic Book. Her most recent book, *Mother Nature: A History of Mothers, Infants, and Natural Selection* (1999), was chosen by both *Publishers Weekly* and *Library Journal* as a Best Book of 1999, was a finalist for the PEN USA (West) 2000 Literary Award for Research Nonfiction, and won the Howells Prize of the American Anthropological Association.

# I. MATERNAL LOVE AND ITS AMBIVALENCE IN THE PLEISTOCENE, THE EIGHTEENTH CENTURY, AND RIGHT NOW

*Over my heart in the days that have flown,*
*No love like mother-love ever has shown;*
*No other worship abides and endures,*
*Faithful, unselfish and patient like yours...*

MARY AKERS ALLEN, 1860

*It was all very well to say that it was the common lot of women to bear children.*
*It wasn't true. She, for one, could prove that wrong.... she did not love her chil-*
*dren. It was useless pretending.*

KATHERINE MANSFIELD, 1922

*...maternal love or maternal hatred, though the latter fortunately is most rare,*
*is all the same to the inexorable principle of natural selection....*

CHARLES DARWIN, 1859

## INTRODUCTION

"Mother-love" is a powerful emotion, rivaled only by the strength of each person's preconceptions about it. For every human life is shaped by being a mother, by having a mother, or by wishing we had one. Phrases like "maternal instinct" are used every day to refer to love or unconditional devotion to children. Yet who knows what this phrase actually means? We observe mothers caring for infants, but where do those nurturing emotions come from? Are they inborn? Are they learned? Do only mothers experience those emotions?

Scientists debate fiercely among themselves whether in the case of creatures so flexible as we humans are a term like "instinct" can mean

I am indebted to Kristen Hawkes, Jon Seger, and Mary Jane West-Eberhard for discussion and comments.

much. For there exists no species-typical suite of behaviors all women engage in right after birth, say licking off the amniotic fluids or eating the placenta, before placing the baby on our breasts to suckle there. There is a dearth of "fixed action patterns" in our species, and mothers respond to babies in myriad ways, from Mary Akers Allen's celebrated "mother-love" that "abides and endures" to Katherine Mansfield's description of disinterest so absolute that the mother feels it is "useless pretending."

Viewed from the privileged vantage point of postindustrial Westerners who cache infants inside predator-free walled nurseries, take out medical insurance, and do their foraging in supermarkets, we take it for granted that mothers will care for each infant they bear. How then to explain headlines like the one that appeared recently in my local paper: "The number of children who died in Sacramento as a result of abuse or neglect in Sacramento county last year was among the highest ever..." (*Sacramento Bee,* July 28, 1998)?

"Highest ever." The accuracy of that claim has to depend on "where?" and on "when?" Compared to northern California fifteen years ago, it's probably true. But compared to Paris in the eighteenth century, Sacramento and Salt Lake City are models of conscientious parenting. Compared to the Pleistocene, the period between 1.6 million and 10,000 years ago, we're doing better than our nomadic hunter-gatherer ancestors in some respects, far worse in others.

Across cultures and through time, including the modern era when official records began to be kept, precise data on infant neglect, abandonment, and infanticide have always been hard to come by. With or without exact figures, there is a general consensus that the numbers in the United States have been increasing of late. One indication is the fact that the number of children taken into foster care has doubled since the 1980s. Such data as we have, together with rivetingly sensational media coverage of selected cases, have provoked legislators into action.

Resulting policy includes a series of stopgap measures intended to insure the physical safety of babies abandoned right after birth. In my home state of California Governor Gray Davis just repealed an old law that made it a crime for mothers to abandon an infant and signed California Assembly Bill 1368, which went into effect January 1, 2001. Bill 1368 permits mothers to abandon infants without penalty, provided they do so at a hospital emergency ward within seventy-two hours of birth. Similar laws (sometimes designating fire stations rather than hospitals as the depository) have just been passed in Utah, Minnesota, and Texas. These states are following the lead of European countries like Hungary, where an incubator was recently set up on the sidewalk outside Budapest's major hospital. In Hamburg, Germany, social workers now give demonstrations on how to deposit babies safely in "letter boxes"—glass cabinets with a tiny mattress on the bottom.

California's new law was a well-meaning bipartisan response to "reports of abandoned babies found in trash bins, restrooms and parking lots," such as the case in New Jersey where "a high school student attending her senior prom delivered in a restroom, hid it in the trash...."[1] Legislators had in mind a specific profile. They envisioned a teenager from a "respectable" family, desperate to keep her pregnancy a secret. The underlying assumptions here might be statistically reasonable for a population with available birth control and a prosperous economy, but otherwise not. After all, abandonment and infanticide are protean and variable phenomena that go back a long time.

Beyond acknowledging the role of infanticide in the history of our species, though, there is little agreement among scholars as to the cause. In ivory towers distant from the legislative assemblies, fire stations, or dumpsters, academics have been debating among themselves for decades why some mothers exhibit so little interest in the well-being of their children. To the best of our ability to know, around half of the homicides right after birth are by teenage mothers. Unquestionably, young maternal age, closely spaced births, and lack of social support are primary risk factors. But it's worth noting that just over one-half involve mothers older than twenty (Overpeck et al. 1999). Such mothers do not necessarily fit the profile of an unwed teenager seeking to avoid disgrace that Sacramento legislators had in mind.

The most obvious generalization about infanticide and abandonment is that they increase when other forms of birth control are unavailable. Apart from this generalization, risk factors vary. Examining infant abandonment across species and through historical and evolutionary time broadens our perspective. It cautions us not to rely on familiar assumptions, projecting personal expectations upon humans at large.

---

[1] Quotations are taken from the press release issued by the bill's principal co-author, Republican state senator Jim Brulte.

Broader perspectives and deeper time-depth help guard against ethno-centrism and keep us from confusing wishful thinking with "natural laws."

## "Essentialists" versus "Social Constructionists"

For most modern Americans, phenomena like infant abandonment and infanticide are deeply disturbing and hard to explain. After all, if fe-males evolved to be mothers, why would any woman ever want to do anything other than turn her life over to meeting the needs of her little gene replicator? At first glance, the prevalence of infant abandonment would appear to disprove a biological basis for mother love. Or else (as defenders of essentialism are quick to point out) it is only *unnatural* mothers who abandon their babies. The equation of "good mothering" with psychological health, bad mothering with pathology, explains why half the women incarcerated in Broadmoor during the first part of the twentieth century, spending long stints in Britain's state asylum for the criminally insane, were put there for committing infanticide.

From the nineteenth century deep into the twentieth, essentialist ideas about females were woven into Darwinian perspectives. Darwin knew that under duress "primitive" women sometimes abandoned young, particularly when ill-timed infants were too closely spaced. But Darwin assumed infanticide was rare. Other evolutionists, however, could only view infanticidal mothers as depraved. The fact that women are primates only strengthened expectations about instinctive devotion, since monkey and ape mothers are famous for carrying their infants everywhere they go, suckling them several times an hour. In all Old World monkeys and among apes like ourselves, long periods of gesta-tion result in a single infant; and provided that baby clings to its mother's fur after birth and manages to negotiate its way to her breast, the mother becomes attached and thereafter carries her precious cargo no matter what. Even the corpse of a dead infant will be carried for days.

In many thousands of scientist-hours of observation, no wild mon-key or ape mother has ever been reported to injure her own infant delib-erately, although first-time mothers are often incompetent. Even counting such inexperienced mothers, though, observations of aban-donment among primates are exceedingly rare with the exception of humans and one other family of monkeys, the Callitrichidae, about whom more later.

Being female was seen as synonymous with bearing and nurturing as many offspring as possible. No wonder then that a mother's responses were assumed to be reflexive and automatic, as inevitable as the uterine muscle contractions that ushered her baby into the world. Such devotion was subsumed under the scientific-sounding label "maternal instinct." Accordingly, mothers who abandon infants were viewed as unnatural. Even mothers who merely feel ambivalent must need counseling.

Since, according to this line of reasoning, mothers had evolved to care full-time for infants, it followed that human infants evolved to need a full-time, completely committed, constantly-in-contact mother in order to feel secure and develop normally. This meant that any woman who gives birth and does not then stay at home to provide same must be unnatural. It was taken for granted that this stay-at-home mom required a husband to support her.

Neither side of this essentialist coin was popular among critics of biological determinism. Feminists pointed out how neatly preconceptions about what was "natural" conformed to 1950s stereotypes about how the two sexes should behave. No wonder feminists felt they had a vested interest in denying the existence of innate sex differences, since it was the parent with the double XX chromosomes who was uniquely qualified to care for infants.

From the 1950s onward, dogmatic assertions about "maternal instincts" prodded feminists to join French philosophers and social historians searching for "social constructionist" alternatives to such essentialist claims. The increasingly well documented history of infant abandonment, beginning in antiquity and peaking in eighteenth-century Europe, became the centerpiece for arguments that—if one granted the starting assumption that animals naturally nurture their young—were both logical and very flattering to humanity's self-image. What if, social constructionists proposed, humans, with their higher brain functioning and seemingly open-ended capacity for language and symbolic thought, operate differently from other animals, transcending "nature"? In short, what if maternal instincts have been lost in the human species? If devotion to infants is a learned emotion, no wonder attitudes toward children vary so much.

The idea that maternal emotions are socially constructed, more nearly maternal "sentiments" than innate biologically based responses, can be traced back to the French social historian Philippe Ariès (with *Centuries of Childhood* first published in French in 1960 and in English in 1962) and to his successors, Edward Shorter in Canada (*The Making of the Modern Family,* 1975), Elizabeth Badinter in France (*Motherhood: Myth and Reality,* 1981), and Nancy Scheper-Hughes in the United States (*Death without Weeping,* 1992). After studying desperately poor mothers in Brazilian shanty-towns, for example, anthropologist Scheper-Hughes concluded that maternal love, "far from universal and innate," was a "Bourgeois Myth": "...anything *other* than natural and instead represents a matrix of images, meanings, sentiments and practices that are everywhere socially and culturally produced" (341).

Shorter and Badinter had already reached Scheper-Hughes's conclusion after researching mothers in eighteenth-century France at a time when 95% of newborns in urban areas like Paris were sent away to be suckled by strangers, the custom known as wet-nursing that resulted in appallingly high rates of infant mortality. Few historians now dispute the numbers. Such lapses in maternal commitment were, if anything, more widespread and extensive than social constructionists originally imagined: hundreds of thousands of babies delegated to distant wet-nurses if not abandoned outright. Yet many of these less-than-solicitous mothers were married, older than twenty, not necessarily destitute, and their pregnancy was not a secret. Presumably they had some choice in the matter. According to Shorter, they simply "did not *care* and that is why their children vanished in the ghastly slaughter of the innocents that was traditional child rearing" (1977:204). If mother love was indeed "natural" and "spontaneous," Badinter asked, how could mothers treat their own flesh and blood this way? How could any mother differentiate between offspring, caring for one, while sending another away? "I am not questioning maternal love," she said. "I am questioning maternal instinct" (1981:ix).

I admired authors on both sides of this yawning divide between the old-fashioned "essentialists" and the late-twentieth-century "social constructionists," especially Badinter and Scheper-Hughes, feminists intent on situating women in historical context. But I was also taken aback by the way the debate had come to be framed as a dichotomy between nature and nurture, with "nurture" recast here as historical circumstance. The baby, as wriggling, messy, and interactive as any other living organism, was being thrown out with the essentialist bath water. Completely overlooked was just how dynamic the multiple social and biological processes contributing to the emergence of maternal commitment—what humans mean by love—were likely to be.

## GENDER IS A PROCESS, BUT SO ARE ALL PHENOTYPES...

By this point, though, who was still listening? In the minds of "social constructionists," gender and all its trappings (including, in the case of women, motherhood) referred to socially transacted processes. Anyone comparing humans to other animals, or talking about what nonhuman animals were doing in the natural world, was assumed to be biased by prescribed categories. *A priori,* such views were prejudged "essentialist" and hence tainted.

By the last quarter of the twentieth century ethologists (scientists who study animals in their natural habitats) and sociobiologists (who seek to understand the biological basis for social behaviors and rely on comparison across species to help them do so) were moving away from moralistic projections toward systematic study of what animals in the natural world were doing. In particular, females were being studied as individuals, leading to a new awareness of the extent to which one female differed from another. A female of the same species, even the same individual at different times in her life, might behave very differently according to her circumstances. By this point, though, social constructionists, flushed by their success in demonstrating how biased by their own preconceptions scientists could be, failed to notice the morphing of their opponents or to acknowledge just how many scientists already concurred with them about the all-too-human problem of observer bias. Unnoticed by social constructionists, there had been a sea change in how females were conceptualized by sociobiologists.

By the late twentieth century anyone with a grounding in evolutionary biology and behavioral ecology took for granted that the same genotype could be very variably expressed depending on local ecological or historical conditions. Virtually all the relevant phenotypic traits— body size, reproductive condition, social status, gender—were viewed as processes, the outcomes of just how genetic instructions became expressed in the course of development. Biologists were increasingly sceptical of dogmatic assertions about species-typical and sex-typical universals, so that "biological determinists" were getting hard to find.

For critics of essentialism had made their point: history and circumstances have to be taken into account. But not because context is *all*-important. Rather, history is important because it is within historically produced social and ecological contexts that innate biological responses—instincts if you must—are expressed. As ethologists and sociobiologists were increasingly forced to confront the problems of observer bias, they revamped observational methods and set about correcting many of the erroneous assumptions that had distorted the way several generations of evolutionists understood selective pressures on females.

Once biases were identified, field researchers studying the reproductive behavior of insects, birds, mammals, or people sooner or later set out to correct them. But this, after all, is the real strength of science compared to more ideologically based ways of knowing: Sooner or later (and in this case it was often later) wrong assumptions get corrected. From 1975 onward, this reformulation brought new respect for how much individual variation there was among females. Some females were mothers, others were not. Nor were all mothers equivalent, and the same mother could behave quite differently from one stage of her life to another. This highly variable female, a strategic juggler coping with all sorts of tradeoffs, was quite different from the romanticized stereotype of a nonstop breeder intent on rearing every offspring she produced. She might as well have been a new life form.

With this new life form in mind, it is time to revisit the eighteenth century, when so many European mothers either abandoned infants or sent them to wet-nurses, the paradigmatic case study that supposedly *proved* how socially constructed rather than instinctive human maternal emotions have always been. It is time to rethink the options and constraints that shaped their behavior from both historical and sociobiological perspectives. I will explain why I think the infamous "wet-nursing era" has been widely misinterpreted and why, far from *invalidating* the existence of maternal instincts, this extraordinary period in European social history provides insights into the biological underpinnings of maternal commitment. This done, I will return to contemporary efforts to cope with infant abandonment, new legislation like California Assembly Bill 1638, an area where confusion over what we mean by "maternal instincts" is likely to lead to unintended consequences.

## THE WET-NURSING ERA IN CONTEXT

Travel with me, then, back to eighteenth-century Europe. The year is 1781, right at the peak of France's "heyday of wet-nursing." Imagine walking toward a substantial stucco house in a prosperous town just north of Paris. The wife of a government official, Madame Roland, is climbing the limestone steps to pay a visit to her neighbor, who gave birth to a daughter the day before. Here's how she described what she saw: "Her husband [who was hoping for a son] is completely ashamed of it; (his wife) is in a foul mood.... The poor baby was sucking its fingers, and drinking cow's milk in a room far removed from its mother, waiting for the hired woman who was to nurse it...so the little creature could be sent to the village..." (cited in Sussman 1982:80).

This image of a newborn sent off posthaste, in the custody of strangers, strikes us as unaccountably odd. Even a contemporary observer like Madame Roland is taken aback by the seeming callousness of her neighbor giving up her baby right after birth. Soon an itinerant baby transporter will arrive at the house, perhaps with a cart, bringing the wet-nurse to pick up her charge, or else leading a mule with baskets strapped to its back, an arduous and risky way to transport neonates. According to police reports from the time, babies occasionally fell out or were lost on the trip. After a journey of indeterminate duration, the baby arrived at a rural destination and was turned over to a nurse who was supposed to be lactating. But who knew?

This apparent "indifference" of mothers became the centerpiece for late-twentieth-century feminist arguments debunking the existence of maternal instincts. According to statistics maintained by the Paris police—who eventually started to track this extraordinary traffic in babies—20,000 of 21,000 babies born in Paris in 1780 were nursed by another woman, usually a "wet-nurse," a recent mother herself who was also lactating. The luckiest babies, born to propertied parents, would be placed directly with wet-nurses chosen by the parents. In the best-case scenario, the wet nurse came to live with the family under maternal supervision—a long-standing European practice among elites. An infant wet-nursed in-house would have the same 80% chance of surviving as if the mother breastfed the baby herself.

More typically, though, babies were sent away, or parents might have the designated heir nursed at home and supernumerary children sent out. The majority of mothers swept up in the wet-nursing business

Fig. 1. *La privation sensible* (The Painful Deprivation) by Jean-Baptiste Greuze (1725–1805) depicts the pick-up of a newborn by an itinerant entrepreneur who will transport the baby to a wet nurse in the countryside. (Courtesy of Bibliothèque Nationale, Paris)

at this time did not have a lot of leeway. For they belonged to working families for whom the wife's labor was essential to keep the butcher shop or other enterprise afloat. Records from the Bureau of Wet Nursing show that survival rates for babies sent away to wet-nurses varied between 60 and 70%. These were the fortunate babies, whose parents were actually involved in and contracted for their care.

The *unluckiest* babies were born to desperately poor mothers, many of them young and/or unmarried, who risked both reputation and their sources of livelihood if they kept the baby. By abandoning her baby, the mother ceased to be directly involved. From medieval times onward, mothers could deposit unwanted babies in foundling homes, often by placing them in a rotating barrel called a *tour,* ring a bell, and fade anonymously into the night.

In an era without other reliable means of birth control, thousands of babies every year were abandoned. Charities and state-run foundling homes had to compete for wet nurses with paying parents. Prices rose, so that parents had to lower their standards and seek nurses farther and farther away. Often there was a dangerously long lag between birth and placement, or else several babies were assigned to the same nurse.

Foundling homes served as magnets for parents with unwanted children, producing unintended consequences on a massive scale. Insufficient wet nurses along with crowding and infectious diseases led to dismally low survival rates. In 1781 only 10–40% of babies abandoned in Paris that year made it to their eighth birthday. Medical professionals and civic authorities were becoming increasingly alarmed, both by these staggeringly high rates of infant mortality and by what was viewed as the "unnatural" behavior of their mothers and the decline in "public morality" it seemed to signify.

## EXPLAINING MATERNAL INDIFFERENCE

Reform movements gathered steam. By the nineteenth century government committees were listening to testimony about the "sacred duty" of motherhood and drafting legislation to curb infant abandonment and monitor the wet-nursing business. Reformers intent on romanticizing instinctive maternal devotion had a vested interest in equating the use of wet nurses with the worst possible motives. They lumped a range of different parental choices in one category—wet nursing—and then equated anything less than self-sacrificing motherhood with the worst possible motive: infanticide.

According to the nineteenth-century French reformer Dr. Alexander Mayer, mothers abandoned "a cherished being...to a coarse peasant woman whom one has never seen, whose character and morality one does not know," "with the desire of not seeing them again" (cited in Sussman 1982:122).

Using wet-nurses came to be viewed as a nonprosecutable form of infanticide, which made for effective propaganda. In England and Germany *angelmaker* and its equivalent *Engelmacherin* were the slang for a wet nurse. In France the name *faiseuse d'anges* was used for both wet nurses and, later, abortionists. The underlying logic was that any woman who got pregnant and then did not carry the fetus to term or who did not care for the infant after birth at any cost, including suckling it, was worse than unnatural. She was thought to be *murderous.*

In 1865 Dr. Mayer prophesied that "[t]he whole thing is so revolting to good sense and morality that in twenty years people will refuse to believe [that wet-nursing] ever happened." And, indeed, a generalized amnesia about this period in Western history does seem to have set in. Of the psychoanalysts and historians who still refer to it, most remember wet-nursing from Dr. Mayer's perspective: "It must have been common knowledge," writes the twentieth-century psychoanalyst Maria Piers (1978) in her book *Infanticide,* that the wet-nurse was "a professional feeder and a professional killer."

By this point, wet-nursing had become the prime exhibit in the social constructionist case against the existence of maternal instincts in the human species. Social constructionists like Ariès argued that the concept of childhood itself had only gradually emerged between the Middle Ages and the eighteenth century. As evidence, Ariès pointed to the iconography of fourteenth-century Italian madonnas with the baby Jesus depicted as a little grownup. Demographic historians stressed doubling of European populations between 1650 and 1850, bringing desperate poverty and high infant mortality rates. Mothers conditioned to seeing children die, it was argued, withheld love as emotional self-defense. More overtly politicized anthropologists laid the blame for maternal indifference on colonial and capitalist oppression of third-world peoples.

Clearly such arguments are pertinent. But by themselves they do not explain the phenomenon of maternal indifference. After all, wherever assistance in rearing infants is in limited supply and other forms of birth control are not available, mothers in all societies practice infanticide. Long before the population explosion in eighteenth-century Europe, from classical and medieval times onward, parents coped with excess heirs or unwanted children by selling them, giving them to the church as oblates, or abandoning them on roadsides. Across cultures, many hunter-gatherer societies suffered high rates of infant mortality without compromising close emotional ties between mothers and the infants they are committed to rear. For example, the !Kung San woman who is the heroine of Marj Shostak's wonderful biography *Nisa* lived in a population where 50% of children died before adulthood. All five of Nisa's own children died. Yet she experienced unbearable grief at each death. "[I] almost died of the pain," Nisa recalled (Shostak 1981:312).

Early diaries (kept mostly by literate men rather than by mothers) and ethnographies describe the same continuum of emotions that we find among a cross-section of modern parents. Maternal responses range from sensual adoration of her baby to neglectful or even abusive.

No doubt some fraction of eighteenth-century French mothers were infanticidal. Others were desperately poor and short on options. Yet it is hard to sustain the argument that hundreds of thousands of mothers who could have afforded to rear their children sent them away to wet nurses instead as a legal, nonprosecutable way of killing them. Rather, it looks to me as if mothers whose labor was needed were taking advantage of wet-nursing, a custom that had originally developed among elites, to reduce the opportunity costs (mother's lost labor) of rearing infants. These mothers were adjusting maternal effort to their circumstances.

In a world where the amount paid out in French livres is equivalent to the number of months the baby would be nursed, there was a near-linear correlation between how much parents paid and the probability that the infant would survive. Abandoning an infant right after birth cost the least—in material terms at least. But abandonment also resulted in the lowest survival rates. During much of this period only 10–20% of abandoned infants would be lucky enough to make it. If a mother could manage to pay just forty-odd livres for half a year of wet-nursing before she defaulted and the unpaid nurse was forced to turn the baby over to a foundling home, survival rates would double. Historian

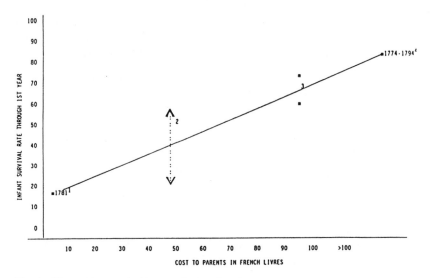

Fig. 2. There is a nearly linear relationship between the amount expended by parents to pay wet nurses and the probability of infant survival.
Notes on how survival rates were calculated:

1. Mortality rates during the first year of life for infants deposited in Parisian foundling hospitals reached 68.5% in 1751 and rose to 85.7% by 1781; 92% of these children would die by their eighth birthday (from data in Sussman 1982).

2. According to Sussman, roughly 10% of parents who sent children to rural wet nurses subsequently defaulted on their payments, with the result that their infants were eventually deposited in foundling homes. Infants who were wet-nursed for six months before this happened had higher survival prospects than those abandoned at birth. The cost here is calculated at one-half the yearly rate for a rural wet nurse.

3. A Parisian artisan might earn twenty to twenty-five livres per month, his wife one-half that. Seven to eight livres per month went to pay the rural wet nurse. Mortality for these wet-nursed infants was 25–40%, rising some-what over time as good wet nurses became increasingly hard to find. Records kept by the Bureau of Wet-Nursing indicate that mortality had risen to 42% by 1794.

4. Infants tended by live-in wet nurses in their mothers' homes enjoyed roughly the same 80% prospect of survival as infants nursed by their own mothers.

George Sussman calculated that about 10% of parents went this route. If parents managed to increase their payments to 90 livres for an entire first year of wet-nursing, survival chances rose to 60%.

The closest parallel I can think of for parents who seem to me more nearly cost-conscious than infanticidal would be working parents today, parents just barely hanging on to a middle-class status while seeking affordable care so that the wife can keep working or else single working mothers without a supportive kin group who have no choice but to scramble to find whatever daycare they can. The main difference is that in the days before pasteurized milk and rubber nipples eighteenth-century working mothers needed 24-hour *night and day* care from another woman who was lactating and often several days' commute away.

If the goal had been to eliminate infants, as the reformers suspected, sending her baby to a wet nurse scarcely solved the working mother's problem. Freed from lactational amenorrhea, most non-nursing wives became pregnant again within months, which is one more reason why infanticide is such a poor form of birth control. Maurice Garden's (1970) remarkable demography of eighteenth-century Lyon documents nearly annual births in the families of butchers and silk-makers who sent babies off to wet nurses. Mothers routinely produced twelve to sixteen children, one mother as many as twenty-one in twenty-four years. The toll taken by such hyperfecundity could be measured not just in infant mortality, but in maternal anemia, prolapsed uteruses, and early deaths. These bad outcomes came as a consequence of foregoing frequent breastfeeding and with it the more natural three- to five-year birth spacing that would have been typical of our ancestors living as nomadic Pleistocene foragers.

There is little to indicate that mothers used wet nursing as a legal form of infanticide. Rather they were economizing on what rearing infants cost them. But more to the point, there was never any reason in the first place to assume that if some mothers were infanticidal this constituted grounds for assuming maternal instincts had been lost in humans.

ELICITING MATERNAL RESPONSES

It's time to return to the question of what we can possibly mean by the term "maternal instinct." Even though human mothers don't *automatically* rear each infant they give birth to, systematic rather than selective observations of other mammals make it clear that they don't do so either. Typically mammals in poor condition just don't get pregnant— the most common form of birth control. But if they do conceive, and circumstances drastically deteriorate, some mammals (like langur monkeys or gelada baboons) spontaneously abort. Other mammalian mothers may carry on but cull or abandon after birth. In his long-term study of wild prairie dogs, biologist John Hoogland (1995) found that about 10% of litters were abandoned at birth. The mothers who abandoned litters tended to be underweight and in poor condition. In certain populations of house mice, mothers choose among pups to concentrate maternal investment on the most robust.

Learning and prior experience caring for babies are particularly important in primates, compared to other mammals. More experienced moms make more competent moms. This is why, across primates, mortality rates among firstborn infants are so high, due to the mother's immaturity (she is not yet full grown) and also to her inexperience. Learning how to care for infants is even more important in the case of human primates. And, as for all primates, the best antidote to maternal inexperience is assistance from other group members. A range of studies of both nonhuman primates and humans, including foraging peoples such as the Hadza, the Efé, and the Aka, demonstrate that having older matrilineal kin nearby reduces the risk of a firstborn dying in infancy. Not surprisingly, perhaps, it is customary among many foraging peoples for young women to remain near their natal families until *after* the birth of their first child.

New mothers learn how to care for their babies, but they also learn to recognize the baby as an individual with whom they feel a special kinship. Because primate babies are born immobile, there is no chance that any baby will wander away and latch on to the wrong mother. There is no way for the mother's milk to get embezzled by the wrong baby. Evolutionarily this is important, because it means that primate mothers *don't have to imprint on their babies right after birth* the way sheep and other ungulates whose babies run around right after birth do; and they don't. Primates are very flexible in this respect. The mother's emotional attachment to her infant *can* begin right after birth; but bonding is an ongoing process, so that the actual window of opportunity stretches out for weeks and months. This is why cross-fostering, the switching of an unrelated infant for the female's own, is accomplished so easily in primates, although the earlier the better.

For all primates, there is a lag on the order of seventy-two hours—roughly equivalent to the delay between birth and the onset of lactation—during which a mother learns to identify her own baby. Within days, though, a human mother can pick out her own baby's clothes by smell alone. Once lactation is established, she not only recognizes her infant, but elevated prolactin levels produced by the baby's sucking (the body's work order for "more milk") intensify her feelings of protectiveness. The more the baby sucks, the more milk the mother produces and the higher her prolactin levels. Pressure of milk built up behind her nipples guarantees discomfort should the mother, for any reason, be separated from her baby and unable to nurse. In addition to the growing bond between the mother and her infant, this is another, quite literally pressing reason for a mother to seek out her baby.

The lag in formation of these bonds turns out to be critical for understanding the willingness of eighteenth-century French mothers to give up their babies. Recall Madame Roland's observation: the baby is kept *in a room far away.* The situation is structured to prevent the mother from responding to infant cues, and by and large events are scheduled to take place before nursing gets under way. It is worth noting that California Assembly Bill 1368 unintentionally does the same thing, decreasing rather than increasing the chances that a mother ambivalent about keeping her infant will become attached to the baby and decide she wants to care for it, a point I will return to.

## Conscious and Unconscious Bases of Maternal Commitment

An odd experiment from early-nineteenth-century Paris illustrates what I mean. As described by historian Rachel Fuchs, 24% of women who gave birth at the state-run charity hospital La Maternité in 1831 subsequently walked across the street and abandoned their babies at the foundling home conveniently situated there. A group of reformers intent on reducing child abandonment decided to force one subset of indigent women to remain with their infants and to breastfeed them for eight days after birth. An experiment that most human subjects review boards would not permit today proved extraordinarily effective: the proportion of new mothers who abandoned their babies fell from 24 to 10% (though, of course, we don't know how these stories end).

It is as if two separate systems inform the mother's actions. One involves her practical, conscious decisions that take into account her economic plight, cultural norms, and her uniquely human awareness of the future: "I cannot afford to keep this baby!" The other system is informed by her tactile and emotional experience with the baby. And in this context it's worth noting what so often goes unremarked in the social constructionist literature debunking maternal instinct: *none* of the "indifferent" mothers from eighteenth-century France or the differentially neglectful mothers in the shanty towns of Brazil—the mothers thought to prove that there was no biological basis to mother love—were breast-feeding.

It is indisputably true (as pointed out by the anti-essentialists) that there is no one root source of emotion or urge equivalent to "the maternal instinct." There *are* a range of biologically based maternal responses to a range of circumstances, however, that, taken together, make it more or less likely that a given mother will become committed to her offspring. The best way to visualize this complicated and multifaceted process is to consider specific features of the mother's condition that increase—or decrease—the chances that she will respond to the various cues produced by a new baby. Given just how important it is for a mother to respond appropriately, it is not surprising that "mother nature" has built multiple redundancies, checks, and failsafes into a system that generally speaking is biased toward inducing a mother to nurture her baby.

Because of the way primate ovaries function, a woman would not normally ovulate or conceive in the first place unless she had the bodily resources to sustain both pregnancy and the costly period of lactation that follows. All through pregnancy, physical changes in the mother's body are under way, lowering her threshold for responding in a positive way to babies. The placenta itself, the baby's supply line, produces progesterone that helps sustain the pregnancy and contributes to changes in estrogen and progesterone levels that ready or "prime" the mother to respond maternally. During the birth process itself, further endocrinological changes, particularly secretion of oxytocin (from the Greek for "swift birth"), produce the muscle contractions that push the baby out. Oxytocin also has an opiate-like, soothing effect, preparing the mother for her first encounter with a tiny stranger.

Physical transformations within the mother's body continue after birth. Continuous proximity to the infant, along with the act of caring for it, produces endocrinological and neurological changes. Care-taking inscribes new pathways in the brain. These retraceable paths in turn lower the threshold of stimulation needed to elicit maternal responses in the future. Memories interact with existential experience. Stimulation from a baby's sucking on her nipples releases oxytocin, making a woman feel relaxed. At the same time (based on work with birds and lab rodents) higher circulating levels of prolactin may increase maternal protectiveness toward infants. Across many species (even in birds or in male mammals that are not lactating) higher prolactin levels are correlated with protective and caring responses. In some mammal mothers, higher prolactin levels are correlated with the fierce protectiveness of their offspring that animal behaviorists call "lactational aggression."

Even without all of the special hormonal changes associated with being pregnant and giving birth, female primates are attracted by infants. Even females far too young to breed find the sounds, smells, and appearance of infants irresistible. Human females of all ages, and many men as well, are attracted by small creatures with rounded head, tiny features, and big eyes. Add to this the very special role of plumpness, prolonged gazing, and fleeting, soon to become directed, smiles. These are specialities of human babies, not displayed by other apes that are equipped from birth to catch hold of their mother's fur and maintain contact with their mothers.

## WHY HUMAN MATERNAL RESPONSES ARE PECULIARLY CONTINGENT ON SOCIAL CONTEXT

Mothers in a broad range of insects, birds, and mammals rely on other group members to help them rear their young. These helpers, male or female, are called *allomothers,* from the Greek prefix *allo-* meaning "other," as in other than the genetic mother. Allomaternal assistance ranges from casual babysitting to extensive help carrying or provisioning the young. When the genetic father of an infant is also known (difficult to do without DNA testing) scientists can talk about "alloparents," individuals other than the mother *or* father, but more often the identity of the genetic father is unknown. When allomothers remain in the group and to varying degrees help the mother protect, carry, or provision her infants, this shared rearing is termed "cooperative breeding" (Sherman et al. 1995).

Primates are well represented at the casual babysitting end of this continuum—as in the case of infant-sharing among vervet or langur monkeys, where other females, especially young and inexperienced ones, take and carry a baby so that its mother is freed to forage unencumbered. Comparative analyses across primate species show that, where mothers have the option to delegate even a small portion of the cost of carrying babies to allomothers, babies grow faster. Hence, babies can be safely weaned sooner, with the result that mothers breed again after shorter intervals than would mothers without assistance. Based on data from human hunters and gatherers compiled by anthropologist Barry Hewlett, allomaternal assistance contributes to larger completed family sizes among human nomadic foragers, presumably because allomothers help keep children safe from hazards and reduce the energetic burden on the mother (Hewlett et al. 2000).

When mothers in cooperatively breeding species produce large litters or large, especially costly or slow-maturing offspring beyond their means to rear alone, they are essentially gambling on having help. For only with allomaternal assistance can they rear them. Should help not be forthcoming, it is unlikely that their young will survive. Worse, a mother who tries anyway may so deplete her bodily reserves that she dies in the attempt. I assume that this is why maternal commitment in cooperatively breeding species is so contingent on circumstances.

Rarely are primate mothers as dependent on allomaternal assistance as are cooperatively breeding Callitrichidae, the family of South American monkeys that includes tamarins and marmosets. While the prospect of allomaternal assistance permits a staggering reproductive pace— mothers give birth to twins or triplets as often as twice a year—the combined weight of the babies is 20% of the mother's body weight. This is why allomothers are needed to carry infants most of the time, except when the mother is actually suckling them. The allomother in charge of carrying the babies is usually the male, or one of several males, with whom the mother mated. Other males and immatures who are often but not always siblings catch insects to supplement the diet of the juveniles about the time when they are weaned (Bales et al. 2000). For three of these species—moustached tamarins (*Saquinus mystax*), common marmosets (*Callithrix jacchus*), and the spectacularly beautiful golden lion tamarins (*Leontopithecus rosalia;* shown in figure 3)—there is a direct correlation between infant survival and the number of adult males present to help rear them.

Fig. 3. Among cooperatively breeding tamarins, males who have mated with the mother along with pre-reproductive group members help by carrying the heavy twins when they are not suckling and provisioning them with small prey about the time the infants are weaned to help them survive the transition from weaning to independence. In the upper left-hand corner, a male who might be the father takes the infants after the mother finishes nursing them. A subadult in the lower right catches a beetle for them. (Pen and ink drawing by Sarah Landry)

This is full-fledged cooperative breeding where help from allomothers has allowed the evolution of especially large and costly infants that are produced after very short breeding intervals. Such fecundity forces Callitrichid mothers to rely on help. This dependency explains why, compared to other primates, tamarin mothers are so unusually sensitive to their social circumstances.

Although infant abandonment is rare in most nonhuman primates, not so in these tamarins. If her mate dies or there are no young tamarins in the group to help her, the mother bails out, typically within the first seventy-two hours. Based on decades of data from a colony of tamarins (*Saguinus oedipus*) at the New England Primate Center, there was a 12% chance of maternal abandonment if the mother had older offspring to help her, but a 57% chance if no help was available. In these instances abandonment was especially likely in the case of twins or triplets.

The evidence is clear: where allomothers defray the burden of carrying infants, mothers freed to forage more efficiently breed after shorter interbirth intervals without suffering higher infant mortality, a usual consequence of fast-paced breeding. Learning just how much allomaternal assistance can increase maternal reproductive success changes the way we look at this phenomenon. Instead of asking why mothers always care for babies, we are now inclined to ask: why don't mothers delegate care to others more often? The answer is that reliable, willing alloparents are in short supply, and for most primates using allomothers is not a safe option.

So here comes my punch-line: where else among primates do we find such big babies along with tamarin-like sensitivity to social support? In humans, of course, who, I believe, must have evolved as cooperative breeders. How else to explain the most curious puzzle of all about human life histories? How could there have been selection on any ape female to produce babies so far beyond her means to rear alone? In all apes mothers give birth to one baby at a time and then nurse that baby for four or more years. But in nonhuman apes youngsters, once they are weaned, provision themselves. Not so among human foragers, where the diets of children as old as eighteen are still being subsidized by adults. Children are dependent for so long that mothers have a new baby long before weaned older children are on their own. A foraging mother without allomaternal assistance can not possibly provide the ten to thirteen million calories that anthropologists like Hillard Kaplan calculate are needed to rear offspring to independence. So who helps?

## FATHERS ARE IMPORTANT, BUT NOT ALWAYS RELIABLE, PROVIDERS

Since Darwin, anthropologists have assumed that hominids evolved to be bipedal and then men evolved to be uniquely clever because smart, large-brained hunters were best able to provide for their families. Yet these long-standing assumptions are not consistent with other assumptions simultaneously being made. It was taken for granted that husbands provisioned wives and offspring within the context of a "nuclear family." Yet human males were also presumed to be hardwired to desire sexual novelty and to seek to copulate with additional women when they could, inclined to polygyny when feasible. What happened, then, when a man's desire for sexual novelty came into conflict with providing for the wife (or wives) and children that he already had?

The idea that Pleistocene mothers relied on a "sex contract" in which wives exchanged sex for provisioning by a husband when motherhood rendered her most needy is not consistent with what men say. As anthropologist Kristen Hawkes has pointed out, men in foraging societies are candid when interviewed. They bluntly explain, for example, that they find pregnant women less attractive than nonpregnant women and the smell of mother's milk repulsive. Disapprove if you like, but think about it. Surely there is a reason why perfume manufacturers in our society select names like "Pheromone" or "Obsession." When was the last time any of us bought a perfume named "Mother's Milk"?

There *are* species out there, like the famously paternal California mice or titi monkeys, where the highest priority of males is to remain near their immature offspring. Not surprisingly, perhaps, mothers in such species are often more anxious to stay near their baby-lusting mates than near their own offspring. And no doubt even in species like our own, where males fall short of this high standard, some men are very tender toward infants and motivated to care for them hour after hour. But only a small proportion. Furthermore, eliciting such "paternal" care requires particular circumstances. Usually it takes intimate and prolonged exposure.

For by and large humans do not act like titi monkeys and the other species in which males have evolved a very low threshold for responding to infants. Some textbooks still depict stone-age fathers as dutifully subsidizing their mates and their highly dependent, slow-maturing young, but in reality it seems unlikely that stone-age men were any more singleminded than modern men are. According to the United Nations report from the Commission on Status of Women, one in four households in the world today are designated "female-headed." Scanning the world around us, relatively few such women receive child support from husbands. In the United States alone, the White House reports that some $34 billion in child support due goes unpaid annually, while according to a 1994 study by the Children's Defense Fund fathers "are more likely to make car payments than pay child support" (Associated Press 1994). Arguably, supporting children from defunct relationships is not a top priority for males in our species.

Recently Kristen Hawkes and her collaborators (1998) have focused attention on this disconnect by demonstrating that fathers in foraging societies are often more interested in prestige-enhancing grand gestures than in maximizing protein yield. Hunters, she argued, were more inclined to "show off" by seeking large, elusive prey like eland than to bring home more reliably bagged small game. The same effort applied to catching tortoises and hares, for example, would yield higher protein returns on average, because the effort expended and the failure rates are both so high for big prey items.

So what happens when meat is in short supply? The gap between what weaned children need and the amount of gathered food mothers can supply is met by other group members—typically kin. Even among the !Kung, a foraging people famous for close and nearly exclusive maternal care of infants, anthropologists Pat Draper and Ray Hames (2000) found that children with many siblings, especially older siblings, were more fertile in adulthood, suggesting that siblings must be doing something important to keep nieces and nephews alive. Other categories of kin are also important. Among Hadza foragers of Tanzania, weaned still-dependent offspring grow faster and are more likely to survive if they have a postreproductive kinswoman helping to dig up something (literally)—in this case probably underground tubers—for immature kin to eat. Hawkes and O'Connell make a compelling case that reliance on gathered food like tubers—-and with it the opportunity for kinswomen to contribute—dates far back in human prehistory to the emergence of *Homo erectus* 1.7 million years ago.

To sum up, then, I am arguing that humans evolved as cooperative breeders. Whether living in the Pleistocene, in eighteenth-century Europe, or in the United States right now, mothers have sought help rearing their children from fathers, other males, female relatives, or anyone else they could rely upon. As a consequence of this dependency, the emergence of maternal commitment, always a complicated process in mammals, is unusually contingent on social circumstance. Mothers lacking allomaternal assistance are forced to take chances or bail out altogether.

The surprisingly high levels of maternal abandonment for some times and places, long assumed to distinguish us from other animals, are in fact predictable when our evolutionary history is taken into account. Rather than proving that women lack maternal instincts, the noteworthy thing about eighteenth-century France or twentieth-century Brazilian shanty-towns is how poorly prevailing social arrangements accommodated the needs of a cooperatively breeding ape. This brings me back to California Assembly Bill 1368.

BACK TO THE PRESENT

*It was ridiculous {Dr. Guttmacher} told the committee, to blame mothers on welfare for having too many children when the clinics and hospitals they used were absolutely prohibited from saying a word about birth control. So we took the lead in Congress in providing money and urging...that in the United States family planning services be available for every woman....*

U.N. AMBASSADOR GEORGE BUSH, 1973

No question about it, abandoned babies are better off in emergency wards than in dumpsters. New laws like CAB 1368 are an improvement over the old ones aimed at punishing mothers rather than protecting infants. But what of the unintended consequences? History warns us that if we set up depositories for "unwanted" infants human mothers are likely to avail themselves of them. Nor will all these abandoned infants be born to teenage mothers whose top priority is keeping their pregnancy secret. If the economy deteriorates, and allomothers remain scarce, young women twenty and older, unmarried or married, will also avail themselves of an opportunity to delegate care of their infants to others.

An all too obvious by-product of "safe havens" for abandoned infants will be even more infants in state custody. This might not be a bad thing, were it not for the fact that our foster care system is notoriously overburdened and with few exceptions inadequate. I will not belabor a point already widely discussed (as in the November 13, 2000, cover story in *Time,* which focused on "The Shame of Foster Care" in America). There is a cruel, yawning divide between having all infants, born or unborn, "protected by law" (the pro-life position) and what I regard as the more humane proposition that "every child should be a wanted child" (the position of Planned Parenthood).

A brief examination of the comparative evidence for primates and for women giving birth in different times and places warns that specific features of the new legislation may be counterproductive. For example, it is precisely during the first seventy-two hours after birth that primate mothers are at greatest risk of terminating investment in an infant, especially for inexperienced, first-time young mothers and cooperatively breeding primates.

If policymakers want to reduce the numbers of abandoned infants entering a floundering foster care system as well as protect the well-being of those infants, why limit amnesty to seventy-two hours? For a mother ambivalent about keeping her infant, the chances of her deciding to abandon it are *greatest* in the first seventy-two hours, before there has been an opportunity for the hormonal and neurological changes that would otherwise occur in a mother in close and secure proximity to her infant—especially if she is breast-feeding. Although the new law provides that the mother can reclaim her baby within fourteen days simply by presenting the identifying code she was given when she left the baby, how likely is this? Why not, then, safe but anonymous—and hassle-free—havens for new mothers and infants? I say hassle-free because I assume that most young women giving birth in secret to an unwanted infant almost by definition lack social support. They are likely to be deeply suspicious and frightened off by any intrusion from what they may perceive as a hostile and judgmental "system." Why not extend the grace period to weeks rather than hours?

The answer has more to do with politics than with infant needs. Fairly obviously, the figure of seventy-two hours was not arrived at on the basis of scientific research. No one familiar with the primate evidence would have chosen a time limit that *precedes* the onset of lactation in primates. It's a time limitation that will if anything *decrease* the chances of an abandoning mother changing her mind and keeping her infant. Rather, it turns out, the figure of seventy-two hours was arrived at as a political compromise between the bill's authors and legislators who wanted the grace period even shorter.[2]

Similarly, for reasons that are more political than sensible, policymakers focus on the physical safety of abandoned babies—a symptom of the problem rather than talking about the problem's source. This is because talking about the source of the problem would require policymakers to discuss sex education and contraception, not to mention abortion, and they view even nonsensical social policies as preferable to the prospect of political suicide.

Looked at comparatively, rates of teenage pregnancy (which happen to be higher in the United States than in any other developed nation) have less to do with moral decline than with changes in the nutritional

---

[2] Telephone interview with Gloria Mengino-Ochoa, counsel to the California Senate Judiciary, December 12, 2000.

status of human beings over the last tens of thousands and hundreds of years. Teenage pregnancy, then, is very much a human-made problem, a human-solvable public health issue, not a moral one.

That is, even though we talk about "the problem of teenage pregnancy," the problem is more nearly one of "failed contraception," an undermining of evolved safeguards that under conditions more typical of human existence protected young girls against inopportune pregnancies. As in all apes, human ovaries evolved to factor how much fat a woman's body had stored. For a still partially dependent girl living among nomadic hunter-gatherers, this indicator of nutritional status would have been synonymous with how much social support she had. Among nomadic foragers, where youngsters depend on shared nutritional subsidies from other group members, a young girl's fat reserves provided a fairly good indicator of how much social support she could expect from parents, grandparents, boyfriends, her mate perhaps, as well as other group members.

By and large, the plumper a girl is, the sooner she matures. Girls growing up in nomadic foraging society on the African savanna remained active, intermittently fed, and very lean, menstruating for the first time closer to sixteen than twelve, the average age of girls today in sedentary, hypernourished Western societies. Menarche would typically have been followed by a long period of adolescent subfecundity, which made conception even in a sexually active girl unlikely. Instead, first births tended to fall around nineteen years or older.

Even in the Pleistocene, *some* girls may have matured and conceived earlier, but only under conditions of spectacular abundance, and if—and this is important—the teenager was enmeshed in a supportive network of kin and other group members willing to provision her. These same supportive group members who shared food with her would presumably have helped her rear any infant she bore. Today, however, adolescents in industrialized nations can lack all manner of social and economic support yet still be well enough nourished to reach menarche at twelve, able to conceive shortly after. Crudely put, the amount of fat girls have on board has become a dangerously misleading physiological cue, telling a girl that it is an auspicious time to go ahead and reproduce, when it is anything but.

No amount of legislation can ensure that mothers will love their babies. But fortunately this particular problem, the problem of artificially produced hyperfertility in U.S. teenagers, is (as Ambassador Bush pointed out) readily solvable.


## II. ON WHY IT TAKES A VILLAGE: COOPERATIVE BREEDERS, INFANT NEEDS, AND THE FUTURE

*...the maternal instinct is the root whence sympathy has sprung and that is the source whence the cohesive quality of the tribe originated.*

ELIZA BURT GAMBLE, 1894


### SO WHY *DOES* SHE CARRY HER BABY?

Anyone who has ever spent time watching chimpanzees will be familiar with the cozy image of a mother tenderly using one arm to hold her newborn baby snug against her body. How natural this seems! The mother-infant bond is the first, the most crucial, and in many social creatures the most enduring social relationship. Who would bother to ask: "Why is that mother carrying her baby?" The answer seems obvious: that's just what primate mothers do. We take it for granted that among our closest primate relations mothers carried their babies all the time, just as we assume our Paleolithic ancestresses must have.

With few exceptions (and most of these include ruffed lemurs and other prosimians still so "primitive" as to stash their litters in nests), primates bear one baby at a time. The mother then carries her single baby wherever she goes. In ancestral environments, infants left on their own would quickly have succumbed to starvation or predation. This was humankind's "Environment of Evolutionary Adaptedness" according to John Bowlby (1969), who in the 1950s was arguably the world's first evolutionary psychiatrist. No wonder *all* baby primates desperately seek "the set goal" of physical contact with somebody and find it comforting to be close to their mother, said Bowlby. No wonder baby monkeys become emotionally attached to whichever warm and familiar creature reliably responds to their needs. Most often, that individual is the mother.

Today Bowlby's theory of attachment is basic to our understanding of infant development. But breast-feeding aside, are mothers the only individuals qualified to provide babies with a secure base? This brings us back to the question of *why* chimp mothers carry their babies.

For anyone who has ever had to care for a newborn baby (especially one that can't cling to body hair the way a chimp can) it scarcely comes as news that carrying a baby is awkward, reduces efficiency, and interferes with activities like hunting or even socializing. Adolescent chimps, for example, travel gregariously in groups. Yet after they become mothers chimps are almost invariably solitary because their slowness puts them at a competitive disadvantage in foraging for ripe fruit (Wrangham 2000). As gregarious as almost all primates are, chimp mothers carrying babies cannot afford to be. So why doesn't the mother hand her infant over to a babysitter, say her adolescent daughter pushily eager to take hold of the baby? The answer is: it's not safe for a chimp mother to do this.

Wild chimps are hunters with a lust for animal flesh. There is a real danger that other chimps in the community might try to wrest and eat a baby. A subadult allomother might not be able to prevent that. Unable to take advantage of allomaternal assistance, a chimp mother carries her baby everywhere not because this is what the mother instinctively "wants" to do, or because it is essential for her infant's healthy development, but because she lacks safe alternatives.

Not long ago, I was visiting a colony of bonobos in Holland and happened to be watching a mother with her baby. A keeper had just given the bonobos some sugarcane. Using one hand to hold the stalk, each bonobo was using the other hand to strip off sweet portions to eat. But this was a daunting challenge for a young, and also subordinate, mother who could not hold her baby and eat at the same time. In order to do so, she moved away from the other bonobos (who in any event were preoccupied with their own treat) and set her baby down on the straw on the bottom of the cage—something she would never do in the wild. Then she tore into her sugarcane. Clearly, this mother's object was to protect her infant, not necessarily to carry it everywhere. When she had a safe alternative to toting her infant everywhere, she used it. Human apes confront the same tradeoff between keeping the infant safe and keeping themselves fed.

## HOMO DAYCARENSIS?

True, *Homo sapiens* is clever enough to manufacture special devices— woven slings, leather *karosses,* or modern *snuglis*—that make it easier to work with a baby on the mother's body, as well as hammocks and cradles that position infants safely off the ground. We build houses with walls to keep predators out of nurseries. Still, the more incompatible with childcare the mother's work is, the more pressure on mothers to delegate care. The more available, willing, and competent allomothers are, the more readily a mother uses them. Consider the case of the Efé of Central Africa, the most traditional of pygmy peoples. The Efé still hunt small prey communally with nets, much as archeologists believe humans were doing tens of thousand of years ago (Soffer et al. 2000).

Among the Efé, infants are passed around among group members on the first day of life. By three weeks of age, babies are with allomothers 40% of daytime, with mothers the rest. By eighteen weeks, hours with allomothers (60% of the time) exceed time with the baby's own mother. Infants average fourteen different caretakers, including fathers, brothers, sisters, aunts, grandmothers, as well as unrelated individuals living in the village—orphans fostered in from other families are especially active caretakers. Similar childcare patterns have been reported for some—but by no means all—foraging peoples (e.g. the Aka, Agta, or Andaman Islanders). Yet we take it for granted that the chimplike pattern of *mother exclusively*—which is the pattern made famous for hunter-gatherers like the !Kung—is the normal one. Hence even the anthropologists studying them still assume that communal care systems like the Efé's are "unique" (Ivey 2000), unusual for our species. I'm not so sure.

In just the last quarter-century, as anthropologists and sociobiologists have started to compare notes, one of the spectacular surprises has been how much allomaternal care goes on, not just among village and urban as well as foraging people, but also—once we started to look— among animals generally. Diverse organisms have converged on cooperative caretaking as a way to rear large litters, or offspring that are especially large, or (as in the human case) infants that are both especially large and slow maturing and also (for an ape) closely spaced. In general, cooperative breeders are characterized by unusually flexible and opportunistic breeding systems, as well as by various adaptations that increase the availability of allomothers (group members other than the mother who help her rear her offspring).

Where it occurs, cooperative breeding permits mothers to produce especially costly young or to rear more offspring than otherwise would survive. Among wild jackals, for example, parents raise about two extra pups for every alloparent in the group helping them. Anyone who has ever wondered how social insects—bees, wasps, and termites—managed to expand to fully one-third of the animal biomass in Amazonian rainforests need look no further than the world's most extensive and reliable communal nurseries. While honeybee queens specialize in doing what they do best, devoting their enormous abdomens to the task of squeezing out 2,000 eggs a day, nonreproductive group members (genetically equivalent to queens, but fed ordinary fare instead of ovary-building "royal jelly") work away at what they do best: tending the hive and the next generation (Wilson 1975).

Cooperative breeding allows animals to take advantage of processes and resources (like honey-making or coordinated hunting) as well as allowing them to move into, and even dominate, new habitats that otherwise would not be available. The cooperatively breeding Florida scrub jay, for example, persists where other jays can not. These avian hunters and gatherers, living on lizards, frogs, and berries, breed in relict patches of scrub oak in spite of unrelentingly heavy predation pressure on their nests from hawks and snakes. They manage to fledge at least a few young by relying on help from young jays who have not yet started to breed, who serve as lookouts and helpers. Since suitable habitat is scarce, helpers benefit as well by remaining in the group until a breeding position opens up (Woolfenden and Fitzpatrick 1990). It was cooperative breeding, with its divisions of labor, sharing, and extra help for mothers, that permitted scrub jays and naked mole rats to occupy novel habitats and social insects and wolves to spread over vast geographic areas. With the emergence of the genus *Homo,* cooperative breeding was to permit a hunting and gathering ape to spread more widely and swiftly than any primate ever had before, moving out of Africa 100,000 years ago, gradually covering and (temporarily at least) dominating the globe.

## FLEXIBLE PHENOTYPES

Cooperative breeding is an option only for creatures that already live in groups. The story begins with offspring remaining near their mothers in *philopatric* associations—from the Greek for loving one's natal place "home country." Benefits of philopatry include remaining safe in familiar terrain (migrating is dangerous) and continuing to take advantage of remaining near kin, near known resources such as safe sleeping places, fruiting trees, and stored food. On average, these benefits from philopatry must outweigh the advantages from dispersing: leaving competitors behind, finding a new territory, starting to breed in one's own right. Delayed dispersal, along with delayed maturation, means that "pre-reproductive" group members—teenagers, "spinster" aunts, real and honorary uncles—will be on hand with little better to do (in a Darwinian sense) than stay alive and help kin rear young. But helpers need to be ready to shift to breeding mode should the opportunity arise. Thus cooperative breeding requires phenotypic flexibility. The same individual has to be prepared morphologically, physiologically, and behaviorally to assume different roles at different life stages and in response to different opportunities. A female marmoset may be a helper this year, a mother the next. She may have one mate or several.

Phenotypic flexibility lies at the heart of cooperative breeding and has led to fascinating adaptations. Many of these involve delayed or suppressed reproduction, with some fairly bizarre side effects, as in allomothers who, without ever being pregnant or giving birth, start to lactate and suckle babies.

An alpha female wolf, paired for life with one male, will typically be assisted by younger group members, who hunt and devour prey then return to the den to regurgitate partially digested meat for her pups to eat. Sometimes the belly of one of these subordinate females will swell up as if she were pregnant. During this pseudopregnancy, she undergoes hormonal transformations similar to real pregnancy and begins to make milk. Vestiges of cooperative breeding frequently crop up in domestic dogs, distant descendants of cooperatively breeding wolves. I once observed a pseudopregnant Jack Russell terrier chase away a mother cat and then adopt and breastfeed *her* kittens. Suckling young of another species is scarcely adaptive behavior, but in the environment of evolutionary relevance where this female's responsiveness to infant cues evolved, pseudopregnancy followed by lactation increased the milk available to large litters.

So why doesn't a subordinate female breed herself instead of helping out? In a number of cooperatively breeding species, like wild dogs, wolves, hyenas, dingos, dwarf mongooses, and marmosets, the reason is: if she did, the alpha female would most likely destroy her young. Worse still, sometimes (as has been observed among wild dogs and marmosets) not only are gestational resources from the subordinate female wasted on doomed young, but thereafter even more somatic resources are diverted to the dominant female's babies, who use the subordinate as a wet nurse (Digby 2000). The threat of coercion makes postponing (or "suppressing") ovulation the better part of valor, the least bad option, for females who then wait to breed until the coast is clear (Solomon and French 1997).

Women did not evolve to suppress ovulation or spontaneously lactate to nurse someone else's baby—although humans have sometimes consciously converged upon this pattern by hiring or enslaving wet nurses. But even without suppressed ovulation, human life histories assure the availability of unusually well qualified allomothers. Delayed maturation means pre-reproductive babysitters are usually on hand, but even better—and uniquely among primates—long lifespans after menopause (Hawkes et al. 1998) make post-reproductive kin available. Lacking infants of their own, their own reproductive careers behind them, such allomothers are likely to be as dedicated and single-minded in caring for immature kin as they are experienced.

## THE USEFULNESS OF EXTRA "FATHERS"

Although cooperative breeders are often monogamous, they may also be found in polygynous groupings (one male, several females) or in polyandrous ones (one female, several males) when circumstances permit. Since Darwin, we have assumed that humans evolved in families where a mother relied on one male to help her rear her young in a nuclear family; yet, as mentioned above, the diversity of human family arrangements (encompassing as it does the full spectrum of monogamous, polygynous, and polyandrous permutations) is better predicted by assuming that our ancestors evolved as cooperative breeders.

Looking across traditional societies, mothers can be found in monogamous, polygynous, or polyandrous unions. In some traditional matrilineal societies, mothers remain among their kin without a mate in residence at all. Yet nowhere is it feasible for a mother to rear children on her own. Even in the modern world, where terms like "single mother" are widely used, survival of mother and young can not be considered apart from shelter and food provided within a larger social framework. The one absolute constant is that a mother needs assistance, although, as is typical of cooperative breeders, women are flexible and opportunistic concerning just who provides the help they need.

Indeed, human symbol-generating cultural capacities offer interesting bonuses in this regard. Social customs and propaganda are used to increase availability of allomaternal assistance. I like to imagine that it was a cagey white-haired grandmother who first invented—thousands of years ago—the folktale to beat all folktales in terms of its helpfulness to her daughters. According to this folk mythology—which by now has spread over a vast area of South America, encompassing peoples belonging to six different language groups—each foetus has to be built up from installments of semen contributed by all the men that a woman has had sex with in the ten months or so prior to birth. Although in fact women do not bear litters sired by several fathers the way wolves, jackals, and other cooperative breeders do and there is no such thing as a human baby with more than one genetic father, this biological fiction about partible paternity has proved extremely convenient for mothers who needed to elicit extra assistance rearing their young and getting their children fed.

However it came to pass, from the Aché of Paraguay in the south, to the Mehinaku, Kaingang, Arawete, and Curipaco peoples of central and eastern Brazil, then westward to the Matis of Peru and northward to the Yanomami and Bari in Venezuela, mothers rely on this convenient biological fiction to line up multiple honorary fathers who will help provision them and their children (Beckerman and Valentine, in press). Based on data from the Aché when these people still lived as nomadic foragers, anthropologist Kim Hill found that 63% of children were ascribed to more than one father and survived better with two men helping. Among the Bari, a fishing-horticultural people, two dads were similarly optimal. According to Steve Beckerman and his co-workers, 80% of 194 children with one secondary "father" in addition to their primary "father"—the man the woman is married to—survived to age fifteen, compared to a 64% chance of survival for 628 children without a secondary father. This makes sense in societies where provisioning by males is unpredictable—as is often the case with fishing and hunting—and where fathers have a high probability of dying or defecting, relying on several fathers has the same beneficial effects as the presence of many males in marmosets. Not surprisingly, as soon as a woman suspects pregnancy she attempts to seduce one of the better fishermen or hunters in her group, which may be the flip side of the finding that the best hunters and the best fishermen have the most lovers.

Across cultures, polyandrous arrangements take many forms. Often polyandrous unions are temporary. For example, among the Shirishana Yanamamo, all marriages begin monogamously; thereafter, if the husband gets his way, an extra wife is added. But if wives are in short supply, or there are other problems to be solved, it is an extra husband who is temporarily added to the family unit. The Yanamamo are best known as "the Fierce People," among whom men raid other groups to steal many wives for their harems. But this is only part of their story. Many Yanamamo women spend at least some portion of their married lives in polyandrous unions, a time-honored standby to insure that children get provisioned and tended in a part of the world where children without fathers are at a serious, even lethal, disadvantage.

The South American belief in partible paternity facilitates cooperative provisioning. But even without this myth, an informal style of clan-based polyandry produces the same outcome in parts of central Africa and Asia. Should a husband die, his real and fictional clan brothers will look out for his children.


## ETHNOCENTRIC STEREOTYPES

Forget the image of promiscuous women having "fun." At stake is a serious endeavor: mothers making do under difficult circumstances. Mother-centered models force us to rethink long-held assumptions about the nuclear family. Not long ago, a *Wall Street Journal* editorial entitled "Feminism isn't anti-sex: It's only anti-family" complained that feminism and especially birth control are responsible for the contemporary breakdown of families in America, with special reference to what is going on in America's inner cities. But given that polyandrous mothers probably predate by thousands of years that most modern of postindustrial luxuries known as "feminism," we would do better to focus instead on demographic and economic realities constraining maternal choices: high rates of male mortality, imprisonment, and defection and job prospects that translate into poor "hunting" prospects, making it impractical for a mother to rely on one man.

Just as surely as romanticized preconceptions about what mothers instinctively want and should do shaped our understanding of what mothers actually did do, so too ethnocentric stereotypes about mothers evolving in nuclear families shaped the way we viewed the world around us. Even when we observed allomothers caring for young, we assumed the helper must be a co-parent and the mother's only mate.

It has been known since the eighteenth century, for example, that male marmosets are attracted to and carry babies; when zookeepers reported that infants fared better when a male was in the same cage as the mother, primatologists—with the ethnocentrism so characteristic of our species—assumed that Callitrichids must be monogamous, adapted to live in nuclear families. Since marmoset mothers do have better luck rearing young with their mate in the cage with them, the matter might have ended there, had primatologists not noticed that mothers, when they could, mated polyandrously with *several* males. Furthermore, these mothers with help from multiple males weaned babies sooner, bred even faster, and had an even higher proportion of their young survive. From the mother's point of view, reproductively monogamy is fine, but polyandry is even better.

Male care is essential in all the Callitrichids; but for three of the four genera (*Callithrix jacchus, Saquinus mystax, Leontopithecus rosalia*), the more adult males in the group, the higher a mother's reproductive success. Extra males (who may also have mated with the mother) help the parents to carry the infants and provide solid food for the rapidly growing twins so the mother can wean them sooner (Bales et al. 2000; Snowdon 1996).

PRIMABILITY OF CARETAKERS

It would not make a shred of difference, though, how many allomothers were on hand, were not other group members inclined to respond to infantile cries or gaping beaks or outstretched hands by picking babies up, delivering food to them, and so forth. Neural and endocrine systems that can be activated, and once activated lead to nurturing, have to be in place. For cooperative caretaking to happen, allomothers have to be susceptible to infant charms and solicitations, amenable to priming.

Fortunately for infants, individuals in many species—including *all* primates—find babies at least interesting and under some circumstances irresistibly attractive. Furthermore, where shared caretaking has paid off, and was selected for over time, thresholds for responding have fallen lower, making allomothers more sensitive to the tantalizing signals babies emit.

Typically it is tougher to elicit nurturing responses from a pre-reproductive female or from a male than from a recent mother. But it is rarely impossible. Sufficiently primed by the right circumstances, a virgin female or a male eventually responds—even in species where nurturing is not a commonly observed part of the male repertoire. This is one reason why the annals of primatology abound with astonishing adoptions, orphaned chimps adopted by older brothers who never before seemed much interested, or abandoned babies left in the forest and picked up by a female belonging to some other species. As it happens, we know most about priming in rodents.

When male mice encounter a strange pup, they either ignore it or eat it. When sufficiently "primed," however (that is, presented with pup after pup until the males become sensitive to pup signals), males finally quit cannibalizing and caretake: licking pups, gathering them in nests, hovering over them to warm them with their bodies. Primed males do just about everything mothers do, short of lactating. The hormonal basis of such maternal-seeming behavior in males—including humans—is only beginning to be studied.

One reason for the delay was preconceived ideas about which individuals "mother." The flip side of the notion that all mothers are nurturing was the idea that "maternal instincts" will be confined to mothers. This was a mistake. When Alan Dixson discovered that male marmosets carrying babies had higher prolactin levels than males not exposed to babies, the first reaction was skepticism. Even after Dixson's finding was replicated, higher prolactin levels were interpreted as paternal care by a monogamous mammal. Only in the last few years has it become clear that elevated prolactin levels can be found in *any* allomother defending or nurturing immatures, not just in genetic parents. Prolactin levels in yearling scrub jays, for example, go up when they are carrying food back to nestlings. Among cooperatively breeding primates like marmosets, close contact with infants stimulates release of prolactin in nonreproductives (among *Callithrix jacchus:* Roberts et al., in press) as well as leading to reductions in testosterone (among *Callithrix kuhlii:* Nunes et al. 2000). The longer the male carries the infant, or the more experienced the male is prior to caretaking, the stronger are these effects.

The biggest surprise, though, was discovering that changes in hormonal levels during a woman's pregnancy might play a role in priming nearby men. Prolactin levels in men living with pregnant women go up over the course of their pregnancy, as do cortisol levels and to some extent estradiol. The most significant effect was the 30% drop in testosterone in men right after birth. Declining testosterone might increase "paternal" behaviors simply by reducing male involvement in other behaviors that divert them from nurturing—like competing with other males. The more responsive to infants men are, the more likely it is that their testosterone will continue to drop (Storey et al. 2000; Wynne-Edwards and Reburn 2000).

No one is suggesting that fathers are equivalent to mothers, male caretakers to female ones. Indisputably, hormonal changes during pregnancy and lactation are far more pronounced in mothers than the modest but still detectable changes in men consorting with them. But the point is that *both* sexes are primable in the sense that their threshold for responding to infants will be lowered by proximity to pregnant mothers and newborn babies. By themselves, proximity and involvement can elicit nurturing. This explains why a fully engaged father, in frequent contact with his infant, can be even more committed to infant well-being than a detached mother. This point tended to be overlooked in early studies because it was taken for granted that mothers evolved to be the sole caretakers of their infants. Attention was riveted by the mother-infant pair, ignoring the social unit around them.

The general primability of both mothers and allomothers helps explain why genetic relatedness by itself can be a surprisingly unreliable predictor of involvement. The fact that humans turn out to be quite primable helps us understand, for example, why adoptive parents, wet nurses, or daycare workers can become so emotionally attached to the infants they care for. Based on DNA data, both !Kung San and Aka men have roughly equivalent (95%) chances of being the father of their mate's children, yet the former engage in relatively little infant care, the latter a great deal. The likeliest explanation is the opportunity for priming to matter among Aka men, who remain in close proximity to infants—within arm's reach—roughly 47% of the time (Hewlett 1988).

In the environments in which humans evolved, immature group members were more likely than not relatives. Predispositions to help them evolved according to Hamilton's Rule. But practically speaking, our ancestors did not think in terms of genes. What mattered were cues from infants processed at an emotional level. This brings us to the source of all these appealing signals: human infants.

## THE TWOFOLD TASKS OF HUMAN BABIES

*As soon as we become convinced love is not possible, love becomes impossible.*
                                        RANDY NESSE, 2000

Right from birth, newborns are powerfully motivated to stay close, root—even creep—in quest of nipples, which they instinctively suck on. These ancient primate urges to stay close and to get lactation under way are the first instinctive behaviors any of us engage in and are among the most powerful in the human repertoire. But maintaining contact is harder to do for little humans than for other primates. For starters, the newborn's mother has no hair for the baby to catch hold of. The mother herself has to position the baby on her breast and go to some trouble to keep him or her there. The mother must be motivated to pick up her baby hours and days before lactation is under way. There follow myriad decision points where a mother can invest to the fullest extent or take shortcuts.

The mother's commitment to her infant is the single most important determiner of survival prospects. But a long evolutionary history of cooperative breeding has meant that both a mother's commitment to her newborn and the level of support she is able to provide are linked to how much social support she herself has. More than in any other ape, a mother's love is contingent on her circumstances. So what (in an evolutionary sense) have been the consequences for human infants of their highly precarious dependence?

Within days of birth, human babies are capable of the same kind of contact calls and piteous cries that other primates make, but in addition they can read and perform all sorts of facial expressions, fully engaging in eye-to-eye contact with people who put their faces within the range that babies can see (around eighteen inches). Babies may reward such attentions by imitating the faces peering at them. Orang and chimp babies are also interested in their mothers' faces and take a brief look now and then. But they do not gaze deep into the mother's eyes like lovers in the early phases of a relationship, what pediatricians call *en face* socializing, the way human babies and their caretakers do. To the extent that psychiatrists and pediatricians thought about this at all, they tended to assume they were witnessing the artifacts of human mental agility and our ability to use language. Interactions between mother and baby, including all the vocal play and intermittent babble, were interpreted (following Colwyn Trevarthen) as "proto-conversations." Yet even babies lacking face-to-face stimulation (say babies born blind) learn to talk. Furthermore, very few other primates engage in such continuous contact noises or "babbling" (Papousek et al. 1991; Elowson et al. 1998); and although none of these babbling monkey babies learn to talk, all, rather curiously, belong to the cooperatively breeding Callitrichidae, little primates that like human babies may have a more pressing need than most other primates to engage allomaternal attentions. (This is not to say that babbling is not important for learning to talk, only to question which came first: babbling so as to learn to talk or being predisposed to evolve into a talker because that creature was born a babbler!)

But back to my point: infancy is the most perilous life phase—why linger there? Why not grow big as fast as possible, into a juvenile? Yet instead of using available energy to outgrow their vulnerability, human babies are diverting calories into sophisticated, metabolically costly neurological machinery for eye contact, imitation, emotional expression—into equipment that other primates (who also need to be attached to their mothers) manage perfectly well without.

What is all this energetically quite costly infantile face-watching about? One possibility is that the infrastructure for later human cognition is so intricate that babies need to start early. But there is an alternative, not necessarily mutually exclusive, explanation. The baby may also be monitoring his or her mother, learning to read her moods and assaying her level of commitment. If human infants have had to become connoisseurs of maternal responsiveness, this would explain why babies become so upset when experimenters ask their mothers to wear expressionless plastic masks. It could also explain why babies become so unnerved when mothers are depressed.

## AMBIVALENT MOTHERS AND PATHOLOGICAL OUTCOMES

To the Darwinian-minded John Bowlby, each infant was a composite put together from innumerable past lives forged from what Bowlby (1969) called "the Environment of Evolutionary Adaptedness." Separation from the mother meant death by predation, so that any ape that survived to reproduce must have managed to stay attached. Being attached was normal and led to security; being detached was abnormal.

For mid-twentieth-century attachment theorists, children could be divided into those that were securely attached to their mothers and those that were "maternally deprived," insecurely attached children, at risk for developing into delinquents—the youngsters Bowlby designated in his early writings as "juvenile thieves." These were children who grow up unmotivated to respect "authority," short on "compliance," empathy, and conscience, less liable to dwell on social consequences and on how others would feel, and liable to take things without asking or paying.

One of the strongest case studies consistent with Bowlby's belief that maternal deprivation put children at risk derives from data compiled in the book *Born Unwanted* (Dytrych et al. 1988). The centerpiece is a study of 220 children in Prague, Czechoslovakia, born between 1961 and 1963 to married women who had twice sought and twice been denied abortions. On this basis, the mothers' subsequent infants were designated "unwanted." In this study 110 of the "unwanted" boys and 110 "unwanted" girls were pair-matched with controls of the same age, school class, sex, and birth order who had the same number of siblings and whose mothers were all matched for age and socioeconomic status as determined by the husband's educational level. All were from two-parent homes. (Had young and/or unmarried mothers been included the results would presumably have been even more dramatic.)

When Professor Zdenek Dytrych, a psychologist at Charles University, and his co-workers relocated 160 of the unwanted pregnancies and 150 of the controls twenty-two years later, following up on the initial "Prague Cohort," more than twice as many of the "unwanted" children had received criminal sentences (41 versus 19), and more than twice as many (22 versus 9) had been sentenced to prison, all statistically significant differences.[1] Children born "unwanted" were also less likely to describe themselves as happy or satisfied with life, but I focus on the criminal records because the results seem more clear-cut.

This is a remarkable study consistent with the hypothesis that children born unwanted are at greater risk for the behaviors that our society considers deviant. But why? Nothing is known about actual childcare.

Much of the research on unwanted children has been done by those advocating particular social agendas. It is not a domain that invites

---

[1] One reason we don't hear more about studies like the Prague Cohort and others has to do with concerns about stigmatization or what might be seen as "developmental profiling"—so-and-so is just bound to turn out poorly—as well as with concerns about the pressure such findings put on mothers to love children unconditionally.

dispassionate analysis. Furthermore, and as always, it is difficult to evaluate causal relationships when many different factors are involved. Was the mother the critical variable? Or was her unwillingness to bear the child merely symptomatic of a nonsupportive social situation when she was pregnant, the same situation that the developing child picks up on after birth? (Note that the Prague study controlled for many variables, but not allomaternal interventions.) And what of all the subjects that did not end up with criminal records? Some mothers may of course have grown more committed, or else their "sociopathic" children just did not get caught. But we also want to know: who else might have been involved in rearing these children? No doubt Bowlby was right about pathological outcomes for the most extreme cases of maternal and social deprivation. (Neurological and other deficits in the most neglected victims of Nikolae Ceausescu's Romanian orphanages come to mind.) But the idea that insecurely attached youngsters grow up at risk of developing into sociopaths has itself developed in interesting ways since Bowlby.

## Why We Need to Consider Models
## Based on Cooperative Breeding

So far, most researchers studying development have presumed the antiquity and the normalcy of the nuclear family with a fixed division of labor (mother nurturing, father providing). Variables studied included (1) availability and responsiveness of the mother; (2) presence or absence of the father; and (3) whether or not the baby was in daycare or mothercare. Studies with this model in mind reveal that children with less responsive mothers are at greater risk for being noncompliant, becoming aggressive, and doing less well in daycare and later in school.

I know of no studies designed to take into account the possibility that humans evolved as cooperative breeders so that infants are cued to the traits most relevant in that context, namely: (1) availability and responsiveness of mother along with (2) availability and responsiveness of allomothers. That is, in terms of developmental outcomes the most relevant variables might be secure versus insecure, rather than securely or insecurely attached to the mother. Even though we do not know what kind of childcare characterized our ancestors in the Pleistocene, it is worth noting that the most comprehensive study we have on the effects of allomaternal care is just as compatible with predictions generated by the hypothesis that humans evolved as cooperative breeders as the same results are with predictions generated by the hypothesis that human babies are adapted to be reared exclusively by mothers.

Alarmed by statistics showing that 62% of U.S. mothers with kids under age six are currently working outside the home and that the majority of these mothers are back at work within three to five months of giving birth, the National Institute of Child Health and Human Development (NICHD) set out to study how the children of these women were faring in different childcare arrangements. Beginning in 1991, 1,364 children and their families from diverse ethnic and economic backgrounds were studied in ten locations around the United States. The main finding of the study was that the maternal and allomaternal sensitivity to infant needs was a better predictor of subsequent developmental outcomes (in terms of traits like respect for others or "compliance" and self-control) than actual time spent apart from the mother was. In other words, the critical variable was not the presence of the mother per se, but how secure infants presumably felt when cared for by familiar people who the infants had learned would be sensitive and responsive to their needs.

## AN ASIDE ON WHY WE STILL NEED TO WORRY ABOUT DAYCARE

Those convinced that babies need full-time care from mothers were no doubt surprised by the results of the massive NICHD study. The study found no ill effects from rampant daycare, even daycare for infants. No doubt, advocates of daycare felt vindicated. The additional information that allomaternal care is not particularly unusual in nature, and may even have been part of our Pleistocene heritage, might tempt some to think that the book is now closed, and daycare is not something we need to worry about. This would be tragically irresponsible.

Keep in mind what the NICHD study actually showed: daycare was better than mother care if the mother was neglectful or abusive—no one's idea of a good situation. Excluding these "worst" cases, there were no detectable ill effects of daycare *provided* that infants had a secure relationship with parents to begin with (which I take to mean that babies felt wanted) and care was of a high quality, meaning plenty of staff, the same caretakers all the time, and caretakers sensitive to infant needs—in short, daycare workers who are going to behave like committed kin. These conditions are not easily met.

Where it exists at all, this caliber of infant daycare—unless family volunteers happen to be available—is expensive. Down the price range, there can be long waiting lines even for inadequate daycare. Such daycare as is available may be unlikely to foster secure relationships. *Average* rate of turnover among all workers in daycare centers is 30% per year. At least one reason for this is obvious. Daycare workers are paid an average hourly wage of $6.12, less than parking attendants ($6.38). Family providers earn even less—$3.37 per hour (from U.S. Bureau of Labor Statistics for 1998, cited in Shonkoff and Phillips 2000:315). Yet daycare places can be so hard to come by that mothers desperate to get back to work may forget to ask "What is the ratio of caretakers to infants?" in their eagerness to inquire "When can we begin?"

So we return to the crux of the matter: why should good daycare be so developmentally indistinguishable from mother-only care?

### Sociobiologists Move beyond Bowlby

Over the last twenty years, researchers familiar with natural history and a broader array of ethnographic cases have started to move beyond the preconceptions that characterized early attachment theory. New disciplines like sociobiology have led to a greater awareness of just how variable mothers themselves, their circumstances, and their level of commitment might be. Along with that awareness came the growing realization that there might be caretakers on the scene *other than the mother* (Hinde 1982; Lamb et al. 1985). So what about all the conditions intermediate between the two extremes of a totally committed mother and no caretaker at all? And what about the role of allomothers in developmental outcomes?

Since Bowlby, evolutionary-minded developmentalists have speculated that infants are monitoring mothers and other caretakers not just to keep caretakers engaged but also to learn about the kind of world they have been born into and developing accordingly (Hewlett et al. 2000). A Pleistocene mother responsive enough to make her baby feel secure was likely to be a mother embedded in a network of supportive social relationships. Without such support, few mothers, and even fewer infants, were likely to survive.

This takes us back to the suggestion that babies are up to more than just maintaining the relationship with their mother, the hypothesis that babies are monitoring mothers to gain information about their social world. Impressed by just how variable rearing conditions could be, evolutionary-minded anthropologists and psychologists including Pat Draper, Michael Lamb, Jay Belsky, Jim Chisholm, and Mary Main recognized that over evolutionary time babies who used their mothers as a cue to determining the kind of world they had been born into, and who developed accordingly, might have a survival advantage. It would be important for a baby to know: Is this world filled with people who are going to help me survive? Can I count on them to share? Can I myself afford to share, and to count on others, or should I just take what I need however I can?

The optimal way to behave might differ very much depending, say, on whether the father was around or whether the mother had kin to help. Perhaps one parent was dead, and the infant was being reared by someone else. In that case the baby needs to know: "Will I be better off in this life predisposed to reciprocate and share, or should I be looking out for what I can get and taking it?" Being extremely self-centered or selfish, being oblivious to others or lacking conscience, traits that early attachment theorists assumed to be pathological, might in fact be adaptive, making an individual without much support from kin better able to survive.

As Bowlby was well aware, there would have been pitifully little opportunity among Pleistocene foragers for infants without committed mothers to survive. And if humans evolved as cooperative breeders, few mothers without social support would have been likely to commit. Nevertheless, with increasingly sedentary lifestyles, survival chances for children—even those without committed mothers—go up. Over the last tens of thousands of years, as people lingered longer in one place, eliminated nearby predators, built walled houses, stored food—not to mention came to use rubber nipples and pasteurized milk—infant survival became to some extent decoupled from continuous contact with mothers and other caregivers.

Ragged bands of street urchins or orphans in refugee camps come to mind, surviving all manner of neglect. Even in our own homes, children routinely survive caretaking regimens that an Efé or a !Kung mother would view as appallingly negligent: what kind of mother leaves her baby alone at night—and on this point our babies would agree. Miraculously, we can leave our infants in a crib and come back hours later to find them still healthy, all ten fingers and ten toes intact. Never before in the history of humankind have so many infants deprived of social contact and continuous proximity to caretakers survived so well to reproduce themselves so successfully.

## EVEN IF WE PERSIST, WILL WE STILL BE HUMAN?

*The truth is that the least-studied phase of human development remains the phase during which a child is acquiring all that makes him most distinctively human....*

JOHN BOWLBY, 1969

There are all sorts of humanitarian reasons to worry about this situation. But from my peculiar evolutionary perspective, there is even more at stake here than individual suffering. What I see at stake is loss of the very traits that define us as what we are. When I hear people fretting about the future of humankind in the wake of global warming, emergent diseases and rogue viruses, crashing meteorites, and exploding suns, I find myself wondering: but even if we persist, will our species still be human?

Arguably, the capacity to empathize with others has served humans well. The reason our species managed to survive and proliferate to the tune of this planet's six billion current occupants has more to do with how readily we learn to cooperate than with what good conquerors we are. It is no accident that humans are so good at remembering who gave us what or invited us to dinner, predisposed to learn that sharing and reciprocating are rewarding and make us feel good. Reciprocal exchange was part and parcel of our long stint as hunters and gatherers, permitting two families to eat even though providers in one had come home empty-handed (Cashdan 1985; Wiessner 1996).

It is because humans are so good at cooperating that we can coordinate complex activities that allow us to exploit resources so effectively. Indeed, it is only because our *Homo ergaster* ancestors could cooperate and share that human mothers could afford to bear such slow-maturing *Homo sapiens*–like babies in the first place. But this type of sharing and cooperation breaks down without trust. Emotional habits like being able to notice what others feel and need, caring about them, and being able to respond to them are learned in the first three years of life.

At a rudimentary level, all sorts of creatures are good at reading intentions and movements and anticipating what other animals are going to do. Predators from gopher snakes to lions have to be able to anticipate where their quarry will dart. Other apes can figure out what another individual is likely to know or not know—say about where an experimenter hid some bananas. But compared to humans, this capacity to entertain the psychological perspective of another individual (what psychologists call "perspective taking") is crude.

The novelist Edmund White has defined compassion as "taking an interest in all the details of (other peoples') existences and understanding their fears and motives, their longings and griefs and vanities." Cognitive neuroscientists like Marc Hauser describe compassion as being able cognitively and emotionally to put oneself in someone else's shoes and articulate how that person feels. This is why humans spend time and energy worrying about those they have never even seen—for example, AIDS orphans in Africa. This capacity for articulate empathy is uniquely well developed in humans; so much so, that many people (including myself) believe that along with language and symbolic thought this capacity for compassion is quintessentially human—what along with language defines us as human.

This capacity for articulate compassion is uniquely human. But its expression in any particular human varies with both innate propensities and each person's experiences in the course of development. Heritable capacities and development, nature and nurture, are both involved. First, there is each individual's emotional, empathetic component, which studies show is to some degree heritable. Already by fourteen months of age, identical twins (who share all genes in common) were more alike in how they responded when an experimenter pretended to pinch her finger on a clipboard and went "ooooh" than were fraternal twins who share only half their genes (Emde et al. 1992; Davis et al. 1994). Second, there is a learned component, having more to do with analytical skills than emotion, as each individual learns to look at the world from someone else's perspective. In most people, learning to adopt someone else's perspective occurs in the context of their earliest relationships with mothers and allomothers, where children are also learning to trust or count on other people.

And this is where someone standing back and taking a long-term view of our species sees a serious problem. There is no reason to think that just because humans have evolved to be smart enough to chronicle our histories and speculate on our origins, evolution has come to a standstill. For gene frequencies in human populations have not ceased to change. Rather, they are in constant flux, which is all evolution ever meant—changes in gene frequencies. (A classic example would be the genes that permit people to continue digesting milk after infancy. They are common in populations with a history of herding and milking cattle, absent among those who never did.) But no matter how useful it might be, natural selection can not operate on a genetic potential, only on traits that are expressed in the course of development. For example, no one doubts that fish benefit from being able to see. Yet fish reared in darkness, like the small cave-dwelling characin fish of Mexico, never develop their capacity to see. In populations of characins long isolated in caves, youngsters no longer develop eyesight even when reared in the light because through evolutionary time traits never expressed are lost.

And this is why the idea of so many children reared without learning to trust in others is so worrisome. Selection only works on developmental outcomes, on phenotypes. But if the human capacity for compassion develops only under certain circumstances, and if an increasing proportion of the species is surviving to breeding age without developing these capacities, it won't make any difference how beneficial compassion was among our ancestors. There is no opportunity for this trait to be selected for. Like sight in cave-dwelling fish, the capacity to empathize will be lost. No matter what the dividends might have been in terms of high levels of interpersonal cooperation, natural selection can not continue to favor a genetic potential that is not expressed. Worse, as larger proportions of people who never had occasion to develop their capacity for empathy survive, empathetic tendencies themselves become less valuable. Who, after all, will there be worth empathizing with?

No doubt our descendants thousands of years in the future will be bipedal symbol-generating apes. They will be adept at utilizing sophisticated technology. But will they still be human in the way we—shaped by a long heritage of cooperative breeding—currently define ourselves?

## REFERENCES

I have tried to keep the number of references to a minimum. For those wishing more complete documentation, please consult the extensive bibliography in *Mother Nature: A History of Mothers, Infants and Natural Selection* (New York: Pantheon, 1999).

Associated Press. 1994. Parents Better at Car Payments Than Child Support, Group Says. *Sacramento Bee,* June 18, 1994, p. A8.

Badinter, Elizabeth. 1981. *Mother Love: Myth and Reality.* New York: Macmillan Publishing Co.

Bales, Karen, James Dietz, Andrew Baker, Kimran Miller, and Suzette Tardif. 2000. Effects of Allocare-Givers on Fitness of Infants and Parents in Callitrichid Primates. *Folia Primatol.* 71: 27–38.

Beckerman, Stephen, and Paul Valentine, eds. In press. *Partible Paternity: The Theory and Practice of Multiple Fatherhood in South America.* Gainesville: University Press of Florida.

Blurton-Jones, N., M. C. R. Ferreira, M. Farquhar Brown, and L. Macdonald. 1979. Aggressions, Crying and Physical Contact in One- to Three-Year-Old Children. *Aggressive Behavior* 5: 121–33.

Bowlby, John. 1969. *Attachment.* Middlesex, England: Penguin Books (reissued 1971).

Cashdan, Elizabeth. 1985. Coping with Risk: Reciprocity among the Basarwa of Northern Botswana. *Man* 20: 454–74.

Davis, Mark H., Carol Luce, and Stephen J. Kraus. 1994. The Heritability of Characteristics Associated with Dispositional Empathy. *Journal of Personality* 62, no. 3: 369–71.

Digby, Leslie. 2000. Infanticide by Female Mammals: Implications for the Evolution of Social Systems. In *Infanticide by Males and Its Implications,* ed. Carel van Schaik and Charles Janson, pp. 423–46. Cambridge: Cambridge University Press.

Draper, Patricia, and Raymond Hames. 2000. Birth Order, Sibling Investment, and Fertility among Ju/'Hoansi (!Kung). *Human Nature* 11, no. 2: 117–56.

Dytrych, Zdenek, Zdenek Matejcek, and Vratislav Schuller. 1988. The Prague Cohort: Adolescence and Early Adulthood. In *Born Unwanted: Developmental Effects of Denied Abortion,* ed. H. P. David, Z. Dytrych, Z. Matejcek, and V. Schuller, pp. 87–102. New York: Springer Publishing.

Elowson, A. Margaret, Charles Snowdon, and Christina Lazaro-Perea. "Babbling" and Social Context in Infant Monkeys: Parallels to Human Infants. *Trends in Cognitive Sciences* 2, no. 1: 31–37.

Emde, Robert N., Robert Plomin, JoAnn Robinson, Robin Corley, John De-Fries, David W. Fulker, J. Steven Reznick, Joseph Campos, Jerome Kagan, and Caroyn Zahn-Waxler. 1992. Temperament, Emotion and Cognition at Fourteen Months: The MacArthur Longitudinal Twin Study. *Child Development* 63: 1437–55.

Garden, Maurice. 1970. La démographie de Lyonnaise: L'Analyse de comportements. In *Lyon et les Lyonnais au XVIIIe siècle,* pp. 83–169. Bibliothèque de la Faculté des Lettres de Lyon. Paris: Editions "Les Belles Lettres."

Hawkes, K., J. F. O'Connell, N. G. Blurton-Jones, H. Alvarez, and E. Charnov. 1998. Grandmothering, Menopause, and the Evolution of Human Life Histories. *Proceedings of the National Academy of Sciences* 95: 1336–39.

Hewlett, Barry S. 1988. Sexual Selection and Parental Investment among Aka Pygmies. In *Human Reproductive Behaviour: A Darwinian Perspective,* ed. Laura Betzif, Monique Borgerhoff Mulder, and Paul Turke, pp. 263–76. Cambridge: Cambridge University Press.

Hewlett, Barry, Michael E. Lamb, Birgit Leyendecker, and Axel Scholmerich. 2000. Internal Working Models, Trust and Sharing among Foragers. *Current Anthropology* 41, no. 2: 287–97.

Hinde, Robert A. 1982. Attachment: Some Conceptual and Biological Issues. In *The Place of Attachment in Human Behavior,* ed. J. Stevenson-Hinde and R. Murray Parkes. New York: Basic Books.

Hoogland, John. 1995. *The Black-Tailed Prairie Dogs: Social Life of a Burrowing Mammal.* Chicago: University of Chicago Press.

Ivey, Paula A. 2000. Cooperative Reproduction in Ituri Forest Hunter-Gatherers: Who Cares for Efé Infants? *Current Anthropology* 41, no. 5: 856–66.

Lamb, Michael, Ross A. Thompson, William Gardner, and Eric Charnov. 1985. *Infant-Mother Attachment: The Origins and Developmental Significance of Individual Differences in Strange Situation Behavior.* Hillsdale, N.J.: Lawrence Erlbaum Associates.

Nunes, Scott, Jeffrey Fite, and Jeffrey French. 2000. Variation in Steroid Hormones Associated with Infant Care Behaviour and Experience in Male Marmosets (*Callithrix kuhlii*). *Animal Behaviour* 60, no. 6: 857–65.

Overpeck, Mary D., A. C. Trumble, H. W. Berendes, and R. A. Brenner. 1999. Risk Factors for Infant Homicide: Reply. *New England Journal of Medicine* 340, no. 11: 895–96.

Papousek, Hanus, Mechthild Papousek, S. J. Suomi, and C. W. Rahn. 1991. Preverbal Communication and Attachment: Comparative Views. In *Intersections with Attachment,* pp. 97–122. Hillsdale, N.J.: Lawrence Erlbaum.

Piers, Maria W. 1978. *Infanticide.* New York: Norton.

Roberts, R. Lucille, Kosunique T. Jenkins, Theodore Lawler, Jr., Frederick H. Wagner, Janet L. Norcross, Deborah E. Bernhards, and John D. Newman.

In press. Prolactin Levels Are Increased after Infant Retrieval and Carrying in Parentally Inexperienced Common Marmosets. LR123G@NIH.gov.

Sherman, Paul, E. A. Lacey, H. K. Reeve, and L. Keller. 1995. The Eusociality Continuum. *Behavioral Ecology and Sociobiology* 6: 102–8.

Shonkoff, Jack, and Deborah A. Phillips, eds. 2000. *From Neurons to Neighborhoods: The Science of Early Childhood Development.* Washington, D.C.: National Academy Press.

Shorter, Edward. 1977. *The Making of the Modern Family.* New York: Basic Books.

Shostak, Marjorie. 1981. *Nisa: The Life and Words of a !Kung Woman.* Cambridge, Mass.: Harvard University Press.

Snowdon, Charles. 1996. Infant Care in Cooperatively Breeding Species. *Advances in the Study of Behavior* 25: 643–89.

Soffer, Olga, J. N. Adovasio, and D. C. Hyland. 2000. The "Venus" Figurines: Textiles, Basketry, Gender and Status in the Upper Paleolithic. *Current Anthropology* 41 (August/October 2000).

Solomon, Nancy, and Jeffrey French. 1997. *Cooperative Breeding in Mammals.* Cambridge: Cambridge University Press.

Storey, Anne E., Carolyn J. Walsh, Roma L. Quinton, and Katherine E. Wynne-Edwards. 2000. Hormonal Correlates of Paternal Responsiveness in New and Expectant Fathers. *Evolution and Human Behavior* 21, no. 2: 79–95.

Sussman, George D. 1982. *Selling Mother's Milk: The Wet-Nursing Business in France, 1715–1914.* Urbana: University of Illinois Press.

Wiessner, Polly. 1996. Leveling the Hunter: Constraints on the Status Quest in Foraging Societies. In *Food and the Status Quest: An Interdisciplinary Perspective,* ed. P. Wiessner and W. Schiefenhovel, pp. 171–91. Oxford: Berghan Press.

Wilson, Edward O. 1975. *Sociobiology: The New Synthesis.* Cambridge, Mass.: Harvard University Press.

Woolfenden, G. E., and J. W. Fitzpatrick. 1990. Florida Scrub Jays: A Synopsis after Eighteen Years of Study. In *Cooperative Breeding in Birds: Long-term Studies of Ecology and Behavior,* ed. Peter B. Stacey and Walter D. Koenig, pp. 241–66. Cambridge: Cambridge University Press.

Wrangham, Richard W. 2000. Why Are Male Chimpanzees More Gregarious Than Mothers? A Scramble Competition Hypothesis. In *Primate Males: Causes and Consequences of Variation in Group Composition,* ed. P. Kappeler, pp. 248–58. Cambridge: Cambridge University Press.

Wynne-Edwards, Katherine, and Catharine J. Reburn. 2000. Behavioral Endocrinology of Mammalian Fatherhood. *Trends in Ecology and Evolution* 15, no. 11: 464–68.

Zahn-Waxler, Carolyn, JoAnn L. Robinson, and Robert N. Emde. 1992. The Development of Empathy in Twins. *Developmental Psychology* 28, no. 6: 1038–47.

# The Practice of Value

*JOSEPH RAZ*

THE TANNER LECTURES ON HUMAN VALUES

Delivered at

University of California, Berkeley
March 19, 20, and 21, 2001

JOSEPH RAZ is professor of the philosophy of law and fellow of Balliol College at Oxford University. He is also visiting professor of jurisprudence at Columbia Law School. He was educated at the Hebrew University and at Oxford, where he received his Ph.D. He has been a visiting professor at a number of universities, including the Australian National University, the University of Toronto, the University of California at Berkeley, the University of Southern California, Yale, and Michigan, and a visiting Mellon Fellow at Princeton. He is a fellow of the British Academy and an honorary foreign member of the American Academy of Arts and Sciences. His publications include *The Authority of Law* (1979); *The Concept of a Legal System* (1980); *The Morality of Freedom* (1986), which won the W. J. M. Mackenzie Book Prize and the Elaine and David Spitz Book Prize; *Practical Reason and Norms* (1990); *Ethics in the Public Domain* (1995); *Engaging Reason* (2000); and *Value, Respect and Attachment* (2001).

# I. SOCIAL DEPENDENCE WITHOUT RELATIVISM

## 1. The Landscape

"Man is the measure of all things; of what is, that it is; of what is not, that it is not," said Protagoras, launching one of those philosophical ideas that reverberate through the centuries, acquiring meanings of their own or providing inspiration for various doctrines, some quite removed from their originator's. "Man is the measure" is such an idea, a thought that many, not only philosophers, find irresistible, while others find in it nothing but confusion.

Even though I will not follow Protagoras's views,[1] the spirit of his maxim will hover over these lectures. My concern, though, will not be with all things, only the value or disvalue of things. Is Man the measure of value? Clearly not, where what is of instrumental value only is concerned. Things are of mere instrumental value when their value is entirely due to the value of what they bring about, or to the value of what they are likely to bring about or may be used to bring about. The instrumental value of things is at least in part a product of how things are in the world, of the causal powers of things. These lectures will consider the case for thinking that Man is the measure of intrinsic value. This narrows the field considerably. For example, the value of the means of personal survival, such as food, shelter, and good health, is merely instrumental.[2]

In matters evaluative Protagoras's maxim seems to dominate our horizon. Its triumph seems to have been the gift, or the price, depending on your point of view, of secularism and of the rise of a worldview dominated by the physical sciences. But in what way exactly do values depend on us? That is not a straightforward question, and the history of philosophy is littered with a vast array of very different answers.

---

[1] Whose interpretation is in dispute. He is taken to be a subjectivist, believing that whatever one believes is true for one, or an objectivist, holding that whatever anyone believes is true, or (by Plato in *Theaetetus* 177b) a relativist, holding that whatever the city decides is just is just in the city. I will not be tempted by any of them.

[2] That is, *qua* means of survival their value is merely instrumental. Those same things may also have value for other reasons.

The view I will explore is most closely related to social relativism, which I reject, and to value pluralism, which I accept. I will emphasise my difference with the first today, and my debt to the second tomorrow. Social relativism, holding that the merit or demerit of actions and other objects of evaluation is relative to the society in which they take place or in which they are judged, is a popular view. Indeed some mild forms of it cannot be denied. Who would deny that in Rome one should behave as the Romans do, at least on a natural understanding of this view, which, among other things, does not take the maxim itself to be socially relative? Such partial or moderate social relativism is surely true in some form or another, and yet it is too tame to do justice to Protagoras's maxim. True, it can take a thorough form, generalising the Roman maxim (normally understood to have restricted application to some kinds of matter only) to all actions, taking the value or rightness of any action to be a function of, say, the practices in its locality. But even so, local relativism[3] is not relativistic through and through. Local standards, those that bind only members of some community, are so binding because they are validated by universal principles, not themselves relativistic. Thoroughgoing local relativism makes the application of all nonrelative standards be mediated by others that are socially dependent, and therefore relativistic. But it is still local relativism, in being moored in universal and socially independent principles of value.[4] It does not hold that Man is the measure of all value. Some values remain socially independent, and those that are socially dependent are so because of them.

Radical social relativism goes further. It not only makes the value or rightness of action depend on social factors, it makes all evaluative standards socially relative: they are valid only where they are practised, or they are subject to some other social condition. Radical social relativism

---

[3] I use the expression "local relativism" to indicate forms of relativism (a) in which the rightness or value of at least some actions is determined by norms that make it dependent on the practices of the place where they were performed or where they are judged; and (b) which include norms whose validity is universal, i.e., they apply timelessly, or to all times and all places. Thoroughgoing local relativism makes the value and rightness of all actions a function of some social practices, but the norms that determine that this is so, or at any rate some of them, are not themselves relative.

[4] These characterisations are precise enough for their purpose here, but admittedly they leave much unclear, much room for further distinctions. My purpose below is to exploit this unclarity to advance the view I find more promising, which can be regarded either as a special variant of local or of radical relativism or as different from either.

risks contradiction, for it has to explain whether the claim that all value is socially relative is itself socially relative.[5]

Some thoroughgoing forms of relativism escape contradiction; to do so it often takes the form of perspectival relativism, taking truth to be truth in or relative to some perspectives.[6] But other problems remain. Radical relativism is charged with making it impossible for us to have the opinions we think we have. We take some of our views to be true absolutely, and not qualified by being relative to a perspective. Similarly, certain disagreements that we believe we have with others are either said not to be disagreements at all or turn out to have a character very different from what we thought they had.

How damaging this point is to radical relativism is a moot question. Radical relativism is a response to a felt crisis that undermines our confidence in evaluative thought due to the persistence of irresolvable disagreements, and other chronic diseases of evaluative thought. Its cure is to reinterpret evaluative thought, preserving much of it, but changing it enough to rid it of its ailments. To complain that the remedy involves change is somewhat ungracious. How else is it meant to work?

And yet the reforming aspect of perspectival relativism makes it an option of last resort. It is a response to a perception of a host of insoluble problems that bedevil evaluative thought and require its reform. What if the problems are illusory? What if their perception is a result of a blinkered theoretical understanding or, rather, misunderstanding of the phenomena? In that case we do not need the cure, with its prescribed amputation of aspects of our evaluative thought. Indeed, we should avoid it as a distortion of a healthy practice.

I will argue for social dependence without relativism, that is, for the view that values, and therefore also reasons, rights, virtues, and other normative phenomena, which depend on them, are socially dependent, but in a way that doesn't involve radical relativism, which does not imply that what is valuable is valuable only in societies that think that it is,

---

[5] The argument is that if it is not then radical social relativism is false, for at least one standard of value, this one, is not socially relative. If it is socially relative then it is true, but only locally, relative to some societies or some perspectives, and therefore radical relativism is false because it is false that necessarily any standard is true only relative to a society or a perspective. If the standard that says so is nowhere accepted then no standard is relative.

[6] See, for one example, S. D. Hales, "A Consistent Relativism," *Mind* 106 (1997): 33–52.

nor that evaluative or normative concepts, or the truth of propositions about them, are relative.

It would be pleasing to be able to say that unlike relativism the view I will explore explains evaluative thinking without reforming it. But that is not quite so. My hope is, however, that we can dissociate the social dependence of value from relativism, and that in doing so we are better able to explain the basic features of evaluative thinking. The suggestion is that most of what social and perspectival relativism promises to explain is explained by the social dependence of value. Radical relativism is detachable from the thesis of social dependence, and adds no merit to it. We can settle for the less radical and less revisionary view I offer, and remain more faithful to the basic features of our evaluative thinking.[7]

## 2. THE THESIS IN BRIEF

### A. The Thesis

It is time to put some flesh on the enigmatic remarks made so far. The social dependence of values, or at least the aspect of it that concerns me, can be expressed as the combination of two theses:

> *The special social dependence thesis* claims that some values exist only if there are (or were) social practices sustaining them.
> *The (general) social dependence thesis* claims that, with some exceptions, all values depend on social practices either by being subject to the special thesis or through their dependence on values that are subject to the special thesis.

This formulation is vague in various ways. In particular it does little to identify which values are and which are not subject to the theses. I will consider later the reach of the two theses. But first, let us dwell on the special thesis for a moment, using the sort of examples of which it is most likely to be true, without worrying about its reach.

---

[7] A word of clarification: I introduce the lecture by contrasting my view that follows with relativism. I do not, however, intend to follow with a critique of relativism. The difficulties with relativism have been ably discussed by various writers. My purpose is to expound the virtues of my account of the social dependence of value. I introduce it by highlighting the ways it differs from relativism to preempt any misunderstanding of it as a form of relativism.

Regarding any value there is in any population *a sustaining practice* if people conduct themselves approximately as they would were they to be aware of it, and if they do so out of (an openly avowed) belief that it is worthwhile to conduct themselves as they do (under some description or another).

I identify sustaining practices in this way to allow that the people engaging in them may not be aware of the value their conduct is sustaining, or that they have only a dim and imperfect knowledge of it, or that they mistake it for something else, which is in fact of no value at all, but which leads them to the same conduct to which the value in question, had it been known to them, would have led them. At the same time, sustaining practices cannot consist merely of conduct identical, or close, to the one that the value would lead one to adopt. This coincidence cannot be purely arbitrary. It must result at least from belief in the value of such conduct.

It may be objected that to count as sustaining a value those whose practice it is must have that value as their reason to engage in the practice. This objection misconceives the nature of the thesis. It does not explain some intuitive notion of a sustaining practice. We have only the vaguest intuitive grasp of that notion, and I am using it in a regimented form to make a theoretical point.

The reasons why the weaker condition that I stipulated seems the better one are three. First, it avoids the awkward question of how adequate people's grasp of the nature of the value must be before their practice can be regarded as sustaining it. The difficulty is not that any attempt to set such a test would be vague. The difficulty is that for the purpose of relating value to practice there is no reason to expect a good understanding of the nature of the value. We cannot expect people to come to a correct view of its nature by examining the practice.[8] Therefore, while practices entail common knowledge of their terms, i.e., of what they require, we need not expect the practices to be informed by a good understanding of the values that could justify or make sense of them.

Second, more general values are put into practice through more specific ones, as when we express our respect for freedom by adherence to the value of the rule of law, among others. While I will not discuss these matters in detail, I share the view that it makes sense to say that a

---

[8] See section C, "Dependence without Conventionalism."

culture or civilisation, or country, respected a general value on the ground that it recognised and sustained in practice many of the more specific values that implement it in the conditions there prevailing. That may be so even if they did not have the concept of the more general value. And if so, it becomes necessary to allow that the sustaining practices of the more specific values sustain the more general one, which they manifest.

Third, as we shall see, values are open to reinterpretation, and to leave that possibility open while maintaining the social dependence thesis we need to leave the relation between value and practice fairly loose and flexible; otherwise the practice will block too many possible reinterpretations.[9]

The examples of opera, intimate friendships, and others show that most often the practices will relate to a set of interrelated values. One may not be able to identify separately practices relating to singing, conducting, etc., in operas. The sustaining practices, which consist of attending operas, music school, listening to CDs, discussing them, writing and reading about them, etc., relate to various aspects of the art, some of which may be related more directly to one or more practices, but which still derive sustenance from all of them.

The dependence of value on practice that the thesis affirms is not simultaneous and continuous. The thesis is that the existence of values depends on the existence of sustaining practices at some point, not that these practices must persist as long as the value does. The usual pattern is for the emergence, out of previous social forms, of a new set of practices, bringing into life a new form: monogamous marriage between partners chosen by each other, the opera, and so on, with their attendant excellences. Once they come into being they remain in existence even if the sustaining practices die out. They can be known even if exclusively from records, they can get forgotten and be rediscovered, and the like. Their meaning may change with time, and I will return to this tomorrow. Sometimes they are kept alive, as it were, by small groups of devotees. The important point is that once they are brought into being through an existing practice they need not ever be lost again, except accidentally, and that regardless of the passing away of their sustaining practices.

You can see now why this form of social dependence does not involve

---

[9] See Lecture III, section 2 ("Interpretation") below.

social relativism. There is no suggestion that what is of value is so only in societies where the value is appreciated, nor that rights, duties, or virtues exist only where recognised. Once a value comes into being it bears on everything, without restriction. But its existence has social preconditions.

The asymmetry between initial emergence and continued existence lies at the root of the special dependence thesis. It is entrenched in the way we think about cultural values: Greek tragedy was born in a nest of sustaining practices; neither it nor the forms of excellence it brought with it existed before. But they exist now, even though the attendant practices have long since disappeared. Moreover, the theoretical motivations for the social dependence thesis do not require continuous social support. For example, the existence and knowability of values can just as well be explained by reference to practices now defunct, and so can the dependence of values on realisation through valuers. But I have gone ahead of myself. Before I turn to the justification of the thesis a few more clarifications are necessary.

## B. Dependence without Reduction

It is sometimes thought that social dependence is a normatively, or ethically, conservative thesis. Since it affirms that value depends on social practices it must, it is concluded, approve of how things are, for according to it all the values by which we judge how things are derive from that very reality. This is a *non sequitur.*

The first point to note is that bads as well as goods are, according to the social dependence thesis, dependent on social practices. The very same social practices that create friendships and their forms of excellence also create forms of disloyalty and betrayal, forms of abuse and exploitation.

If both goods and bads, both positive and negative values, are socially dependent, what determines whether what a practice sustains is a positive or a negative value? Do goods and bads have the character they have because they are taken by participants in the practice to have it? Not quite. The worry arises out of the thought that the social dependence thesis is reductive in nature. That is, it may be thought that it commits one to a two-step procedure: first one identifies a sustaining practice in value-free terms, and then one identifies, by reference to it, the character of the positive or negative value it sustains. Such a procedure seems to me hopeless. There is no way we can capture the variety and nuance of various concepts of values and disvalues except in evaluative terms, that is, by using some evaluative concepts to explain others. The social dependence thesis is not meant to provide any form of reductive explanation of concepts. Reductive explanations only distort the phenomena to be explained. Evaluative concepts provide ways of classifying events, things, and other matters by their evaluative significance. Nonevaluative classifications, even if they succeed, *per impossibile,* in bringing together everything capable of being identified by nonevaluative criteria, which falls under an evaluative concept, cannot make sense of the reason they are classified together, nor can they sustain counterfactuals and determine what would belong together were things significantly other than they are.[10] Sustaining practices can be identified only in normative language, referring to the very values they sustain.

This claim appears neutral between the concepts of true and of false values. That is, the claim is that value concepts are explained by reference, among other things, to other value concepts, and it seems not to matter whether the concepts used in the explanations are of true or of illusory or false values. But appearances are misleading. Concepts of false values cannot have instances. Schematically speaking, if there is no value V then the concept of V is a concept of a false or illusory value and there is nothing that can have the value V (because there is no such value). We inevitably try to explain any concepts, whether we take them to be of what is real or of the illusory or impossible, by the use of concepts that can have instances. Concepts that cannot have instances do not connect the concepts they are used to explain to the world or to anything in it, and thus they fail to explain them. It is true that to explain the concept of an illusory value we need to point to its connections, should it have such, to other concepts of other illusory values. These concepts are likely to be part of a system of (incoherent or flawed) beliefs, and to understand any of them we need to understand their interrelations. But unless they are also related to concepts that can have instances they remain unattached to anything real, and their understanding is locked in a circle of notions detached from anything possible. To have a better grasp of such concepts we need to relate them to concepts with possible instantiation at least by reference to their aspirations. That is, those concepts are taken

---

[10] A point first explained by J. McDowell in "Aesthetic Value, Objectivity, and the Fabric of the World," reprinted in *Mind, Value, and Reality* (Harvard University Press, 1998).

to be in earnest, in joke, or in fiction related to something real, and we need to understand these aspirational connections to understand the concepts.

Thus people's understanding of concepts generally—and value concepts are no exceptions—depends, among other things, on their understanding of their relation to concepts that can have instances. In the case of value concepts that means that it depends on their understanding of concepts of true values.[11] This establishes that the social dependence thesis is in no way a reductive thesis of evaluative concepts.

We can now see why the charge of conservatism is unjustified. The charge is that the special thesis entails acceptance of what people take to be good practices as good practices, and what they take to be bad practices as bad practices, that it is committed to accepting any practice of any kind of evaluative concept as defining a real good or a real bad, as its practitioners take it to do. To which the answer is that it does not. The existence of a sustaining practice is merely a necessary, not a sufficient, condition for the existence of some kinds of values. The special thesis does not in any way privilege the point of view of any group or culture. It allows one full recourse to the whole of one's conceptual armoury, information, and powers of argumentation in reaching conclusions as to which practices sustain goods and which sustain evil or worthless things, which are, perhaps, taken to be good by a population.[12] Of course, deficiency in our conceptual, informational, and argumentational powers may well make us blind to some goods or lead us to accept some evils. But that must be true in any case. The special dependence thesis would be to blame only if it denied that such limitations lead to mistakes and privileged the concepts or information of some group or culture. But that it does not do.

---

[11] The implication is that if people come to realise that their understanding of value concepts depends on concepts of false values (e.g., of religious values) they realise that it is defective and has to be revised and reorientated by relating it to concepts of true values. I am inclined to believe that people who have value concepts necessarily have some concepts of true values. But there is no need to consider this question here. The remarks above about the priority of concepts with possible instances are consistent with recognition that people's understanding of concepts they possess can be, and normally is, incomplete. I discussed some of the issues involved in "Two Views of the Nature of the Theory of Law: A Partial Comparison," in *Hart's Postscript,* ed. Jules Coleman (Oxford: Oxford University Press, 2001), pp. 1–37.

[12] It also allows one to judge that some groups or cultures miss out on some goods, which are not known to them.

*C. Dependence without Conventionalism*

Another objection to the social dependence thesis is that it turns all values into conventional values. However, this objection is based on another unfounded assumption, that if the existence of a value depends on
a sustaining practice that practice must be a reason for the value, a reason for why it is a value, or something like that. That is the case with
conventional goods, which are goods the value of which derives, at least
in part, from the fact that many people value them. I say "at least in
part," identifying conventional goods broadly, because this seems to me
to conform better with the way we think of conventional goods. Few are
purely conventional in the sense that nothing but the fact that people
generally value them makes them valuable. Paradigmatically conventional goods, like the good of giving flowers as a mark of affection, have
reasons other than the convention. The fragrance, colours, and shapes of
flowers are appealing partly for independent reasons and make them appropriate for their conventional role. Most commonly these independent grounds for valuing flowers are themselves culturally dependent;
they are not, at least not entirely, a product of our biology. But the cultural dependence of our valuing of flowers because of their colours,
shapes, and fragrance is not in itself of the right kind to make their value
a conventional value. We would not value them had we not been im-
bued with culturally transmitted attitudes. But we do not think that
the fact that others value them is a reason why lilies are beautiful. However, the fact that others think it appropriate to give flowers for birth-
days makes them appropriate birthday presents.

Conventionalism should be distinguished from social dependence.
Conventionalism is a normative doctrine, identifying the reasons making what is right or valuable right or valuable. In contrast, social dependence is, if you like, a metaphysical thesis, about a necessary condition
for the existence of (some) values. This does not mean that the existence
of values is a brute fact, which cannot be explained. It can be explained
in two complementary ways. On the one hand, there may be a historical
explanation for the emergence and fate of the sustaining practices. Why
did opera emerge when it did, etc.? On the other hand, there will be
normative explanations of why operatic excellence is a genuine form of
excellence. That explanation is, however, none other than the familiar
explanation of why anything of value is of value: it points to the value of
the form in combining music, dance, visual display, acting, and words,

in providing a form for a heightened characterisation of central human experiences, or whatever.

With these clarifications behind us, let's turn to the reasons for the social dependence thesis.

### 3. JUSTIFYING CONSIDERATIONS

*A. The Dependence of Values on Valuers*

Four considerations, or clusters of considerations, support the social dependence of values. (1) It offers a promising route toward an explanation of the existence of values. (2) It points to a ready explanation of how we can know about them. (3) It accounts for the deeply entrenched common belief that there is no point to value without valuers. No point to beauty without people, or other valuers, who can appreciate it. No point to the value of love without lovers. No point in the value of truth without potential knowers. (4) Finally, and most importantly, it fits the basic structures of our evaluative thinking.

All four considerations support the social dependence of value. None of them requires relativism. So far as they are concerned radical relativism is to be embraced only if it is the inevitable result of the social dependence of value. But that, as we shall see, it is not.

The brief discussion that follows concentrates on the last two considerations, only occasionally touching on the others. Let me start with what I take to be the fundamental thought, namely that values depend on valuers.

The thought is so familiar that it is difficult to catch it in words, difficult to express it accurately. It is also one that can be easily misunderstood and is often exaggerated. Perhaps one way to put it is that values without valuers are pointless. I do not mean that without valuers nothing can be of value. The idea is that the point of values is realised when it is possible to appreciate them, and when it is possible to relate to objects of value in ways appropriate to their value. Absent that possibility the objects may exist, and they may be of value, but there is not much point to that.

Think of something of value. Not only is the appropriate response to it to respect it and to engage with it in virtue of that value, but absent this response its value is somehow unrealised. It remains unfulfilled.

The goodness of a good fruit is unrealised if it is not enjoyed in the eating.[13] The same sense of lack of fulfillment applies to a novel destined never to be read, a painting never to be seen, and so on. Not all good things can be thought of in that way. The thought does not quite work for my wonderful friendship with John that is destined never to come about. There is no similar sense of waste here,[14] or of something missing its fulfilment.[15] In such cases the thing of value does not yet exist. Only things of value that exist can remain unfulfilled. Nothing is unfulfilled simply because something of value could exist and does not.

That the value of objects of value remains unfulfilled, if not valued, is explained and further supported by a familiar fact. That an object has value can have an impact on how things are in the world only through being recognised. The normal and appropriate way in which the value of things influences matters in the world is by being appreciated, that is, respected and engaged with because they are realised to be of value. Sometimes the influence is different: realising the value of something, some may wish to make sure that others do not have access to it, or they may destroy it or abuse it, or act in a variety of other ways. But all these cases confirm the general thought, namely that the value of things is inert, with no influence except through being recognised.

Values depend on valuers for their realisation, for the value of objects with value is fulfilled only through being appreciated and is, rhetorically speaking, wasted if not appreciated. That explains the view that there is no point to the value of things of value without there being valuers to appreciate them, and it lends it considerable support. The view I have started defending is now but a short step away.

My claim was not only that the value of particular objects is pointless without valuers, but that the existence of values themselves is pointless without valuers. The thought is now fairly clear: what point can there be in the existence of values if there is no point in their instantiation in objects of value? If this is indeed a rhetorical question my case is made.

[13] I refer to the fruit's intrinsic value as a source of pleasure. The same point can be made of its instrumental value as a source of nourishment.

[14] The notion of waste imports more than just that a good was unrealised, that its value remained unfulfilled. It suggests inappropriate conduct, letting the good remain unrealised in circumstances where this should not have happened. I do not mean to imply that this is generally true of cases where the good is not realised.

[15] If I or John never have friends at all it may be that we are unfulfilled, that our lives are lacking. But that is simply because our lives (or we) would be better if we had friends. The point I am making in the text above is different, though reciprocal. It concerns not the good (or well-being) of valuers, but the goodness of objects with value.

One final consideration may be added here. It is constitutive of values that they can be appreciated and engaged with by valuers. This is plain with cultural values, by which I mean the values of products of cultural activities. It is a criticism of, say, a novel that it cannot be understood. If true, it is a criticism of serial music that people cannot appreciate it and engage with it. This consideration is less obvious with regard to other values, such as the beauty of waterfalls. But it is not surprising, nor accidental, that they are all capable of being appreciated by people. None of this amounts to a conclusive argument for the pointlessness of values without valuers. But it all supports that conclusion.

The dependence of values on valuers does not by any means prove the social dependence thesis. One reaction to the argument so far is to separate access to values from the existence of values. The ability to appreciate and to engage with many values presupposes familiarity with a culture. Typically appreciating them and engaging with them will require possession of appropriate concepts, and concepts are, if you like, cultural products. We have to admit, one would argue, that the existence of sublime mountains is independent of social practice, as is their beauty (unless it is the product of land cultivation, pollution, and the like). But appreciation of their beauty requires certain concepts, and certain sensitivities, which are socially dependent. On this view, the social dependence thesis has the wrong target. We should not be concerned with conditions for the existence of value, but with conditions of access to value.

This conclusion is borne out by the fact that the dependence of value on valuers must be expressed in terms of the pointlessness of values without valuers, rather than anything to do with their existence.

## B. Temporal Elements in Our Value Concepts

Yet there may be a case for going further than the relatively uncontroversial social dependence of access. The social dependence of (some kinds of) values appears to be enshrined in the structure of much evaluative thought. It is easiest to illustrate with regard to values that are subject to the special dependence thesis, that is, those that exist only if there was a social practice sustaining them. Here are some examples. It is difficult to deny that opera (the art form) is a historical product that came into being during an identifiable period and did not exist before that. Its creation and continued existence is made possible by the existence (at one time or another) of fairly complex social practices. The same goes for states, and for intimate friendships (e.g., of the kind associated, though not exclusively, with some ideals of marriage), and in general for all art forms, and for all kinds of political structures and social relations.[16] It is therefore also natural to think that *the excellence* of operas (or excellence in directing or conducting operas, etc.), the *excellence* of the law *qua* law (say the virtue of the rule of law or of possessing legitimate authority as the law claims to do), and the *excellence* of a close friendship (as well as virtue as a close friend) depend on the very same social practices on which the existence of opera, intimate friendships, or the law depends.

The thought that the excellences specific to opera and those specific to intimate friendship, or the state, depend on the social practices that sustain them, and that they depend on them in the same way and to the same degree that the existence of the opera, intimate friendship, and the state does, is reinforced by various commonsensical observations: Could it be that the excellence of Jewish humour existed before the Jewish people? Does it make sense to think of the transformation of the string quartet by Joseph Haydn as a discovery of a form of excellence that no one noticed before?

A further thought reinforces this conclusion. The very idea of opera, friendship, or the state is a normative idea in that we understand the concept of an opera or of friendship or of the state in part by understanding what a good opera is like, or a good or successful friendship, or a good state. When we think of the state, as a creature of law, then the fact that the state claims supreme and comprehensive authority is part of what makes a social institution into a state.[17] The concept of the state is (among much else) the concept of a political organisation claiming supreme authority. It is, therefore, the concept of a political organisa-

---

[16] Of these the temptation to deny dependence on social practices may be greatest with regard to intimate friendship. All one needs for that, some will say, is to have the appropriate emotion toward the other and be willing to act accordingly (when the emotion and willingness are reciprocated). But both the emotion and the actions appropriate to it are socially determined, and cannot be otherwise. I have argued for this view in *The Morality of Freedom* (Oxford University Press, 1986), pp. 308–13.

[17] The thesis that the state is constituted by a legal order was forcefully advanced by Hans Kelsen in his book *A General Theory of State and Law* (New York: Russell and Russell, 1945). John Finnis has argued the case for the normative character of the concept of the law in his *Natural Law and Natural Rights* (Oxford University Press, 1980), chapter 1. In *Practical Reason and Norms* (1975; 2nd ed.: Oxford University Press, 1999), chapter 5, I argued that the law is a normative system claiming authority that is both comprehensive and supreme.

tion that is good only if it has the authority it claims. Its specific form of excellence determines the nature of the state.[18]

Opera, friendship, and other art forms and social forms are more fluid. But they too are to be understood, in part, by their specific virtues. Some art forms are rigid, and rigidly defined, as are Byzantine icons. Most are fluid, and their concept allows for a variety of forms, for realisation in different traditions and in different manners. Quite commonly it also allows for the continuous transformation of the genre. Even so, mastering the concept of any specific art form requires an understanding of normative standards specific to it. Opera, to give but one example, is nothing if not an art form where success depends on success in integrating words and music, such that the meaning of the work, or of parts of it, is enriched by the interrelation of word and music. This of course leaves vast spaces for further specification, articulation, and dispute. Not least it leaves unspecified the way in which music and words have to be related. But it is not empty: it imposes constraints on success in opera, and through this on the concept of opera.

The tendency of some disputes about the quality of art works to turn into doubts about whether they are art at all manifests both the dependence of the concept of art and of different art genres on normative standards and the fluidity of those standards, which makes it possible for artists to challenge some of them at any given time by defying them in practice. The same is true of the state, or of friendship: some friendships are so bad that they are no friendships at all.

If forms of art and forms of social relations and of political organisation are constituted in part by standards for their success, then the thought that the creation of these art forms and of these political organisations is also the creation or emergence of these forms of excellence, while still obscure, seems almost compelling. As art forms, social relations, and political structures are created by, or at any rate their existence depends on, social practices, so must their distinctive virtues and

[18] The claim made here that a normative standard and a form of excellence are part of the concept of the state does not entail that they are part of the necessary conditions for something being a state that it meets those standards. To be a state it needs to claim legitimate comprehensive authority, not to have one. However, as I point out below, at least some concepts allow for something like that. Of some kinds it is the case that objects can belong to them by degrees: this is more of a K than that, we can say. It is more of a holiday than the one we had last year, etc. In such cases the excellence of the kind commonly contributes to the determination of degrees of membership in it. And commonly there is a vague boundary between being a very bad member of the kind and not being a member at all.

forms of excellence depend on social practices that create and sustain them. In these cases, it would seem that not only access to these values but the values themselves arise with the social forms that make their instantiation possible. Similar arguments can show, the suggestion is, that the same is true of many other values.

## 4. Limits of the Special Thesis

So far I have tried to describe and motivate the social dependence thesis, and in particular the special thesis. It is time to say something about its scope and limitations.

The special dependence thesis seems to apply primarily to what we may call cultural values, meaning those values instantiation of which generally depends on people who have the concept of the value, or of some fairly closely related value, acting for the reason that their action or its consequences will instantiate it or make its instantiation more likely. In plain English these are values that people need to know at least something about and to pursue in order for there to be objects with those values. They need to engage in relations with the idea that they want to be good friends, make good law in order to make good law, and so on. The excellences of the various forms of artistic activity and creativity, the values associated with the various leisure pursuits, and the goods of various forms of social institutions, roles, and activities relating to them and of various personal relations are all instances of cultural values. The special dependence thesis applies to them because sustaining practices are a necessary condition for it to be possible for these values to be instantiated, and the possibility of instantiation is a condition for the existence of values.

Four important classes of values are not subject to the special thesis. They are values the possibility of whose instantiation does not depend on a sustaining practice.

1. Pure sensual and perceptual pleasure. Sensual and perceptual pleasures are at the root of many cultural pleasures, but their pure form—the value of the pleasure of some sensations or perceptions—is not subject to the special thesis.
2. Aesthetic values of natural phenomena, such as the beauty of

sunsets. As was noted before, access to them is cultural-dependent, but their existence is not.

3. Many, though not all, enabling and facilitating values: these are values whose good is in making possible or facilitating the instantiation of other values. Take, for example, freedom, understood as the value of being in a condition in which one is free to act.... People can be free without anyone realising that they are free. No sustaining practice is necessary to make it possible for people to be free. I call freedom an enabling value, for its point is to enable people to have a life, that is, to act pursuing various valuable objectives of their choice.

Many moral values are of this kind, though some are more complex in nature. For example, justice is an enabling value, in that denial of justice denies people the enjoyment or pursuit of valuable options or conditions, but it can also be an element of the value of relationships, in that treating the other unjustly is inconsistent with them. Those relationships are subject to the special thesis, but justice as a condition in which one is not treated unjustly is not.[19]

4. The value of people, and of other valuers who are valuable in themselves, that is, the identification of who has value in him- or herself does not depend on sustaining practices.

Moral values, and the virtues, rights, and duties that depend on them, often belong to the last two categories and are thus not directly subject to the special thesis. They are, however, at least partially dependent on social practices indirectly. This is most obvious in the case of enabling values: their point is to enable the pursuit and realisation of others, and to the extent that the others are socially dependent, so are they, at least in their point and purpose.

A similar point applies to the value of people or of valuers generally. The whole point of being a valuer is that one can appreciate and respect values, and to the extent that they are socially dependent there is no point to being a valuer, unless there are sustaining practices making possible the existence of values.

---

[19] According to many views freedom too is not merely an enabling value but a component of other values as well.

Does that mean that values of these two categories are subject to the general thesis, at least in part, that is, at least to the extent that they depend for their point on values that are subject to the special thesis? To answer this question we need to disambiguate the general thesis. As phrased the special thesis is about the existence of some values. The general thesis merely refers to values "depending" on others. Do they so depend for their existence or for their point? I think that for the purpose of providing a general account of values the more significant thesis is the one that focuses on the fact that (with the exception of pure sensual pleasures and the aesthetic values of natural objects)[20] all values depend for their point on the existence of values that are subject to the special thesis.[21]

In discussing the dependence of values on valuers I noted the case for a thesis that there is no point to values without a socially dependent access to them. In many ways that is a more attractive thesis, for there is some awkwardness in thinking of values as existing at all. For reasons I went on to explain it seemed to me that that cultural values are conceived in ways that presuppose that they have temporal existence. They are subject to the special thesis. There is less reason to attribute temporal existence to the values that are not subject to it. We think of them as atemporal, or as eternal. What matters, however, is that they have a point only under certain circumstances. For most values their point depends on it being possible to recognise them and engage with them. They are idle and serve no purpose if this is impossible. In this sense the value of valuers depends on other values, for what is special about valuers *qua* valuers is their ability to engage with values. The point of enabling values is that they enable people to engage with other values. They depend for their point on there being such other values. In these ways values of these categories are partially subject to the (general) social thesis.

They are only partially subject to it, for not all other values are subject to the special thesis, and therefore the values depending on it indirectly are not entirely dependent on it. But the values that can give a meaning and a purpose to life are socially dependent. The purely sensual and perceptual pleasures are momentary pleasures; only when they are

----

[20] And access to those largely depends on social practices.

[21] Which is not to deny that there are some values whose existence depends on the existence of others, and that singling them out may be relevant for some purposes.

integrated within cultural values and become constituent parts of them can they become an important part of people's lives, only then can they give meaning to people's lives, and the same is true of enjoyment of the beauty of nature. Moreover, the same is true of moral requirements and virtues that are not also parts of social relations or of institutional involvement. Being a teacher, or a doctor, or even a philosopher can contribute significantly to a meaningful life. But being a nonmurderer, or a nonrapist, or a person who simply gives away to others everything he or she has (having acquired it like manna from heaven) is not something that can give meaning to life. In sum: the life-building values are socially dependent, directly or indirectly.

Time to stop. Today I tried to delineate some of the outlines of and motivation for a view of the social dependence of values, which is free from relativism, Tomorrow I hope that some of its merits will emerge through a discussion of its relations to value-pluralism, to interpretation, and to evaluative change.

## II. THE IMPLICATIONS OF VALUE PLURALISM

### 1. SPECIFIC AND GENERAL VALUES

Evaluative explanations travel up and down in levels of generality. Sometimes we explain the nature of relatively general values by the way they generalise aspects of more specific ones. We explain the nature of relatively specific values by the way they combine, thus providing for the realisation of different, more general ones. For example, we can explain the value of friendship, which is a fairly general value standing for whatever is of value in one-on-one human relationships of one kind or another that are relatively stable and at least not totally instrumental in character, by reference to the more specific, to the value of various specific types of relationships. Thus, the value of friendship in general is explained by reference to the relatively distinct values of intimate friendships, of work friendships, of friendships based on common interests, and so on. On the other hand, we can explain the value of tragedies by reference to more general literary, performance, and cognitive values that they characteristically combine.

The more general the values, the less appealing appears the thesis of their social dependence. The more specific the values, the more appealing it appears, but at the same time the more prone we are to doubt whether these relatively specific values are really distinct values. These doubts are easily explained. Let me start with a quick word about more general values, like beauty, social harmony, love. We doubt whether there are practices sustaining such values, for their very generality challenges our common expectations of what practices are like. They are, we think, patterns of conduct performing and approving of the performance of, and disapproving failure to perform, actions of a rather specific type in fairly specific circumstances. Things like the practice of annually giving 10% of one's earnings to charity.[1] We do not think of people's behaviour toward issues involving beauty as a practice, for there is no specific action-type, performance or approval of which can constitute the practice of beauty, so to speak.

Our appreciation of beauty can be manifested by almost any conceivable action under some circumstance or other. In large part, the practices sustaining more general values are those that sustain relatively specific values that instantiate these general values (among others). Of course, the general value can be instantiated in new ways, not yet known, as well. Its scope is not exhausted by the scope of its sustaining practices. That the existing practices sustaining specific values through which a more general value is sustained do not address all possible applications of the general value does not detract from the practice counting as sustaining that value, though it may show that people have not recognised, or not recognised adequately, the general value that the practices support.

Turning to more specific values, the doubts change. Here we tend to accept that there are sustaining social practices, but we may doubt whether there are distinct values that they sustain. Is there any sense, one may ask, in regarding the psychological thriller as embodying a distinct form of excellence, and therefore a distinct value, different from that which is embodied in romantic comedies, for example? Is it not the case that both psychological thrillers and romantic comedies are good or bad to the extent that they succeed or fail in embodying general values, such as being entertaining, insightful, beautiful to watch, etc.?

---

[1] This is particularly clear if one conceives of a practice along the lines of H. L. A. Hart's explanation of social rules in *The Concept of Law* (1961; 2nd ed. 1994).

I have to admit that when referring to values *as values,* which merci-fully we do not do too often, we have in mind fairly general values like freedom, beauty, dignity, or happiness. However, it is impossible to un-derstand the value of everything that has some value as merely an in-stantiation of one or more of these general values. What is good about romantic comedies is not just that they are optimistic, generous about people, well-plotted, etc. (and not even all of these are very abstract val-ues) but also the special way in which they combine these qualities, which may be all that distinguishes some romantic comedies from some domestic dramas, which otherwise may display the same values. Many specific values, specific forms of excellence, have this structure: objects belonging to the relevant kind instantiate that relatively specific value if they combine various other values in a particular way. They are dis-tinct values because of the special mix of values they are. When talking of genres—or of kinds—constituting values I will have such values in mind.

The concept of a genre or a kind of value combines two features: it defines which objects belong to it, and in doing so it determines that the value of the object is to be assessed (*inter alia*) by its relations to the defining standards of the genre.

Each literary or artistic genre or subgenre is defined by a standard, more or less loosely determined, setting the criteria for success in the genre, the criteria for being a good instance of the genre. The standard of excellence set by each genre is identified not only by the general val-ues that go to make it, but by their mix, the nature of their "ideal" com-bination. This is not to deny that there usually are also other criteria definitive of genres and other criteria for being an instance of a genre (like ending with a wedding).[2]

Some may object to the suggestion that all appreciation in litera-ture, music, and the visual arts is genre-dependent. In any case a serious question arises whether these conclusions can be generalised outside the arts, even assuming that I am right about them.

Do we still rely on genre in the evaluation of works of literature, art,

[2] Is it not necessary that there be additional criteria for belonging to a genre? Not so. Some genres may be such that any item belongs to them if, were it to belong to them and be judged by their standard of excellence, it would be ranked higher than if it were to belong and be judged by the standard of any alternative genre. In such cases the value specific for the genre provides the specific content for the criterion of being an instance of the genre. But this is a special case, and most genres have additional criteria of membership, though rela-tive success may be one of the criteria.

or music? Have not composers abandoned the categories of symphony, concerto, etc.? Have not the boundaries of novel, novella, short story been eroded? Has not the very distinction between a narrative of fact and fiction been successfully challenged? In any case, can one hope to detect genre-based thinking outside the understanding and appraisal of literature and the arts?

These doubts are exaggerated. It is true that writers and composers have broken loose from the hold of what we may call traditional genres. It is also true that the process was not one of replacing new genres with old ones, at least not if genres are understood as imposing the same stringent rules that the old ones obeyed.[3] We are in a period of greater fluidity and flexibility. But that does not mean that evaluative thought in general is not genre-based. That notion allows for all these flexibilities.

I have contributed to the misunderstanding on which the objection is based by using the term "genre," alluding to formal musical and literary genres. It seemed helpful to start with an analogy to a familiar application of what I call genre-based or kind-based thought, namely its application to works that fall squarely within the boundaries of a specific and fairly well-defined genre, such as a Shakespearean sonnet, or a sonata form, or a portrait painting. It is time to abandon the analogy and allow for the full flexibility and complexity of the idea.

Its gist is in the two-stage process of evaluation: we judge the value of objects by reference to their value or success as members of kinds of goods. Is this a good apple? we ask. Or, did you have a good holiday? Was it a good party? Was it a good lecture? Is he a good father? In all these cases the noun ("apple," "party," etc.) does more than help in identifying the object, event, or act to be judged. It identifies the way it is to be judged.[4] This object has some value because it is a good apple; it was

---

[3] The failure of twelve-tone technique to take hold is an instructive example.

[4] Evaluation with reference to kinds has, of course, been often discussed by philosophers. For example, J. Urmson in "On Grading," *Mind* n.s. 59, no. 234 (April 1950): 145–69, and *The Emotive Theory of Ethics* (London: Hutchinson, 1968) used it to introduce an element of objectivity into evaluative thought at a time when emotivism seemed to reign; Philippa Foot, in *Virtues and Vices, and Other Essays in Moral Philosophy* (Oxford: B. Blackwell, 1978), relied on it to establish the relativity of evaluations to points of view, as part of a rejection of universalist ethical views such as utilitarianism. See also Georg von Wright, *The Varieties of Goodness* (London: Routledge and Kegan Paul, 1963), for a more complex view. The view explained here differs from theirs by (1) claiming that objects can relate to kinds in a variety of ways, of which exemplification is only one; and (2) allowing for detachment, that is, for transition from good of a kind to good, while retaining the umbilical cord to one's kind as the ground for the detached judgment.

time well spent because it was a good party, that is, because the event was good as a party, etc. The habit of evaluating by kinds is so instinctive that we may fail to notice it: it is odd to say, "The lecture was good because it was a good lecture." But that is how it is. The lecturer's activity is of value because it was successful as a lecture. The two-stage procedure is essential to the idea of what I call a genre-based evaluation, and these examples illustrate how pervasive is its application outside the arts.

Perhaps paradoxically, membership in a genre is not, however, essential to the process. Truman Capote's *In Cold Blood,* we may say, is neither a novel nor a documentary but creates a new terrain somewhere in between. We then appreciate it in relation to the standards of excellence both of reportage and of novels, judging whether it deviates arbitrarily or sensibly, whether the deviation contributes to its merit or detracts from it. Genre-dependent evaluation is marked by the fact that objects are evaluated by reference to kinds, to genres. But there are different relations they can bear to the genre. Straightforward membership or exemplification of the kind is only one of them. Two elements determine how items can be evaluated. First is the definition of the kinds of goods to which they relate, which includes the constitutive standards of excellence for each kind. Second are the ways the item relates to the kinds. It may fall squarely within them. Or it may, for example, relate to them ironically, or iconoclastically, or as a source of allusions imported into something that essentially belongs to another kind, to create ambiguities, so that the item under discussion enjoys a duck/rabbit effect: you see it belonging to one kind one moment and to another kind the next moment.

Both kinds and ways of relating to them are sustained by social practices and are defined in part by standards of excellence specific to them. Some periods, formal ones, tend to hold kinds rigid, allowing little change, and tend to restrict the ways objects can relate to a kind to a few well-defined patterns. Others, and our time is one of those, allow, even encourage, great fluidity and openness to change in their recognised kinds and a fluid, rich variety of ways in which items can relate to them.[5] But these ways of relating to evaluative kinds or genres are themselves fixed by criteria that explain what they are and how they

---

[5] Compare the example of fashion, and the different ways of relating to it, discussed in my book *Engaging Reason* (Oxford: Oxford University Press, 2000), pp. 147–48.

work, and therefore how objects or events that exploit them are to be assessed.

I do not claim that all objects of evaluation are instances of good or bad kinds, nor that all objects that are either good or bad are instances of such kinds, nor that those that are instances of kinds of goods or of bads are evaluated exclusively as instances of the kind. Saying this is merely to repeat the obvious. A novel may be a superb novel and yet immoral for advocating wanton violence, etc.[6] I dwelt on genre- or kind-based values because they illustrate clearly the possibility of social dependence without relativism.

## 2. DIVERSITY WITHOUT RELATIVISM: THE ROLE OF GENRE

Value pluralism has become a fairly familiar doctrine in recent times. Its core is the affirmation (a) that there are many distinct values, that is, values that are not merely different manifestations of one supreme value, and (b) that there are incompatible values—incompatible in that they cannot all be realised in the life of a single individual, nor, when we consider values that can be instantiated by societies, can they be realised by a single society. A person or a society that has some of them is necessarily deficient in others. It is commonly understood to mean that the values that we fail to realise, or some of them, are as important as the values that we can realise, and that this is generally true both for individuals and for societies. So that even if individuals and societies are as good as they can be they are not perfect, nor can they be ranked according to the kind of value they exemplify.[7]

In spirit,[8] as I see it, value pluralism is committed to the view that

---

[6] There is, of course, the familiar claim that being immoral makes the novel bad as a novel. I think that the verdict on this one is: it depends. Sometimes it does, sometimes it does not. It depends on whether the objectionable aspect is well integrated in the work or is relatively isolated within it.

[7] Various alternative understandings of pluralism abound, from mere satisfaction of the first condition above to forms of pluralism that include hostility or competitiveness between supporters of different values. My characterisation of pluralism here is stronger than mere satisfaction of the first condition, for my interest is in those aspects of pluralism that force people to choose among values, force them to give up on some in order to pursue others (at all or to a higher degree).

[8] That is, this feature is not entailed by the two characteristics by which I defined value pluralism, but is assumed by many of its supporters, and is an essential part of their general view of value.

there are many incompatible and yet decent and worthwhile routes through life, and that they are as available to people in other civilisations, and were as available to people in other generations, as they are to us. Such views, which underlie the writings of Isaiah Berlin and of Michael Walzer, to name but two, reject the hubris of the moderns who believe that our ways are superior to those of all other human civilisations. I mention this here because the spirit of value pluralism courts contradiction.

Values are contradictory when one yields the conclusion that something is good, and the other the conclusion that this very thing is, in virtue of the same properties, without value, or even bad. The spirit of pluralism in affirming the value of different cultures, their practices and ideals, runs the risk of affirming contradictory values. Can one affirm value diversity without contradiction? Can one do so without abandoning our critical ability to condemn evaluative beliefs, regardless of their popularity, and regardless of their rootedness in some culture or other?

Relativism handles apparent contradictions by confining the validity of values to particular times and places or to particular perspectives. In doing that, however, social relativism runs the risk of having to recognise the validity of any value that is supported by the practices of a society, so long as no contradiction is involved in the recognition. It has too few resources for criticising the evaluative beliefs of other societies.[9] The social dependence thesis avoids this pitfall. Unlike social relativism it does not hold that social practices limit the application or validity of values. The test of whether something is valuable or not is in argument, using the full range of concepts, information, and rules of inference at our disposal. So far as the soundness of claims of value is concerned, the social dependence of value is neither here nor there. It makes no difference.[10]

Can, one may therefore wonder, the social dependence thesis accommodate the spirit of pluralism?[11] Is it not condemned to judge most

---

[9] Not that every relativist will acknowledge that as a difficulty. It is a reform of our ways of thinking about values that relativists are committed to.

[10] At least in general it makes no difference. I do not mean to deny the possibility of some views about specific values that are inconsistent with the social dependence thesis, and therefore refuted by it.

[11] The thought of the possibility of accommodation is meant to leave it open whether in any particular case an apparent contradiction is a real contradiction.

apparently contradictory values to be really contradictory? I think that the spirit of pluralism can be accommodated within the framework of the social dependence thesis partly because it can embrace local relativism, as can any other view, but mainly because evaluative thought is so heavily genre- or kind-dependent.

We are intuitively familiar with the phenomenon in our understanding of literature, music, films, art and architecture, and others. But the same applies to values in other domains. We can admire a building and judge it to be an excellent building for its flights of fancy and for its inventiveness. We can admire another for its spare minimalism and rigorous adherence to a simple classical language. We judge both to be excellent. Do we contradict ourselves? Not necessarily, for each displays the virtues of a different architectural genre, let us say romantic and classical.[12]

The vital point is that judgments of merit (and of demerit) proceed in such cases in the two steps discussed earlier: we identify the work as an instance of one genre and judge it by the standards of that genre. If it is a good instance of its genre then it is a good work absolutely, not only good of its kind. Judgments of works as being good of their kind do not yield the appearance of contradiction. No suspicion of contradiction is aroused by judging one church to be an outstanding Byzantine church and another to be a very good Decorative Gothic church, even though conflicting standards are applied in the judgments, that is, even though features that make one good (as a Byzantine church) would make the other bad (as a Decorative Gothic church). The appearance of contradiction arises when we generalise from genre-bound judgments to unrestricted evaluative judgments, finding both of them good for apparently contradictory reasons. This may lead one to endorse an evaluative account we may call genre-relativism, permitting genre-relative evaluations, but holding that unrestricted evaluations are meaningless. However, we regularly indulge in such unrestricted evaluations, and there is in fact nothing wrong with them.[13] The point to bear in mind is that

---

[12] To simplify the presentation I will revert to referring only to simple instantiation of one kind in the examples, leaving out the complex relationships objects can have to kinds, as explained above.

[13] This does not mean of course that it is always possible to rank works belonging to different genres by their degree of excellence. Quite often such works are of incommensurate value. The points made in the text apply primarily to noncomparative but unrestricted judgments of value, though they signify that one necessary precondition of comparative judgments obtains.

unrestricted judgments are based on genre-related standards. The work is good because it is good by the standards of its genre.[14] While the verdict (good, bad, or mediocre) is unrestricted, its ground is always relative to a particular genre. Thus contradiction is avoided.

The same ways of resolving apparent contradictions apply outside the arts. One system of criminal justice is good to the extent that it is a good adversarial system; another is good to the extent that it is a good prosecutorial system. Excellence in being an adversarial system consists, in part, in features absence of which is among the conditions of excellence in being a prosecutorial system of justice. Nevertheless, the two systems may be no worse than each other, each being good through being a good instance of a different, and conflicting, kind.

Are not the examples I give simple cases of local relativism? Local relativities, of the "in Rome do as the Romans do" kind, are obviously important in facilitating the spirit of pluralism. Manifestations or applications of local relativism are usually taken to be, and some are, independent of genre- or kind-based considerations. They rely on nothing more than the fact that to apply to a particular set of circumstances, a relatively general value has to be realised in a way that will not be suitable for other circumstances.

We are used to appeal to such considerations to explain why different, incompatible forms of marriage, and of other social relations, were valuable at different times. We rarely test the hypothesis that this was made necessary by differing circumstances, and I suspect that often no such justification of diversity is available. The factual considerations involved are too complex to be known. True, in many such cases the local forms of relationships are suitable to local circumstances simply because they took root there, and people have become used to them, to living by them. This is a good reason for not disturbing them if they are valuable. But they are not valuable because they are the only way to implement some general value. Rather they are one of several possible valuable but incompatible arrangements to have. The argument for their value depends on a genre- or kind-based argument to defend their value against

---

[14] Among the many questions this view brings to mind: how is membership of genre determined? Criteria of membership in a genre are themselves genre determined and may differ from genre to genre. They are, in other words, determined by the sustaining practices of the genre. Since the standards of each genre determine membership in it, multiple membership is possible, and not all that rare. This may lead to diverse judgments, as the work may be good in one genre and not so good, or even bad, in another, leading to indeterminacy regarding its unrestricted standing.

charges of contradiction because of their incompatibility with other valuable arrangements.[15]

Many of the diversities in forms of personal relations, as well as the case of adversarial v. prosecutorial systems of criminal justice,[16] and many others, can be reconciled only via a local relativism that, to explain away apparent contradictions, relies on, and presupposes, genre- or kind-based evaluations.

## III. CHANGE AND UNDERSTANDING

### 1. UNDERSTANDING AND VALUE

To the extent that it is possible to distinguish them, my emphasis so far has been on ontological questions, on the existence of values. It is time to shift to questions of understanding of values, remembering all along that the two cannot be entirely separated.

Understanding, rather than knowledge, is the term that comes to mind when thinking of evaluative judgments. Judgment, rather than mere knowledge, is what the practically wise person possesses. Why? What is the difference? It is a matter of degree, with understanding and judgment involving typically, first, knowledge in depth, and secondly, and as a result, knowledge much of which is implicit. Understanding is knowledge in depth. It is connected knowledge in two respects. First, knowledge of what is understood is rich enough to place its object in its context, to relate it to its location and its neighbourhood, literally and metaphorically. Second, knowledge of what is understood is also connected to one's imagination, emotions, feelings, and intentions. What one understands one can imagine, empathise with, feel for, and be disposed to act appropriately regarding. Understanding tends to involve a

---

[15] I have discussed the application of this form of local relativism as applied to constitutions in J. Raz, "On the Authority and Interpretation of Constitutions: Some Preliminaries," in *Constitutionalism,* ed. Larry Alexander (New York: Cambridge University Press, 1998).

[16] Needless to say there can be shortcomings in each system that have to be remedied and that sometimes can be remedied by borrowing elements from another system, even one that is based on incompatible principles. But respect for valuable diversity is not to be confused with conservative opposition to sensible reform.

good deal of implicit knowledge precisely because it is connected knowledge. Its richness exceeds our powers of articulation.

Understanding is displayed, and put to use, through good judgment. To illustrate the point, think of a simple example of good judgment. Jane, we may say, is a good judge of wines. Ask her which wine to serve with the meal. John, by way of contrast, has perfect knowledge of the bus timetable. You should ask him which bus to take, but it would be odd to think of him as being a good judge of bus journeys, or as having a good judgment of bus journeys, in the way that Jane is clearly a good judge of wine because of her excellent judgment regarding wines. The difference is that John's views, perfect though they are, are based on one kind of consideration, whereas Jane is judging the bearing of a multitude of factors on the choice of wine. Moreover, the ways the different factors bear on each other, and on the ultimate choice, defy comprehensive articulation. If Jane is articulate and reflective (and to possess good judgment she need be neither) she may be able to explain every aspect of every one of her decisions, but she cannot describe exhaustively all aspects of her decisions, let alone provide a general detailed and content-full[1] procedure for arriving at the choices or opinions she may reach on different real and hypothetical occasions, as John can.

It is not difficult to see why values call for understanding and judgment. The connection is most evident regarding specific values. They are mixed values, constituted by standards determining ways for ideal combinations of contributing values, and criteria for various relationships that objects can have to them (simple instantiation, inversion, etc.). Their knowledge requires knowledge of the various values that combine in their mix, and of the way their presence affects the value of the object given the presence of other values. Regarding these matters whose complexity and dense texture defy complete articulation, knowledge is connected and implicit, amounting, when it is reasonably reflective and reasonably complete, to understanding, and its use, in forming opinions and in taking decisions, calls for judgment.

The case of general values may be less clear. The more general the value, the more homogeneous and simple it is likely to be. Can one not have knowledge of it without understanding, and apply it without

---

[1] It is always possible to provide thin descriptions of such procedures: you consider the impact of all relevant factors on your overriding goal, and, mindful of the need to protect other matters of concern to you, you reach a decision that will be best in the circumstances. I do not mean formal or thin descriptions like this.

judgment? The apparent simplicity of general values is, however, misleading. To be sure, one can have limited knowledge of them, as one can of more specific values, without understanding. One can know that freedom is the value of being allowed to act as one sees fit. Such one-liners are true so far as they go. We find them useful because we have the background knowledge that enables us to read them correctly. Relying on abstract formulations of the content of values, and *denying* that they need to be understood in context and interpreted in light of other related values, leads to one of the most pernicious forms of fanaticism.

As I have already mentioned, more general values are explained at least in part by the way they feed into more specific ones. The point can be illustrated in various ways, appropriate to various examples. There could be forms of friendship different, some quite radically so, from those that exist today. But one cannot pursue friendship (a relatively general value) except through the specific forms it has (this comment will be somewhat qualified when we discuss innovation and change below). Therefore, knowledge of the value of friendship is incomplete without an understanding of its specific forms, with their specific forms of excellence.

## 2. INTERPRETATION

I hope you found my remarks on the connectedness of knowledge about values, and its relation to understanding and judgment, persuasive. If so you may be wondering how much we can know about values.

The problem arises out of the fact that so much of our evaluative knowledge is implicit. This means that a considerable degree of disagreement is inevitable. Transmission of implicit knowledge depends on personal contacts. In mass mobile societies disagreements are liable to sprout. Disagreement about values undermines the very possibility of evaluative knowledge, at least so far as cultural values are concerned, and for the remaining time I will discuss only them.[2]

The nature of cultural values is determined in part by a standard of excellence, implicit knowledge of which is part of the conditions for possessing the value-concept. The concept and the value are thus inter-

---

[2] Much of what I will say applies, if at all, to other values as well, but the arguments that establish this will not be considered here.

dependent. The standard, you will remember, depends on a sustaining practice. The novel, for example, emerged as a distinct genre with its distinctive standard of excellence with the emergence of a sustaining practice. It could have been otherwise. A different value might have emerged had that practice not developed, and another one, sustaining a different standard, had emerged in its place. The process is continuous: the early Victorian novel developed into the mid-Victorian novel as the standard by which novels were judged changed with changes in the underlying sustaining practices, that is, with changes in the concepts involved, or, if you like, with the emergence of new concepts referring to the modified standards by which novels came to be judged.

Disagreements about the application of the concepts, those that cannot be explained by faulty information or other factors, mean that matter lies within the area regarding which the concept is vague. Here then is the problem: the value is determined by the standard of excellence set by the sustaining practice and enshrined in the value-concept. Where the value-concept is vague, because due to disagreements about it there is no common understanding of its application to some cases, what are we to think?

One temptation is to go down a radical subjectivist escape route and deny that evaluative disagreement is anything other than a difference of taste. There is no fact about which people disagree. They just like different things. Nothing in the story so far would, however, warrant this extreme reaction. The disagreement is limited, and does not warrant denying that we know that Leo Tolstoy is a better novelist than Elizabeth Gaskell, or that a fulfilling relationship can make all the difference to the quality of one's life, and many other evaluative truths. Furthermore, the nature of the disagreements we are considering tends to affirm rather than challenge the objectivity of values and the possibility of evaluative knowledge. For these disagreements are contained within a framework of shared views: that being imaginative contributes to the excellence of a novel, that being loyal contributes to the excellence of a relationship, and so on. The disagreement is about the way the elements relate, about their relative importance, and the like. It is bounded disagreement that makes sense only if the agreement makes sense, and the agreement is that regarding these boundary matters people are justified in their claim to knowledge. We need to find a way of dealing with the intractability of local disagreements without denying the possibility of evaluative knowledge in general.

What other options are there? The epistemic option[3] is not available. That option claims that the vagueness of evaluative concepts is due to people's ignorance of their precise nature, and hence their tendency to make mistakes in their application. In truth regarding each case there is, according to the epistemic option, a fact of the matter: either it is or it is not an instance of the value. In cases of vagueness we are, perhaps inescapably, unaware of it. Groping in the dark, we—not surprisingly—disagree. This option is not available because, given that the value-defining standard is set by the sustaining practice, if the sustaining practice is vague there is no fact of the matter ignorance of which renders our understanding of the value and the value-concept incomplete. There is nothing more to be known.[4]

You may think that there is no problem here. If those who disagree recognise that they are dealing with a vague case, and because of that the question whether the value-concept applies to the problem case admits of no clear answer, their disagreement will evaporate. They will both withdraw their conflicting claims and say that there is no answer to the question. But that option is not generally available either.[5]

First, the condition cannot always be met in cases of vagueness. That is, it cannot be the case that when a concept is vague those who have it always recognise when it is vague. If it were so the concept would not be vague. Rather it would be a concept that precisely applies to one range of objects, does not apply to a second range of objects, and the question of its application to a third range does not arise: regarding them it neither applies nor does not apply.

Regarding cultural values the problem is worse. The existence of a sustaining practice is a condition of their existence because the possibility of their instantiation requires that people understand something

---

[3] Associated with T. Williamson's (in his *Vagueness* [London: Routledge, 1994]) and R. Sorensen's account of vagueness generally, and with R. M. Dworkin's treatment of the vagueness of what he calls "interpretive concepts."

[4] In this regard the concepts of cultural values differ from the generality of concepts whose object does not depend on them, or on other closely related concepts, for its existence. Dedicated coherentists will say that the concept is determined by a coherent idealisation of the practice that resolves its vagueness. I agree that the concept cannot be gauged from a statistical headcount of people's behaviour. It is, if you like the phrase, a theoretical construct based on that behaviour. But it is not subject to a completeness requirement simply because there are not enough resources to prefer one way of completing it over the others. For my discussion of concepts, which depends on some aspects of T. Burge's account, see "Two Views of the Nature of the Theory of Law: A Partial Comparison," in *Hart's Postscript,* ed. Jules Coleman (Oxford: Oxford University Press, 2001).

[5] Though it is available in some cases.

about their nature, and that understanding will be implicit and requires a practice to be generated and transmitted. But the practice is not what explains why the standard of excellence is a standard of excellence. That is explained by reference to ordinary evaluative considerations. Therefore, where some people believe that the value-concept applies to an object and others deny that it does both sides appeal to evaluative considerations in justifying their views. Neither side appeals to the sustaining practice. The fact that it does not settle the issue cannot be invoked by either side. Therefore, the option of simply acknowledging that the case is a vague case and that none of the rival views is true is not always available to them.[6]

Moreover, retreat from a disputed domain is possible where there is something to retreat to. This is easy with concepts that admit of degree: he may not be quite bald, only balding, or something like that. But with cultural values that option is not usually available. The conflicting views, once fleshed out, are conflicting accounts of the standard of excellence for the kind.[7] While sometimes a relatively small retreat from each of the rival accounts can resolve the difference, allowing for an undetermined terrain, this is not always so. The rival accounts may cut across each other, leaving no room for such mutual retreat.

This makes this kind of evaluative disagreement resemble cases of aspect seeing or Gestalt shifts. Think of a duck/rabbit shape. I look at it and see a duck. I look again, and, usually with some effort, I switch and see a rabbit. I still know that it is a duck as well. Both perceptions are correct. Thinking about values does not rely on direct perception in this way. But disagreements due to the underdetermination of values, and the vagueness of value concepts, bear analogy to aspect seeing.[8] In them too one can, if one tries, appreciate the force behind the other person's account of the value. Yet that does not open the way to a partial modification of these accounts. Rather, typically one remains faithful to one's own account while acknowledging that the other's has force to it as well. Sometimes one does not. One can come to have both accounts and rely on each on different occasions.

[6] It is sometimes available, that is, when considerations other than appeal to the sustaining practices can be relied upon to establish the vagueness. This point will resurface below.

[7] Cf. R. M. Dworkin, *Law's Empire* (Cambridge, Mass.: Harvard University Press, 1986).

[8] On aspect seeing, see S. Mulhall, *On Being in the World: Wittgenstein and Heidegger on Seeing Aspects* (London: Routledge, 1990).

Can the holders of rival and incompatible views both be right? In spite of the initial implausibility, and the difficulties that this view creates, I believe that this is often the situation. We are not considering any disagreement about the value. In many disagreements at least one side is in the wrong. We are concerned only with disagreement where the sustaining practice underdetermines the issue. That is why it is tempting to say that there is no fact of the matter that can settle the dispute. Disagreements of this kind have two features: they are fairly general, and they cannot be explained away by ignorance or mistake.

Remember that the relations of concepts and of the values that depend on them and their sustaining practices are rather loose. Practices underdetermine the nature of the values they sustain when, owing to the relatively loose connection required, while they can rightly be claimed to support some particular standard of excellence, the claim that they support it is no better than the claim that they support another standard. When people's disagreements about the nature of a value are irresolvable they are so because they have, or can develop, ways of understanding the value that all conform with the commonly understood features of the value, what I called the boundaries of agreement, but diverge in their view of how they fit together, how they relate to each other, about their relative importance and whether they contribute to the value in dispute for one reason or another.

People unfamiliar with the value-concept would not be able to participate in the argument at all. Both diverging accounts have a good deal in common, and both present an attractive standard of excellence. Of course, one may like objects that excel by one standard better than objects that excel by the other standard. But that possibility is inherent in the approach to value I am developing. Values guide action, they guide our imagination and our taste; but there are many of them, and one's taste may favour some rather than others. Articulate people familiar with the value-concept can give a (partial) account of it, and I will assume that they are not making mistakes. Nevertheless, their account will inevitably be vague in some ways in which the concept is not, and not vague in some ways in which the concept is. It may be as good an account as one can give and yet there will be others no worse than it, but different, and incompatible in that they cannot all be part of one account.

This is why accounts of values deserve to be regarded as interpretations of the values they are accounts of. Interpretations are explanations (or displays) of meaning that can be rivalled. That is why we feel that they are more subjective: Alfred Brendel's interpretation of Schubert's B-flat sonata is no less good than, though very different from, that of Kovasovich, and it tells us something about Brendel as well as about the sonata. An explanation of how genes determine people's eye colour is not an interpretation, not because there can be only one such explanation, but because all the explanations are compatible with each other. They tell us little about those who give them other than their ability to explain.

Explanations are interpretations where there is a possibility of diverse incompatible explanations being correct. This multiplicity of correct rival interpretations explains why they are so revealing of their authors.[9] But it does not show, as some suppose, that interpretations are no more than a matter of taste. Some interpretations are straightforwardly wrong; others though holding some truth are inferior to their rivals. In short, the concept of interpretation provides us with the features we wanted: it is governed by objective standards, yet it allows that the phenomena underdetermine their interpretation and can be interpreted in various ways, none worse than the others. This allows them to be revealing of the interpreters, as well as of those who prefer one interpretation to the others.

Like aspect-seeing, interpretations admit both of fixity and of flexibility. That is, it takes an effort for people to see the sense of rival interpretations, and the common belief that if I am right the other must be wrong is no help in this. Even after one sees the merit of a rival interpretation there may be only one that one feels at home with. Yet some people can be at home with various ones and feel free to rely on them on different occasions.

We display this complexity by regarding some interpretive statements as true or false, others as right or wrong, and others still as more or less correct, or as good interpretations, an appellation that allows for the possibility of others no less good. We need to free ourselves from the rigidity of the divisions of domains of thought into those that are either objective and entirely governed by true/false dichotomy and those that are entirely subjective and are mere matters of taste. There are many

---

[9] Though, of course, mistakes and wrong interpretations can also be revealing of their authors.

other reasons for breaking out of this straightjacket. But unless we do so we will not be able to understand our understanding of values.


## 3. Interpretation and Change

One way of putting my response to doubts about evaluative knowledge that derive from the perennial nature of some kinds of evaluative disagreement is that we can know more than those who deny the possibility of evaluative knowledge suppose, and less than many of their opponents think, or that we can know something, but less than is sometimes imagined. My tendency to explain the possibility of knowledge at the expense of many knowledge claims was evident in my account of the kind- or genre-based nature of many evaluative judgments. Since many value judgments are genre-based, they allow for knowledge, based on the defining standards of the genre, and avoid contradiction, since different objects that belong to different kinds can be judged by otherwise contradictory standards.

The underdetermination of value by practice, which is an inevitable consequence of the social dependence of value, confronted us with a different problem. However, my response was similar. I claimed that both sides in such disputes can be right. This time recognition of this fact requires not realisation that criteria of value are kind-based, but a loosening of the rigid divide between matters of knowledge and matters of taste, between the domain of truth and that of preference. The realisation both of the kind-dependence of value judgments and of the interpretive nature of many value judgments requires greater toleration of diversity than is common. It requires abandoning many claims to exclusive truth. But those are also required of us if we are not to make claims that the subject does not warrant.

The tendency to account for evaluative knowledge through moderating its ambition is common to important strands in contemporary philosophy.[10] My motivation differs from that of most of these writers in that I am not concerned with reconciling evaluative knowledge with a naturalistic metaphysics, nor with the alleged problem of how evalua-

---

[10] See, in very different ways, Alan Gibbard, Peter Railton, and Christine Korsgaard among others.

tive beliefs can motivate.[11] This may account for some of the differences in the positions we favour.

The softening of the distinctions between knowledge and taste, truth and preference, which I am urging, arises out of the social dependence of value, with the result that, at least where cultural values are concerned, the proper contours of values are vague and their existence is in a flux. This results in the centrality of interpretation in evaluative thinking. Interpretation also provides the bridge between understanding of what there is and creation of the new. The crucial point is to see how this transition can be gradual, almost unnoticed. Of course it is not always like that. We are familiar with pioneering, revolutionary social movements as well as with self-consciously revolutionary movements or individual attempts in the arts. The social dependence of values points to caution in understanding the contribution of such revolutionary innovations. History is replete with examples of revolutionary impulses leading people to abandon, as out of fashion or worse, the pursuit of familiar values, in search of some vision of the new and better. It is much rarer for those visions to come true as intended. The new forms of the good take time and require the density of repeated actions and interactions to crystallise and take a definite shape, one that is specific enough to allow people intentionally to realise it in their life or in or through their actions. When they settle, they commonly turn out to be quite a bit different from the revolutionary vision that inspired them.

Be that as it may, it is of interest to see how the familiar fact that change can be imperceptible is explained by the facts adumbrated so far. Two processes are available, and the distinction between them is often too vague to allow a clear diagnosis when one or the other occurs. First, one may like a variant on the norm, and that may catch on, and become the standard for a new norm. Second, one or another of the interpretations of a value, even if it is no better than its rivals because the value is underdetermined, may gain wide acceptance and affect the practice, shifting it to a new standard. In this case the change is relatively conservative, typical of the way kinds drift over time, imperceptibly, or at least unperceived at the moment. What has been undetermined by the old kind becomes the clear standard of the new kind.

---

[11] My response to the first issue is outlined above in Lecture I, section 2, and to the issue of motivation in chapter 5 of *Engaging Reason.*

The important point to make is that the social dependence of values enables us to understand better such developments and their general availability. It enables us to reconcile the objectivity of values with their fluidity and sensitivity to social practices, to shared understanding and shared meanings. It enables us to combine holding to a fixed point of reference, which is essential to thinking of values as objective and to our being able to orient ourselves by them, either by trying to realise them or through more complex relations to them, and realising that their fixity is temporary and fragile, which explains how change is often continuous, and no different from their further development in one way rather than another, which was equally open. None of this is explainable unless we take seriously the contingency at the heart of value.

*American Culture and the Voice of Poetry*

*ROBERT PINSKY*

THE TANNER LECTURES ON HUMAN VALUES

Delivered at

Princeton University
April 4, 5, and 6, 2001

ROBERT PINSKY is a poet and professor of English at Boston University. He was educated at Rutgers and at Stanford, where he received his Ph.D. He is a fellow of the American Academy of Arts and Sciences and the American Academy of Arts and Letters and is the recipient of numerous awards, including the Shelley Memorial Award, the *Los Angeles Times* Book Prize in Poetry, and the Lenore Marshall Prize. He was the thirty-ninth Poet Laureate of the United States (1997–2000) and in that capacity undertook the Favorite Poem Project, a video archive of American citizens discussing and reading their favorite poems. He co-edited, with Maggie Dietz, the resulting anthology *Americans' Favorite Poems.* His volumes of criticism include *The Sounds of Poetry* (1998); *Poetry and the World* (1988), which was nominated for the National Book Critics Circle Award in Criticism; and *The Situation of Poetry: Contemporary Poetry and Its Traditions* (1978). He is the author of numerous collections of poetry, including *An Explanation of America* (1980), which won the Saxifrage Prize; *The History of My Heart* (1984), which won the William Carlos Williams Prize; *The Want Bone* (1990); *The Figured Wheel: New and Collected Poems, 1966–1996* (1996), which was nominated for the 1995 Pulitzer Prize in Poetry and was awarded the Ambassador Book Award in Poetry; and *Jersey Rain* (2000).

# I

I hope to respond to the large-minded rubric of the Tanner Lectures on Human Values, and at the same time to avoid becoming drunk on the term "Human Values," or intimidated by it. My goal will be to look at great things through the aperture of my metier. So while "American Culture" is an immense term, by "the voice of poetry" I mean something quite literal and practical: the voice of a person saying a poem. My examples will be specific, drawn from the Favorite Poem Project, a kind of accidental, oblique experiment—or something less scientific, a venture—in American culture.

I'll begin with some general formulations.

The term "culture" with its old agricultural and biological connotations has taken a new, surprisingly central place in recent thought. Even we unsystematic readers of magazines and newspapers notice that in economics, in American electoral politics, in the geo-political analysis of different peoples and their national systems, culture has become a kind of ulterior cause of causes. It has been proposed that culture determines the power of a nation to achieve economic development, and that cultural differences underlay the recent contest between George Bush and Al Gore. Even the directions and conceptions of science have been seen in cultural terms.

In its former, rather frumpy state, the term "culture" (as in the antiquated phrase "a person of culture") had no aura of dread (despite Marxist or Freudian analysis of the mere social fear that one might seem "uncultured"). In its contemporary form, however, the notion of culture evokes anxiety of two contradictory, indeed more or less opposite, kinds.

There is the nightmare of undifferentiation, a loss of cultural diversity comparable to the loss of bio-diversity. Hundreds of languages have died in the last century, with their alphabets and epics and delicate structures. In the terrible closing pages of *Tristes Tropiques,* Claude Lévi-Straus indicates how the mere breath, the very glance, of the observer rapidly destroys differences that evolved for centuries, homogenizing and sterilizing the former abundance. This vision of destruction by a dominant culture reminds us of the etymological link between "culture" and *"colon,"* the one who cultivates or scratches the soil, the colonialist.

But the other, obverse dread is of a vicious, tribalized factionalism, the coming apart of civic fabrics through fragmentation, ranging from the paranoid brutality of ethnic cleansing to the division of mass culture into niches. Religious difference, racial difference, linguistic difference, even generational difference can seem compounded and hypertrophied by information-age forces: the fanatical obsession with difference and its exploitation by tyranny have been multiplied and accelerated by modern technology. The swiftness and pervasiveness of contemporary broadcast propaganda parallel the heightened efficiency of contemporary killing squads. In this disturbing vision, the etymological ghost is culture's relation to "cult," a word denoting arcane forms of worship: the sinister difference of strangers.

On one hand, we are afraid of becoming so much like one another that we will lose something vital in our human nature—and on the other hand, we are also afraid of becoming so different, so much divided into alien and murderously competitive fragments, that we cannot survive. In what ways do these opposed, even contradictory cultural anxieties share a single root?

For an American poet, the fear of lost differentiation and the fear of excessive differentiation do indeed embody a single, in fact familiar anxiety: the fear of being cut off from memory. It is memory that tempers the imagined extremes of culture, the polarities of explosion and undifferentiation. Memory resists uniformity because it registers fine gradations; memory resists the factional because it registers the impure, recombining, fluent nature of culture. The mother of the muses is memory, and the traditional Greco-Roman crown of the poet is made of leaves that when picked remain green.

The most profound observers of the United States have seen in our manners, and in the cultural correlatives of our democracy, a version of fragmentation, the dread that we become too unlike one another. Alexis de Tocqueville, in the *locus classicus* for this viewpoint, associates the separation of individuals into fragments or atoms horizontally, from their peers, with the separation of individuals vertically, from their past and future. Tocqueville writes:

> Thus not only does democracy make every man forget his ancestors, but it hides his descendants and separates his contemporaries from him; it throws him back forever upon himself alone and threatens in the end to confine him entirely within the solitude of his own heart. (*Democracy in America,* Henry Reeve text rev. by Francis Bowen, ed.

Phillips Bradley [New York: A. A. Knopf, 1945], vol. 2, chapter 2,
p. 99)

This passage recalls the great classical tag, found in *Gulliver's Travels* as
well as in *King Lear,* which notes that the human animal is a puny creature: its patchy fur and flimsy hide give inadequate protection; its claws
and little teeth are poor weapons. It is a mediocre climber and swimmer,
and even its best specimens cannot run as fast as the young or aged of
many other species.

This commonplace trope is deployed to emphasize certain redeem-
ing human qualities, such as the capacity for reason or memory. Tocqueville, in comparing democracy with aristocratic culture, directs us
toward memory, and a particular aspect of memory: the processes of culture. The creature is not only clever, not only *capax rationis:* it has developed ways to extend memory beyond its lifetime. Its unlikely survival
has depended upon its devising means of communication not only horizontally, with its contemporary peers, to co-operate in gaining food or
shelter, but also vertically, with its predecessors and successors, so that
the experience of past lifetimes can be used.

For this purpose of communal memory and transmission, the animal
has devised the binary code of digital media, and printed marks before
that, and incised or written marks before that—and before those technologies of marks, the creature made a technology of its own body, with
a highly refined system of grunts, emitted through its feeding orifice.
Like the griots in Alex Haley's *Roots,* who call up across the centuries information about dynasties, family relations, property rights, the human
animal through the amazing grunt-code of speech can retain subtle
shades of information: which food is available at what time of year, what
customs for mating or burial will best serve the community, information as precise or subtle as "bring me a pound of galvanized ten-penny
nails" or "I love you but not that way." Patterns like rhythm artfully
render the grunt-information more memorable, and more memorizable.

I have come to realize that it is this process that I mean by "culture":
the process of shared memory that Tocqueville sees as transformed, even
threatened, by the conditions of American democracy. The concept of
culture, Stephen Greenblatt has pointed out, "gestures toward what
appear to be opposite things: *constraint* and *mobility*" (*Critical Terms for
Literary Study,* ed. Frank Lentricchia and Thomas McLaughlin [Chicago:
University of Chicago Press, 1995])—terms roughly parallel to the
uniformities of the colonialist and the divergences of the cultist. The

process of culture, a form of memory, controls us and also enables us. In their extremes those actions of control and liberty manifest the envisioned dystopias of global homogenization on one side and fragmentation on the other. More precisely, culture is a process of both memory and resistance to memory, curatorship and transformation.

Consider poetry, an art that in European languages has roots in aristocratic courts with their flirtations and imperial visions, or in folk sources like the ballad and the hymn. That is, practically speaking, the art of poetry has been preserved in many cultures either by a social class that considers itself the hereditary caretaker or by a cottage life, passed along through the generations along with the jokes, recipes, dances and songs of the grandparents. In other words, poetry in such societies has either snob value or the values of a unifying folk culture: two sources of continuity that the USA, relatively speaking, does not have.

Some Americans used to sentimentalize the Soviet-era poetry readings held in athletic stadiums and attended by thousands. But those events depended upon the exploitation of ancient tastes and attitudes: specifically, they joined the power of totalitarian government with the cachet of poetry in a country where an angry driver will shout at another: "You have no culture!" This is not an American insult. We must strain our imaginations to conceive of countries where the politicians must at least pretend to love the great national poet, and perhaps memorize a line or two.

Relatively speaking, in the United States the high bourgeoisie has not preened itself on curatorship of poetry. Nor do we have a single, unifying folk culture. The Italian-American grandmother, the Cuban-American grandmother, the Yankee grandmother, the African-American grandmother, insofar as they pass on the jokes and recipes and rhymes, will have different ones.

In place of the aristocratic or folk idea, we have, quite characteristically, improvised and patched together a place for the art of poetry, in various ways—journalistic, middle-class-domestic, professionalized, academic, self-conscious—many of them well represented in John Hollander's two-volume anthology of nineteenth-century American verse. The American invention of "Creative Writing" is another example of that improvisation.

I don't mean to deprecate American culture on these grounds, nor to elevate it chauvinistically. We are not Persians or Bengalis. (Though I suppose that some of us are indeed Persian-Americans or Bengali-

Americans.) That in those highly unified cultures most people quote, recite and compose poetry as part of a life is attractive, and in each case reflects a certain culture. Certain forms of memory, relatively speaking, are settled and available. But the eccentricities of Emily Dickinson and Walt Whitman explore the soul's dependence on memory, and its resistance to memory, with strangely improvised instruments. Her skewed hymns and his breakaway arias both reflect a culture where imported, inherited and invented elements jangle or coalesce; where the provinces are in no more clear a relation to any capital than the present is to the past; where the wrestling of curatorship with transformation is palpably strenuous. Underlying that contest, and inspiring invention, is the possibility of a vacuum, of failed memory.

That threatening vacuum is in keeping with Tocqueville's most explicit pronouncement about American poetry—a pronouncement that, out of context, can seem comically harsh:

> Nothing conceivable is so petty, so insipid, so crowded with paltry interests—in one word, so anti-poetic—as the life of a man in the United States. (*DIA*, p. 74)

But in fact Tocqueville, after observing that the principle of equality "has dried up most of the old springs of poetry," proceeds to ask "what new ones it may disclose." Legends of heroes and gods or angels and demons, old traditions and rituals, all viable material for the poet in aristocratic societies, he says, will not serve poetry in America. He has an interesting notion about the first thing poets in the new world would turn to:

> When skepticism had depopulated heaven, and the progress of equality had reduced each individual to smaller and better-known proportions, the poets, not yet aware of what they could substitute for the great themes that were departing together with the aristocracy, turned their eyes to inanimate nature. As they lost sight of gods and heroes, they set themselves to describe streams and mountains....Some have thought that this embellished delineation of all the physical and inanimate objects which cover the earth was the kind of poetry peculiar to democratic ages. But I believe this to be an error, and that it belongs only to a period of transition.
>
> I am persuaded that in the end democracy diverts the imagination from all that is external to man and fixes it on man alone. Democratic nations may amuse themselves for a while with considering the productions of nature, but they are excited in reality only by a survey

of themselves. Here, and here alone, the true sources of poetry among such nations are to be found....

Among a democratic people poetry will not be fed with legends or the memorials of old traditions....All these resources fail him; but Man remains, and the poet needs no more. The destinies of mankind, man himself taken aloof from his country and his age and standing in the presence of Nature and of God, with his passions, his doubts, his rare prosperities and inconceivable wretchednesses, will become the chief, if not the sole, theme of poetry among these nations. (*DIA,* pp. 75–76)

And in a rather ringing final paragraph to his chapter, Tocqueville concludes:

Such are the poems of democracy. The principle of equality does not, then, destroy all the subjects of poetry: it renders them less numerous, but more vast.

From these provocative ideas, rich in implications to develop or refute, suggesting an abundance of examples and suggestions, I would like for now to extract only one main notion of Tocqueville's chapter, as it is germane to the Favorite Poem Project: the relation between the ancient art of poetry and democratic culture. I mean the ideas that take him from the characterization "petty,...insipid...antipoetic" to the ringing conclusion about "the destinies of mankind" and materials "less numerous, but more vast."

Those formulations suggest useful insights into American literature. For instance, how does the poetry of Whitman or Dickinson confirm or refute Tocqueville's expectation that American poetry would reach for profundity not through historical figures, heroes and legends, and not through gods or demons and angels, but by concentration on the individual soul? Can it be that this young Frenchman in effect actually predicted Whitman and Dickinson? And what about Henry Wadsworth Longfellow's conscious effort to create American legends and heroes? Or Herman Melville's? But my subject for the moment is poetry less in relation to American poets than to American readers and reading.

The response to the Favorite Poem Project has surprised me, in its scale and its intensity. With very little publicity, the invitation to name a poem one would be willing to read aloud for an audio and video archive, and to say a few sentences about the poem's personal significance, produced more than eighteen thousand written responses. (These letters and e-mails themselves are an interesting archive.) In fact, my co-workers on the project and I closed the invitation at that point, before the first CNN television piece about the project, because too many letters would have overwhelmed our selection process, which rested on a few graduate student screeners.

My first names for the undertaking were along the lines of "The Say a Poem Project" and various ideas incorporating the phrase "giving voice." These titles all seemed cumbersome or corny, and it was my co-editor Maggie Dietz and Sam Miller of the New England Foundation for the Arts, our first sponsor, who came up with "Favorite Poem," a title that emphasizes the second of the two principles, vocality and autonomy, guiding the project.

As editor, my goals included maintaining a certain level of literary quality, without merely imposing my own tastes; also, representing a range of ages, regions, ethnicities, economic classes, kinds of education. Additionally, Maggie Dietz and I decided that although certain writers and kinds of writing should be represented (for example, African-American poets, Dickinson and Whitman, Shakespeare) the poems should not all be American. Indeed, to reflect American readers and culture— people devoted to Rainer Maria Rilke or Pablo Neruda in translation, for example, and people with native tongues other than English—it would be necessary to include poems written in many different languages. That decision was consistent with the terms of our National Endowment for the Arts grant: to create a portrait of the United States, in the year 2000, through the lens of poetry.

Another question I hoped the project would explore is the place of poetry in relation to a tremendously powerful, often brilliant and certainly elaborate mass culture. In one way or another, every American poet and reader must respond to that amazing constellation of genius and vulgarity, vitality and turpitude, of which the greatest products, perhaps, are jazz and the American feature film.

I find some insight into that question in letters sent to the project, as quoted in the anthology along with the poems, and in the statements of people we recorded reading poems. John Doherty, in his initial correspondence, wrote the sentence "I guess a ditchdigger who reads Shakespeare is still just a ditchdigger." And indeed, in the video segment, we see him digging a ditch, wearing his hard hat, as part of his work as a construction worker for the Boston Gas Company. After talking briefly about his work, he reads some well-chosen selections from Whitman's "Song of Myself." "Poetry," he says in his remarks, "was definitely intimidating at first. It just looked like a lot of words that were out of order and out of place, that did not belong together." He adds, "It takes a lot of reading and re-reading to grasp it."

I believe that in many countries social constraints of one kind or another might suppress or temper this candor, requiring more respect or less discovery. This freedom to judge the art of poetry itself as a consumer, intimidated by the art's difficulty but not by its social prestige or authority, feels American to me, for good or ill. It is echoed by a number of the participants, including Seph Rodney, who early in his unforgettable discussion of Sylvia Plath's "Nick and the Candlestick" remarks that he had always thought of poetry as merely "grandiose" and "for want of a better term, a high-falutin'…not very *real* way of using language." Like Doherty on Whitman, Rodney on Plath presents his attachment to her work as a kind of conversion experience to poetry itself.

Poetry's place in the world and in a particular life seems more self-evident and authoritative for some of the participants who came here from other places, such as Lyn Aye, the Burmese-American anesthesiologist in San Jose, who reads a poem by Zawgee in Burmese and in English translation, or Jayashree Chatterjee, the New Jersey librarian who reads Rabindranath Tagore in Bengali and in English.

What is striking in all four of these instances is a note of personal conviction in both the delivery of the poem selected and the statements about the poem. The slightly accented Burmese and Indian voices both speak about exile or loss of place, and in what I consider another characteristic American gesture they select poems that simultaneously sharpen and soothe those feelings of immigrant dislocation.

In short, the intimacy and introspection of these readers, in their approach to the poems they read, correspond to Tocqueville's proposition about poetry in a democracy. The subject of each poem as they describe it begins with the condition of a soul: material, to borrow Tocqueville's terms, more "vast" for each reader than it is various or "numerous." (Though an overall variety characterizes the undertaking as a whole.)

Concentration on the individual human soul is audible in the construction worker's remarkable reading of Whitman's closing passage. The poem's familiar, bizarre mixture of grandiloquence and comedy, egotism and generosity, takes on new overtones as the young man in the video, sitting on an earth-mover, reads the first-person lines:

The spotted hawk swoops by and accuses me…he complains of my
    gab and my loitering.

I too am not a bit tamed.…I too am untranslatable,
I sound my barbaric yawp over the roofs of the world.

The last scud of day holds back for me,
It flings my likeness after the rest and true as any on the shadowed
    wilds.
It coaxes me to the vapor and the dusk.

I depart as air.…I shake my white locks at the runaway sun,
I effuse my flesh in eddies and drift it in lacy jags.

Whitman's vision of his death and his endurance are insightfully read
by Doherty as an address to the reader, on a quite practical level. "You
will hardly know who I am or what I mean," he reads, and "Failing to
fetch me at first keep encouraged, / Missing me one place search another, / I stop somewhere waiting for you." This advice was written, and
in this instance was read, in a particular spirit of direct address, an im-
mediacy that means to redefine poetry itself, and views the personal occasion as transcendent.

The mass medium of video, perhaps paradoxically, thus dramatizes
something I consider crucial about the medium of poetry: a poem takes
for its medium the reader's breath and hearing. That is, even in silent
reading, the reader imagines the sounds of the words and sentences.
When I read a poem, aloud or not, I am aware of it as something to say,
or that could be said. The vehicle for that awareness is in my bodily
senses—the vehicle also for memory, as when I chant the phone number
or the grocery list, some evolutionary link between vocal rhythm and recalled information.

The reader is not merely the performer of the poem, but an actual,
living medium for the poem. In relation to mass media, this distinction
seems to me crucial: if the medium is any one reader's voice, or any one
reader's ears, then the art is by its nature, inherently, on an individual
and personal scale. In that intimacy and human presence reading a poem
resembles a live performance, as distinct from a mass-produced image
such as a movie. But insofar as its text is fixed, the poem is distinctly less
ephemeral than the live performance. Poetry's dual qualities of human
scale and permanence are roughly parallel to the dread of homogenizing

uniformity on one side and the fragmented life of the Cyclopes on the other side. That is why poetry's voice—its literal, actual voice—takes on a heightened poignancy, and a heightened value, in a culture rich in dazzling performative art that is produced, duplicated and marketed on a mass scale. In the setting of mass culture, the voice of poetry, in ways show business cannot, embodies something crucial: an essential respect for individuals.

To put this another way, I have been surprised to find from this project that in a perhaps unique sense one can see a person read a poem. That is, I can watch your face while you listen to music, watch a movie or look at visual art—but I am not witnessing your experience of that work. The same goes for watching a reader deep in a novel. To watch someone saying a poem aloud can be to witness that person's experience of the poem. The readers in the videos, though they know that they are being filmed, make visible the intimate and individual nature of the art. Their "performances" of the poems are not actorly presentations of the poem's emotions and ideas—though those are surely present—but something subtly and crucially different from that: presentations of what it is like to read a particular poem.

Tocqueville's speculations about equality, on one hand, and on the other contemporary mass culture with its emphasis on performance, on lavish spectacle and reproduction, combine to make me hear with special urgency the particular reader's voice: its regional accent, its sense of an individual life, and its respect for the words, as it utters:

> You will hardly know who I am or what I mean,
> But I shall be good health to you nevertheless,
> And filter and fiber your blood.

The poem, which is neither its performance nor its characters on a page, is what takes place as a reader literally or figuratively gives voice to the lines, rendering the cadences and the unique currents and energies of the syntax, apprehending the movement of the meanings.

When the Favorite Poem Project has been described approvingly as "populist" I have felt uncomfortable, because I know that our approach was in essential ways elitist. There is a generation that loves the writing of Robert Service, and some of them wrote to us, and some of their grandchildren wrote to us about Shel Silverstein. Some from the generations between those two wrote to us about Rod McKuen, or the lyrics of Bob Dylan—all part of the larger archive of letters and e-mails, but not represented in the book or the recordings, by fiat of us editors.

On the other hand, we were guided by respect for the ways nonprofessional readers read and the ways they describe their reading. This element of the project has excited some negative judgment. Pov Chin, a teenager from California who is represented both in the anthology and in the videos, wrote:

> My interpretation of this poem written by Langston Hughes may not be the same as his. But a poem is what I choose to make of it and this one is a description of me. It explains how I feel about life.

A reviewer of the book took this statement as his leading example of a defect he found in it. After quoting these sentences, he writes:

> This theme—*this is a description of me*—occurs again and again.... Rather than letting poems draw us out of ourselves, making us larger and broader, we are encouraged to make the poems smaller so that we can take them inside us and, in a literal sense, comprehend them....Pinsky and Dietz may simply have assumed that the only way to sell poetry to Americans is to appeal to their inherent narcissism. (Troy Jollimore, *Boston Book Review* [March 2000])

In its way, this makes a certain sense. (The reviewer, incidentally, quotes de Tocqueville about American pettiness and self-centeredness, but not about the more vast subjects for poetry.) The terms of the Favorite Poem invitation did invite the volunteers to say something about their particular, personal reasons for selecting the poem. Indeed, the explicit criterion we developed for selection was the intensity and interest of what the person had to say about the poem. It could be argued that this editorial inclination vulgarized the project, or at least distorted it toward the personal or introspective, and away from the poem as a means of discovery about the world, or as a highly developed work of art.

But the cliche of American narcissism does not adequately describe what these people actually say. Let me return to the example of Pov Chin, who says of a poem that it is "a description of me." Her voice and accent in the video are those of a California teenager, and this prefatory statement of hers (a statement I think of diffidence) can sound glib or self-centered. The poem is an extremely short one by Langston Hughes, far from his most impressive work:

Minstrel Man

Because my mouth
Is wide with laughter
And my throat
Is deep with song,
You do not think
I suffer after
I have held my pain
So long?

Because my mouth
Is wide with laughter,
You do not hear
My inner cry?
Because my feet
Are gay with dancing,
You do not know
I die?

The little paradigm of this poem, as plain as a folk song, takes on rich overtones and vibrations in relation to the American minstrel tradition of blackface—makeup that was sometimes worn by black, as well as white, performers. The grinning minstrel-show performer, bursting with joy, represents a terrible and complicated process of cultural appropriation and distortion, all sorts of sublimated guilts and envies and myths, comforting and disturbing.

Of all that, the high school student Pov Chin appears to be unaware. When she found the poem and copied it out, she tells us, she had not heard of Langston Hughes. It is not clear if she knew at the time that he was African-American, or what the information signifies to her, particularly since she was born in Laos of Cambodian parents. Yet what she says about the poem is germane, and perhaps increases one's respect for the poem. In the book, she writes:

> …I am not free. I am a female Cambodian growing up in America but I am raised in the old-fashioned Cambodian ways. Asian tradition for daughters is very strict. It is so hard for me to see my friends having a sleep-over and the only person missing is me. I walk around school with a big smile on my face but inside I am a caged bird just waiting to be free. Life has never been easy for me especially with my parents' problems. Their problems started during the Khmer Rouge genocide in the early '70s. Two of their sons passed away in front of

their faces, killed by the Khmer Rouge. They still had the courage to get out of Cambodia and find refuge for us in America.

This is not literary criticism, nor does it pretend to be. But the word for it is not "narcissism," either, and as an explanation of why the writer values "Minstrel Man" by Langston Hughes, it is forceful and appropriate. The association of freedom and cultural restraint with performance and the equation of "big smile" with being caged represent an insightful tribute to Hughes's poem. To the extent that Pov Chin didn't know much about the author, it is remarkably intuitive. Even the exclusion from the American high school custom of sleep-overs and the delicate euphemism "passed away" for the murdered children testify to a rich and respectful relation to the poem.

The distinction between the narcissistic and the personal, abundantly clear in this letter quoted in the anthology, is even more clear in the video segment artfully filmed by Emiko Omori. In the opening shot Pov Chin begins speaking in the foreground; in the background, behind her, we see a suburban-looking interior and first a television set playing something with Asian faces and then, as the camera pans upward, the seated figure of a woman. This watchful figure, present throughout the shot, is Pov Chin's mother, silently following the interview as though she is not about to let this, one of her remaining children, out of her sight. We see a shrine, and some incense being lit and some family photographs: of children posing in front of a very modest house; of an unsmiling elderly woman.

A notable aspect of Pov Chin's narration comes with her explanation that during the family ordeal and the murder of the little boys she was not yet born; the mother was pregnant. "It was not only us," she says, "it was my granny, too, and they killed my granny." The first person plural of "only us" is striking to me: "they rounded us up," she says at another point. This unself-conscious first person plural, like the watching maternal figure, embodies the powerful familial and social component of the sentences quoted in the anthology and echoes similar questions of the generic and the individual, inside and outside, cultural cage and cultural sustenance, in Hughes's poem. "I am not free" is related to "they rounded us up"; both sentences acknowledge the great conundrum of each person's connection to others. Whatever one understands that "we" to represent, it is not narcissism.

I have quoted a somewhat negative response to the project (and the review I've quoted from is in fact only partly negative) less to argue with

it or to score points against it than to suggest the range of cultural and
literary responses that this undertaking has called up, partly by accident. A scrap about an anthology, or about what is narcissistic, what is
personal, is one eddying current in a great flood of ambiguities and agi-
tations. My proposition is that the reviewer's gesture against a leveling
uniformity and the Favorite Poem Project's gesture toward a unifying
cultural ground, though they seem like opposite actions, both express a
defense of shared memory.

A successful, inventive mass culture, together with Tocqueville's
"principle of equality" from which the mass culture partly grows, creates a certain need to define, and perhaps construct, the social place of an
ancient art. This pressure should not be seen as merely negative: it, too,
is enabling as well as controlling. The mass culture itself struggles to
adjust memory and change, and like the poets sometimes it succeeds
and sometimes it collapses into pretension or banality. In the absence of
the settled aristocratic idea, and in the absence of the unifying folk-cul-
ture, Americans have been pressed to supply new forms of memory. Responding to this pressure, Whitman became somewhat broken-hearted
by his inability to create (and fill) the role of national bard. That sadness
was reenforced for me by my own surprise at how journalists responded
to President Clinton's gift of *Leaves of Grass* to Monica Lewinsky: they
thought of Whitman not as the quintessential American poet, but as
the author of a rather hot book.

Nonetheless, the vacuum or pressure that created and frustrated
Whitman's ambitions also inspired his poetry. And the unsettled place
of poetry has continued to inspire great works as well as blather and despair: the poetry of both William Carlos Williams and Wallace Stevens,
for example, can be seen as growing more or less explicitly out of the
question of poetry's place in national manners. "The spirit and space,"
writes Stevens in his poem "The American Sublime": "The empty
spirit / In vacant space. / What wine does one drink? / What bread does
one eat?" To take a less sublime example, improvising the figurative
bread, the wine, the place, Americans have invented Creative Writing,
with all of its still-evolving virtues and defects. The audio recordings,
videos and anthology of the Favorite Poem Project are one more gesture
of this kind of improvisation, and in some measure give an account of it,
as well.

I'm afraid that to make my point I may have exaggerated the
uniqueness of the United States. All culture, after all, like any living

person's memory, perpetually adds and rearranges, drops and inflects its material: it is a process of change, not a static entity or a list of works. The more I knew about Iran and India, the more, I am sure, I would have to modify my assumptions about Persian and Bengali poetry, the more flux and ambiguity I would perceive.

Still, American culture as I have experienced it seems so much in process, so brilliantly and brutally in motion, that standard models for it fail to apply. The Mandarin notion of a privileged elite preserving cultural goods on an old-world model is swamped by the demotic genius of characteristic makers like Whitman, Duke Ellington, Buster Keaton. The Arnoldian model of cultural missionaries bringing along the masses wilts not only for the same reason but because modern political history has discredited the notion that intellectual or artistic figures can automatically serve as moral leaders. The Mandarin's complementary opposite, the Philistine model, would accept the marketplace entirely: whatever is consumed, is good. This idea collapses before the omnivorous, strangely vaunting aspiration of actual Americans—with the Favorite Poem Project one current example. Another model, the idea of mass culture as our only real culture, cannot do because culture is a process of memory, and as mass cultural products speed by, the popular culture of each decade is winnowed to be preserved in the care of universities, libraries, foundations. A serious task of criticism is to assist in that winnowing process. In the archives of curatorship, classic jazz and silent comedy and blues await any of the best of our sitcoms or rap performers that deserve remembering. And the model of American culture as a mere confederation of ethnic or regional or religious or gender-based cultures cannot suffice because all of our greatest achievements—a poem by Dickinson or a chorus by Charlie Parker—are as mixed, syncretic and eclectic as our inventions in food or clothing. In that polyglot, heuristic and erratic flux, each of the nonprofessional readers of this poetry project, anchored by the vocal attachment to a poem, offers a still point.

In my second lecture, I will try to trace certain ways that American poets of the past century have brought social materials, and even a kind of social comedy, into the introspective lyric poem: expanding, and perhaps breaking through, the prescient terms of Alexis de Tocqueville. But I hope it will be appropriate, in relation to what I have said, to end with a personal response to a poem. The project asks for "a" favorite, not one single favorite. I will say a little about my own attachment to one of perhaps a hundred poems I might have chosen.

When I arrived at Rutgers from a town on the New Jersey Shore, the first person in my family to attend college, I found something lordly and exhilarating in the assumption that I was entitled to read the greatest works of art. Though I understood William Butler Yeats's "Sailing to Byzantium" only imperfectly, I recognized something of the spiritual force Yeats attributes to such monuments of magnificence. "Once out of nature," I read, and that phrase meant immeasurably more to me than *after I die.* "Once out of nature I shall never take / My bodily form from any natural thing, / But such a form as Grecian goldsmiths make / From hammered gold and gold enameling."

I can echo Pov Chin here, and say that whatever Yeats meant by these lines, they described me. The alien, elaborate texture of his invented Byzantium, the remoteness from me of the historical Byzantium and of Yeats himself, the stylized and perhaps even absurd image of the mechanical bird—all the strangenesses I heard in the poem—seemed to gain force from their very distance. Those golden quanta of artifice were not American, they were not of New Jersey, they were neither Christian nor Jewish. But the act of putting those strange forms into my actual or inner voice seemed to recognize something already in me—perhaps the past, all the history that had been assimilated unconsciously and in a blur, but in a unique and individuating blur.

The voice of the poem was, precisely, a "bodily form." Because that form could embrace my experience with magisterial ferocity, it spoke to anxieties that perhaps prefigured this lecture's notion of cultural anxieties about fragmentation and sameness. Half-comprehended phrases like "the artifice of eternity" suggested that the soul did not have to be lost in an enveloping mass, nor isolated as a provincial—one was not necessarily doomed to be a cipher or a galoot. The imagined city of Byzantium's differences from what might seem my nature called up that nature—a particular soul tied to a particular dying animal—in a way that, say, a work about Jewish lads from New Jersey whose grandfathers were barkeepers, might not.

The voice of artifice, I secretly half-dared to think, had always been there. Now, maybe, it was ready to wake up and guide what I hoped would be a progress of the natural thing I thought I had been as a child and high school pupil, toward the shimmering world of art, encompassing classical learning and television, a world of hammered phrases and dying animals, of gold and enamel and neon, a world that included and transformed all, where the drowsy emperor of the will might become alert, where memory endlessly discovered semblances and distinctions: the world, in a word, of poetry.

## II

I want to say something about social reality in American poetry of the twentieth century. Alexis de Tocqueville formulated American poetry as introspective, concentrated on the aperture of the individual soul; I mean to look at ways the poetry of the past century has turned his formulation inside-out. Tocqueville wrote:

> The destinies of mankind, man himself taken aloof from his country and his age and standing in the presence of Nature and of God, with his passions, his doubts, his rare prosperities and inconceivable wretchedness, will become the chief, if not the sole, theme of poetry. (*DIA*, vol. 1, p. 76)

The story of twentieth-century American poetry could be told as a series of brilliant inventions for including material not "aloof" from country or age: not so much departing from Tocqueville's larger definition as extending and deepening it to include manners and community.

I'll begin with some general speculations about social reality and the nature of poetry.

Dire abandonment, I have read, often makes institutionalized souls, especially children, croon and rock rhythmically, a heartbroken ritual music, fearsomely minimal. A medical name for this behavior is auto-stimulation. The embarrassing hint of masturbation in that term, the grotesque unease or nervous giggle of that association, perhaps reveals an eerie recognition. Just outside the membrane enclosing that wounded isolation, made visible by contrast, is my ordinary consciousness: engaged yet furtive, communicative yet shamed, teeming with a host of wants and taboos—the word "taboo" embodying the price of our charmed admission to the world of social stimuli. The regular cadence of the outcast creates a rudimentary other, an illusion of response, that we recognize; the covert sexual fantasies of what we call normal life are only one example of a similar principle at work.

On what I'll call a more formal level, the regular, monotonous chant recalls certain vocalizations of normal, humdrum solitude: little repetitious charms of invocation amid the frustration of some misplaced object—*keys keys keys keys keys;* the staccato repetition of a one-syllable obscenity, like a muttered ceremony of rage or desperation; the happier spells of celebration recited at good news or some gratifying experience (*yes yes yes yes yes*); and—perhaps most interesting of all, and closest to the cadenced moans of the devastated—the little half-sung noises made to ease a painful awareness of embarrassment. I confess that remembering a fetid, grade-A *faux pas* can make me half-whisper a syllable like *"dah"* in *prestissimo* monotone to the rhythm of *The Stars and Stripes Forever* or *The Mexican Hat Dance.*

These ephemeral proto-poems share an interesting duality with the auto-stimulation of total distress. The unvarying, solitary rocking or crooning, with its reduction or stylization, perhaps substitutes mimetically for its opposite: a varying, attentive social presence, listening as I lament my lost car keys, curse my mistake or celebrate the letter announcing good news for me.

The instance of embarrassment is more complex: the tuneless tune I murmur brings back the social world where I brought shame on myself, and imitates the all-too-responsive real presence of others, but in a rudimentary, dwindling simulacrum that distracts me from the awfulness of the actual remembered scene. And this little mimesis, like the cadenced grunts of loss, has its parallel in poetry.

Nervous muttering resembles a work of art in that it simultaneously sharpens and dislocates a feeling, calling it up but transforming it, maybe blunting it a little by incorporation. Insofar as rhythm and repetition accomplish this double action, the little repeated, one-word proto-poem differs significantly from anecdote. Anecdote is sociable; perhaps narrative itself is sociable. Life among others in a novel, even a novel entirely in dialogue, is in some essential way told-about. The novel overtly tells us what people say and do, immersing us in social reality with an illusion of presentation. In a play, presentation is actual: communal reality, in theatrical performance, exists both as though it were happening and as actually happening.

In a poem, the social realm is invoked with a special intimacy at the involuntary level of voice itself. Communal life, whether explicitly included or not, is present implicitly, in the cadences and syntax of language: a somatic ghost. In such a theory, the Industrial-Revolution art form, fiction, reflects the conversation or letters of middle-class people in a town or city—the panicked verbosity of Pamela, the homey enumerations of Crusoe, the word-wound, shopper-like roaming of Leopold Bloom, all create a social scene from the manufactured web of discourse. The older form of theater is more like a ritual: performance creating actual presences. Maybe that is why theater so often involves the cloying yet somehow apt word "magic." The social world in poetry, according to this paradigm, is neither told about nor presented: it is, precisely, *invoked:* brought into being by the voice. Incantation, rather than ritual.

Real works blur and explode such distinctions, defying tidy generic modes of social reality. So too do new forms: film art and opera, both of them influencing and influenced by literature, can give presence a virtually assaultive vividness, as enveloping and fluid as dreams. Technologies like film and broadcast media dismantle any tidy definition of art forms from without, as artists do from within. We routinely recognize qualities in a novel as "poetic" or in a poem as "novelistic" or "dramatic."

Nevertheless, the kinds of art retain attributes, with characteristic terrains—and something deep in poetry operates at the borderland of body and mind, sound and word: region of the subtle knot that John Donne says makes a man. George Oppen calls up that transitional territory in the fifth section of his poem "Of Being Numerous," with bold contrasts and overlaps among physical fact, cultural artifact and mind itself:

> The great stone
> Above the river
>
> In the pylon of the bridge
>
> '1875'
>
> Frozen in the moonlight
> In the frozen air over the footpath, consciousness
>
> Which has nothing to gain, which awaits nothing,
> Which loves itself.

This passage gains in physicality from the abstract—or at least formal —chiasmic arrangement of vowel-sounds and words in the phrases "frozen in the moonlight in the frozen air" and "nothing to gain, which awaits nothing." Pronouncing such symmetries audibly, or feeling their virtual sound, quickens our sense of physical breath stirring into social speech: the poetic quality that poets writing about their art have associated with a conversation heard through a door, a drunken song a few streets away, a distant singer in a foreign tongue. The chiasm of "nothing to gain...awaits nothing" is an artifact like the bridge, recognized before it is interpreted.

Even a dramatic monologue, or a narrated dialogue like Robert Frost's "Home Burial," makes its voice or voices present to our imagination partly in the half-conscious way I have attributed to poetry: somatically, by invocation, by something linked to the reflex of auto-stimulation or of its diametric twin embarrassment, a mimesis in rhythmical sound of social life. In Frost's poem, the blank verse becomes more than a vehicle; it is a physical presence: as corporeal as the infant's corpse at the center of the poem's marital argument, and as conventional as the social world that surrounds and infiltrates that same argument. The play of the social and the intuitive is part of the couple's contention, and it is manifest in their voices:

'God, what a woman! And it's come to this,
A man can't speak of his own child that's dead,'

'You can't because you don't know how to speak.
If you had any feelings, you that dug
With your own hand—how could you?—his little grave;
I saw you from that very window there,
Making the gravel leap and leap in air,
Leap up, like that, like that, and land so lightly
And roll back down the mound beside the hole.
I thought, Who is that man? I didn't know you.
And I crept down the stairs and up the stairs
To look again, and still your spade kept lifting.
Then you came in. I heard your rumbling voice
Out in the kitchen, and I don't know why,
But I went near to see with my own eyes.
You could sit there with the stains on your shoes
Of the fresh earth from your own baby's grave
And talk about your everyday concerns.
You had stood the spade up against the wall
Outside there in the entry, for I saw it.'

'I shall laugh the worst laugh I ever laughed.
I am cursed. God, if I don't believe I'm cursed.'

This passage of fewer than two hundred words—barely room for a prose narration to clear its throat—establishes forcefully the two contending people with their agonized grief, and within both of the agonists two elements contending for recognition: physical reality on one side, and sensitive decorum or ceremony on the other. Both elements are in the verse. The extreme compression, the more remarkable because the dialogue is credible as speech, is enabled by a physical component, by the artist's arrangements of vocal noises at the threshold of consciousness. The occasional end-rhyme is the least of it: "I saw you from that very window there, / Making the gravel leap and leap in air, / Leap up, like that, like that, and land so lightly / And roll back down the mound beside the hole." Analysis can trace such steps only clumsily and approximately: it is not only the syncopation of repeated words, and not only the vowel in "down the mound" but the contrasting vowel of "hole" that ends the sentence with a rather thudlike rhyme on "roll."

In a way the most powerful moment in this conversation is a strange, apparent irrelevance, just before the closing. She has said that "one is alone" and "dies more alone," that "Friends make pretense of following to the grave, / But before one is in it, their minds are turned." His speech in response culminates in the bizarre line, "Amy! There's someone coming down the road!"

After what she has just said about the underlying frailty, even hypocrisy, of human attachments—"The world's evil"—his sudden, exclamatory concern about a passing neighbor or stranger is grotesque, pathetic, absurd in a way that I think is precisely like life. Embarrassment—a halting consciousness of other people, the sudden barricade of social awareness, obstructing emotion and threatening to take over the mind—is in a way the most basic, irreducible manifestation of social reality. For Frost's characters it is both an obtrusion on their argument and part of its essence. In this unexpected line, bursting from the character as he is about to be left, embarrassment and abandonment join.

To some extent, poetry cannot exclude the social realm because poetry's very voice evokes the attentive presence of some other, or its lack. And in twentieth-century American poetry's incorporation of explicit social material, the tension of embarrassment and abandonment recurs. Perhaps the most widely admired poem named by participants in the Favorite Poem Project, appealing to readers of very different ages and levels of sophistication, is "The Love Song of J. Alfred Prufrock," a poem that probes social isolation and social terror with tremendous eloquence. Many high school students seem to intuit that the poem was written by a very young man—T. S. Eliot inventing a middle-aged, first-person protagonist as vehicle for the sexual and social diffidence of youth.

Eliot's poem is of course about many other things as well: for example, it is about culture as a burden, as oppressively controlling and discouraging as it is enabling, perhaps more so. Prufrock in this sense is very close to the figure of the exhausted aesthete, the wistful dandy. If he had confidence, he might be a dandy. For the dandy, experience is somewhat tainted or corrupted by culture. (Though Oscar Wilde might reverse that statement.) As embarrassment is akin to abandonment—feeling excessively distinct from the attentive social world—the aesthete's jadedness is a feeling of sameness. In the terms of Wallace Stevens's "The Man Whose Pharynx Was Bad":

> Mildew of summer and the deepening snow
> Are both alike in the routine I know

This is partly the voice of the nineteenth-century or Romantic life of sensation, in a state of exhaustion. It is an exaggerated, comic version of the pre-modern poets—Algernon Charles Swinburne, Ernest Dowson?—who were the immediate predecessors of the Modernist generation. Frost parodies that hyper-sensitive aesthete in himself, writing in "To Earthward,"

> I craved strong sweets, but those
> Seemed strong when I was young.
> The petal of the rose
> It was that stung.

The expressively inverted syntax, "The petal of the rose / It was that stung," is like a gently derisive tone of voice.

What is the point of parodying the dandy or aesthete in oneself, for Stevens or Frost? It is, partly, a way of parodying both poetry itself and the American culture that has no ready place for poetry. Like embarrassment, like the warning "There's someone coming down the road!" it acknowledges the presence of others and the tension aroused by that presence. I hear this serious joke on the voice of poetry in William Carlos Williams, too. In "These," a poem partly about pathos and death, he writes the terrible then momentarily comical lines:

the people gone that we loved,
the beds lying empty, the couches
damp, the chairs unused—

Hide it away somewhere
out of the mind, let it get roots

and grow, unrelated to jealous

ears and eyes—for itself.
In this mine they come to dig—all.
Is this the counterfoil to sweetest

music? The source of poetry that
seeing the clock stopped, says,
The clock has stopped

that ticked yesterday so well?

Of course all clocks, before they stop, tick—presumably "well." The
rhetorical question, repeating the observation, resembles the ancient
wisecrack about even a stopped clock being right twice a day. The poem
evokes the terror of death and loss, and then for a moment questions el-
egy and all other attempts to verbalize loss, as tautological or obvious.
"Stupidity" has been an element in the poem from the rhetorical snap of
its opening sentence:

THESE

are the desolate, dark weeks
when nature in its barrenness
equals the stupidity of man.

The audacity of this, like the almost-parodic repetition of "the clock has
stopped," has a virtuoso quality, in its deadpan, downright way almost
as dandified as Stevens's exotic ambushes of vocabulary. There is even a
note of the exquisite in the rarefied word "counterfoil," which sounds
like music or fencing but denotes the stub of a check, where the date and
amount are recorded.

Like one who recalls "The petal of the rose / It was that stung," and
like the sensibility that finds the white of summer mildew and the

white of snow "alike," Williams's voice here momentarily concedes an embarrassing absurdity in its discourse, and in the roots of its discourse. The stopped clock once ticked well, then it stopped—poetry sees this and in effect strikes its brow, speaking its question to marvel at the obvious. It is a moment that places poetry into something a little like a roomful of people, with Williams simultaneously among them, regarding poetry as quizzically as any, but also presenting its power to them—as he does with the two lines that follow the relatively comic question:

> The source of poetry that
> seeing the clocked has stopped, says
> The clock has stopped
>
> that ticked yesterday so well?
> and hears the sound of lakewater
> splashing—that is now stone.

With characteristic speed, restlessly varying idioms and levels, Williams takes the memorializing gesture from somewhat hapless record-keeping—the counterfoil noting the stopped clock—to a somber image, with a kind of classical dignity.

The aesthete, stung by the petal, seeing the mildew and the snow as alike, is in a way the poet reduced to a social type. In these poems, a touch of the hyperbolically exquisite allows poetry to acknowledge its own nature: by some social standards, an art of preposterous, goofball metonymies and far-fetched resemblances. In a mode that is a mirror-reversal of the dandyish, it sees that the clock has stopped and says, "the clock has stopped," adding that it ticked quite well yesterday. In each case, a tiny particle of social comedy infuses a brilliant phrase. The self-consciously dandyish and its mock-naive reversal both acknowledge poetry's exorbitant, nearly embarrassing qualities and at the same time make those qualities irresistible and even—because they have a social meaning—somehow familiar.

Poetry, then, has roots in the moment when a voice makes us alert to the presence of another or others. It has affinities with all the ways a solitary voice, actual or virtual, imitates the presence of others. Yet as a form of art it is deeply embedded in the single human voice, in the solitary state that hears the other and sometimes re-creates that other. Poetry is a vocal imagining, ultimately social but essentially individual and inward.

Insofar as Tocqueville was prescient about American poetry's concentration on the human soul, "aloof" from society and from ages, there is perhaps a special drama in our poetry to this play between social and individual, outward and inward voice.

Elizabeth Bishop delineates that drama explicitly and compactly in the crucial passage of her poem "In the Waiting Room":

Suddenly, from inside,
came an *oh!* of pain
—Aunt Consuelo's voice—
not very loud or long.
I wasn't at all surprised;
even then I knew she was
a foolish, timid woman.
I might have been embarrassed,
but wasn't. What took me
completely by surprise
was that it was *me:*
my voice, in my mouth.
Without thinking at all
I was my foolish aunt,
I—we—were falling, falling,
our eyes glued to the cover
of the *National Geographic,*
February, 1918.

The voice comes "from inside"—inside the dentist's office and inside the child. The possible embarrassment ("I might have been...but wasn't") may be prevented by the strangeness of this moment, which could be a primal moment for poetry, or for individual consciousness, or both. As she begins to faint, the child gazes at the undifferentiated landscape of "shadowy gray knees, / trousers and skirts and boots / and different pairs of hands" and asks, "Why should I be my aunt, / or me, or anyone? What similarities... / held us all together / or made us all just one." The bizarre, alien assemblage of knees, boots, hands, as a vision of the social world outside the self, fragmentary and dizzily provisional, may be peculiarly American.

What makes us all one—and what makes us all different—seems deeply involved with a voice: a voice that is both imagined and actual; both inner and social; both mine and someone else's; that separates me and includes me. It will not do to sentimentalize this voice; at the climax of Bishop's poem is the sentence "The War was on." Each of these dualities involves struggle, perhaps even combat. But the voice of poetry is uniquely situated as audible yet not necessarily performative.

I have proposed in both of these lectures that the voice of poetry is intimate, on an individual scale. It penetrates and in a sense originates where the reader's mind reaches toward something heard or uttered as though vocality were one of the senses. This medium is different from the poet's intonations and personality shining forth at a poetry reading, and different from a skilled actor's gifts. It is inside a reader. It is vocal and emotive and intellectual.

This intimacy and human scale have special meaning within a mass culture extraordinarily rich in performance, with show business providing an industry, an aristocracy, an all-but-universal measure. American mass culture is a mighty achievement, and its works have included poetry and been included in poetry. But American poetry also plays a vital role as a contrast to mass culture, somewhat resistant precisely because the poetic medium is essentially individual.

This contrast explains the frequency with which one is asked a certain question. In its various forms, it is the question that the news media cannot resist asking any poet. Broadcast or print; highbrow, lowbrow or middlebrow; national or local—uppermost in the reportorial mind is always the same inquiry, sometimes presented as the product of original thought, a conceptual innovation. Like many cliches, the question picks up the truth by precisely the wrong end, with the grip that cripples or neuters.

The inevitable Question, however it is presented, amounts to: shouldn't poetry be part of show business? Or even, why does it seem out of step with so much else? And because the query is wrongheaded, one's answers are always a bit feeble. It might be, "Have your poems been set to music?" Well yes, but to paraphrase a great poet, I thought I was doing that when I wrote them. Or, "What do you think of rap music?" Don't know much about it, but my guess is that as with "literary" poetry most of it is ordinary, a little of it is very good and a little is contemptible. I have heard Yusef Komunyakaa express distrust of it insofar as it makes a commodity out of rage. "And poetry slams?" Probably a good thing for poetry, though as part of the entertainment industry poetry will always be cute and small; as an art it is immense and fundamental. "How can I learn to read poems aloud?" By reading poems—for instance, poems by Emily Dickinson and Gerard Manley Hopkins, among others who might not have been hits on the poetry reading circuit. "Do you write for the page or for the stage?" I hope that I compose with my voice, and that I read with my voice. I do own pens, and word-processing equipment, and I use them.

But the interrogation is hopeless, because it begins with the assumption that poetry's tremendous strength, in the American context, is its weakness. Poetry mediates, on a particular and immensely valuable level, between the inner consciousness of the individual reader and the outer world of other people. To take poetry from that profound terrain to a more familiar platform would be to tame it.

And perhaps American poetry, where society so often appears more as an imagining than as an experience, is untamed in particular ways. It has been proposed that while the United States is a great nation the Americans are not—or not yet?—a great people. We are not defined by blood and we are perhaps not yet defined by the alternative of shared memory. The Constitution, the Civil War, the cultural achievements of Walt Whitman, Willa Cather, Duke Ellington, John Ford—are they, quite, part of a shared memory? Do they supply the place of a mythological origin as dragon's teeth or wolf-babies? In this view, even our racial divisions are only one egregious part of the ongoing project of becoming a people.

In another way of looking at it, perhaps it is the spirit of American culture to resist becoming "a people," or to continue that project indefinitely, always morphing or discarding—not resting with, for example, Longfellow's Paul Revere and Hiawatha. In its way, the unlikely, almost unreadable landscape of Bishop's waiting room, prosaic yet delirious, is more like a national myth, closer to Whitman's barbaric and unanticipated yawp. In the project of inventing a culture, or of an ever-prolonged imagining one, the voice of poetry is essential because of its unique place between silence and speech, between the single soul and the community, between marketplace and dreamlife, between the past and the breath of the living.

Culture, in all its forms of memory, can preserve us from excessive sameness on one side and fanaticism about difference on the other side. Culture also can be oppressive, even nightmarish: genocides, holocausts, the destruction of ancient cultures, massacres, imperialisms, police states and prison states all can be seen as cultural manifestations. Poetry is not the voice of virtue and right thinking—not the rhyme department of any progressive movement; in fact, great poets have espoused repulsive politics. But the turns of verse, between justified and ragged, the regular and the unique, the spoken and the implied, the private and the social, profoundly embody a quest—perhaps the democratic search, and endless—for life between a barren isolation and an enveloping mass.

I will quote another poem—one I have written about before, in an account of my home town on the Jersey Shore. My excuses for writing about the poem again are aptness to the present subject and the poem's magnificence. Written near the beginning of the twentieth century by Edwin Arlington Robinson, "Eros Turannos" epitomizes for me the tidal forces within lyric poetry that draw it toward the social. The poem's peculiar, rather spectacular form embodies those forces and their "War," as Bishop calls it, with something private and interior.

Robinson's poem begins with the situation of one person: a woman who must choose between a love affair that she well knows will be a calamity or no love affair at all. The extraordinary account of her psychology turns out, partway through the poem, to be spoken by a town:

## EROS TURANNOS

She fears him, and will always ask
    What fated her to choose him;
She meets in his engaging mask
    All reasons to refuse him;
But what she meets and what she fears
Are less than are the downward years
Drawn slowly to the foamless weirs
    Of age, were she to lose him.

Between a blurred sagacity
    That once had power to sound him,
And Love, that will not let him be
    The Judas that she found him,
Her pride assuages her almost,
As if it were alone the cost.
He sees that he will not be lost,
    And waits and looks around him.

A sense of ocean and old tress
    Envelops and allures him;
Tradition, touching all he sees,
    Beguiles and reassures him;
And all her doubts of what he says
Are dimmed with what she knows of days—

Till even prejudice delays,
    And fades, and she secures him.

The falling leaf inaugurates
    The reign of her confusion;
The pounding wave reverberates
    The dirge of her illusion;
And home, where passion lived and died,
Becomes a place where she can hide,
While all the town and harbor side
    Vibrate with her seclusion.

We tell you, tapping on our brows,
    The story as it should be,
As if the story of a house
    Were told, or ever could be;
We'll have no kindly veil between
Her visions and those we have seen,
As if we guessed what hers have been,
    Or what they are or would be.

Meanwhile we do no harm; for they
    That with a god have striven,
Not hearing much of what we say,
    Take what the god has given;
Though like waves breaking it may be,
Or like a changed familiar tree,
Or like a stairway to the sea
    Where down the blind are driven.

The poem's astoundingly deployed rhymes make it a kind of hyper-ballad: a ballad to the ballad power, as though the woman's isolation and shame call up some longing for a folk-tradition that her country does not have. The first-person plural impersonates the communal, but also heightens the poem's loneliness and lack. I take that sense of lack partly from what I know of Robinson's career. For the long first part of it, he was indigent, lonely, spurned by magazine editors, embittered with his provincial town in Maine and with the New York where he also found the going hard.

But on the other hand, the town does notice the woman's fate, and notices it with awe. On this subject, let me quote the letter about this poem printed in *Americans' Favorite Poems*—the only letter in the anthology that we print anonymously:

I discovered the poem many years ago as a newly married girl living in a small town, which in fact possesses a harborside. My husband had an intractable (it seemed then) drug and alcohol problem and was away a lot for his job. I didn't have a job at the time, knew no one, and spent many days in solitude riding my bike, reading, and reflecting on what my life had become since my decision to marry. I did not then comprehend what the line "for they that with a god have striven" meant. I just recognized completely the state of wishing to be united with a man because of what I knew or thought I knew about the onward years. I lived then and now in an ancient house left me by my father, whose father left it to him, whose father left it to him. It is one mile from the ocean, surrounded by old trees. These facts made up no small part of my husband's decision to marry me. I copied that poem into the journal I kept then and it sits before me on the table as I write. I have always felt the woman was as I was. The knowledge that I've gained about "the god" has lent a retrospective dignity to events experienced as utter failure. The discovery of the poem, with its eerily large number of coincidences with my own situation, was like a gift, or maybe a clue in a giant game of charades, from "the god" himself, who saw he had perhaps misjudged his opponent.

This personal account of the poem is as remarkable as the coincidences it notes. Its viewpoint is perhaps more psychological and social than literary. The writer, for all her power and eloquence, does not choose to consider the ways that the poem's story may be Robinson's story, a transformed account of his own frustration, loneliness, dignity and rage. But this insightful, anonymous letter also suggests something like the classical relation of tragic hero and community, or touches on that idea with the words "a retrospective dignity." In the poem, the community gains a certain stature from its awareness that in it is one who has wrestled with a god; the individual gains dignity from the witnessing of that struggle. The man, who "waits and looks around him," is in ways less important than the god or the town. The poem is less about two people than it is about one person, love as a ruling force, and a social setting.

The form of poetry in the poem, the chiming and symmetrically swirling rhymes, creates the voice of a great solitude, a desolation that communicates itself to the very landscape. "A sense of ocean and old trees" is vague partly as a mocking evocation of the man who looks around him, lightly comic in ways like those I have noted; but the phrase also has a specificity that relates it to Robinson's concluding image, the "stairway to the sea / where down the blind are driven." The nightmare ritual or flight suggested by that image implies a social world more ancient or more fantastically barbarian than can be known. The voice of the poem, in our heads and in our breath, brings that world and the solitude of the protagonist together, with terror and majesty.

"Eros Turannos" was published in the same issue of *Poetry* magazine as Carl Sandburg's group of *Chicago Poems,* including "Chicago"—the well-known anthology piece (it is in the Favorite Poem anthology), the apostrophe that begins "Hog Butcher for the World" and ends "Freight Handler to the Nation." "Chicago" is not a bad piece of writing, though by "anthology piece" I have indicated its limits. In no way does it begin to equal "Eros Turannos" in emotion, in formal penetration or invention. But Sandburg's group was made the leading item in that issue of *Poetry* and that year received the magazine's Levinson Prize, which Yvor Winters in his book on Robinson says was "the most considerable prize offered for poetry in the United States at that time" (*Edwin Arlington Robinson,* p. 11).

This is very far from the most impressive anecdote about literary awards and recognitions: it's a familiar tale that Marcel Proust, Henrik Ibsen and James Joyce all failed to win the Nobel Prize in Literature. The lists of poet laureates include many ciphers. With the arrogance of the living, we may deceive ourselves that nowadays we know better. What's germane here is the way these two poems approach their subjects, and their implied subject of how poetry will situate itself in relation to American life.

It may be that the judges found Sandburg's epithets and participles vital: "Laughing the stormy, husky, brawling laughter of Youth, half-naked, sweating, proud to be Hog Butcher...." Indeed, they may have found his poem engaging and engaged precisely in relation to my subject in these lectures: poetry's voice in American culture. Where "Eros Turannos" might have seemed laudable but modest in scope, Sandburg's dithyrambic embrace of Chicago as "laughing with white teeth" may have seemed not only original but *avant-garde.* (But *avant-garde* may be a contradiction in terms in our culture, where the model of mass media makes being part of some *garde* too available, and perhaps too prized, when the crucial issue is, precisely, distinction.)

Comparison of the two poems helps define a place for American poetry, its profound role of both engaging and resisting the rather Sandburg-esque giant of a society that is at once dazzling and banal, provincial and global, menacing and hopeful. Poetry's voice participates in that society and its culture, but by its nature also resists them: by nature singular where they are plural, memory-driven where they are heedless, personal where they are impersonal—luxuriously slow where they are rushed, and thrillingly swift where they are plodding.

I speak as an enthusiast of modern life: I enjoy the possibilities of jet travel, the DVD and the VCR, am devoted to my computer and my cell phone, appreciate the marvels of contemporary plumbing, medicine, dentistry. Like Frank Bidart in his recent poem "For the Twentieth Century," I am grateful for the technologies that make Callas, Laurel & Hardy, Szigeti available at a touch of the PLAY button, turning their art into "pattern, form / whose infinite // repeatability within matter / defies matter." But the voice that appreciates the artists and the "thousand / technologies of ecstasy" that preserve them is also idiosyncratic, not duplicable, and resistantly inward as well as outward.

What Robinson resisted in 1911 was a provincial vacuum, the nightmare of us small-town watchers who can gossip and tap our brows but cannot make tragedies or ballads. A village stinginess haunts his work and this poem in particular, recalling Tocqueville's description of American life: "Nothing conceivable is so petty, so insipid, so crowded with paltry interests." There is something heroic in Robinson's simultaneous resistant loathing and meticulous love for the provincial settings and figures he imagined, the lonely grandeur of his hypertrophied ballad stanzas and saturated ironies. Sandburg has considerable merits, but by comparison his poem's rebellions are trivial, and its celebrations coarse.

Robinson, like the hero of his poem, wrestled with something larger than himself, and his wrestling deserves a grave and delighted communal awe. His command of specificity and abstraction and his managing of idiom and lines resist in an anticipatory way any invitation to make American poetry something that goes down easily: a part of show business, or a branch of literary theory, or any other diminished thing. I believe that there are great poems being written now, by living American poets. Almost by definition, such poems are grounded partly in resistance. Almost by definition, we may not be giving them laurels. "Eros Turannos" is arresting and spectacular, in the chamber of spirit and ear that I have suggested is the place of poetry. Its distinction answers a cultural need as a more eager rhetoric of community cannot. In certain ways "Eros Turannos" is in itself and in its place in the world a little aloof, not automatically or easily visible. It is great as a work, negligible as a commodity. That is the way of the world. Fortunately, art too has its way: not tamed by expectation, untranslatable by journalism or pedantry, outlandish, even barbaric, sounding its yawps somewhere over our worldly roofs, or beyond them.

*A Promise of Happiness:*

*The Place of Beauty in a World of Art*

*ALEXANDER NEHAMAS*

THE TANNER LECTURES ON HUMAN VALUES

Delivered at

Yale University
April 9 and 10, 2001

ALEXANDER NEHAMAS is Edmund N. Carpenter II Class of 1943 Professor of Humanities at Princeton University, where he is also professor of philosophy, professor of comparative literature, director of Hellenic studies, and head of the Council of Humanities. He was educated at Swarthmore College and at Princeton, where he received his Ph.D. He has been a visiting professor at a number of universities, including the University of Calfornia, Berkeley and the University of Pennsylvania, and has served on the editorial board of *American Philosophical Quarterly, History of Philosophy Quarterly, Journal of Modern Greek Studies, Dialogos* and others, as well as *The Garland Encyclopedia of Aesthetics* and *The Cambridge Dictionary of Philosophy.* He is a fellow of the American Academy of Arts and Sciences and recipient of the Mellon Distinguished Achievement Award and the 2001 International Nietzsche Prize. He is the translator, with Paul Woodruff, of both *Plato's Phaedrus* (1995) and *Plato's Symposium* (1989), and the author of *Nietzsche: Life as Literature* (1985), *The Art of Living: Socratic Reflections from Plato to Foucault* (1998), and *Virtues of Authenticity: Essays on Plato and Socrates* (1999).

# I

What happens to us when something—something we see for the first time or have perhaps known for long—reveals its beauty to us, and, suddenly transfigured, takes our breath away and makes time stand still? This is Plato's answer:

> When someone sees a godlike face or a bodily form that has captured Beauty well, he shudders and a fear comes over him...; then he gazes at him with the reverence due a god.... Once he has looked at him, his chill gives way to a sweat and a high fever, because the stream of beauty that pours into him through his eyes fires him up and waters the growth of his soul's wings.... Nothing is more important to that soul than the beautiful boy. Mother, brothers or friends mean nothing to it; it willingly neglects everything else and couldn't care less if it lost it all for his sake.[1]

And this is Arthur Schopenhauer's:

> Then all at once the peace, always sought but always escaping us on the former path of the desires, comes to us of its own accord, and it is well with us. It is the painless state Epicurus prized as the highest good and as the state of the gods; we are for the moment set free from the miserable striving of the will; we keep the Sabbath of the penal servitude of willing; the wheel of Ixion stands still.[2]

Plato and Schopenhauer agree on one thing: the beautiful object is not an end in itself. Plato believes its beauty leads those who can follow it further to more worthy beauties, to wisdom and virtue, to the true happiness only philosophy (he thought) could secure. Schopenhauer finds in beautiful things the real nature, the "persistent form," of their species, removed from the details and freed from the travails of ordinary life, pulling along its beholders, who also shed their individuality

I am very grateful to Richard Rorty and Elaine Scarry for their comments on these lectures when I first presented them at Yale University in April 2001 as well as to Yale's Whitney Humanities Center and its director, Peter Brooks, for their invitation and hospitality.

[1] Plato, *Phaedrus,* trans. Alexander Nehamas and Paul Woodruff (Indianapolis: Hackett Publishing Company, 1995), 251a–52a, modified.

[2] Arthur Schopenhauer, *The World as Will and Representation,* trans. R. B. Haldane and J. Kemp (London: Kegan Paul, Trench, Trubner, 1883), Book III, sec. 38.

and become "that *one* eye of the world which looks out from all knowing creatures." Beyond that common ground, there is a world of difference.

When Plato thinks of beauty, he first thinks of beautiful people—most often, beautiful boys. Paederastic desire is the initial step toward the higher beauties he values; but these—the beauty of souls, of laws and ways of life, of learning—however abstract, persist in provoking passion and longing. Even the philosopher who finally grasps, through reason alone, the intelligible Form of Beauty itself wants of it just what ordinary men want of the boys whose sensual beauty strikes and distracts them: intercourse.[3] Modeled on the human form and its power, beauty is for Plato inseparable from yearning and desire.

The beauty of the human form, to the extent that it is an object of passion, is irrelevant to Schopenhauer.[4] He turns his back to it with an almost desperate determination. Beauty is for him to be found only in works of art, in pretty landscapes, and, sometimes, in the recollection of the distant past. Desire, yearning, and passion are just what Schopenhauer wants to escape from; beauty, as he conceives it, is the surest means of liberating us from the shackles of the will, which, since it "springs from lack, from deficiency, and thus from suffering," can never be content and is the source of constant misery. All satisfaction is ephemeral, "like the alms thrown to a beggar, which reprieves him today so that his misery may be prolonged until tomorrow." The will is "the wheel of Ixion"; beauty stops it temporarily by removing us for a moment from its demands.

It is hard to imagine a starker opposition. Schopenhauer denounces just what Plato celebrated when he personified the desire for beauty as the son of two minor gods, Resource and Poverty: "Now he springs to life when he gets his way; now he dies—all in the same day. Because he is his father's son, he keeps coming back to life, but then anything he finds his way to always slips away, and for this reason [he] is never completely without resources, nor is he ever rich."[5] And although Plato never really thought of works of art as beautiful, Plotinus, who did, be-

---

[3] Plato, *Symposium,* trans. Alexander Nehamas and Paul Woodruff (Indianapolis: Hackett Publishing Company, 1989), 211d6 (*sunontas*), d8 (*suneinai*).

[4] Except as a fit subject for painters and sculptors; Schopenhauer, *The World as Will and Representation.*

[5] Plato, *Symposium,* 203e.

lieved that "whatever is beautiful produces awe and a shock of delight, passionate longing, love and a shudder of rapture."[6]

Plato and the long tradition that followed him take beauty to be the object of love (*erōs*)—that is the name of the desire for beauty I coyly omitted from my quotation from the *Symposium* just above. They can use the risky language of passion because a vast philosophical (and, later, religious) picture allows them to think that love of beauty, dangerous as it is, can lead, when practiced correctly, to love of truth, wisdom, and goodness—to moral perfection or, more modestly, moral improvement. Once that picture began to fade, however, only the dangers of beauty remained visible in the traces it left behind. And so human beauty was reduced to good looks: superficial, morally irrelevant, even suspect—no longer a subject worthy of philosophy. To the extent that beauty mattered, it came to be confined to art and the wonders of nature—museums and national parks.

Not that works of art cannot provoke the most extraordinary reactions. Think, for example, of the young man who left on the Cnidian Aphrodite the physical evidence of the consummation of his passion for the statue; think of Mark Twain on Titian's *Venus of Urbino,* "the foulest, the vilest, the obscenest picture the world possesses": "I saw," Twain writes, "a young girl stealing furtive glances at her; I saw young men gazing long and absorbedly at her; I saw aged infirm men hang upon her charms with a pathetic interest."[7] The erotic has always been essential to our love of the arts, but, for complicated reasons, it has come to seem deeply inappropriate. The proper, "aesthetic," reaction to the beauty of nature and art has gradually been divorced from passion and longing completely. Schopenhauer in fact follows Immanuel Kant, who claimed that beauty produces a "disinterested pleasure," a pleasure bereft of desire, and is in turn followed by almost everyone else. In 1914, Clive Bell became famous for defending early Modernist art on the grounds that "to appreciate a work of art we need bring with us nothing from life, no

---

[6] Plotinus, *Enneads,* I 6.4.15–18.

[7] Mark Twain, *A Tramp Abroad,* cited by David Freedberg, *The Power of Images: Studies in the History and Theory of Response* (Chicago: University of Chicago Press, 1989), p. 345. The Cnidian Aphrodite story appears in Pliny, *Natural History,* 36.21. It is discussed, along with several other similar cases, by Leonard Barkan in "Praxiteles' Stained Aphrodite, and Other Tales of Sex and Art" (unpublished manuscript, 2001). Barkan, very cautiously, suggests that perhaps all aesthetic pleasure may be a form of erotic delight. I would prefer to see them on a continuum: the attraction of beauty always includes an erotic aspect, but not every form of eroticism need manifest itself sexually.

knowledge of its ideas and affairs, no familiarity with its emotions…we need bring with us nothing but a sense of form and colour and a knowledge of three-dimensional space."[8] He should also be famous for following that thought to its conclusion and excluding beauty from art altogether, since for most people "'beautiful' is more often than not synonymous with 'desirable.'"[9] And in 1938, R. G. Collingwood, precisely because he knew that Plato saw that love is what beauty deserves, insisted that "the words 'beauty,' 'beautiful,' as actually used, have no aesthetic implication…. The word 'beauty,' wherever and however it is used, connotes that in things in virtue of which we love them, admire them, or desire them…. To sum up: aesthetic theory is not the theory of beauty but of art."[10]

The idea that art and beauty have little to do with each other is reinforced by the commonplace that evaluating a work of art marks the end of our interaction with it, the goal toward which all criticism aims. In 1949, Arnold Isenberg wrote that "it is a function of criticism to bring about communication at the level of the senses, that is, to induce a sameness of vision, of experienced content. If this is accomplished, it may or may not be followed by agreement, or what is called 'communion'—a community of feeling which expresses itself in identical value judgments."[11] In 1995, Alan Goldman restated essentially the same view: "The purpose of interpretation itself [is] to guide perception toward maximal appreciation and therefore fair evaluation of a work."[12] Mary Mothersill, who wants to bring beauty back into the philosophy of art, believes that the critic's "aim is to remove obstacles to appreciation and to present a particular text, performance, or object perspicuously, that is to say, in such a way as to enable its audience to arrive at a fair estimation of its merits."[13] But, like most philosophers of art, she takes "beautiful" as a "generic aesthetic predicate," a general term of appraisal.[14]

[8] Clive Bell, *Art* (New York: G. P. Putnam's Sons, 1958; originally published in 1914), pp. 27–28.

[9] Ibid., p. 21.

[10] R. G. Collingwood, *The Principles of Art* (Oxford: Clarendon Press, 1938), pp. 38–41.

[11] Arnold Isenberg, "Critical Communication," in his *Aesthetics and the Theory of Criticism,* ed. William Callaghan et al. (Chicago: University of Chicago Press, 1973), p. 164. Perhaps these are not, in the end, distinct possibilities. It could be that "immediate experience" refers not to the first experience of a work of art but to the perceptual experience that is induced in a work's audience once the critic has communicated the features to which attention needs to be paid.

[12] Alan H. Goldman, *Aesthetic Value* (Boulder, Colo.: Westview Press, 1995), p. 102.

[13] Mary Mothersill, *Beauty Restored* (Oxford: Clarendon Press, 1984), p. 31.

[14] Ibid., p. 3.

Such a generic kind of aesthetic value, if it exists at all, becomes apparent much later, and after much longer investigation, than the feature Joseph Addison had in mind when he wrote that "we immediately assent to the Beauty of an Object without enquiring into the particular Causes and Occasions of it."[15] Although that was not Addison's intention, the beauty he spoke of became associated with desire and good looks, and as it did, the arts joined the rest of our world and became suspicious of it themselves. By contrast, aesthetic value, difficult to discern and appreciate, seemed tailor-made for the art of Modernism. Think of the difference between Botticelli's *Birth of Venus* and Picasso's *Seated Bather;* of the disparity between Keats's "La Belle Dame Sans Mercy" and Wallace Stevens's *The Hand as a Being;* of the dissonance between Mozart's *Marriage of Figaro* and Schoenberg's *Moses und Aron.* Modernist works, and the rhetoric that accompanied them, made being difficult and inaccessible a virtue: how can I know whether I do or should like a Modernist work that is so difficult to understand in the first place? If to be beautiful is to look or sound good, to be in general immediately attractive, most Modernist works are not beautiful. And if Modernism, as many of its defenders argued, shows what is essential to all art, then beauty may be as irrelevant to *The Birth of Venus,* "La Belle Dame Sans Mercy," *Dove sono,* even perhaps to the *Apollo Belvedere,* as it seems to be to Damien Hirst's sectioned, eviscerated, and preserved cows in his *Some Comfort Gained from the Acceptance of the Inherent Lies in Everything.*

If beauty is irrelevant to *art,* surely it is irrelevant to the serious aspects of the rest of our lives, while aesthetic value, if it is relevant to art, has been defined so as to have no connection to anything else that matters to us—sex, morality, politics, religion.[16] We can always say that we should value poems and paintings "just as" poems and paintings and nothing else, but such slogans usually mean simply that we shouldn't allow the sexual, moral, political, or religious aspects of poems or paintings to determine their value: what remains, remains a mystery. Unless, then, we are willing to identify aesthetic value, in part or completely, with one or more of these values, we can't connect what matters to us in the arts with anything else that matters to us in life. Worse, we can't even say why the arts matter to us in the first place. And to take aesthetic values seriously, to take them as *human* values, as I believe we

---

[15] Joseph Addison, *The Spectator* (1712), 411.

[16] Immanuel Kant, *Critique of the Power of Judgment,* trans. and ed. Paul D. Guyer (Cambridge: Cambridge University Press, 2000), §§1–5.

should, risks seeming not serious, calling to mind a purple suit, a green carnation, a penchant for paradox, and a general air of irresponsible insouciance. There's nothing wrong with purple suits, green carnations, or the penchant for paradox, but they are only accidental features of taking aesthetic values seriously; and although irresponsible insouciance may be occasionally wrong, it is not a necessary feature of admiring the aesthetic. Aesthetic considerations form a distinct kind. Although they are most evident in the arts, they are not confined to them (and pretty sunsets). But we will not be able to recognize their role as long as beauty is denied entrance both in the arts and in the rest of what matters to us. Dave Hickey has called beauty "the invisible dragon." What denies it entrance, the visible dragon that must be slain before beauty can shine forth once again, is the view that criticism is a kind of intellectual layer cake, "descriptions supporting interpretations,...lower-level statements supporting higher-level ones, and...critics arguing for evaluations by means of interpretations,"[17] the idea that to evaluate a work of art is to finish with it, the goal and end of our involvement with it.[18]

It is true that we cannot arrive at a final evaluation of anything without first understanding it fully, and it is plausible to think that the aim of criticism is the evaluation of works of art. We tend to consider what Kant called the judgment of taste, the statement "This is beautiful," now taking "beautiful" as shorthand for a general evaluation, to be the culmination of our aesthetic interaction with things. That is why many philosophers agree that the purpose of criticism is to reach a "verdict" regarding the works of art it addresses, even though they dispute whether this verdict can be supported by the same sort of reasons as a legal or moral verdict or, indeed, whether it can be supported by reasons at all. But although this is plausible, it is not true.

What is true is that one part of aesthetic discourse aims at verdicts: that part, interestingly, that is most likely to contain the vocabulary we commonly characterize as "aesthetic"—words like "powerful," "swift," "fluid," "deep," "solid," "sharp," "eloquent," and "delicate," the terms, we are told, on which evaluation depends. My list is not haphazard. It

---

[17] Ann Sheppard, *Aesthetics: An Introduction to the Philosophy of Art* (Oxford: Oxford University Press, 1974), p. 84.

[18] Richard Rorty has pointed out that it is not necessary to deny that some beautiful things may provoke the kind of reaction Schopenhauer values in order to argue that Plato's view is also correct. That is a very valuable idea, and I intend to develop it more fully in a future version of these lectures.

comes from Arthur Danto's book on the philosophy of art, *The Trans-figuration of the Commonplace,*[19] and he, in turn, has taken it from a review of an exhibition of André Racz's drawings of flowers. That, I believe, is not an accident. And I suspect that the idea that all criticism aims at verdicts, as well as the extraordinary interest of philosophers in the nature and logical features of "aesthetic" terms, derives from the fact that most of us, when we think of criticism and aesthetic discourse in general, actually think of reviewing, which both aims at verdicts and depends heavily on "aesthetic" descriptions. These are some of the terms, for example, that Michael Fried used in less than two pages while reviewing a Hans Hofmann show: "a surprisingly warm grayish brown," "warm, autonomous colors," "forceful streak of blue," "vibrant with energy," "flare into resonant life," "passionate note," "integrated," "coloristic strength," "impatience with contrivance that is itself perhaps a bit contrived," "power, delicacy, and subtle intelligence," "exploratory and liberating." It may not come as a surprise that Fried concluded that Hofmann's was one of the two "finest" shows that month in New York and not to be missed (although, of course, a review can equally often reach a negative verdict).[20]

Reviews aim to let us know whether or not we should visit an exhibition, read a book, or attend a performance. What is fascinating is that the vocabulary itself is almost never enough to convince us one way or the other. Our attitude toward the reviewer is also—perhaps even more—crucial: If you are familiar with Fried's views, tastes, and preferences and find them abhorrent (as I don't), you may well decide, precisely on the strength of his praise, to give Hofmann a miss. Critics are in that respect like artists: We cannot understand an individual work in isolation, without a knowledge of its maker's style; just so, we need to be familiar with the critics we read if we are to rely on their recommendations.

Let me stay with that idea a moment. Kant famously claimed that the judgment of taste is "not based on concepts." What he meant was well expressed by Arnold Isenberg when he wrote that "there is not in all the world's criticism a single purely descriptive statement concerning which one is prepared to say beforehand, 'If it is true, I shall like that

[19] Arthur C. Danto, *The Transfiguration of the Commonplace: A Philosophy of Art* (Cambridge, Mass.: Harvard University Press, 1981), p. 155.

[20] Michael Fried, "New York Letter: Hofmann" (originally published in 1963), in *Art and Objecthood: Essays and Reviews* (Chicago: University of Chicago Press, 1998), pp. 294–96.

work so much the better.'"[21] Isenberg, like Kant, would say that if we smuggled in terms that are not purely descriptive—terms like "forceful" or "integrated" in contrast to "large" or "written in 1917"—then the conclusion would be more likely to follow. If, though, we rely on critics whose style we already generally know, it is not only "purely descriptive statements" about a work that fail to show that it is beautiful: no account of the work, however many aesthetic terms it contains, will by itself imply that you will like that work better, even though aesthetic terms always evaluate whatever they describe.[22] What Fried describes as "a forceful streak of blue," given your view of his taste, may be more likely to repel rather than attract you. It's not that Fried is *wrong* to call the blue streak forceful: you can see just what he means, but, also, you just don't like it. You might even say, "That's exactly *why* I don't like it." His commendation is your condemnation.

The notion that we can understand the complex practices of criticism by generalizing from reviews seems to me as hopeless as the dream that we can capture the many ways the arts matter to us by isolating and studying a group of special words. Aesthetic terms are by themselves both insignificant and double-edged. Arthur Danto, for one, would disagree with both these pessimistic claims. He writes that the aesthetic terms he mentions

> echo terms of praise in common life; it is difficult to imagine a context in which it is discommendatory to speak of something as "powerful." Power, speed, sureness, fluidity, are qualities we praise in things, or at least things we rely upon, and it is useful here to consider them, not least of all because, as examples, they are markedly less shopworn than the commonplace vocabulary of aesthetic discourse, at least as this is represented in philosophy.[23]

To me, these terms—"powerful," "swift," "fluid," "deep," "solid," "sharp," "eloquent," "delicate"—seem quite as shopworn as any others that have appeared in philosophical discussion: you will know little—and that, very vague—about Racz's drawings if that is what you know of them. And they are, as I said, double-edged. With the possible exception of "powerful," it is easy to imagine, and possible to find, instances

[21] Isenberg, "Critical Communication," p. 164.

[22] Danto, *Transfiguration,* p. 156.

[23] Ibid., p. 155.

where they are used to condemn rather than praise: delicacy, to take the most obvious case, could be a serious defect in a depiction of a brutal execution;[24] sharpness of tone is not a quality prized by opera singers; Jake and Dinos Chapman's *The Un-nameable* is repellent partly because their demented figures of little girls flow so fluidly into one another; while it is because it is hollow (the contrary of solid) that Robert Morris's *Untitled: Ring with Light* exerts its magnetic attraction.

The ability to cut both ways applies even more to the much more complex, almost technical terms that critics sometimes use to summarize a complicated general approach to art, terms that have little to do with the limited aesthetic vocabulary we have looked at so far. Fried, again, rejected the minimalism (or "literalism") of Donald Judd, Sol LeWitt, Robert Morris, and Tony Smith for being, in contrast to the work of Frank Stella or Kenneth Noland, "theatrical" in a very intricate and specific sense—a notion he has used in order to develop a general approach to the art of Modernism. The virtues of Modernism, as he sees it, are absorption, autonomy, and self-sufficiency, an effort—perhaps impossible—to act as if they have no audience, while Minimalism is essentially audience-oriented and flattering. Minimalism, for Fried, aims to produce works that are just objects in literal space, explicitly attracting their spectators' attention to them: "For Judd, as for literalist sensibility generally, all that matters is whether or not a given work is able to elicit and sustain (his) interest. Whereas within the modernist arts nothing short of *conviction*—specifically, the conviction that a particular painting or sculpture or piece of music can or cannot support comparison with past work within that art whose quality is not in doubt [without, that is, any concern for what its audience think of it]—matters at all."[25] Thirty-seven years later, however, Peter Schjeldahl praises Minimalism precisely for the features for which Fried had condemned it, for producing "a visceral conviction of utter reality—actual space, heartbeating time; it was the dawn of a new world...a true revolution had occurred—

---

[24] Danto himself makes a related and very interesting point when he argues, taking his cue from Robert Motherwell's *Elegies to the Spanish Republic,* that sometimes it might even be inappropriate for a work to be *beautiful*—if, for example, it depicts a savage and horrible subject: "A painting—a work of art in general—can have an internal beauty and be a failure if, in fact, the beauty is inappropriate or unfitting. But that means that there are works that are better off for not being beautiful, since they might be artistic failures if they were, so to speak, aesthetic successes." See his "Beauty and Morality," reprinted in *Uncontrollable Beauty: Toward a New Aesthetics,* ed. Bill Beckley with David Shapiro (New York: Allworth Press, 1998), p. 31.

[25] Michael Fried, "Art and Objecthood," in *Art and Objecthood,* p. 165.

one that shifted the focus of art experience from the created work to the self-conscious viewer."[26] Dave Hickey, for his part, is more explicit and more irreverent: "Our twentieth-century characterizations of the work of art as this ravishing, autonomous entity that we spend our lives trying to understand, that makes demands on us while pretending that we are not there, is simply a recasting of the work of art in the role of the remote and dysfunctional male parent in the tradition of the Biblical patriarch. Even art critics deserve some respite from this sort of abusive neglect."[27] Of course, one could always dismiss criticism as an expression of differences in taste masquerading as argument, but that in turn would express an impoverished understanding of the role of both taste and argument in our lives.

For over forty years, philosophers have tried to distinguish descriptive terms ("blue"), which apply to things on the basis of public criteria, and aesthetic terms ("elegant"), which lack criteria and require the exercise of taste, with which only some people are blessed.[28] That the evaluation, and so the value and significance, of art depends on a particular set of aesthetic features has now become an institutional self-evident commonplace. The *Encyclopedia of Aesthetics,* which was published in 1998, has this to say in its entry "Qualities, Aesthetic": "To say that a particular painting has a blue spot in the upper right corner is not to say or suggest anything about the value of the painting; such a statement is clearly not relevant as grounds for aesthetic praise or blame of that painting"— in contrast, for example, to its being garish or unified.[29] But the actual practice of art criticism reveals that this thin, anemic picture is only a poor caricature. In the Mannheim version of Edouard Manet's *Execution of Maximilian,* there is a streak of red paint between the legs of a soldier in the firing squad. In the painting's earlier versions, the streak represents the stripe on the trousers of the squad's commander, who is standing behind them. In the Mannheim version, the officer has disappeared,

---

[26] Peter Schjeldahl, "Less Is Beautiful," *New Yorker,* March 13, 2000. And see Fried, *Art and Objecthood,* pp. 43–44.

[27] Dave Hickey, "Prom Night in Flatland: On the Gender of Works of Art," in *The Invisible Dragon: Four Essays on Beauty* (Los Angeles: Art issues. Press, 1993), pp. 46–47.

[28] The project originated with Frank Sibley's "Aesthetic Concepts," in *Art and Philosophy: Readings in Aesthetics,* ed. W. E. Kennick (New York: St. Martin's Press, 1964), pp. 351–73. Sibley's influential essay has been discussed extensively since its original publication in 1959; a good response is in Ted Cohen's "Aesthetics/Non-Aesthetics and the Concept of Taste," *Theoria* 39 (1973): 113–52.

[29] Göran Hermeren, "Qualities, Aesthetic," in *Encyclopedia of Aesthetics,* ed. Michael Kelly, 4 vols. (New York: Oxford University Press, 1988), vol. 4, p. 98.

and critics have been arguing for years about the significance of the streak. Michael Fried, after considering all the possibilities, decides that this is just what it is: a streak of red paint, which is, as such, crucial to his interpretation and evaluation of the work:

> On close inspection the streak of paint is merely that and nothing more: it absolutely resists being assimilated to the work of representation, by which I also mean that it escapes the categories of finish and nonfinish that indefatigably structured contemporary responses to Manet's work.... Perhaps it too is best thought of as a *remainder...*, something left over after the task of representation was done and which stands for everything in Manet's art which adamantly resisted closure, which was irremediably disparate, which pursued a strikingness that could not be kept within the bounds even of the excessive, which repeatedly interpellated the beholder in ways the latter could only find offensive and incomprehensible, and which in fact continues to defeat our best efforts to make reassuring sense of his paintings by inserting them in a historical context, no matter how that context is defined.[30]

If a streak of red paint can make such a difference, it is ludicrous to believe that criticism is exhausted by a specific "aesthetic" vocabulary. We will learn little about the arts if we concentrate on their elegance, garishness, fluidity, unity, or forcefulness. The fact is that there is no special class of aesthetic terms or qualities that only some people can discern while the rest of us remain trapped within the prosaic world of description. The best we can say about terms like "elegant" or "garish" is that if they apply to an object at all, they are (unlike other terms) always relevant to its aesthetic value—but not particularly useful in letting us see what that is. The fact is that everyone uses aesthetic terms all the time: they are part of the texture of our life. There is, actually, no word that cannot on some occasion or other be used aesthetically: even "blue"—for example, in Mary's mantle in *The Virgin Visited by Angels at the Temple* in the *Visconti Hours,* in almost any work by Yves Klein, in William Gass, who wrote a whole book on the word and turned it into object and tool of aesthetic attention at once:

> *Blue,* the word and the condition, the color and the act, contrive to contain one another, as if the bottle of the genie were its belly, the lamp's breath the smoke of the wraith. There is that lead-like look.

[30] Michael Fried, *Manet's Modernism, or the Face of Painting in the 1860s* (Chicago: University of Chicago Press, 1996), pp. 359–60.

> There is the lead itself, and all those bluey hunters, thieves, those pigeon flyers who relieve roofs of the metal, and steal the pipes too. There's the blue pill that is the bullet's end, the nose, the plum, the blue whistler, and there are all the bluish hues of death,[31]

and in what seems like a cosmic joke on philosophy, the blue spot at the upper right-hand corner of Damien Hirst's *Alantolactone* (1992)![32] Aesthetic terms are everywhere: every word can be one. They are, for that reason, less of a problem than aestheticians have thought. It is not, as many have believed, that some people just fail to detect delicacy or balance and therefore lack "taste, perceptiveness, or sensitivity."[33] It is that they don't find them where we do; their taste differs from ours. No one lacks taste, if taste is simply the ability to see *some* of the aesthetic features of things: the only question is whether that taste is good or bad.

Reviews, we have seen, end in verdicts, but in verdicts that are peculiarly thin, and the reviews themselves tell us little about the works they concern. Talk of power, swiftness, fluidity, or delicacy is an invitation to look at, to read, or to listen to the works for ourselves, often to get acquainted with them for the first time. It is a promise that time spent with them will (or will not) be worth our while, and how reliable the promise is depends partly on the reviewer's record and reputation. Reviewers are like people, ideally friends whose judgment I trust, eager to introduce me to someone they think I will enjoy meeting.

Now suppose I accept the invitation: I read the book, I visit the gallery, go to the opera, watch the TV show. Am *I* also trying to reach a verdict, to decide whether the work is or is not valuable? That I *will* reach a verdict of some sort is likely, but it is neither my goal nor, if it is positive, the end of my interaction with the work.

The human parallel has something to teach us here. When I meet someone on your recommendation, I do so in the *hope* that I will enjoy the meeting but not *in order to* enjoy it, and certainly not in order to *de-*

---

[31] William Gass, *On Being Blue: A Philosophical Inquiry* (Boston: David R. Godine, 1976), p. 11.

[32] In *The Prose of the World* (Evanston: Northwestern University Press, 1973), p. 62, Maurice Merleau-Ponty writes that André Malraux once told a story about an innkeeper at Cassis, who saw Pierre Renoir working by the sea and went over to observe him: "'There were some nude women bathing in some other place. Goodness knows what he was looking at, and he changed only a little corner.'...The blue of the sea had become that of the brook in *The Bathers*.... This vision was less a way of looking at the sea than the secret elaboration of a world to which that depth of blue whose immensity he was recapturing pertained." I am grateful to Sean Kelly for this reference.

[33] Sibley, "Aesthetic Concepts," p. 351.

*cide* whether it is worth enjoying. My *goal* is not to enjoy the meeting, but to get to know someone new. If the meeting turns out as all of us had hoped, if, that is, I decide it was enjoyable (although, I repeat, making that decision was never my goal), I shall want to know that person better. My "verdict" is not, as long as it is positive, the end of the matter; on the contrary, it is a desire to make that person a larger part of my life, a sense that your friend has more to offer than I was able to see on that occasion. The positive verdict doesn't signal the end of our interaction, but expresses my realization that it should go on. In other words, it is not a verdict.

If enjoyment seems too trivial or banal a reaction, imagine that, either on your suggestion or by chance, I find myself with someone who strikes me as utterly beautiful. I don't mean someone whom, so to speak, I merely judge to be beautiful or good-looking, but someone whose beauty actually attracts me. At first, of course, I will just want to keep on looking. But that, if the beauty continues to strike me, will soon give way to the desire to approach, to spend some time with that person then and there, to get to know them better. I won't always act on my desire (I may be shy, afraid of rejection, considerate of the feelings of someone else, afraid of my action's consequences for myself), but sometimes I will. And now suppose I do.

We are now on delicate and dangerous ground. I am arguing that when I find someone beautiful I am attracted to them; and that is to have a sense that my life would in some way be better (by no means primarily, or even marginally, moral), more worthwhile, if that person were part of it. Sometimes, half-knowingly, I allow myself to believe that people whose looks I admire are more intelligent, engaging, serious, or sensitive than I know they are. That could be because I am unwilling to acknowledge the sexual aspects of my attraction or, more generously, because I hope that in time I will find such features in them. Often, in fact, to say that an attraction is merely sexual (more probably that it *was* merely sexual, since such an acknowledgment usually comes after the fact) is to say that I found nothing further to attract me to a particular person; it is an evaluation of a relationship that didn't, sometimes against my own desires and expectations, go anywhere. Sometimes, knowingly, I disregard the fact that they are not intelligent or engaging because I am willing to admit that my attraction is mostly sexual: that is when beauty becomes identical with good looks. Sometimes, someone I find beautiful also strikes me as intelligent, engaging, serious, or sensitive. Sometimes, attraction turns into love. In all these cases, to find someone beautiful (or even just good-looking) is nothing like issuing a verdict and very like a desire to continue interacting with them, to know them better, to make them—to whatever extent and in whatever way—my own.

The expression "to make someone my own" should not sound a sour note, suggesting possession, mastery, control, or any of the many other relations we have come officially to disapprove of in recent years. I am not thinking of Swann's desire to possess Odette so completely that merely hearing that she owns a dress he has not seen nearly shatters him because it shows him that her life has aspects of which he is not aware.[34] Such things occur often enough, but in the love and friendship to which I want to liken that aspect of our relation to the arts that matters most in life, the desire to make someone my own is inseparable from the desire to make myself their own as well. Even in cases where I simply enjoy your company without being your intimate friend or lover, I can exhibit a willingness to change as a result of interacting with you: the extent of such a willingness is a matter of degree. I am not inclined to spend my time with you because I already know what I want to get out of you, having a settled sense of myself and of what you can give me. Rather, I suspect that you can give me something I don't yet have a conception of, I hope that you will make me want something I have not wanted before.[35] In doing so, I make myself emotionally and intellectually vulnerable to you.[36] I put my identity at risk, and the risk is great because I don't yet know how you will eventually affect me—and if you feel as I do, your problems are exactly like mine. But then, as the ancient proverb said, friends have everything in common.

Aristotle, who made much of that proverb, believed that the best kind of friends love each other for their own sake, "as another self." He thought that this is possible only for the virtuous, who love one another not on account of the profit or pleasure they can derive from their friendship, but on account of their virtues, which are essential to who one is,

[34] Marcel Proust, *Remembrance of Things Past,* trans. C. K. Scott Montcrieff and Terence Kilmartin, 3 vols. (New York: Random House, 1981), vol. 1, pp. 262–63.

[35] See Richard Rorty, "The Pragmatist's Progress: Umberto Eco on Interpretation," in *Philosophy and Social Hope* (London: Penguin, 1999), pp. 144–45.

[36] See J. David Velleman, "Love as a Moral Emotion," *Ethics* 109 (1999): 338–74. Velleman's views, especially his criticisms of various common conceptions of love, are very valuable, and his own phenomenology of love is extremely attractive. His Kantian conclusion that love is directed at the rational nature of our lovers, however, is not easy to accept.

and, therefore, for themselves.[37] Unless your conception of virtue is very broad, that makes friendship much too rare a phenomenon, and, besides, it flies in the face of experience—not every captured criminal, after all, turns state's evidence. But we can turn Aristotle's picture around: friendship is not limited to the virtuous, but friends find in each other features they consider to be virtues, rather than merely pleasant or profitable. With profit and pleasure, you generally know what to expect. Virtues, in this context, manifest themselves in the most unexpected ways and (as we shall see more clearly when we return to the arts) belong to your friend and to your friend only—which is the reason we say we love our friends for themselves and part of the reason it is impossible to say why we love them at all. Your friends, then, are the people from whom you don't already know what you want to get, but whom you trust enough to give yourself to in the hope that they too will give themselves to you, both of you becoming something you can't at this stage even imagine. To love your friends for themselves does not prevent you from loving them for your own sake as well. It is, though, to put yourself in their hands and give them a part in determining what your sake actually is, what your self will turn out to be as a result of your friendship.

Still, you can be wrong, and put your trust in the wrong person. That is one of the great dangers of beauty. Now, you may ask, how did beauty come into this discussion of friendship? Surely it is not necessary to find our friends beautiful. That is true, but it is also impossible to be a friend of someone you actually find physically repulsive, even ugly.[38] David Lynch gives a brilliant demonstration of it in *The Elephant Man.* Lynch manipulates the physical point of view of the camera and the fictional point of view of Frederick Treves, the physician who saved John Merrick from a freak show on purely humanitarian grounds, and shows Treves ceasing to mind Merrick's appearance as he gradually realizes that Merrick's horrible physical disfigurement does not reflect a psychological wasteland and comes to be actually fond of him. At the very same time, and through the same mechanism, Lynch makes his character appear

[37] Aristotle, *Nicomachean Ethics,* VIII–IX.

[38] To find someone ugly is not simply to judge that they are ugly—which is to say that you can understand why someone might think of them as ugly, how someone *else* might find them ugly—but to be directly struck by them as ugly, to be, to that extent, repelled by them. The case is parallel to finding someone beautiful, which implies being actually attracted to them, not just realizing that others might find themselves in that position.

more human to the audience, whose fondness for Merrick reflects Treves's transformation. In Nicholas Ray's *Rebel Without a Cause,* Natalie Wood's character, desperate about her father's moral disapproval, cries out, "He looks at me as if I was the ugliest thing in the world!" In her memoir, *Paula,* Isabel Allende recalls her feelings for the man who raised her:

> The first time I saw my Tío Ramón, I thought my mother was playing a joke. *That* was the prince she had been sighing over? I had never seen such an ugly man.... [T]en years later...I was at last able to accept him. He took charge of us children, just as he had promised.... He raised us with a firm hand and unfailing good humor; he set limits and sent clear messages, without sentimental demonstrations, without compromise. I recognize now that he put up with my contrariness without trying to buy my esteem or ceding an inch of his authority, until he won me over totally. He is the only father I have known, and now I think he is really handsome![39]

Intimacy reveals beauty; perhaps it goes with it hand-in-hand.

Allende's mother, who loved Ramón, did not even have to wait to find him handsome. For love, as Plato saw, is beauty's attendant and constant companion. To love someone just is to find them beautiful. One of the first signs that love has withdrawn is a sense (I would not call it a "realization") that our lover no longer seems beautiful, that a particular feature, which may once have been attractive, gradually turns into a cause of aversion. Love for someone whom I actually find ugly, though perhaps possible, is pathological.[40] That is the love of Shakespeare's Dark Lady sonnets: "My love is as a fever, longing still / For that which longer nurseth the disease" (147). And so strange a love it is that even Shakespeare's best readers seem to shy away from it. When Helen Vendler, whose reading of the sequence is a brilliant dissection of its paradoxical voice, comes to its final sonnet—"In loving thee thou know'st I am forsworn...For I have sworn thee fair: more perjured eye / To swear against the truth so foul a lie" (152)—she feels forced to put "love" in quotation marks in her discussion: The speaker's "own complicity is what shocks

---

[39] Isabel Allende, *Paula,* trans. from the Spanish by Margaret Sayers Peden (New York: HarperCollins, 1994), pp. 48–49.

[40] I am not thinking of that version of Christian love that is addressed to everyone indiscriminately, simply as a child of God. But even there, the practice, for example, of kissing lepers' wounds during parts of the Middle Ages suggests that nothing about those we love can provoke repulsion.

him, as he discovers that it is precisely her *unworthiness* that raises 'love' in him." Such "love" is merely sexual passion: the poem is "a bitterly shaming acknowledgment of one's own least acceptable sexual proclivities," and "the reader admires the clarity of mind that can so anatomize sexual obsession while still in its grip."[41] I doubt the paradox disappears if we exchange sexuality for love: sexual passion must still find *something* attractive in its object. But love, which can survive contempt, dislike, disgust, and even hate, can't ever live with ugliness. Eros, Plato wrote, "was born to follow and serve Aphrodite, because he was conceived on the day of her birth. And he is by nature a lover of beauty because Aphrodite herself is especially beautiful" (*Sym.* 203c).

As long as I find someone beautiful—which is, in different degrees, a matter of love—I commit myself to its being worthwhile for that person to be—to whatever extent—part of my life and for me to be, in turn, part of their own life as well. Without that forward-looking element, and all its risks, attraction and love wither and disappear: love, as Plato knew and Proust wrote (though Proust is tormented by a thought I find exhilarating), "in the pain of anxiety as in the bliss of desire, is a demand for a whole. We love only what we do not wholly possess."[42] And as with love, so with beauty: beauty fades and dies out when it can promise nothing it has not given already.

And so, also, with art. A work we admire, a work we love, a work we find, in a word, beautiful sparks within us the same need to rush to converse with it, the same sense that it has more to offer, the same willingness to submit to it, the same desire to make it part of our life. I don't want to understate the differences, but I also don't want to lose sight of the similarities. We can't hurt works of art, nor can they hurt us, in all the ways we hurt one another, but overlaps persist. When Dave Hickey personifies the Modernist work as a dysfunctional father capable of indifference, abuse, rejection, or humiliation, what he says—although not true of Modernism generally—is still true, if only as a metaphor, of many works, both Modernist and not. Still, even the least possessive among us don't usually rush to share our lovers with others, not even our

---

[41] Helen Vendler, *The Art of Shakespeare's Sonnets* (Cambridge, Mass.: Harvard University Press, 1997), pp. 643, 645. The same scare-quotes around "love" occur in G. Blakemore Evans's commentary on Sonnet 152 in his edition of the sonnets for *The New Cambridge Shakespeare* (Cambridge: Cambridge University Press, 1996), p. 152.

[42] Marcel Proust, *The Captive,* trans. C. K. Scott Montcrieff and Terence Kilmartin and Andreas Mayor (New York: Random House, 1981), p. 102. That, of course, is also the starting-point of Socrates' speech on Eros in the *Symposium.*

friends. While we want our lovers to be admired, it can be disturbing to find them loved by someone else, and devastating to discover that their love has found another object. And yet we eagerly allow, encourage, expect, and sometimes even require others to love the works we find beautiful. We want to converse, to interact further with beautiful people directly; we want them primarily for ourselves (in another sense of that term). But when I am moved by a novel, my desire to get to know it better is one and the same as my wish for others to read it and discuss it with me. When I think that a work is beautiful, I believe others should think so too. And if that, as I have claimed, is to think that my life would be more worthwhile if that work were to be part of it, I also believe that the lives of others would also be more worthwhile if they felt about the work as I do. Our feelings for art are essentially promiscuous. Here is Dave Hickey again, after being bowled over by Gustave Flaubert's *A Simple Heart* at age fifteen on a sunny afternoon in a small Texas town:

> I started calling my friends. I wanted them to read the story immediately, so we could talk about it; and this rush to converse, it seems to me, is the one undeniable consequence of art that speaks to our desire. The language we produce before the emblem of what we *are,* what we know and understand, is always more considered. This language aims to teach, to celebrate our knowledge rather than our wonder.... The language that we share before the emblem of what we lack, however, as fractious and inconsequent as it often seems, creates a new society.[43]

I am trying to say that the judgment of taste—the statement "This is beautiful"—is neither a conclusion I reach by interacting with a work nor, since it is not a conclusion and thus not supported by reasons, purely subjective—though, as Kant rightly saw, it is based on, and expresses, a feeling toward that work. Far from freeing us from the demands of desire, as Schopenhauer thought, beauty provokes them. He thought that to perceive a beautiful object is to grasp its "Platonic Idea," its real nature, to come to understand it fully and in itself, apart from its relations to anything else. I think of beauty in exactly the opposite way. Beauty is, in every case, the object of love. Both last as long as the sense that I am standing before something I do not yet fully understand to which I am willing to submit in order to come to know it bet-

[43] Dave Hickey, "Simple Hearts," in *Air Guitar: Essays on Art and Democracy* (Los Angeles: Art issues. Press, 1997), p. 30.

ter—not through the mediation of others, since that, we shall see, is impossible in aesthetics, but directly, on my own. But far from being solipsistic, my desire to possess the beautiful thing on my own is essentially social. Part of it is the desire that others have that desire as well; as Peter Schjeldahl has written, "An experience of beauty entirely specific to one person probably indicates that the person is insane."[44] Part of it is the desire to know how these others react to the work, to depend on them as I continue to shape my own understanding and to return the favor to them. For these reasons, I am willing to spend part of my life in their company, literally with those with whom I discuss it, less strictly with those whose views of the work I may read or discuss with my friends. The social nature of the judgment of beauty is, as I shall argue in the next lecture, one of art's great pleasures and one of its greatest dangers.

All I have accomplished in this lecture is to claim that the judgment of beauty is not a verdict on the features of persons or things but a sense that our life will be more worthwhile if they are part of it. It is a sense that can be wrong—as long as love and beauty last, the jury, so to speak, is always still out—and, we shall see, capable of great harm even when it is right. The values of art have nothing to do with a specific set of "aesthetic" features: any feature can be aesthetic that is relevant to interpreting, and thus evaluating, a work and there is no way of knowing in advance which features are relevant and which are not. Our attitude toward works we find beautiful is similar to our attitude toward beautiful persons. It also differs from it in some ways, and these reveal that the judgment of taste has an essentially social aspect. The social nature of the judgment of taste—the fact that it is not purely private, that it involves, somehow, the agreement of others—raises the possibility that to say that something is beautiful is to make a genuine judgment, one that, in Mary Mothersill's words, is "contingent, hence either true or false,...such as to admit testing by anyone who cares to take the trouble and [for which] there are determinate confirmation procedures that can be sketched in advance...consistent (or inconsistent) with other judgments...eligible to play a role in inference, support entailments and so forth"—a judgment as genuine or objective as saying that something is blue.[45] But then, as Mothersill knows, "someone who found nothing remarkable in [what I take to be beautiful] would strike me as slightly

---

[44] Peter Schjeldahl, "Notes on Beauty," in *Uncontrollable Beauty,* ed. Beckley and Shapiro, p. 58.

[45] Mothersill, *Beauty Restored,* p. 164.

defective—as if something blocked his perception or impaired his sensibility."[46] Let me leave you with that thought. We all have it, all the time. It implies that, since tastes differ everywhere, everyone in the world finds everyone else defective. That is disturbing, but the thought also envisages an ideal world, free of contempt, in which everyone's taste would then be exactly the same. That is more than disturbing: it is truly frightening. Why? That is the question with which I begin my next lecture.

II

Almost everyone knows that when he heard a witty remark of James Whistler's, Oscar Wilde cried, "I wish I'd said that!" and Whistler replied, "You will, Oscar, you will." What not everyone may know is what "that" was that Whistler had said. It was this: "My dear fellow," the painter told Humphry Ward, the art critic for the *Times,* who had been judging Whistler's work during an opening, "you must never say this painting is good or that bad. Good and bad are not terms to be used by you. But you may say 'I like this' or 'I don't like that,' and you will be within your rights. Now come and have a whisky: you're sure to like that."[1]

I am interested in what happens to me when I say to myself that something is beautiful and not merely that I like it. In my first lecture, I said it is not the conclusion of interpretation—that is why the judgment of taste, as Kant claimed, does not follow from any description of its object: we can give no reasons for it. It is more like hearing something call me, a guess or a hope that if that thing were part of my life it would somehow make it more worthwhile. But when I find something beautiful, even when I speak only to myself, I expect others to join me and make that beautiful thing part of their own lives as well. Whistler did not just put Ward down; he also asked a real question: Does anyone have the right to such an expectation?

The question is raised by the fact that if the judgment of taste expresses something more than a purely private preference, it seems to de-

[46] Ibid., p. 165.

[1] Richard Ellmann, *Oscar Wilde* (New York: Knopf, 1988), p. 133.

mand nothing less than universal agreement. Yet how can we expect *anyone* to accept a judgment for which we can give no reasons? And what of the brute fact that such a demand has never been met? Kant thought that everyone who judges something to be beautiful speaks with "a universal voice,"[2] but all that clamor sounds to me no stronger than the voice of one crying in the wilderness. Universality, at any rate, comes at a very high price, only vaguely hinted at in the third *Critique,* but clear and definite in the works of contemporary Kantians. For if the judgment of taste is a genuine judgment, then, as Mary Mothersill argues, it is either true or false; if it is true, everyone should accept it; there is therefore something wrong with those who don't. Worse, since we all believe our judgments are true (whether or not they really are), we must feel that everyone whose taste differs from ours is "slightly defective— as if something blocked his perception or impaired his sensibility."[3]

Can this be right? I would probably consider defective everyone who refused to acknowledge that I am now standing before you (unless, of course, we were having a philosophical conversation!). I might possibly, in certain circumstances, consider defective someone who, unable to understand some more complex idea, was also unwilling to learn what it took to see that it was true—defective intellectually or defective in character, defects of which I am aware in myself. I would find fault, under very specific conditions, with someone who disputed some particular aesthetic judgment of mine—perhaps a friend from whom I expected better, or someone whose disagreement was based purely on what I considered ignorance or prejudice. But I can't even begin to

---

[2] Strictly speaking, Kant writes that "if one…calls the object beautiful, one *believes* oneself to have a universal voice, and lays claim to the consent of everyone" (*Critique of the Power of Judgment,* ed. Paul Guyer and trans. Paul Guyer and Eric Matthews [Cambridge: Cambridge University Press, 2000], §8, p. 101). He thinks, of course, that this belief is correct. Guyer points out (p. 368n18) that in *Anthropology from a Pragmatic Point of View,* §67, Kant offers "a striking variation on this theme": "Kant describes the judgment of beauty as an invitation (*Einladung*) to others to experience the pleasure one has oneself felt in an object." But that invitation, which is much closer to how I would describe the judgment of beauty, is still an invitation issued to one and all.

[3] Mary Mothersill, *Beauty Restored* (Oxford: Clarendon Press, 1984), p. 165. David Hume, unlike Kant and Mothersill, believed that "there are certain general principles of approbation and blame" (that the judgment of taste, in Kant's terms, is in fact governed by concepts): "Some particular forms or qualities, from the original structure of the internal fabric, are calculated to please, and others to displease." Faced, then, with the fact of widespread disagreement, he accounted for it by claiming that "if they fail of their effect in any particular instance, it is from some apparent defect or imperfection in the organ." See "Of the Standard of Taste," in David Hume, *Essays, Moral, Political, and Literary* (Indianapolis: LibertyClassics, 1987), p. 233.

imagine what it would be like to consider defective *everyone* who disputed my particular taste in painting, literature, or television. I can't
even imagine I would have that reaction toward everyone who found my
taste, say, for television in general an error (the same might be true for
lyric poetry).

Here, now, is another version of the Kantian way of looking at
things:

> When you do not laugh at the jokes I love, or when you do not care
> for baseball, that may sadden or surprise me, but it is a worldly fact
> that I can tolerate, that I can live with. But when I take a thing [the
> reference is to movies and photography—the whole institutions] to
> be art, I take my relation to it to put me in touch with everyone else,
> at least potentially, for I am taking it that the thing ought to be able
> to be the focus of a catholic community.[4]

For me, judgments regarding beauty or art, although not purely subjective, do not have that kind of generality: neither a beautiful object nor
an artistic field creates a catholic community; it creates many different
communities, and not any less serious because they are partial—each is,
from the point of view of those who belong to it, orthodox. When the
same author writes that to consider "that something is art is to understand that this thing is an object for a community of auditors, and that
you belong to this community,"[5] I want to say the same about beauty.
Also, that neither for art nor for beauty is that primarily a matter of *understanding:* it is a matter of hoping, of trying to make the beautiful
thing an object for such a community, of *creating* the community that
centers around it—a community whose boundaries are constantly shifting, whose edges are never stable or impermeable. But that doesn't matter.

It doesn't matter because the community I hope to create around
what strikes me as beautiful is never a universal community. If it were,
if I expected my judgments of beauty to be binding on everyone, then in
the ideal case—apart from those whose sense and sensibility were incorrigibly corrupted—everyone in the world would agree with everyone
else on what is beautiful and what not. C. S. Peirce held that a true belief is a belief fated to be accepted by everyone who engages in scientific

[4] Ted Cohen, "The Very Idea of Art," *NCECA Journal* 9 (1988): 12.
[5] Ibid., p. 10.

investigation[6] and had a vision of an ideal world—a world he thought to be supremely beautiful—in which scientific inquiry would come to an end. Kantianism, from which Peirce drew much of his inspiration, has a similar dream about aesthetics—it dreams of a world where aesthetic judgment provokes no disagreement and, since the judgment of taste is a conclusion regarding the aesthetic features of things, everyone's reasons for making the same judgments as everyone else would also be the same as everyone else's. Is that a dream or a nightmare? Is it any less repulsive than Aldous Huxley's *Brave New World,* where, apart from the incorrigibly corrupt Savage who insists on having his own taste, "everyone is happy nowadays"? A world where everyone liked, or loved, the same things would be a desolate, desperate world—as devoid of pleasure and interest as the most frightful dystopia of those who believe (quite wrongly) that the popular media are inevitably producing a depressingly, disconsolately uniform world culture. Although I say this with serious discomfort, a world in which everyone liked Shakespeare, or Titian, or Bach for the same reasons—if such a world were possible—appears to me no better than a world where everyone tuned in to *Baywatch* or listened to the worst pop music at the same time. What to me is truly frightful is not the quality of what everyone agrees on, but the very fact of universal agreement. Even the idea of *two* individuals whose aesthetic judgments are absolutely identical sends shivers down my spine. In a minute I will try to suggest why.

If the Kantian view is right, then in the less than ideal situation in which we are bound to live, where no one agrees completely on aesthetic issues with anyone else, whoever attaches importance to such issues will certainly end up finding everyone else defective. No doubt everyone feels that way about some people, but I wonder if that is the right way to feel about everyone else in the world. If the idea that the judgment of taste is a genuine judgment implies that our species should be held together by bonds of mutual contempt, then something is wrong with that idea. We must reject it without falling back on the silly relativism for which aesthetic judgments express purely private preferences that we cannot ever discuss or evaluate.

Our aesthetic judgments need a middle ground on which to rest, for they are most consequential. It is not as if I go through life picking one

---

[6] See John P. Murphy, *Pragmatism from Peirce to Davidson* (Boulder, Colo.: Westview Press, 1990), p. 31.

person here, one novel there, one landscape further down and adding them to my stock of what I have judged to be beautiful. Prospective as they are, my judgments determine, literally, my life's course—they direct me to other people, other objects, other habits and ways of being. They are, as I have said, essentially social. Yet their range does not extend to humanity as a whole; if it did, the idea of a world where everyone found the same things beautiful would not be revolting. The reason it is revolting is that what we find beautiful constitutes our taste, and, as Susan Sontag once wrote, although taste "has no system and no proofs... there is something like a logic of taste: the consistent sensibility which underlies and gives rise to a certain taste."[7] Such a consistent sensibility is essential to character: It is our style. And it is central to character and style that they are part of what distinguishes us from the rest of the world, even from those who are the closest to us. *"One thing is needful,"* Friedrich Nietzsche wrote in *The Gay Science:*

> To "give style" to one's character—a great and rare art! It is practiced by those who survey all the strengths and weaknesses of their nature and then fit them into an artistic plan until every one of them appears as art and reason and even weaknesses delight the eye.... In the end, when the work is finished, it becomes evident how the constraint of a single taste governed and formed everything large and small. Whether this taste was good or bad is less important than one might suppose, if only it was a single taste![8]

The subtleties of Nietzsche's view are not important here. What matters is that I can admire you for exhibiting "a single taste," a consistent sensibility, without for that reason admiring the taste you exhibit—at least not in every respect. Who strikes me as having bad taste? Not everyone whose judgment I reject. Not everyone who shares my judgment for reasons I find unacceptable. Those, rather, whose views I cannot connect in an interesting way with the rest of their aesthetical choices. Bad taste, most often, is literally the lack of taste, haphazardness, the absence of style.

Developing a style, as Nietzsche saw, is an accomplishment. As Charles Baudelaire said of Manet, "He will never completely fill the

---

[7] Susan Sontag, "Notes on 'Camp,'" in *Against Interpretation* (New York: Dell, 1966), p. 276.

[8] Friedrich Nietzsche, *The Gay Science,* trans. Walter Kaufmann (New York: Random House, 1974), sec. 290.

gaps in his temperament. But he has *a temperament*—that's what's important."[9] For that reason, when I detect a style, even a style I don't admire, I want to come to know how its elements hang together, the character its possessor's choices manifest. Conversely, I may become reconciled to the fact that those whose style I admire differ from me on specific questions without thinking of that as a lapse, precisely because it fits with the rest of their taste. And so I understand and respect Dave Hickey's admiration for Norman Rockwell, whom I continue to find trite and banal, because Hickey discerns in his work formal complexities put in the service of a widely accessible art (like Raphael's, he would say) that celebrates Hickey's populist democratic values,[10] as I accept Michael Fried's rejection of Minimalism, which I enjoy, because it lacks the seriousness, impersonality, and "conviction" that are the hallmarks of the Modernist works to which Fried is devoted.[11] It is no mean feat to exhibit a consistent sensibility.

But it is also not enough. Consistency that is too obvious and predictable often amounts to the unity that Sontag, in the essay from which I have quoted, called "Camp,...the glorification of 'character.'...What the Camp eye appreciates is the unity, the force of the person.... What Camp taste responds to is 'instant' character...and, conversely, what it is not stirred by is the sense of the development of character. Character is understood as a state of continual incandescence—a person being one, very intense thing."[12] The camp character is so determined that every new action, every new choice, is already anticipated and always exhibits more of the same. This, though somehow suspect, need not be a fault. It is, for example, the defining feature of many movie stars. In film after film, Garbo is just Garbo, and we love her because we know exactly what to expect, because we can recognize everything we *already* knew her to be whatever new situation we find her in. She gives pleasure precisely because she is capable of remaining uncannily the same whatever drama is unfolding around her: the same faraway look combined with

[9] Charles Baudelaire, *Correspondance* (Paris: Editions de la Pléiade, 1966), vol. 2, p. 501.

[10] Dave Hickey, "The Kids Are All Right: After the Prom," in *Norman Rockwell: Pictures for the American People,* ed. Maureen Hart Hennessey and Anne Knutson (New York: Harry N. Abrams: 1999), pp. 115–30.

[11] Michael Fried, "Art and Objecthood," in *Art and Objecthood* (Chicago: University of Chicago Press, 1998), pp. 148–72.

[12] Sontag, "Notes on 'Camp,'" pp. 285–86.

the same passionate intensity, the same yielding lassitude combined with the same cold hard flame, the same (always the same) monosyllabic pelvis. Yet character, as I am thinking of it, in all its unity and consistency, can also surprise: unanticipated actions and novel dispositions can *fit in* with the old, throwing new light on them and, in that very process, changing their significance and coming to compose with them an original but still intelligible whole.

Consistency is therefore one element of an admirable style or character. Its price is uniformity—internal and self-imposed, like camp, or social and derived from others, as happens with all those who let another, either an individual or a group, dictate in one way or another what they are to appreciate and like. If camp is always on the brink of collapsing into doubtful taste, social uniformity (although it has its own uses: think of the punk style or all those men in their grey flannel suits) reveals its radical absence—whether you let Bernard Berenson, Clement Greenberg, Leo Castelli, or Martha Stewart determine your preferences for you, however happy your choices, your taste is no longer yours, but theirs. Style requires originality, and originality demands distinctiveness. It is with us as it is with the arts, and that is one reason we should be careful not to draw too stark a distinction between "art" and "the world." T. S. Eliot once wrote that one function of criticism was "to exhibit the relations of literature—not to 'life,' as something contrasted to literature, but to all the other activities, which, together with literature, are the components of life."[13] I would go a little further: Features we tend to associate only with the arts, because under the sway of Modernism (not Eliot's, this case) we have tried to draw a contrast between the arts and life, are crucial to all these other activities, which, together with the arts, are the components of life. Part of the value of the style, taste, or character for which we admire some individuals derives from their difference from other styles, tastes, and characters, just as the value of works of art depends on their ability to stand out from their surrounding context. Not that difference, which is a catch-all idea, incapable of specifying anything and unable to be a goal in its own right, produces value on its own. Value depends on specific features, which themselves differ from others in specific ways. They are the kind of features that set Jean-Baptiste Chardin apart from his contemporaries,

[13] T. S. Eliot, quoted by Wendy Lesser, *Pictures at an Execution: An Inquiry into the Subject of Murder* (Cambridge, Mass.: Harvard University Press, 1993), p. 10.

which Nicolas de Largillierre missed when he told him, "You have some
very fine paintings there. They must be by a good Flemish painter."[14]
These are the features to which Michael Baxandall has given such careful attention in *Patterns of Intention* and *Shadows and Enlightenment*,[15] the
features that allow him to see that Chardin started from "an old heroic
formula for lighting composition found in such as Guido Reni" and
"transferred [it] to domestic things and to food on tables. But he worked
on it and effectively transformed it, not least by distinguishing more
sharply between illumination and distinctness, distinctness and force of
hue, force of hue and lustre. In effect he asked what the old formula
could be seen as *representing,* and by making it represent perception he
made it something else.... [His pictures] offer the product of sustained
perception in the guise of a glance or two's sensation."[16] That is why
Chardin's painting forces you, as Jed Perl has noticed, to *see slowly.*[17]
Beauty, both in art and in the rest of life, may take a long time to see.
What you then see will be something that stands out, although its
beauty and its value are not identical with its standing out. Even though
the value that derives from standing out does not necessarily conflict
with moral virtue, it does not depend on it: it is a different kind of reason for admiration and praise, blame and contempt.

I have said that to find something beautiful is to want to make it part
of your life and of the life of those whose taste you already admire; also to
want to find others who have made it part of their own lives, in the hope
that something about it that you have not yet seen will make your life
worthwhile. I have said nothing about what makes a life worthwhile in
the sense I intend, and I must try to do so now. In the ideal case, what
you find in or through the beautiful thing and the many relationships
into which the beautiful thing leads you will be something no one has
seen before; as a result, you will turn into someone interestingly, perhaps
admirably, different from everyone else. The judgment of beauty, which
is a judgment of value, implicates you in a web of relationships with

[14] The anecdote, reported by Cochin, is repeated by Pierre Rosenberg, "Chardin: The
Unknowing Subversive?" in Pierre Rosenberg et al., *Chardin* (Paris: Editions de la Réunion
des Musées Nationaux, 2000), p. 29.

[15] Michael Baxandall, *Patterns of Intention: On the Historical Explanation of Pictures* (New
Haven: Yale University Press, 1985), ch. 3; *Shadows and Enlightenment* (New Haven: Yale
University Press, 1995).

[16] Baxandall, *Patterns of Intention,* pp. 98–99.

[17] Jed Perl, *Eyewitness: Reports from an Art World in Crisis* (New York: Basic Books, 2000),
pp. 311–30.

people and things, and leads toward individuality. It is neither completely objective nor entirely social nor purely private. It is personal.

It is also aesthetic. The aesthetic features of things are those features they share only with those objects from which they are indistinguishable.[18] This idea underlies our sense that the little patch of yellow wall in Jan Vermeer's *View of Delft* that brought the dying Bergotte, like the dying Proust himself, out of his bed to pay homage to it was not, as Proust's fictional critic had written, beautiful just by itself, "like a priceless specimen of Chinese art," but only within the context of Vermeer's work.[19] It allows me to understand why I admire Piero's *Baptism of Christ* for its geometric balance, while Rockwell's equally balanced *After the Prom* leaves me cold; why the violence of Steven Seagal films makes them distasteful while the violence—the "particular" violence—of *Oz* is one of its glories; why the endless philosophical discussions of *The Magic Mountain,* which may sound quite silly in themselves, are essential to the novel's greatness, while the discourses of *Siddhartha* make the book unreadable. It permits any feature to be aesthetic in a particular context, and every object to have aesthetic properties.

Beauty does not depend only on elegance, grace, harmony, unity, and the other isolated features that appear in the pathetic lists of our textbooks. Beauty is the object of love: Anything can provoke it, and even a streak of red paint or a blue spot on the upper right-hand corner of a painting that any "person of normal intelligence and eyesight" can perceive can turn out to be aesthetic in a particular context. You don't need taste or sophistication to become aware of the aesthetic features of things—you need taste to focus on the right ones, in the right way.

---

[18] In this, I follow Mothersill, who follows Sue Larson; see *Beauty Restored,* pp. 343–45. The issue is very complicated and needs to be discussed in detail. For example, it may be that two vases may be identical in shape but different in color: can't they share some aesthetic features in respect of their shape? There is also an issue whether being indistinguishable is a transitive relation, whether "$a$ is indistinguishable (by $A$) from $b$" and "$b$ is indistinguishable (by $A$) from $c$" imply that "$a$ is indistinguishable (by $A$) from $c$." If it does not, as Nelson Goodman, for example, argued in *The Structure of Appearance* (Cambridge, Mass.: Harvard University Press, 1951), p. 230, and also in *Languages of Art* (Indianapolis: Bobbs-Merrill, 1968), pp. 99–112, then none of the properties of $a$ can be aesthetic. If, for instance, $a$ is $F$ and we suppose that $F$ is aesthetic, then $b$ also is $F$, since $a$ and $b$ are indistinguishable. But then $c$ is also $F$, since $b$ and $c$ are indistinguishable. In that case, $F$ is not an aesthetic property of $a$, since it shares it with at least one object from which it is distinguishable. Delia Graff, however, has recently argued that the relation is transitive, and, if she is right, this particular problem can be avoided ("Phenomenal Continua and the Sorites," *Mind,* forthcoming). But the question is far from settled.

[19] Marcel Proust, *Remembrance of Things Past,* trans. C. K. Scott Montcrieff and Terence Kilmartin, 3 vols. (New York: Random House, 1981), vol. 3, p. 185.

What you do need is to examine those things for yourself, since if they share their aesthetic features at all, they share them only with what looks exactly like them. That in turn explains why the aesthetic and the perceptual are so closely connected, even though, as many have often noticed but seldom squarely faced, they are not the same: both require direct contact with their object, but for different reasons. Aesthetic awareness is perceptual only if its object is itself perceptual, which is why discussions of aesthetic properties always revolve around painting, to which perception is crucial, and are so embarrassed by literature, in which perceptual features like assonance, alliteration, and rhythm are a small part of what matters. Finally, this idea explains why interpretation must also be direct. No matter how much I tell you about a painting or a novel that has changed my life, no matter how well you learn my account, my interpretation will never be yours unless you are able to work it out directly on your own; until then you will only be accepting mine. Unlike knowledge and like understanding (also not a perceptual matter), interpretation cannot be transmitted from one person to another. Making beautiful things part of my life is not a metaphor: I must literally spend it in their presence and company. I know what I think of Walter de la Mare's *Epitaph,*

> Here lies a beautiful lady,
> Light of step and heart was she;
> I think she was the most beautiful lady
> That ever was in the West County,

but not if he was right (though I have my suspicions), nor what the beauty of his lady was like.

I do know that Manet's *Olympia* (fig. 1) is one of the world's great paintings. Art historians, I suppose, would find that to verge on the banal (although some *would* disagree, and most of the rest of the world would have no idea what I was talking about). What I said tells you nothing about the painting; it may tell you something—a little—about me. I am magnetized by the work, have looked at it long and hard, spoken about it with friends and colleagues, tried to find people who share my feelings for it and others who dispute them, and I have read about it. I have rushed to converse both with the *Olympia* and about it. I have learnt about the social structure of 1860s Paris, about the way prostitution became identified with the working classes and the effect the depiction of such a working-class woman in a classic pose had on Manet's

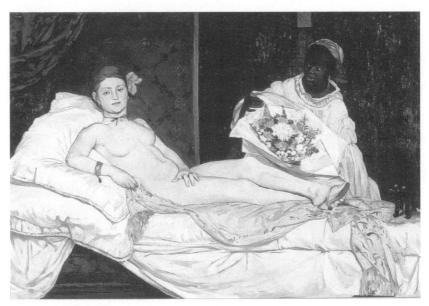

Fig. 1. Edouard Manet, *Olympia*. (Copyright Réunion des Musées Nationaux/ Art Resource, NY)

contemporaries, and about the significance of the disjointed way the body is painted:

> The achievement of *Olympia*...is that it gives its female subject a particular sexuality as opposed to a general one. And that particularity derives...not from there being *an order* to the body on the bed but from there being too many, and none of them established as the dominant one. The signs of sex are present in plenty, but they fail, as it were, to add up. Sex is not something evident and all of a piece in *Olympia;* that a woman has a sex at all—and certainly Olympia has one—does not make her immediately *one thing,* for a man to appropriate visually; her sex is a construction of some kind, or perhaps the inconsistency of several.[20]

I have also learnt about the work's sources, about the relation between Manet and what Michael Fried calls the generation of the 1860s, painters like Henri Fantin-Latour, Whistler, and Alphonse Legros, about the way Manet's works of that period face their beholder in a way that might help explain the sheer incomprehension with which contem-

---

[20] T. J. Clark, *The Painting of Modern Life: Paris in the Art of Manet and His Followers* (Princeton: Princeton University Press, 1984), ch. 2. The quotation is from p. 132.

porary critics received the work—an incomprehension I still feel when I look at the painting:

> Manet, in his struggle against absorption, found himself compelled to seek not just an alternative compositional route to intensity and strikingness, but also an alternative mode of execution, one that would be consistent with, that would somehow "project," the facingness and instantaneousness that were his main resort.... The means by which he tried to bring this about not only were powerless to enforce such a reading, they threatened, by their glaring departure from traditional norms of finish, to doom his already difficult art to total incomprehensibility.[21]

I also learnt that the figure who for Clark is simply a "Negress" or a "maid" and for Fried a "black maid" was probably based on a woman by the name of Laure,[22] who was born in Paris, to parents unnamed, on April 19, 1839, and whom Manet had sketched at least once before he put her in his painting. She is not simply "black," just as Victorine Meurend is not simply "white," not just a stock character, but an African-Caribbean-French woman, a native of the city. Dressed in a typical Parisian dress at least a size too large for her, and so either a hand-me-down or bought at a secondhand shop, she is herself, like Olympia, a working-class woman, not simply a figure of "primitive or exotic sexuality,"[23] or "inert and formulaic, a mere painted sign for Woman in one of her states."[24] *Olympia* is, then, also connected to the popular Orientalist paintings of the time, which displaced actual desire and sensuality to an imaginary Orient: The categories that painters like Jean-Léon Gérôme were projecting to this imaginary construction were present in the everyday world in which the painting's audience moved and lived. The work's

> doubled femininity...places the painting in a critical relation to Orientalist myth by making its modernity explicit both through what the painting does to locate the white woman in time, space and class relations and through its calculated and strategic revisions to

---

[21] Michael Fried, *Manet's Modernism, or the Face of Painting in the 1860s* (Chicago: University of Chicago Press, 1996). The quotation is from p. 307.

[22] Clark, *The Painting of Modern Life,* pp. 133, 138; Fried, *Manet's Modernism,* p. 318. And see the general discussion in Theodore Reff, *Manet: Olympia* (New York: Viking Press, 1977), ch. 3.

[23] Reff, *Manet: Olympia,* p. 93.

[24] Clark, *The Painting of Modern Life,* p. 133.

the trope of the African woman—now also signalled as a figure located in time, space and class relations, that is in the history of the
present, as another Parisian proletarian.[25]

All that, of course, forced me to turn to other paintings, contemporary with, earlier than, and later than the *Olympia.* I had to learn more
about Manet himself, his sources, the work of his contemporaries, art
criticism in mid-nineteenth-century Paris, the Orientalist tradition in
painting, the history of the nude. Each of these projects in turn sent me
to still other works, which I then discussed with people or read about.
Of course, I looked at the obvious works the critics discuss—Titian's
*Venus of Urbino,* Francisco de Goya's *Naked Maja,* Jean Ingres's *Venus
Anadyomene* and *Large Odalisque,* Diego Velázquez's *Venus with a Mirror*
(which, I found out, was once hanging not demurely on the walls of the
National Gallery, but salaciously from the ceiling over its owner's bed,
for reasons both obvious and disturbing to a naive aesthete like me),
Robert Morris's performance piece *Site,* Mel Ramos's *Manet's Olympia,*
and scores of others. And I also saw, for myself, that Manet is playing
havoc with François Boucher's portrait of his wife (fig. 2). Madame
Boucher, of course, is dressed, lying on her proper *chaise-longue,* coyly
glancing away, surrounded by symbols of domesticity—books, letters,
sewing materials, bibelots—while Olympia lies naked on a messy bed
that has no place in a bourgeois home, gazing, somehow, at the beholder. Yet, apart from their right arm,[26] their poses are strikingly similar. Both women lift themselves from the plush pillows behind them;
each has her left hand between her legs—although Madame Boucher's
gesture, of course, is not a dare to the spectator; their slippers are alike,
and in both cases one is dangling slightly. The naked Olympia seems to
have kept the bracelet and neck ribbon of the dressed Madame Boucher,
while the bow on Madame's headdress has turned into an orchid—a
transformation that did in fact not prove easy to recognize: Olympia's
flower has often been interpreted as a bow.[27] The flower draws the eye to
the left, where her hair, pulled back in front, frames her forehead in a

[25] Griselda Pollock, "A Tale of Three Women," in her *Differencing the Canon: Feminist
Desire and the Writing of Art's Histories* (London: Routledge, 1999), pp. 247–317. The quotation is from p. 294.

[26] Manet had experimented with that position in a number of preliminary sketches for
*Olympia* and in other works; see Reff, *Manet: Olympia,* pp. 67–74.

[27] See ibid., p. 108.

Fig. 2. François Boucher, *Madame Boucher.* (Copyright The Frick Collection, New York)

stern curve recalling the shape of Madame Boucher's neat cap. Madame Boucher's hair, naturally, is thoroughly tucked in under her cap, while the rest of Victorine's red-brown hair floats like a cloud—extremely difficult to see and, once seen, to keep in sight[28]—over her left shoulder. And just as Victorine's hair hovers in and out of sight as we look at the

[28] It may actually have been missed by many in the work's early audiences (as it still is by many casual observers today). The many contemporary caricatures of the *Olympia* leave it out altogether. Clark, *The Painting of Modern Life,* p. 137, suggests that this was because the flowing hair, once you see it, changes the overall effect: "[T]his body has abundance after all; it has a familiar sex." Though seeing Victorine's hair does make a serious difference, I am not sure it has quite that effect. If anything, it complicates the already complex and inconsistent information the painting provides about its subject: the face is still sternly framed by the pulled-back hair, but an *additional* softness is added to Victorine. Clark writes that it is difficult to make it "part of the face it belongs to." Face and hair are incompatible." My own reaction is that it is Victorine's hair itself that does not add up to one thing—not just the hair and her face. It is important to note that Henri Fantin-Latour (1883), Paul Gauguin (1889), and Pablo Picasso (1901) all omitted that shock of frizzy hair from their sketches or caricatures of the work (in contrast to Paul Cézanne's version of 1875–77 and Gauguin's full copy of 1890–91).

*Olympia,* so Olympia hovers in and out of sight as we look at *Madame Boucher.* Manet kept the screen and drapery of Boucher's painting, but transposed them from right to left, as in a mirror image. When we look at the luminous, respectable Madame Boucher, what we see, through a glass, darkly, is the questionable shadow of Olympia.

I still feel the magic of that painting, which attracts me with the promise of a secret it is still keeping back. I am focused now on Olympia's eyes. Michael Fried writes that Victorine Meurend confronts the viewer directly,[29] but that can't be right, for I cannot lock eyes with her. Her look, which is as direct as it is vague, as confrontational as it is yielding, as arrogant as it is tender, acknowledges me precisely as it ignores me. If she is smiling, is she indicating surrender, defiance, resignation, or indifference? Does she look affectionate, professional, jaded, or sad? Is she looking at me or somewhere over my left shoulder? That is not the look of the traditional nude.[30] It directs me to something else altogether; perhaps blasphemously, Victorine Meurend's regard reminds me of eyes I have sometimes seen in Byzantine and post-Byzantine icons, particularly of the Virgin Mary, like the anonymous Athonite *Galaktotrophousa* or its contemporary *Virgin Paraklesis* painted in 1783 by Michael of Thessaloniki.

My attraction to the *Olympia* has literally changed the shape of my life. Its beauty has in no way removed me from the everyday, as Schopenhauer might have thought, unless we take that to mean that it created a different everyday than I would have faced without it. It has directed me to paintings and literary works that I would have paid no attention to or that I would have understood quite differently if I did not have Manet in mind. It has led me to people I would not have known otherwise, per-

[29] Fried, *Manet's Modernism,* p. 469n26.

[30] I believe Clark, *The Painting of Modern Life,* pp. 132–33, has something similar in mind when he contrasts Olympia's look to the look of *Venus Anadyomene* or the *Venus of Urbino* and describes it as "blatant and particular, but also...unreadable, perhaps deliberately so...candid but guarded, poised between address and resistance." By contrast, he finds that Laure, whom as we have seen he does not consider an individual character, expresses simple compliance. But, once alerted to the particularity of Laure and its implications for the interpretation of the work, we can begin to see that her look, too, is complex and elusive. There is no simple compliance there. Is she looking at Victorine with a trace of contempt, as she offers the flowers to her? Or is there a hint of pity in her eyes? If she is smiling, does her smile (as faint and enigmatic as Victorine's own) indicate pride in the small triumph that the extravagant bouquet represents? Or is it a sign of uncertainty, the quizzical expression on the face of someone who doesn't yet know how Victorine is likely to react? Laure, once we begin to see her as a concrete individual, becomes pictorially as well as ideologically complex.

sonally or through their writing. I am reasonably sure that none of these friends, colleagues, and authors has been bad for me. I am not as sure about the works to which my fascination with the *Olympia* has steered me: I don't know whether the motives that led me to the vast numbers of female nudes I have looked at or the pleasures I have received from them are altogether innocent. I really don't know exactly how they have affected me, whether, from a currently relevant moral point of view, they have caused me benefit or harm. Not that after a half hour with the *Rokeby Venus* in the National Gallery I came home with a keener appreciation for pornographic pictures of women's naked bodies. Culture, as Plato was the first to notice, works in subtler ways, gradually and imperceptibly.[31] He never thought that a performance of Euripides' *Medea* would cause its audience to go home and strangle their children (although some have thought that he did). He was worried whether his citizens were over the long run being "brought up on images of evil, as if in a meadow of bad grass, where they crop and graze in many different places every day until, little by little, they unwittingly accumulate a large evil in their soul."[32] I don't know, and I may possibly never learn, whether my love of the *Olympia* has led me to such a meadow of bad grass.

What I do know, and what I hope my discussion has intimated, is that the further I go into the *Olympia* itself, the more I need to know about ever more other things. By inducing us to look for the aesthetic features of things, the sense of beauty attracts us to what is most distinctive and individual in the objects we love. To capture a beautiful thing in its particularity we must see how it differs from others, and to do that we must come to know, as exactly as we can, what those things are, and how each one of them in turn differs from the rest of the world. Loving something is inseparable from wanting to know and understand it. We cannot love what we are not absorbed in, but the contrary of absorption is not always theatricality. Far from closing us off from the rest of the world, absorption often leads further into it. As always, Plato was there first: the *Symposium* and the *Phaedrus* give voice to his vision of beauty's power to draw its lover further along. A metaphysical picture may have led him to think that beauty ultimately leads to a world of its own, but

---

[31] See M. F. Burnyeat, "Culture and Society in Plato's *Republic,*" Tanner Lectures, Harvard 1997.

[32] Plato, *Republic,* translated by G. M. A. Grube and C. D. C. Reeve (Indianapolis: Hackett Publishing Company, 1993), 401c.

his vision doesn't require that picture: "What happens when there is no immortal realm behind the beautiful person or thing is just what happens when there *is* an immortal realm behind the beautiful person or thing: the perceiver is led to a more capacious regard for the world."[33] We understand things better not when we delve into their depths, in mutual isolation, but when we see how they are like and unlike every thing that surrounds them—and that, in the end, is everything.

We often think interpretation discounts an object's appearance and uncovers the real meaning hidden behind it. That image, once forcefully expressed by Susan Sontag, led her to reject interpretation altogether: "Interpretation says, Look, don't you see that X is really—or, really means—A?…Interpretation…presupposes a discrepancy between the clear meaning of the text and the demands of (later) readers…. The manifest content must be probed and pushed aside to find the true meaning—the latent content—beneath."[34] Interpretation, she argued, "is the revenge of the intellect upon art," even "upon the world,"[35] based on "an overt contempt for appearances."[36] "In place of a hermeneutics," it was her famous conclusion, "we need an erotics of art."[37]

But hermeneutics and erotics, as Plato knew, do not exclude each other; that's why Socrates was the great erotic. Love and interpretation cannot be separated. We want to interpret the object of our love, and we want to be interpreted, and affected, by it. That is to place the beautiful object in as broad a context as possible in order to see how it differs from everything else, how it accomplishes something—if it does—that nothing else accomplishes. Interpretation does not proceed from how something merely seems to what it really is but, rather, from how it seems or is (the difference now hardly matters) at first to how it seems or is when we have come to know it better. And to know it better is to know how it is similar to and different from all the things to which we can connect it. Since these are indefinitely many, interpretation, like our sense of beauty itself, is in principle inexhaustible.

[33] Elaine Scarry, *On Beauty and Being Just* (Princeton: Princeton University Press, 1999), pp. 47–48. Scarry, I think, believes that when I perceive the beauty of one thing, I become open to the beauty of others. That is true. What is also true, and what I am trying to say here, is that to perceive the beauty of one thing, which is in most cases not a one-time affair but a longer story, sometimes even an affair of a lifetime, is *identical* with perceiving the beauty of others.

[34] Susan Sontag, "Against Interpretation," in *Against Interpretation,* pp. 5–7.

[35] Ibid., p. 7.

[36] Ibid., p. 5.

[37] Ibid., p. 14.

That is, I believe, what Proust's narrator finally recognizes, despite his talk of uncovering the meaning and essence of things through the part of himself that exists outside time—that part to which, sitting in the library of the Guermantes, he attributes the happiness he had once felt while tasting a madeleine dipped in tea and finding himself transported to his childhood in Combray or when, on his way to the Guermantes', he stepped on two uneven paving stones that unaccountably brought him back to Venice.[38] For, having finally decided to begin working on his book, during his long reflection on its nature, he comes to see "that it would be impossible to depict our relationship with anyone whom we have even slightly known without passing in review, one after another, the most different settings of our life." Nothing is what it is independently of anything else; no moment, person, or thing has a meaning in and of itself:

> Life is perpetually weaving fresh threads which link one individual and one event to another, and…these threads are crossed and recrossed, doubled and redoubled, to thicken the web, so that between any slightest point of our past and all the others a rich network of memories gives us an almost infinite variety of communicating paths to choose from.

Marcel modifies his earlier thoughts on timeless objects that carry their meaning in themselves. His story will be a story of time, in time. And his awareness that, to take account of these communicating paths, the story of his life will have

> to use not the two-dimensional psychology which we normally use but a quite different sort of three-dimensional psychology added a new beauty to those resurrections of the past which my memory had effected while I was following my thoughts alone in the library, since memory by itself, when it introduces the past, unmodified, into the present—the past just as it was at the moment when it was itself the present—suppresses the mighty dimension of Time which is the dimension in which life is lived.[39]

---

[38] Proust, *Remembrance of Things Past,* vol. 3, pp. 900–904.

[39] Ibid., vol. 3, pp. 1086, 1087. I have discussed that idea in more detail, again in connection with Proust, in "Writer, Text, Work, Author," in *Literature and the Question of Philosophy,* ed. Anthony J. Cascardi (Baltimore: John Hopkins University Press, 1987), pp. 267–91; Richard Rorty has recently given his own version of it in "Being That Can Be Understood Is Language," *London Review of Books,* March 16, 2000, pp. 23–25.

If interpretation is interminable and if we can never know to what and to whom it will lead us, how the search for beauty will affect our moral character remains always unpredictable. Many people believe that attention to the arts is important because it is morally beneficial. For Richard Rorty, Vladimir Nabokov and George Orwell are valuable because they make us more aware, and less tolerant, of the ways in which we are cruel to one another. Interpreting a particular image in Nabokov's *Pale Fire,* Rorty writes: "That poor lame boy trying to get his spastic brother out of the range of the stones hurled by schoolchildren will remain a familiar sight in all countries, but a slightly less frequent one in countries where people read novels."[40] That is a view I wish I could share, but I can find no reason for it. For Elaine Scarry, beautiful things promote our sense of justice.[41] I can't see that: not that they can't, but that they simply don't have to. The ancient Athenians adored beauty, practiced democracy, and were vicious to friend and foe alike. Again and again, history has smashed to pieces Plato's idea that to love the beautiful is to desire the good ("Good speech…good accord, good shape and good rhythm follow upon goodness of character").[42] Beautiful villains, graceful outlaws, tasteful criminals, and elegant torturers are everywhere about us. Salome, Scarpia, and Satan do not exist only in fiction. And neither, of course, does Quasimodo.

Perhaps, one might say, the moral dangers of the arts are small, whatever their benefits. But let me confess that when my eyes get tired of trying to catch Olympia's elusive gaze, they often turn to the vicious, violent world of *Oz*—not simply to relax or "just" for entertainment, but for the serious pleasures in it. How do I know these pleasures are serious? Well, I have watched a lot of television, I have written a little about it, I talk to people who also watch it a lot, and I read those who write about it. Am I wasting my time and ruining my character or are you missing something that could add to your life? The questions now sound more urgent. The dangers of the popular arts seem greater, aesthetically and morally, since the jury, so to speak, is still out and they don't yet have a place within the higher halls of culture. It is less risky to take it for granted that they lead to degradation: we can then wait safely until they are either admitted into those halls or left to disappear. That

[40] "Introduction" to Vladimir Nabokov's *Pale Fire* (New York: Everyman's Library, 1992), p. xvii.

[41] Scarry, *On Beauty and Being Just,* ch. 2.

[42] *Republic* 400d–e.

assumption has a long history. It goes, once again, back to Plato, who used it against tragedy—not to play it safe, of course, but actually to make it disappear. He failed, as we can see by the fact that it is Greek tragedy (along with Plato himself—how he would have hated that!) to which we now appeal in order to denounce the popular media. Plato's assumption has always been with us, for the very same reason that popular art has always been and will continue to be with us. Henry Prynne excoriated Shakespeare by appealing to the Bible, Samuel Taylor Coleridge appealed to Shakespeare in order to show that the novel destroys the mind, and a German tract of 1796 condemned reading itself in the most uncanny anticipation of the language and imagery of today's attacks against mass culture, television, or popular music:

> Readers of books…rise and retire to bed with a book in their hand, sit down at table with one, have one lying close by when working, carry one around with them when walking, and who, once they have begun reading a book are unable to stop until they are finished. But they have scarcely finished the last page of a book before they begin looking around greedily for somewhere to acquire another one; and when they are at the toilet or at their desk or some other place, if they happen to come across something that fits with their own subject or seems to them to be readable, they take it away and devour it with a kind of ravenous hunger. No lover of tobacco or coffee, no wine drinker or lover of games, can be as addicted to their pipe, bottle, games or coffee-table as those many hungry readers are to their reading habit.[43]

None of this is to say that watching television is bound to be morally benign. Works of art—and some works of television are works of art—have often had significant moral and political effects—some for good (one thinks of Charles Dickens, perhaps of Goya), some for bad (here all today are likely to think of *Triumph of the Will;* some, of Richard Wagner; others, perhaps, of the nude), and most in ways that are deeply debatable (what should we say of Virgil's championing of Augustus? of Caravaggio's advertising for the Counter-Reformation? of Jacques-Louis David's glorification of revolution and empire?). The judgment of taste, even at its most specific, implicates a vast number of other works and a large variety of other people: it commits you to nothing less than

[43] Quoted in Guglielmo Cavallo and Roger Chartier, eds., *A History of Reading in the West,* trans. Lydia G. Cochrane (Amherst: University of Massachusetts Press, 1999), p. 285.

a whole mode of life. What that life will bring is impossible to predict: you can't know in advance the sort of person it will make you. You can't even know for sure that what you will eventually find is something you will consider to have been worth your while. Perhaps you will feel about the work you once loved as Swann came to feel about Odette after all the time he devoted to her: "To think that I have wasted years of my life, that I've longed to die, that I've experienced my greatest love, for a woman who didn't appeal to me, who wasn't even my type!"[44] Perhaps—that might be worse—the beautiful thing or person you loved may have actually led you to a degraded life, which, degraded as you have become, you can no longer recognize for what it is.

Beauty, Stendhal said, is a promise of happiness. To take that seriously, as I do, is to be willing to live with ineradicable uncertainty. Nothing can match the elated conviction that comes at the moment a new beauty enters our life; what's to come is still unsure. I know, now, that I want what beauty promises, but not what it is, whether I'll get it, or what will become of me if I do. Beauty and certainty, Nietzsche saw, are in conflict:

> One day the wanderer slammed a door behind himself, stopped in his tracks, and wept. Then he said: "This penchant and passion for what is true, real, non-apparent, certain—how it aggravates me! Why does this gloomy and restless fellow keep following and driving *me?* I want to rest, but he will not allow it. How much there is that seduces me to tarry! Everywhere Armida's gardens beckon me; everywhere I must keep tearing my heart away and experience new bitternesses. I must raise my feet again and again, weary and wounded though they be; and because I must go on, I often look back in wrath at the most beautiful things that could not hold me— *because* they could not hold me."[45]

Uncertainty is essential to life, suffusing it so completely that we are no longer aware of it. Beauty is its visible image, a call to look more attentively at ourselves and the world and, so, to see how little we see.

Why, then, tarry in Armida's gardens? Why, if seeing better need not reveal better things? Why pursue beauty if it can lead to harm? Because, perhaps, in finding it we may produce it ourselves. Nietzsche, again: "I want to learn more and more to see as beautiful what is necessary in

[44] Proust, *Remembrance of Things Past,* vol. 1, p. 415.

[45] *The Gay Science,* p. 309.

things; then I shall be one of those who make things beautiful."[46] But making beautiful things is a way of being beautiful—and that is reason enough. For beauty is valuable, although its value is always in question—perhaps precisely because its value, like the value of life, is always in question.[47]

Beautiful things are not produced only by great artists. Sometimes they don't even have to be particular artifacts. They can be the aesthetical choices through which we manifest our character and style—the range of things we find beautiful and what we find beautiful about them. In the end, the justification of all aesthetic action depends on whether it manages to constitute a whole that is coherent enough to stand as an object in its own right and different enough from others in a way that provokes admiration and interest; then others will be attracted to us not only for the things to which we give them access, but for our own sake as well. Our style will be itself a thing of beauty. Proust wrote that

> style for the writer, no less than colour for the painter, is a question not of technique but of vision: it is the revelation, which by direct and conscious means would be impossible, of the qualitative difference, the uniqueness of the fashion in which the world appears to each one of us, a difference which, if there were no art, would remain the secret of every individual.[48]

[46] Ibid., p. 276.

[47] Elaine Scarry has pointed out that although one can pursue goodness, justice, or truth in the hope of becoming good, just, or knowledgeable, "it does not appear to be the case that one who pursues beauty becomes beautiful. It may even be accurate to suppose that most people who pursue beauty have no interest in becoming themselves beautiful." She argues that producing beauty is not enough of a parallel because those who pursue goodness want two distinct things: to produce greater goodness *and* to become themselves good (*On Beauty and Being Just,* pp. 87–88). But I am not sure that these are really distinct. One can, of course, do good for all sorts of base motives, but that doesn't qualify as pursuing goodness, and no one can be good without doing good: to be good is just to do good for the right reasons. Scarry also argues, on her way to claiming that beauty ultimately leads to justice, that one might think that people who pursue beauty "become beautiful in their interior lives" but rejects the idea because of the essential connection between beauty and external appearance (pp. 88–89). Here, I believe, the distinction between external appearance and interior life is too stark. Not everyone who looks at beautiful things, of course, is capable of producing them as well (just as not everyone who pursues justice or goodness succeeds at becoming just or good—"knowledgeable," by the way, does not seem to me parallel). But those who do thereby acquire the unity of style or character that, I am arguing, constitutes a way of being beautiful that transcends that stark distinction. Not every thing or person I find beautiful is *good-looking:* Most people, in fact, are found beautiful by someone or other in the course of their lives, and most are certainly not good-looking; good looks are the last thing one would associate with Francis Bacon's tortured paintings and "external" beauty is not an obvious feature of Arnold Schoenberg's compositions.

[48] Proust, *Remembrance of Things Past,* vol. 3, pp. 931–32.

I can see such a difference revealed not only in artists, but also in critics I read and people I know. I think I can see it in everything and everyone I find beautiful. It is what makes me find them beautiful, what draws me to them with the promise that it is a difference worth making part of the fashion in which the world appears to me.

Our world is a world of art. Beauty, which has a place in both, makes life and art continuous. Some people are admirable, despite their moral defects, because their achievements display the power, the originality, and the distinctiveness—the beauty—that are essential to great works of art. As long as we discern a single taste, we detect something of value, whatever other defects it may reveal, however questionable its contents. The great enemy of the beautiful is not the ugly, which at least engages and provokes and may for that reason eventually reveal an unexpected beauty, but the indifferent, the common, the nondescript, what we are not able even to notice. Although, of course, others might do so some day, and in that way redeem both what we ignored and themselves.

Individuality and distinctiveness, the demonstration that more is possible than we had imagined before, are values not only of art but of life. But individuality and distinctiveness presuppose coherence and unity: without them, nothing can stand on its own as an object either of admiration or of contempt. If those are discernible in my aesthetical choices, in what I have found beautiful, in what I have in turn found of beauty in it, in the various groups to which my choices have led me, in what I received from them and what I in turn had to give them—if my choices both fit with one another and also stand out from the rest, then I have managed to put things together in my own manner and form. I have established, through the things I have loved, a new way of looking at the world and left it richer than I first found it.

In "The Soul of Man under Socialism," Wilde wrote:

> A man is called selfish if he lives in the manner that seems to him most suitable for the full realization of his own personality; if, in fact, the primary aim of his life is self-development. But this is the way in which everyone should live. *Selfishness is not living as one wishes to live, it is asking others to live as one wishes to live.* And unselfishness is letting other people's lives alone, not interfering with them. Selfishness always aims at creating around it an absolute uniformity of type. Unselfishness recognizes infinite variety of type as a delightful thing, accepts it, acquiesces in it, enjoys it.[49]

[49] *The Works of Oscar Wilde,* ed. and with an introduction by G. F. Maine (London: Collins, 1948), p. 1040.

There is a dimension of life of which this is true, and we must finally admit its importance—we cannot continue to keep our eyes closed to the central role of aesthetic features in our interactions with one another. I doubt that the primary aim of life is self-development, since I doubt that life has a primary aim. And for that reason I also doubt there is an "infinite variety of type." There are in fact many types, as there are many tastes. That no single type is best of all doesn't mean that every type is as good as another. But, in the end, the question is not how to rank these types but what to make of them, how to appreciate them, understand them, and use them to create a type, a taste, that is, if we are able and lucky, truly our own. The passion for ranking and judging, the fervor for verdicts, which has for so long dominated our attitude toward the arts, and our lives, is simply another manifestation of selfishness.

# The State and the Shaping of Identity

*KWAME ANTHONY APPIAH*

THE TANNER LECTURES ON HUMAN VALUES

Delivered at

Clare Hall, Cambridge
April 30 and May 1, 2001

KWAME ANTHONY APPIAH is professor of Afro-American studies and philosophy at Harvard University, where he is also director of undergraduate studies. He was educated at Clare College and received his Ph.D. in philosophy from Cambridge University. He is a member of the African Literature Association, the American Philosophical Association, the Aristotelian Society, and the Modern Language Association, and has been president of the Society for African Philosophy in North America and chair of the Joint Committee on African Studies of the Social Science Research Council and the American Council of Learned Societies. His numerous publications include *For Truth in Semantics* (1986); *Necessary Questions: An Introduction to Philosophy* (1989); *In My Father's House* (1992), which won the Annisfield-Wolf Book Award and the Herskovits Award; and *Color Conscious: The Political Morality of Race* (1996, with Amy Gutmann), which won the Annual Book Award of the North American Society for Social Philosophy and the Ralph J. Bunche Award of the American Political Science Association. He is co-editor, with Henry Louis Gates Jr., of *The Dictionary of Global Culture* (1996) and they are also co-editing the *Perseus Africana Encyclopedia.* He has published a series of mystery novels, of which the most recent is *Another Death in Venice* (1995). He is preparing, with his mother Peggy Appiah as the major author, *Bu Me Bé: Proverbs of the Akan,* an annotated edition of 7,500 proverbs in Twi, the language of Asante in his home country of Ghana.

# I. INDIVIDUALITY AND IDENTITY

In contemporary philosophical discussion in the English-speaking world, there is a broad consensus on the outlines and the history of a liberal political tradition. It is conventional, for example (as, of course, you all know) to suppose that this liberal tradition owes much to John Locke's conception of religious toleration *and* his theory of property; that the language of human equality and human rights, which was developed in the French and American revolutions, is central to the heritage; that liberals care about individuality, in ways well articulated by John Stuart Mill in *On Liberty;* that it is natural for a liberal to speak of human dignity and to suppose that it is (*ceteris,* no doubt, as usual, *paribus*) equally a possession of each human being. We may have learned to think of these core elements of the liberal tradition as contested: so that, to put it crudely, liberals are not people who *agree* about the meaning of dignity, liberty, equality, individuality, toleration, and the rest; rather they are people who *argue* about their significance for political life. We may have learned, that is, that the liberal tradition—like all traditions—is not so much a body of doctrine as a set of debates. Still, it is widely agreed that there *is* a tradition that has debates about these topics at its core.

It is an important question whether we can, in fact, identify traditions of thought that include these elements; and this is, of course, a question that would require serious historical inquiry. My own suspicion is that if you began such an inquiry, the intellectual antecedents of the politics of Mill or L. T. Hobhouse or Isaiah Berlin or John Rawls would turn out to be more multifarious than singular, and that what we now call the liberal tradition would look less like a body of ideas that

One attractive feature of the issues I shall be discussing in these lectures is that almost everyone one meets is interested in them, and almost everything one reads provides material for thinking about them. So I am sure I cannot recall all my intellectual debts here—and, since I do not think of intellectual life as a matter of the creation of property, I am happy that other people's ideas have become integrated with my own. The most substantial debts of which I am aware are to the thought of Charles Taylor and Ronnie Dworkin and to the students in the many classes I have taught on race and identity at Harvard over the last decade. I am also very grateful to those at Cambridge University who invited me to give these Tanner Lectures, even if they have faced me with the terrifying prospect of lecturing at my alma mater for the first time since I ceased to be a student here.

developed through time and more like a collection of sources and interpretations of sources that we now find useful, looking backward, in ar-
ticulating one influential philosophical view of politics. Yet another
instance, so to speak, of the Owl of Minerva's taking wing as the light
fades. One reason—a shallow one, perhaps, but it has impressed me—
one reason for thinking that liberalism is a creation of hindsight is that
the word "liberalism," as the name for a political faith, occurs, so I am
told, nowhere in the writings of Locke or the American Founders, in
whose absence our current story of liberalism's history would be sorely
depleted.

But I am not—as may become, I fear, increasingly evident—a historian. And my interest in these lectures is not a historical one. Rather, I
shall be preoccupied with a set of problems that arise for those of us who
find ourselves broadly convinced that certain values, now associated by
anglophobe philosophers with the word "liberal," are important to ethical life in general, and to political life more particularly. But in order to
explain how these problems arise, it will help, first, to offer an account
of liberalism's core. And now you will understand why I began with a
preemptive expression of skepticism about the idea of *a* liberal tradition. I grant, of course, the interest of the question how well the position
I am going to characterize recognizably reflects a broad consensus of *soi-
disant* liberal thinking; but I think the problems I want to discuss are of
interest and importance, whether or not "liberalism" is the right name
for the project within which they arise. Indeed I hope to be able to persuade you that, though the problems I am talking about arose for me in
thinking about certain questions for the liberal political tradition, they
are important even if, *mirabile dictu,* you do not find yourself disposed to
think of yourself as a liberal at all.

Here, then, is a sketch of the position within which the problems I want
to talk about arise.

Each of us has one life to live. While there are many moral constraints on how we live our lives—constraints that derive from our
obligations to other persons prominent among them—these constraints
do not determine which particular life we must live. We must not live
lives of cruelty and dishonesty, for example, but there are many lives we
can live without these vices. There are also constraints on how we may
live that derive from our historical circumstances and our physical and
mental endowments: I was born into the wrong family to be a Yoruba

chief and with the wrong body for motherhood; I am too short to be a successful professional basketball player, too unmusical to be a concert pianist, and I do not have the mathematical aptitude required to make serious contributions to string theory. Nevertheless, adding these social and biological constraints to the moral ones still leaves me with many degrees of freedom in making a life. And so, once the constraints are acknowledged, each human life starts out with many possibilities. Some people have a wider and more interesting range of options than others. I once had a conversation with the late Nobel laureate Jacques Monod— one of the founding fathers of molecular biology—who told me he had had to choose, at a certain point in his life, between being (as I recall) a concert cellist, a philosopher, and a scientist.[1] So there were various lives the young Monsieur Monod could have led, each of them a life of interest and value, and he made his choices among them. But everybody has—or, at least, should have—a variety of decisions to make in shaping a life.

I assume that, so far, no one here, liberal or illiberal, will disagree. But that is in part because of a number of important changes in the climate of moral philosophy since the days when I studied it here, nearly thirty years ago.

First, we have developed a more capacious sense of the range of ethical concerns. It is a reflection of this more capacious understanding that we have a use now for a distinction between ethics and morals, of the sort that Ronald Dworkin identifies when he says: "Ethics, as I use the term, includes convictions about which kinds of lives are good or bad for a person to lead, and morality includes principles about how a person should treat other people."[2] I shall myself draw on this distinction regularly, though I shall not consistently use Dworkin's verbal convention to mark it.[3] But the diffusion of the understanding that there is a philosophical debate to be had about what lives we should lead, a discussion that must go beyond the question how we should treat others and that defines a well-lived life as something more than a life in which our preferences are

[1] See "Conversation in the Fog at London Airport, with Jacques Monod, Anthony Appiah & Mark Fitzgeorge-Parker," *Theoria to Theory* 9, no. 2 (1975).

[2] Ronald Dworkin, *Sovereign Virtue* (Cambridge, Mass.: Harvard University Press, 2000), p. 485n1.

[3] Bernard Williams, in particular, has argued that there are ethical norms, central to the ways in which we construct our lives, that do not belong to the universalizing institution of morality; see Bernard Williams, *Ethics and the Limits of Philosophy* (Cambridge: Harvard University Press, 1985).

well satisfied, has significantly extended the scope of philosophical reflection.

Second, we have come to recognize a wider range of the distinctively moral virtues than impartial benevolence. There are arguments for partiality all over the place now: to family, lovers, friends, fellow citizens and nationals, and, of course, to ourselves: so much for impartiality. But what we owe to others is not easily limited to wishing them well: so much for benevolence.

Third, there has been a fairly forceful flurry of attacks on the utilitarian assumption (an assumption shared, of course, whether explicitly or implicitly, with some other moral theories) that morality works in a single currency, that all values are commensurable. And fourth, many moral philosophers have come to believe—under the influence of Isaiah Berlin, among others—that there is an incompatibility between some virtues that makes it impossible to conduct a life in which all of them are given their full due. Wisdom and courage may be the virtues of generals: it is difficult to see how, in their profession, impartial benevolence can be given full rein. And there is, some now hold, no further, more fundamental currency of value that we may use to adjudicate among wisdom, courage, and benevolence; and so there is no way to determine whether a life that balances them as the general must is better or worse than a life that balances them after the manner of a bishop.[4]

These issues are important. But I put them aside for now, because the point I want to insist on is one that can be accepted for any and all of these reasons. It is this: unless you think that there is a single best life for each of us (given the historical contingencies that shape our options) you will have to hold that there are choices to be made about how each life is to be given its determinate shape. And for a person of a liberal disposition these choices belong, in the end, to the person whose life it is.

This means, I think, at least two things. First, the value of my life, the standard by which it is to be assessed as objectively more or less successful, depends, in good measure, on my life's aims as specified by me. Second, for a person of a liberal disposition, my life's shape is up to me, even if I make a life that is objectively less good than a life I could have

---

[4] Every one of these three lines of thought, by the way, is consistent with holding that there are objective and determinate answers to a vast range of moral questions and that when there is no determinate answer it is an objective fact that this is so. These new views do not represent the growth of relativism.

made, provided that I have done my duty toward others. All of us could, no doubt, have made better lives than we have: but that, the liberal says, is no reason for others to attempt to force those better lives upon us. True, morality and affection demand a concern for the ethical achievements of others. So thoughtful friends, benevolent sages, anxious relatives will rightly offer us both assistance and advice as to how to proceed. But it will *be* advice, not coercion, that they justly offer. And because coercion will be wrong in these circumstances, it will be wrong when it is undertaken by governments interested in the perfection of their citizens as well. That is what it means to say that—once I have done my duties—the shaping of my life is up to me.

What my duties to others are is, as a result, one of the central questions for liberalism. Making a life as a social being requires making commitments to others. If these are voluntary, it may be proper to enforce them even against my (later) will. But how much does what I owe go beyond my voluntary undertakings? One of Mill's suggestions was, roughly, that what we owed to others, in addition to what we had committed ourselves to, was that we should not harm them; and that leads to interesting discussions about what counts as harm.[5] But if we grant that the mere fact that I do something you do not want me to do does not *eo ipso* count as my harming you, then the view that I should be permitted (in particular, by the state) to make whatever life flows from my choices, provided that I give you what I owe you and do you no harm, seems still to leave me a wide range of freedom. Which, given the centrality of liberty to liberalism, is what you would expect.

In recent years, a new set of issues has arisen for liberalism from a recognition of the fact that the tools with which we make our lives include many socially provided resources: among them, most obviously, language, and other private and public institutions. But there are also what we now call *identities*: genders and sexual orientations, ethnicities and nationalities, professions and vocations. Identities are ethically central, in ways I shall be exploring throughout these lectures, because they are among the most important elements we use in making our lives. For we make our lives *as* men and *as* women, *as* gay and *as* straight people, *as* Englishmen and Englishwomen and *as* Americans, *as* black and *as* white. Mill wrote in *On Liberty* of expressing one's individuality through a "plan

⁵ These issues are extensively discussed in Joel Feinberg's *Harm to Others* (New York: Oxford University Press, 1984).

of life," an idea that is central, too, to Rawls's more recent formulation of liberalism.[6] And, as we shall see, a plan of life is centrally shaped by our identities.[7]

Some people have argued that state acknowledgment of such identities is intrinsically illiberal: precisely because the shaping of my life is up to me, the government should treat me simply as a citizen and should seek to constrain my acts independently of my identities, requiring me only to do my duty to others and avoid harm. Otherwise the state will be in the business of advantaging and disadvantaging particular identities in ways that constrain the individual's freedom to shape his or her own life.

Other, so-called multicultural liberals have argued, to the contrary, that the state *must* recognize these identities because without them individuals will lack some of the essential publicly sustained resources for making a life. A human life is made, in part, by the constitution of an individual identity: and these social identities are among the tools that all of us use in that self-constitution. To the extent that social identities allow people options for making their lives, they are positive resources in that process. And their recognition by the state is part of what makes them available for this purpose. (Because it is sometimes useful to be able to distinguish the individual identity one constructs from these collective identities, I shall sometimes call it one's *individuality*.)

In this dispute, I initially found myself occupying an intermediate position: I thought—contra some anti-multicultural liberals—that the

---

[6] John Stuart Mill, *On Liberty* (Amherst, N.Y.: Prometheus Books, 1986), p. 67; John Rawls, *Political Liberalism* (New York: Columbia University Press, 1993).

[7] Talk of "plans" here can be misleading, because it suggests a life sketched out in advance, a life not only without spontaneity but also insensitive to new knowledge or to changing circumstances. But, of course, what Mill meant by a plan of life doesn't map out your biography in advance. It is not like the plans of those ambitious young women in sex-and-shopping novels, who want to have a husband with a fortune by the time they are thirty. A plan of life is more like a set of organizing aims within which you can fit your daily choices, and elements of it may change as time passes. What makes a life one life ethically is not that it is guided by a single plan. But among the elements that give continuity to a life are our persisting social identities, and the plan of life I have at any particular time will reflect those identities. (I am conscious here that I am responding to comments on a talk on individuality I gave at the New York Humanities Institute in December 1998, particularly from David Rieff. He rightly objected to two possible implications of talk of a life plan: that there was something to be said for a life mapped out fully in advance and that one should avoid changing one's direction in life. But, like Mill and Rawls, I meant by a plan something that could have a fairly open texture: and having a plan, however determinate, doesn't commit you to sticking to it no matter what.)

sorts of social identities I have mentioned are, indeed, resources for the making of lives, but also—contra some multicultural liberals—that this is an argument for toleration of identities not for their recognition. That is, I was inclined to a view about these social identities that is analogous to the position on religious toleration adopted by the American Founders: so far as is possible, no establishment of identities, on the one hand; but, on the other, free exercise (subject to the constraints of duty and harm) as well.[8]

I shall try to say more about what the analogues of non-establishment and free exercise here might be in a moment. But actually to apply such an ideal requires, first of all, some notion of what the relevant social identities are. Here it seems to me that the existence in a society (or subculture) of the sort of social identity that raises questions for ethics and politics consists in three core elements.

First, the availability of terms in public discourse that are used to pick out the bearers of the identity by way of criteria of ascription, so that some people are recognized as members of the group—women, men; blacks, whites; straights, gays. The availability of these terms in public discourse requires both that it be mutually known among most members of the society that the labels exist and that there be some degree of consensus on how to identify those to whom it should be applied. Let us call a typical label for a group "L."[9] This consensus is usually organized around a set of stereotypes of Ls, beliefs about what typical Ls are like, how they behave, how they may be detected.[10] Some elements of a stereotype are typically normatively derived: they are views about how Ls will probably behave, rooted in their conformity to norms about how they should behave. We can say, in a convenient shorthand, that there

---

[8] The American Founders in practice must have thought these principles attached not to individuals but to communities, since they knew that some of the states that came together to form the union did, in fact, have established religions. So I am really drawing on the current understanding of religious toleration, as embodied in interpretations of the first amendment, not on the original understandings of it.

[9] Groups will generally have more than one label, so that part of what one learns in coming to understand an identity is a way of assigning members to the group and a label associated with it. Thus one has, so to speak, an individual concept associated with the group, which is one's own set of criteria of ascription.

[10] I do not use the term "stereotype" in a way that implies that any of the beliefs that constitute it are incorrect. See my "Stereotypes and the Shaping of Identity," *California Law Review* 88, no. 1 (January 2000): 41–54.

must first be a *social conception* of Ls. Stereotypes are rough-and-ready things, and there may be different conceptions of Ls associated with different individuals or groups within the society. For a social conception to exist, it is enough that there be a rough overlap in the classes picked out by the term "L," not that there be a singular determinate extension; nor is it necessary that the stereotypes or criteria of ascription be identical for all users of the term. So it does not matter that the boundary between women and men is not agreed upon (do female to male trans-gendered folk count as men all along, or only after surgery, or never?) or that even given a full specification of his affectional life and sexual habits it might well not be universally agreed whether or not William Shakespeare was what we now call "straight." It follows from this that one cannot always speak of *the* content of a social conception: sketching a social conception requires an ethnography of ways of conceiving of Ls, one that recognizes especially that different stereotypes of Ls may tend to be held by people with different social positions. (African-Americans, for example, may well have characteristically different social conceptions of a black identity from others in the United States; and homosexuals may tend to conceive gay identity differently from heterosexuals.)[11]

A second element of a social identity is the internalization of those labels as parts of the individual identities of at least some of those who bear the label. If the label in question is, once more, "L," we can call this *identification as an L.* Identification as an L means thinking of yourself as an L in ways that make a difference: perhaps thinking of yourself as an L shapes your feelings (so that you respond with pride as an L, when an L triumphs); perhaps it shapes your actions, so that you sometimes do something as an L (offering a helping hand to another L, perhaps, who is otherwise a stranger; or restraining your public behavior by the thought that misbehavior will reflect badly on Ls). Often, then, being an L carries ethical and moral weight: Jews ought to help other Jews and should avoid behaving in ways that discredit the Jewish community. And often, too, there are behavioral norms associated with identities that it seems wrong to dignify with the epithets "ethical" or "moral": men (of-

---

[11] Many people have the idea that the normative content of an identity should be determined essentially by its bearers. Even if that is true—which I doubt, since recognition by people of other identities is often a proper source of their meaning—this would still mean that some people would have the content of their identities determined in part by others, namely, those of the same identity.

ten we say *real* men) walk this way, hold their hands that way, don't cover their mouths when they laugh.

Identification often has a strong narrative dimension. By way of my identity I fit my life story into certain patterns—Confirmation at puberty for a religious identity, tenure in my mid-thirties for a professional one; and I also fit that story into larger stories—for example, of a people, a religious tradition, or a race. By way of an identification as an African-American, you can think of yourself as the first person of African descent to gain a Cambridge doctorate in English literature; by way of an identification as Jewish, you can be the first Jewish president. As I wrote in *Color Conscious: The Political Morality of Race:*

> This is not just a point about modern Westerners: cross-culturally it matters to people that their lives have a certain narrative unity; they want to be able to tell a story of their lives that makes sense. The story—my story—should cohere in the way appropriate by the standards made available in my culture to a person of my identity. In telling that story, how I fit into the wider story of various collectivities is, for most of us, important. It is not just gender identities that give shape (through, for example, rites of passage into woman- or manhood) to one's life: ethnic and national identities too fit each individual story into a larger narrative. And some of the most "individualist" of individuals value such things. Hobbes spoke of the desire for glory as one of the dominating impulses of human beings, one that was bound to make trouble for social life. But glory can consist in fitting and being seen to fit into a collective history: and so, in the name of glory, one can end up doing the most social things of all.[12]

The final element of a social identity is the existence of patterns of behavior toward Ls, so that Ls are sometimes *treated as Ls.* To treat someone as an L is to do something to them in part, at least, because they are an L (where the "because they are an L" figures in the agent's internal specification of her reasons for the act). In the current landscape of identity, the treatment-as that is often in focus is invidious discrimination: like it or not, gender, sexuality, and racial and ethnic identity have been profoundly shaped by histories of sexism, homophobia, racism, and ethnic hatred. But it is as well to recall that not all treatment-as is negative

---

[12] K. Anthony Appiah and Amy Gutmann, *Color Conscious: The Political Morality of Race* (Princeton: Princeton University Press, 1996), p. 97.

or morally troublesome: most sexuality (even bisexuality) requires responding to people as women and as men, and this means that there are patterns of action toward men and toward women that are constitutive of the standard range of sexual orientations. The *New York Times* reported on its front page recently that Bernard A. Friedman, a federal judge in Detroit, had written with sweeping—and injudicious—generality that "[a]ll racial distinctions are inherently suspect and presumptively invalid."[13] This is not only a questionable reading of American law (and the words "suspect" and "invalid" here are legal terms of art), but it is also doubtful as a moral ideal. If—as I fear is pretty close to the truth—black people living in the United States are more likely to suffer race-based disadvantages while white people continue to receive systematically race-based advantages, then it is *not* making a distinction between black people and white people that is morally suspect. But that identity-based responses can be morally positive should be uncontroversial: many of the world's acts of supererogatory benevolence involve treating people as fellow Ls—generosity, then, is often a form of treatment-as.

Where a classification of people by the members of a society as Ls is associated with a *social conception* of Ls, some people *identify as* Ls, and people are sometimes *treated as* Ls, we have a paradigm of a social identity that matters for ethical and political life. That it matters for ethical life—in Dworkin's sense—flows from the fact that it figures in identification, in peoples' shaping and evaluation of their own lives; that it matters for politics flows from the fact that it figures in treatment by others, and that how others treat one will help determine one's success and failure in living one's life.

With social identities thus understood, we can ask the question, once more, what it would mean to allow (the analogue of) free exercise of them while avoiding (the analogue of) establishment. On the establishment side, the idea would be to avoid government policies that amounted to making some identities the official identities of the state, just as disestablishmentarians oppose the maintenance or introduction of an official state religion. So presumably, anything that counted as making, for example, heterosexuality the official sexual orientation, masculinity the

---

[13] *New York Times,* Wednesday, March 28, 2001, p. A1.

official gender, white the official race, or Englishness (conceived ethnically) the official national identity would count as an impermissible establishment in the same way that making Anglicanism the official religion impermissibly establishes a particular Christian denomination.

Now, in a country with an established church it may seem far from obvious what wrong is done intrinsically when one establishes either religious or other identities. Many people in England, including many self-identified conservatives (with a small *c* and with a large one), apparently think that it is not only proper but positively desirable to identify the English state not only with a church, but also with a racial identity. I fear I detected the resonant reverberations of a thousand nodding heads when Charles Moore observed famously some years ago: "You can be British without speaking English or being Christian or being white, but nevertheless Britain is basically English-speaking and Christian and white, and if one starts to think that it might become Urdu-speaking and Muslim and brown, one gets frightened and angry."[14] If I find myself agreeing with Polly Toynbee—who observed: "Let him call us politically correct: I call him a racist"—it is not because I think it is clear what, in general, the prohibition of racial establishment amounts to. Nor is it obvious whether, to offer a different example, the disarmingly named "Defense of Marriage Act" in the United States, which aims (perhaps unconstitutionally) to permit one American state not to recognize a gay marriage contracted in another, amounts to saying, in effect, that the national state identifies with heterosexuals and repudiates homosexuals and thus "establishes" heterosexuality.

After all, the root liberal idea, I have suggested, is that each of us is in command of his or her own life; or, in W. E. Henley's familiar, and suitably first person, poetic formulation:

---

[14] Quoted in Polly Toynbee, "The White Backlash," *Guardian,* Wednesday, March 3, 1999, from an October 1991 *Spectator* article (Charles Moore, "Time for a More Liberal and 'Racist' Immigration Policy"): "You can be British without speaking English or being Christian or being white, but nevertheless Britain is basically English-speaking and Christian and white, and if one starts to think that it might become Urdu-speaking and Muslim and brown, one gets frightened and angry. Next door to me live a large family of Muslims from the Indian subcontinent. We are friendly enough to one another and they have done us various small acts of kindness. During the Gulf War, however, I heard their morning prayers coming through the wall, and I felt a little uneasy. If such people had outnumbered whites in our square, I should have felt alarmed. Such feelings are not only natural, surely—they are right. You ought to have a sense of your identity, and part of that sense derives from your nation and your race."

I am the master of my fate:
I am the captain of my soul.[15]

If this is how things should be, then clearly wresting command of my life from me does me a wrong. Others may sail in the same waters, in command of their own vessels. Rules of the sea may be made, among them rules that prohibit endangering the journeys and the ships of others. But a proscription against taking command of another person's fate cannot rule out every action on the part of others that affects my life, every deed that shapes my choices or influences me in virtue of my various social identities. I shape my life in the light of what I know about the costs of various options, costs that will depend in part on the acts and decisions of other individuals and groups and of the state. Which acts and policies constrain me in ways that amount to taking from me my command of my life? Well, we can say the ones that are coercive, but that doesn't tell us much. For very often what counts as coercion is constraining a person's action to an extent that would ordinarily be illegitimate, and in this case it is precisely what is and is not legitimate that is at stake.

Here, so it seems to me, we will make progress only if we bring in another liberal value as well, namely, equality. Identities as I have been imagining them are important tools in the shaping of one's life. To the extent that we are equals as citizens, the state owes us equal consideration. Insofar as resources—including not only economic but also symbolic and other resources—are made available by the state, they should be made available equally. A state that identified with heterosexuals as such, providing them with material resources (such as tax benefits for couples) or symbolic goods (such as the recognition of their marriages) or practical benefits (such as the laws governing the division of property in the unhappy event of separation), and denied them to homosexuals would be failing to treat people of different sexualities with the required equality.[16] Distinguishing in law between parents and childless couples, in contrast—granted that the having and raising of children is something in which there is a proper public interest—would not be open to the same objection, provided, of course, that there was some reasonable relationship between the distinctions made and the effects sought; and

---

[15] *The New Oxford Book of English Verse,* ed. Dame Helen Gardner (Oxford: Oxford University Press, 1972), p. 792.

[16] My discussion here owes much to Dworkin's *Sovereign Virtue.*

that is true even though "parent" is surely an important social identity, as I have defined that term.[17]

When it comes to free exercise, it may seem more obvious what is required. Free exercise of identity would mean being able to make a life as an L without the government's interfering with our living out our own understanding of what it means to be an L and, in particular, without the government's trying to coerce us not to live as an L at all. Once more, what this means in practice is not, alas, as straightforward as it seems.

To begin with, once free exercise has financial costs (as it inevitably will if the identities matter) there will always be an element of coercion lurking somewhere, since as Robert Nozick reminded us forcefully in *Anarchy, State and Utopia,* taxation is coercive and taxation is where the government gets most of its money. True, it is a different kind of coercion: one of the advantages of taxation as a means of raising resources— as contrasted with forced labor—is that, while it reduces the resources that a citizen has for life-making, it does so in a way that leaves a wide range of choices open. Taxation pays for the national defense, allowing some to opt for the soldier's life, others to spend their youth developing their skills in their chosen lives as mathematicians or soccer players. Conscription leaves you no such choice.

Taxation will, of course, constrain expensive identities more than it constrains cheaper ones: the heir to the Duke of Omnium will rightly see estate taxes as constraining his life as a scion of a landed aristocracy. But the government should not aim, in taxing him, to constrain his identity *as such.* The tax need not be an expression of a view about the

---

[17] Similarly, if being raised by a single-sex couple were always worse than the best available alternative, the refusal of adoption rights to homosexual couples would not be an illegitimate infringement on their identity. Since, however, there is no evidence for the empirical antecedent of this conditional, I do not endorse the consequent (see, for example, Charlotte J. Patterson, "Adoption Of Minor Children by Lesbian and Gay Adults: A Social Science Perspective," *Duke Journal of Gender Law and Policy* 2: 191). It might be worse because people deliberately treated the children of gay couples badly, as a reflection of their homophobia. Then the real problem would be to try to stop that immoral practice. Whether, in the interim, gay adoption should be permitted would presumably then depend on whether it was possible to protect the children from real harm. Even if the refusal of adoption rights to gay people substantially reduced the success of their lives *and* was made necessary by injustice, we should not use children as a means to the end of fulfilling other people's lives: the adoption is for their sake, not the adopters'. There are no principles at stake here that do not apply in other cases of adoption where there is substantial prejudice. In the United States courts have held, for example, that the fact that children's lives may go worse in racially prejudiced communities because their parents are of different races is not a proper ground for refusing adoption to mixed-race couples. Part of their reasoning has been that the state must not give effect to these unjust prejudices. But this is presumably only so where the relevant harms are not sufficiently certain or substantial.

goodness of his life. In constraining his choices through taxation, it is indifferent to the meanings inhering in the identity he is constructing and undiscriminating as to its worth as against other lives with other identities. To repeat the central point: not everything that shapes your choices, even if it stops you from doing what you most want to do, is illegitimately coercive. So it is at least consistent to hold that tax moneys may be spent to permit the free exercise of identity, while holding that state coercion in the sphere of identity is wrong.

I have spoken of identities so far and of their recognition without reflecting on the fact that much recent multiculturalist discussion has been driven by a Hegelian conception of recognition, drawing on the now too familiar discussion of lordship and bondage in *The Phenomenology of Spirit*. There the thought is that my identity as master is constituted in part by the acknowledgement of my status by the bondsman (and, of course, vice versa). I cannot be a master, act as and think of myself as a master, unless the bondsman acts toward me as bondsman to master and treats me as a master. It will be uncontroversial among those who have normal human relations that the responses of other people play a crucial role in shaping one's sense of who one is. As Charles Taylor once put it:

> On the intimate level, we can see how much an original identity needs and is vulnerable to the recognition given or withheld by significant others.... Love relationships are not just important because of the general emphasis in modern culture on the fulfillment of ordinary needs. They are also crucial because they are crucibles of inwardly generated identity.[18]

We may even acknowledge that our identities are sensitive to the responses of strangers. If, as has happened often enough in our time, a black person receives contemptuous glares from white strangers, a Jew sees Gentile strangers turn and spit as she passes, a gay man faces a daily passage through a world of putatively straight men glowering and muttering "filthy queer," only someone with no sense of a normal human psychology would suggest that the proper response is only: "Sticks and

---

[18] Charles Taylor, *Multiculturalism and the Politics of Recognition* (Princeton: Princeton University Press, 1994), p. 36.

stones will break my bones, but words will never hurt me." Taylor is surely also right, then, when he goes on to say that "the projection of an inferior or demeaning image on another can actually distort and oppress, to the extent that the image is internalized."[19]

But to grasp all this is not yet to say what role the state should have in the regulation of such acts of Hegelian recognition and misrecognition. On the one side lies the individual oppressor whose expressions of contempt may be part of who he or she is, and whose rights of free expression are presumably grounded, at least in part, in the connection between individuality and self-expression. On the other, the oppressed individual, whose life can go best only if his or her identity is consistent with self-respect. How, if at all, is the state to intervene? Some writers, Taylor among them, seem to hold that the state itself, through government recognition, can sustain identities that face the danger of self-contempt imposed by the social contempt of others. Others hold that, in regulating the public sphere in a society of diverse identities in order to sustain a regime of mutual toleration, the government should seek to educate citizens of all identities into an attitude of "live and let live." Here the first-order constraint that the state should not take sides for one identity against others may require the regulation of those identities that do not practice public toleration, even if to do so amounts to taking sides against those identities.

My aim here is only to exemplify the sorts of political questions raised by identity. For I believe that progress with such questions requires a deeper understanding of the background of moral and social psychology upon which our identities depend. And a modest contribution to that understanding is one of my aims in these lectures. But I also think that settling such questions in detailed policy terms is not the most useful way in which philosophy can contribute to the political life of our culture. Philosophy, so it seems to me, is most helpful in the political life of democracies when it suggests that certain issues, framed through particular conceptual resources, need to be borne in mind in shaping policy. And if it is to be helpful in this way, it will most often be because it not only identifies the issue—as I have identified the relations of identity and the state—but also provides some mapping of the conceptual territory that

[19] Ibid.

surrounds it. Despite the current vogue for talk of public intellectuals, it seems to me that the life of an intellectual, dominated as it distinctively is by the desire to understand and make sense of our world, is not necessarily the best standpoint from which to make detailed policy prescriptions. For these require a sense for what is possible in the political moment—of what rhetoric will work, what interests can be mobilized and defeated, what actual bureaucracies can currently achieve; and while there are some intellectuals who have the knowledge and the practical wisdom to make such judgments, a philosopher's training does not prepare one for them, and I am happy to admit that these talents are not mine.

I am conscious that the picture I have been sketching of the ethical and its relevance for what states owe their subjects has not obviously been part of the moral repertoire of every age or condition. For many people through much of human history, it has probably seemed that their task was to live the life to which they were born: to work on the lord of the manor's estates or the master's plantation, to be a good wife or daughter or son, to rule as a lawful prince: to occupy a station—however base or exalted—and perform its duties. The ideal of self-creation and self-mastery can easily seem to be the ideal of those who have mastery over others. Many English schoolboys in the heyday of Empire learned the whole of William Ernest Henley's poem, of which I cited earlier only the final couplet. (I have an idea I learned it under the title "Invictus," which implies that it is not a philosophy for the vanquished, though I see that that is not how it appears in *The New Oxford Book of English Verse.*)

Out of the night that covers me,
Black as the Pit from pole to pole,
I thank whatever gods may be
For my unconquerable soul.

In the fell clutch of circumstance
I have not winced or cried aloud.
Under the bludgeonings of chance
My head is bloody, but unbowed.

Beyond this place of wrath and tears
Looms but the Horror of the shade.

And yet the menace of the years
Finds, and shall find, me unafraid.

It matters not how strait the gate,
How charged with punishments the scroll,
I am the master of my fate:
I am the captain of my soul.[20]

We may assume that it did not occur to sufficiently many of those boys who became the political masters of imperial subjects that those subjects might have had the same ideal of self-mastery. But the fact that an ideal was promulgated for a few does not mean that it should not be made available to all of us: what is liberal is not the idea of self-mastery—but the idea that it should be offered to everyone. And I have never met anyone who did not want the opportunity to shape a life of his or her own: even monastics who take vows of obedience have, in an obvious sense, made lives of their own.

It is important, as well, that the ideal of self-creation is not solely Western, at least if my reading of some secondary literature on Confucianism is correct. And this point is worth stressing, because Confucianism, with its talk of the filial piety and loyalty to the emperor, is often thought of (and not only in the West) as precisely an ethic of "my station and its duties."

So consider, for example, Tu Wei-ming's discussion in *Humanity and Self-Cultivation: Essays in Confucian Thought* of *hsieu-shen* (which he translates as "cultivating personal life"). Tu argues that this is an element of *li,* the process of becoming fully human that includes as well "(2) regulating familial relations (*ch'i-chia*), (3) ordering the affairs of state (*chih-kuo*), and (4) bringing peace to the world (*p'ing t'ien-hsia*)."[21] Now *li* has often been translated as "propriety" or "ritual," but Tu Wei-ming argues that it is better understood as the "externalization of *jen*" (which is often translated simply as "benevolence") "in a concrete situation."[22]

---

[20] *The New Oxford Book of English Verse,* ed. Gardner, p. 792.

[21] Tu Wei-ming, *Humanity and Self-Cultivation: Essays in Confucian Thought* (Boston: Cheng & Tsui Company, 1998), p. 27.

[22] Ibid., p. 18. What Tu Wei-ming calls *jen* here is now often transcribed as *ren* and translated as "benevolence" or, in what I believe is the currently favored interpretation, "humanity."

And he also suggests that we should think of *jen* as "a principle of in-wardness" (in the sense that it comes from within rather than outside the self) that is "linked with the self-reviving, self-perfecting, and self-fulfilling process of an individual."[23]

Philip J. Ivanhoe remarks, in a similar spirit, in a recent book enti-tled *Confucian Moral Self-Cultivation* that "[m]oral self-cultivation is one of the most thoroughly and regularly discussed topics among Chinese ethical philosophers" and demonstrates the truth of his claim by follow-ing this theme through from Confucius (551–479 B.C.E.) and Mencius (391–308 B.C.E.) to Xunxi (310–219 B.C.E.), Zhu Xi (1130–1200 C.E.), Wang Yangming (1472–1529 C.E.), Yan Yuan (1635–1704 C.E.), and Dai Zhen (1723–77 C.E.).[24] (These philosophers flourished from the sixth century before Christ to the eighteenth century of the common era: that is, indeed, a long tradition of reflection.)

To see moral self-cultivation at the heart of ethics is not, of course, *eo ipso,* to celebrate what Mill meant by individuality: Confucius and the Confucians by and large regarded moral self-cultivation as a matter of developing a character that would lead one to live a good life, and they did not suggest (so far as I have been able to discover) that what made a life good was in any sense up to the individual. But they *did* have the idea—Immanuel Kant's pietist Protestant idea—that what mattered

[23] Ibid., p. 9. This interpretation fits with one of the more surprising moments in the *Analects* where Confucius is highly critical of the honest—or, as Tu Wei-ming suggests we might say, "hyperhonest"—villager (*hsiang-yüan*). It comes in *Analects* 17, where we find: "The Master said: 'The "honest men" of your prefecture undermine virtue'" (*The Analects of Confucius: A Literal Translation,* with an introduction and notes by Chichung Huang [New York: Oxford University Press, 1997], p. 169; this edition numbers the adage 7.12, but in many editions it is 7.13; and that is how Tu Wei-ming refers to it). Mencius, when asked to explain this passage, said that these "honest men" were (as a different translation has it) "thieves of virtue" according to Confucius because: "If you would blame them, you find nothing to allege. If you would criticize them, you have nothing to criticize. They agree with the current customs. They consent with an impure age. Their principles have a sem-blance of right-heartedness and truth. Their conduct has a semblance of disinterestedness and purity. All men are pleased with them and they think themselves right, so that it is im-possible to proceed with them to the principles of Yâo and Shun. On this account they are called 'The thieves of virtue'" (*The Works of Mencius,* translated, with critical and exegetical notes, prolegomena, and copious indexes by James Legge [New York: Dover Publications Inc., 1970]). (Yâo and Shun are two of the seven wise kings of antiquity that Confucius most admired; see *The Analects of Confucius,* p. 31.) Tu Wei-ming glosses Mencius in a way that makes the centrality of self-cultivation clear: "The real problem with the hyperhonest vil-lager is his total lack of commitment to the Way. Despite his apparent compatibility with the established social norms, he is absolutely devoid of any 'ambition' for self-improve-ment" (*Humanity and Self-Cultivation,* p. 38).

[24] Philip J. Ivanhoe, *Confucian Moral Self-Cultivation* (Indianapolis: Hackett Publishing Company, 2000), p. ix.

was not just doing the right but doing it for the right reason, a reason that flowed from the self one had either uncovered (this is the Mencian line) or crafted (this is Xunxi).[25] And they *did* believe that the work of making one's self was a central ethical task.

Mencius, certainly, would have appreciated the story told about Rabbi Zusha, brother of the celebrated eighteenth-century Jewish scholar Rebbe Elimelech of Liszensk (1717–87), who wandered the woods singing praises to the divinity and was known as the "Fool of God." Zusha is supposed to have said: "When I die and come before the heavenly court, if they ask me, 'Zusha, why were you not as great as Abraham?' I will not be afraid. I will say that I was not born with Abraham's intellectual capabilities. And if they ask me, 'Zusha, why were you not like Moses?' I will say that I did not have his leadership abilities. But when they ask me, 'Zusha, why were you not Zusha?' for that I will have no answer."[26]

Zusha was an eighteenth-century Hasidic rabbi; Mencius, a member of the Chinese gentry born nearly four decades after Plato: I am certain they would have been puzzled by some of Mill's defense of individuality, but they, like Plato, would surely have recognized that he was discussing a topic that mattered to them. And so, to judge by some of our proverbs, would my Akan ancestors: "Wobö bra-pa a, wote mu dé" (If you live a good life you find it sweet) they said; and also: "Öbra ne deé wo ara woabö" (Your life is what you alone have formed). And so I make no apology for suggesting that while I have framed these issues within a particular modern Western tradition, the topic I am adumbrating is part of the common conversation of much of humankind.

I hope I have said enough about the idea of an identity and the liberal response to it that you will have some sense of the territory in which my talk of identity is intended to be located. It is because identities are important in these ways that I believe we need to have an account of them.

And my aim in the remaining lectures is to explore two kinds of presupposition of this whole way of framing a question for ethics and politics. The first set of presuppositions is about the natures of the people whose individualities I have been taking so seriously. The picture of the person that is implicit in much of what I have been saying is of an

---

[25] See ibid., chapters 2 and 3.

[26] Rabbi Joseph Telushkin, *Jewish Wisdom* (New York: William Morrow, 1994), p. 90. I learned this story from my friend Daniel Rose.

individual with needs, tastes, values, identities, and dispositions and a capacity for rational deliberation and action. It is, as Kant suggested, because people are capable of reason that we must respect their right to self-mastery, what he taught us to call their autonomy. A creature driven by instinct and appetite, incapable of planning, unguided by commitments, insensitive to reason or to the demands of morality: such a creature would not be entitled to the concern for its autonomy that the liberal ethical perspective entails. Such a creature would not—in the relevant sense—be making a life.

I want to examine one of these assumptions—that we have a capacity for rational deliberation—in order to ask whether our pervasive irrationality provides grounds for the state's intervention in the making of our individual identities.

The second presupposition of the liberal framing, which I will explore in the final lecture, is about the origins of these individuals. We all start out—do we not?—as infants. Without language, without ambitions, without projects. And the languages, ambitions, and projects we acquire, and the social identities we develop, are not themselves the product solely of our own choices. If we place so high a premium on permitting people to shape their own lives once they are adults, are there not also constraints on how we can shape them as children? Or, to put the matter more positively: we should presumably prepare them, if we can, to take up the task of developing an identity and shaping a life. But how should we do so?

A person's shaping of her life flows from her beliefs and from a set of values, tastes, and dispositions of sensibility, all of these influenced by various forms of social identity: let us call all these together a person's "moral self." A person's self changes over time—beliefs, tastes, sensibilities, even identities change. But each of us has, at any time, a self from which our choices in the shaping of a life derive. In this language we may ask what it is permissible to do to shape each person's self in childhood.

This question seems to me to arise very naturally, in the sort of way I have suggested, out of current liberal preoccupations and debates; and that is how it arose for me. But surely any plausible view of politics will have a view about what terms the state should set for the determination (by itself or by others) of the selves with which each person in the community will reach adulthood.

In conducting and creating our lives we govern our thoughts, plans, and actions. We need to identify our aims, understand how the world in which we are living is constituted, and connect our actions with our aims in the light of that understanding. In making our lives, we must reflect on ends, accumulate evidence, form beliefs, identify options for action, predict and evaluate their outcomes, and then act. The moral self I have spoken of requires these capacities of reason if it is to make a life. In the next lecture I want to take up some questions about how we should understand these demands of reason. This will be important, after all, if we are concerned to help people shape their lives as responsible moral selves, ready to take up the task of making lives of their own: and that will be the topic I shall turn to toward the end of the next lecture and in the final one.

## II. REASON AND THE SELF

If my friend Dorothy is standing outside in her best clothes with an umbrella and it starts to rain, chances are she'll open up the umbrella. If she doesn't, there'll be a reason: she was trying to be inconspicuous; she thought the umbrella wasn't working; she doesn't care about her clothes because her boyfriend has just left her. But if she really *does* realize that opening the umbrella is a way to keep her clothes tidy *and* knows that she can *and* cares about her appearance *and* has nothing else on her mind and she *still* leaves the umbrella tightly furled, we'll just be stumped. And we'll wonder, rightly, if we've got her state of mind right.

Now, our resources for explaining why Dorothy hasn't opened the umbrella are close to unlimited, though, of course, the more we know or think we know about her the more constraints there will be. We might even be willing to accept the occasional deviation from reason. But the more this happens, the less certain we will be of the particular ascriptions of mental states that we have made; and we will eventually come to wonder whether, in fact, Dorothy is responding to the world as a creature with beliefs, desires, hopes, fears, and the rest of the multifarious states we ascribe with careless regularity to ourselves and to others every day and all the time. I shall need a shorthand way for referring to beliefs, desires, intentions, emotions, and the like, so I shall call them, as philosophers usually do, "intentional states." So now we can say: reasonableness of some sort is built into our ascriptions of intentional states.[1]

There are two major kinds of reasonableness that have interested philosophers from the beginning of the Western tradition: one, the epistemic or theoretical, has to do with keeping beliefs in line with evidence, with each other, and with the world; the other, the ethical or practical, has to do with keeping action in line with our beliefs and our purposes. I began with an example of practical reason, but Dorothy could puzzle us epistemically as well: we would be just as stumped if she looked out across the lawn in the teeming rain and remarked how pleasantly sunny it was. If she raised her umbrella now, we should no longer have the practical puzzle. But her using an umbrella as a parasol when there's overwhelming evidence that it's raining now raises a problem of a new, epistemic, kind.

The notion that people have intentional states is not limited to our society, our language, or, more generally yet, our Western tradition. It would be easy to tell the little story I told about Dorothy in Twi, my father's Ghanaian mother tongue. Everywhere people make sense of what others do on the basis of supposing them to have inner states that represent how the world is and how they would like it to be. Everywhere, too, people will have a hard time making sense of someone who seems, on the basis of one set of considerations, to have such intentional states, and yet does not act as they require. It is not that people believe they can always predict what others will do: unpredictability is one predictable element in human action. But we do make assumptions of predictability all the time, and we will want explanations when those assumptions fail.[2] So, whatever your first language or cultural origins and whatever

---

[1] You may take what I have just said as a brief informal gloss on the later teachings of Donald Davidson (see Donald Davidson, *Inquiries into Truth and Interpretation* [New York: Oxford University Press, 1984]). But you should also note that I do not mean to be taking sides in a debate about the reality of the internal states that I have adverted to. Perhaps Daniel Dennett is right and the constraint that we can only sensibly speak of someone's beliefs and desires if that someone is broadly speaking reasonable is built into the adoption of what he calls an "intentional stance" toward them: the essence of the intentional stance being that we predict and explain what people say and do while making them seem reasonable at the same time. Adopting the intentional stance is approaching something *as if* it had intentional states, as we often do with our computers. Taken either way—as an observation about having beliefs and such or about being treated as having them—the claim seems to me correct.

[2] I am of the party that thinks that the reason for this human consensus is that we come equipped with a disposition to understand other people this way; a "module," in the cognitive science jargon, that generates a mental model of others without our having to be taught very much about it. But, once again, for my present purposes you do not need to agree with

your philosophical inclinations, there is a set of questions here to ask: about the relationship between having intentional states, on the one hand, and being in some sense reasonable, on the other.

This question, interesting enough in itself, matters a great deal to the wider project of these lectures, which is to explore some of the presuppositions of the picture of the self that leads us to think that people should be left to make their own lives. The liberal notion that autonomy matters relies, as I said in the last lecture, on the assumption that people are not "driven by instinct and appetite, incapable of planning, unguided by commitments, insensitive to reason." If the ascription of intentional states requires reasonableness, then a creature with commitments and plans will necessarily be sensitive to reason. It will, therefore, be entitled to self-government. If, *per contra,* our states are not rationally constituted, this argument may not go through.

So, what sorts of things are practical and epistemic reasonableness? That is a question you could come at in many ways. But one relatively simple way (a sort of *via negativa*) is to ask what kinds of relations between intentional states—and between intentional states and other states of the world—are grounds for an accusation of *un*reasonableness. Let me offer some simple examples, the first of them on the practical side:

*John prefers this artichoke to this beet and this beet to that carrot. It would seem then that he ought to prefer the artichoke to the carrot. If the schema is generally valid—if you prefer A to B and B to C, then you ought to prefer A to C— then we can say that preferences should be transitive. Suppose, however, that John actually prefers the carrot to the beet.*

What could we say about John?

Here is one line of thought. If John had the carrot right now and you had the beet, he would be willing to give you something of value to persuade you to swap. For if he prefers the beet, then he would rather have the beet than the carrot and so the exchange has some value to him. And the same would be true if he had the beet and you had the artichoke. So far, there is no problem. But if he also prefers carrot to artichoke, then he would offer something for the chance to swap the carrot for the

<hr/>

me about that. Perhaps the reason that people everywhere respond to other people by supposing them to have intentional states is just that something like this is true and everyone has noticed that it is true; or, again, maybe this is not true but it is the easiest way to get along with other people, adopting the intentional stance, and all societies have discovered that it is the easiest way.

artichoke, if he had it: for the carrot is worth more to him than the artichoke. But now it seems that, little by little, you can take away from
him everything he values.

Suppose you have the carrot, the beet, and the artichoke. First just
give him the carrot. (Trust me, it'll be worth the investment.) Now offer him the beet. He will pay you to swap. Now you offer him the artichoke. He will pay you to swap again. Since you retrieved the carrot in
the first swap, you can now offer it to him again, and he will once more
pay you to swap carrot for artichoke. Obviously, you can keep going
round this little circle for as long as you like and, if his preferences don't
change, as I say, you can take away, perhaps in tiny pieces, everything he
values.[3]

Now, if an actual John were actually faced with this actual sequence
of options—faced, that is, not with this story, but with actual artichokes, beets, and carrots—there would be two possibilities. Either he
would go on until he lost everything and then we would think…Well,
it's unclear what we would think. We might think, for example, that he
had come to value playing this game more than anything else in the
world (which is, roughly, the best we can do for a rational explanation of
the gambler who fritters away all his worldly goods). Or we might think
that he didn't realize what was going on. But, failing that, I think we are
likely just to conclude that we don't exactly know what is happening
but that saying, simply, that he prefers artichokes to beets, and beets to
carrots, but carrots to artichokes, doesn't really capture it.

The other possibility is that John would grasp at some point what
was happening and stop the game. Suppose, for example, he said he
would hold on to the artichoke, thank you very much, when offered the
carrot for the fourth time. Then all would be well. For we would now
have grounds for supposing that he didn't prefer the carrot to the artichoke, and we could heave a sigh of relief and record that he no longer
had a preference intransitivity. People can be temporarily irrational and
we will forgive them, provide they put things right when the problem
makes itself manifest.

---

[3] I should underline the fact that this story relies on assumptions not just about preferences but about beliefs, options, and choices as well. The story assumes that John recognizes
beets and artichokes and carrots, knows what options are on offer, chooses to pay for the
swaps, and so on. The focus of our attention is on John's preferences because it is they that
are apparently irrational. If the other apparatus is working as it should, this is what will happen. But if it *isn't,* then the behavior we have elicited may have some other explanation.

On the epistemic side, there are two major kinds of deviation, corresponding broadly speaking to inductive and deductive rationality. On the inductive side, we have people like Dorothy faced with rainstorms who think it's sunny. It seems clear enough that there can be explanations for this sort of thing. Dorothy might think the sky was gray when it wasn't because she believed there was something temporarily wrong with her color vision. But, once again, if someone *has* vision and looks out on a scene in which it is visibly the case that it's raining, we shall have difficulty ascribing to them the belief that it *isn't* in the absence of an explanation of this kind. So, just as we can conclude that, *ceteris paribus,* preferences will be transitive, so we can conclude something like this: sighted people will ordinarily believe what is visibly evidently true.

Let me offer a similar simple example from the deductive domain. Consider Dorothy again.

*Dorothy thinks the umbrella is protecting her from the rain; she also thinks that if the umbrella is protecting her from the rain, she is not getting wet; but she thinks she is getting wet.*

From the first two of these beliefs it seems to follow that she should believe that she is not getting wet. Given that she doesn't, it is hard to say why we should accept that these *are* her beliefs. Once more, there are stories we could tell—I leave them to your imagination. But we surely think that, ordinarily, if someone believes something of the form "If *A,* then *C*" and believes that *A,* she doesn't believe that it's not the case that *C.* Indeed, if they think about the matter at all, they will presumably believe that *C.* Because the logical principle that *C* follows from "If *A, C*" and *A* has long been called *modus ponens,* we can call this idea *applied modus ponens;* and it is an instance of the sort of rationality built into our normal understanding of intentional states.

What I have just dubbed *applied modus ponens,* transitivity of preference, the capacity, when awake, to detect the obvious features of your environment: this disparate little list is meant to exemplify the sorts of things that an assumption of reasonableness amounts to. Let me call the various requirements that together constitute reasonableness the "rules of reason."

What I want to say amounts to this: even though we often deviate from the rules of reason, it is essential to understanding our intentional states that we see them as governed by those rules. We understand what beliefs and desires *are* in us rationally imperfect beings by seeing how they would operate in rationally perfect beings, who thought everything through, never made logical mistakes, saw the world as it was. The rules of reason are the rules a rationally perfect being would live by. We are not such beings; nevertheless, this idealization is central to an understanding of our psychologies.

There will be many of you who will draw on your knowledge of the behavioral economics or psychology literatures, or your dealings with ordinary people away from the study, who will, no doubt, find it incredible that anyone at this late stage should be defending the view that I have just outlined. The names of Daniel Kahneman and Amos Tversky, or Herbert Simon, or Tooby and Cosmides and Gerd Gigerenzer, will spring to your lips. How, you will be thinking, can someone who lives in our time—with all the massive experimental evidence that this is simply not how our mental states work, all the grounds for doubting that we maximize utilities rather than using heuristics—persist in thinking that it is useful to build rationality of this sort into our understanding of intentional states?

The challenge can be simply put. Nobody is even close to being rational in this way: how can it be helpful, then, to understand the beliefs and desires of actual agents in the light of this demanding model of rationality?

One popular reply is that this picture of rationality is indeed false of us, but that this is because it constitutes a normative ideal. What this picture is *for,* on this view, is not predicting or describing behavior—not even the behavior of an idealized agent—but saying how we *should* ideally behave.

If this is meant as an account of the sense in which assumptions about rationality in use by social scientists—among them the classical decision theory that underlies much modern economics and so-called rational choice theorizing—have idealized human behavior, then it is just a *pun* to say that they do so by providing ideals up to which we should live. I am discussing the role of the rules of reason as constitutive of our understanding of human beliefs and desires: and in this context it will do no good to defend the picture from its empirical inadequacies by observing that it would be a better world if people did conform to it. To make this move is just to give up claiming the role I have proposed for the rules of reason in structuring our conception of the mind.

But there is one obvious way in which the normative and descriptive

theories are related. The rules of reason help us to understand the intentional states about which the normative theory makes recommendations. *If* we should conform to classical decision theory, for example, we
should assign our degrees of belief in such a way that their measure has
the shape of a probability-function. But to do that we need to know
what degrees of belief are—and that is exactly what the decision theory,
construed as the expression of what I have called the rules of practical
reason, does.[4]

*Whether* we should try to conform to the norms of the pure classical
theory is another question. But here, too, our rules of reason will help.
For they allow us to explore what might happen if we *did* try; and I shall
suggest in a moment that, once we *do* explore this question, we can see
that the sorts of rules of reason we find in classical decision theory are
not a set of ideals worth trying to conform to.

It is a matter of non-normative fact, of course, what norms individuals and societies respect. On the other hand, there is no doubt that the
beliefs that embody these norms—beliefs about what one should do or
about what one is rationally committed to believing—are not reducible
without residue to accounts of non-normative fact. You don't understand what it is for something to be rationally required simply because
you know how a community of people who believed that it was rationally required would behave.

What else is needed might, perhaps, be put as a slogan like this: to
know what it is for something to be rationally required is to recognize
the demands of reason. Less programmatically: on the practical side, to
know what it is for something to be rationally required is to be disposed, once you see that an act, A, is, indeed, rationally required, to
act—other things, no doubt, as usual, being equal—as is rationally required; to be disposed, then, to try to do A. On the theoretical side, recognizing the demands of reason means seeing that you should believe
what reason requires and being disposed, once you see this, to believe it.

Looked at this way, the particular mode of idealization I have proposed is bound to seem unhelpfully radical. To idealize in this way is to
regard us as governed by the thought that we should aim to think and
do what someone like us whose reasoning was perfect would find it best
to do: and this is risky, because thus to ignore the fact of our rational

[4] *How* it does it is explained in some detail in my book *Assertion and Conditionals* (Cambridge: Cambridge University Press, 1985).

imperfections—our limited capacities for reasoning, our tiny memories—may lead us to be worse off, by the very same standards, than we might be if we opted for less stringent idealizations. There is no guarantee that a rationally imperfect creature that aims at the goals of a rationally perfect creature will end up doing what perfection would entail more often than it would if it used, say, rules of thumb that recognized its imperfections and used its knowledge of its own place in the world. I may well do better, for example, in the long run refusing complex bets from a smart bookmaker at large odds than trying to calculate in every case what pattern of acceptance will maximize my expected gains.

What this thought suggests is that the mode of idealization appropriate to developing strategies for real-life decision should be different from the mode I have adopted so far; and this naturally invites the question once more: "For what purposes is *this* mode of idealization appropriate?"

The answer, I am arguing, is that this mode of idealization is appropriate for the purpose of thinking about what our beliefs and desires would have to be like if they were to do their job as well as possible. What, after all, are beliefs for? Representing the states of the world that are relevant to determining how to bring about what we want. And what are desires for? Representing the way we would like the world to be. Desires shape preferences among states of the world. And a state of the world, A, is preferred to another, B, just in case if we could bring about A or bring about B but not bring about both, we would bring about A. The epistemic rules of reason are meant to show how we should change our beliefs in response to evidence and reflection in such a way as to increase the likelihood that they will represent the world the way that it actually is; the practical rules of reason seek to show how we should choose to act if we are to get as much as possible of what we want most.

But living up to these rules would require us finite, natural creatures to be impossibly perfect. And so we cannot have beliefs and desires that live up to those demands. In a certain sense, indeed, if the rules of reason define belief and desire, we do not have beliefs and desires at all. Or, you might say, we do not have beliefs and desires but we should like to. The idealized agent defined by the rules of reason shows us what that would be like. We can see that such an idealized agent would have a life in which beliefs and desires did best what they are meant to do. But we can also understand, in the light of that theory, why our states are not able to be beliefs and desires; and how to use them, despite their imperfections, to make the best life we can. It is against that ideal theory that we can make sense of the heuristics that are studied by social and cognitive psychologists: for it is only against the ideal theory that we can explain what the heuristics are doing. They are aiming to help us make our imperfect states do what the perfect states would do. That is why, I think, rational choice explanations have the hold they do on the social scientific imagination. These norms are built into what beliefs and desires are for.[5]

How, then, should we *use* the rules of ideal reason?

Well, often we just think things. Often we just form intentions and act on them. But sometimes we don't know what to think *or* what to do. That is when the norms guide us. If we have the time to reflect,[6] we can use our understanding of the rules of reason to decide whether what we are disposed to believe and desire (and thus to do), given our actual psychological processes, is, in fact, likely to get us what we most want. In the simplest sort of case, for example, we learn from our experience with visual illusions that we should not form beliefs in the way we are designed to do in certain circumstances: those where our eyes and brains will regularly be tricked. Illusions reflect a regular form of deviation from the rules of reason. For they cannot normally be overridden and so we cannot normally change these habits of belief-formation in the light of our experience in the way that the rules of reason would seem to require.

[5] There are two natural ways of understanding the claim that representing the world and how we should like it to be is what beliefs and desires, respectively, are meant to do. One is conceptual: this is what they are meant to do in the sense that it is built into our conception of them that this is what they are for. In that sense, you could say, this is what *we* mean them to do. Another is explanatory: this is what they were meant do in the sense that this is their evolutionary (or providential) design.

I do not think it is plausible that beliefs and desires have as evolutionary purposes the purposes I have described. For evolution's purposes, what is important is that we should detect those features of our environment relevant to our survival fast enough to allow us to use that information to help us survive and that we should have those aims that will keep us fed, find us mates, give us offspring, and help them and their genes survive. The inner states that evolution has equipped us with have, clearly, done a good job at that task so far, for they have made us a successful widespread species. Because we have limited computational resources, the way evolution has done this has involved designing us to get the relevant answer to the questions most important for survival in a reasonable time: and that has meant designing us to use not procedures that conform to the rules of reason, but all sorts of *ad hoc* procedures that work faster than applying the rules of reason in the practical contexts in which they are most often to be used.

[6] Whether we have the time is always going to be a matter of judgment based on the beliefs we actually have, which may be mistaken.

People must often deviate from what reason requires because they are not rationally perfect. This fact has led some psychologists to explore how our actual cognitive design (produced as it was by a process of selection of adaptive strategies) reflects these imperfections. So they have proposed that we use "quick and dirty" or "fast and frugal" belief-forming mechanisms, which take advantage of the fact that it is possible to design algorithms for belief-formation that will be extremely reliable within a specific range of environments, even though they would be generally unreliable *outside* that range of environments.[7] One simple example here, due to Gerd Gigerenzer and D. Goldstein, is a mechanism for deciding which of two cities in a certain country is the larger.[8] They propose a two-stage algorithm, which they call "Take-the-Best," the first stage of which is that you should judge that a city you have heard of is larger than one you have not. In the actual world, since the chances that someone who lives in that country will have heard of a place do in fact rise with its population, this step provides a good example of a belief-forming procedure that works in a rough and ready way because of features of the agent's environment and her relation to it. Furthermore, such an algorithm will work just as well for an agent who is unaware of these features as for someone who knows about them in detail.

Nobody proposes that such an algorithm is actually built into human cognitive architecture, the relevant features of our environment (cities and their sizes) being pretty short-range in the evolutionary time-scale; but there may be other features of our cognitive architecture that do reflect longer-term such stabilities. Consider, for example, the fact that people regularly deviate from what the rules of reason seem to require by being risk-averse about losses: of two options with equal expected utility, they will pick one with a lower yield that is close to certain over a potentially higher yielding but riskier option that includes a possibility of loss. Most people, for example, will prefer to keep 1,000 pounds rather than buy a chance of getting 2,010 pounds on the toss of

[7] See "Fast, Frugal *and* Rational: How Rational Norms Explain Behavior," Nick Chater, Department of Psychology, University of Warwick; Mike Oaksford, School of Psychology, University of Wales, Cardiff; Ramin Nakisa, Department of Experimental Psychology, University of Oxford; Martin Redington, Department of Experimental Psychology, University of Oxford. Web address: http://www-psych.stanford.edu/~jbt/224/Chater_Oaksford_fast.html. See also Gerd Gigerenzer, Peter M. Todd, and the ABC Research Group, *Simple Heuristics That Make Us Smart* (New York: Oxford University Press, 1999).

[8] G. Gigerenzer and D. Goldstein, "Reasoning the Fast and Frugal Way: Models of Bounded Rationality," *Psychological Review* 103 (1996): 650–69.

a fair coin. One proposal that has been made as to why this is runs as follows.

In the circumstances of human evolution, acquiring great quantities of an asset was generally not useful, since many things humans wanted were wasting resources, subject to decay even with the best storage technologies; only a limited amount could be consumed by a single individual or family, and the excess could not generally be exchanged for other useful things in the relatively simply economies of our remote ancestors. In contrast, falling below a certain basic minimum of resources guaranteed death or its close evolutionary cousin infecundity; and, since most of our early ancestors were close to the level of subsistence most of the time, risking current assets usually did mean that, if the risk did not pay off, one would fall below that required minimum. So a bias against risking what one has is built into us, even though in the present world most such risks do not pose threats to our survival, and even though most of us would be better off, by the standards taught us by the rules of reason, if we did not have such a bias. (Not all of us, of course: irrational behavior sometimes produces rewards, as the government chooses to remind us regularly by supporting a National Lottery.)[9]

Notice that whether something involves a risk of loss is often a matter of how the choice is framed. Consider the following example from Amos Tversky and Daniel Kahneman. You are told of an outbreak of a disease that will probably kill about 600 people in the population if nothing is done. There are two possible policies. One will save 200 people pretty certainly. On the other policy, there is a 1/3 chance of saving 600 people and a 2/3 chance that they will still all die. Suppose they cost the same. Most people will prefer the first policy.[10] But now frame the case the other way round. On one option, 400 people will pretty certainly die. On the other, there is a 1/3 chance that nobody will die, and

---

[9] This sort of risk-aversion, which involves treating losses and gains asymmetrically, is reinforced, of course, by the structure of our sentiments. The person who loses 1,000 pounds in a perfectly rational bet that would have netted him a couple of pounds if it had paid off is additionally burdened by regret at the loss. Whether or not this feeling itself counts as reasonable, taking account of it, if it is a settled fact of our natures, is certainly reasonable. And so you could say that evolution has built into us, by way of the mechanism of regret, an emotion that makes risk-aversion sometimes rational. (You could also say that regret is often itself irrational, when its propositional content is that I should have done something else than what I did.)

[10] Amos Tversky and Daniel Kahneman, "The Framing of Decisions and the Psychology of Choice," *Science* 211 (1981): 453–58; reprinted in *Rational Choice,* ed. Jon Elster (New York: Oxford University Press, 1986), pp. 123–41. This case is discussed on pp. 124–25.

a 2/3 chance that all 600 will still die. Now most people prefer the second policy.[11]

What makes the difference, arguably, is that in the first case the first policy is described as one of saving 200 people, while in the second it is described as losing 400 people. In the first case, the baseline is the number of people who will be lost if we do nothing and so the 200 people are "gained"; in the second, the baseline is the number of people we have now, and so the 400 people are "lost." And people tend to be risk-averse about gains, but risk-taking about losses, as the evolutionary explanation predicts. (Note, by the way, that no one picks the response that the rules of reason suggest, which is indifference between these policies.)

So here the agent's choices depend on how certain options are described, and this makes a difference even though what is being offered is the same pair of options under different logically equivalent descriptions.[12]

My aim so far has been to defend, first, an account of the rules of reason as constitutive of our understanding of beliefs and desires. That, I think, is why rational choice explanations are so attractive and compelling. But I have also urged, second, that once we grasp the idealization that

---

[11] Most people in these cases meant about three-quarters of a sample of about 150 students at Stanford and the University of British Columbia. Tversky and Kahneman, "The Framing of Decisions and the Psychology of Choice."

[12] This fact is important in real economic choices that people make every day. Consider a taxi-driver whose aim is to make a hundred dollars a day. It's two o'clock in the afternoon, two hours before he has to hand the car over to another driver, and he's made his $100.00. I flag him down and ask him to take me to the airport: a longish trip that will net him $15.00. He has the time to do the job and $15.00 would normally be appealing. But he's made today's account, so he declines. If he'd only made $85.00 so far today, he'd take me. (This example was suggested to me by the discussion of Richard Thaler's work in Roger Lowenstein, "Exuberance Is Rational," *New York Times Magazine,* February 11, 2001, pp. 68–71. Taxi drivers' "accounts" are discussed on p. 71, column 1.) What makes the difference? That he views a day where he makes less than $100.00 from taxi driving as one where he's made a loss. The taxi driver's attitude here is irrational from a profit-maximizing point of view, because whether an offer is worthwhile should depend only on whether your expected profit is higher if you accept it than if you reject it. It shouldn't depend on what you happen to have in your pocket already.

Taking the past into account in this kind of way is at the heart of another favorite irrationality that has been noticed by behavioral economists, that of our tendency to weigh "sunk costs." One of Richard Thaler's standard examples is the fact that we are more likely to go to the stadium if we've bought the ticket already than if we'd merely planned to go to the football game and buy the ticket there. But when you're contemplating going to the game, the ticket money has already been spent and (let's suppose) you can't get it back: so, since nothing you do will bring the money back, it's odd to take account of the expense in deciding whether to go. If you won't enjoy it, then the money's already wasted. If you will, there's a reason to go, independently of the sunk cost.

underlies that understanding—once we see that it involves ignoring our imperfections—it is clear that the rules of reason are impossible to live up to. Third, I have proposed that we *can* use them, when we have the time, away from the pressure of actual decisions, to reflect upon whether our habits of belief and decision are likely to have us believing what it is best to believe and achieving what we most want. And, fourth, I have suggested that, since the evolution of theoretical and practical reasoning has occurred with our actual limited minds, our actual beliefs and desires often deviate from what the rules of reason require because our actual minds in our actual environments can often get the right results by using "fast and frugal" rules of thumb. And when I say "the right results" here, I mean the results that the rules of reason would yield if we had the capacity to use them.

These claims matter for a politics based, as I suggested in the first lecture our politics should be, on respect for the idea that each of us has his or her own life to make. If, for example, it is possible to shape our environments, by state action, in ways that mean that our actual cognitive systems will more often settle on the right answer, as understood by applying the rules of reason, then, so it seems, government could be seen to be helping us to make the lives we really want.

From the fact that we often breach what the rules of reason require, it follows that there can be questions about whether our decisions reflect our beliefs and desires. In practice, there may be lines of thought we should have followed that would have identified for us better courses of action and we may have carried through incorrectly the lines of thinking we did carry through. In cases where this is true, shaping the world so that we will be directed to the right outcome is not an interference in our projects but an aid in their completion.

But another consequence of our imperfection is that we do not have a single consistent picture of the world or a single coherent preference structure. Sometimes, so to speak, we use one mental map, sometimes another, inconsistent one. If we realized the inconsistency, we might do the investigation necessary to correct it, if we had the time. But, since the maps are invoked in different contexts, the fact of their inconsistency may well never come to our attention. Similarly, we may have incoherent collections of preferences. When I am shopping with cash I think of my financial resources in one way; when I am using a credit card I conceive them in another. I know, at some level, that these two forms of money are fungible, and so I have the intellectual resources to recognize the problem. Still, I haven't done anything about it yet (I will, I promise, when I have the time…really), and so it is unclear what my real attitude to money is. As a result, then, both of the inconsistency of our beliefs and of the incoherence of our overall preferences, it may simply not be clear what my projects really are: I have many incompatible projects and I haven't done the work to resolve the inconsistencies.

There is another kind of inconsistency in our desires that is not logical inconsistency. It has to do with the fact that we have second-order preferences, so that, to use the most famous obvious example, I may *both* want to smoke a cigarette *and* want not to have this first-order desire. Some work has been done—notably by Harry Frankfurt—that suggests some principles by which we might adjudicate in such cases, between a mere desire and a person's real will. If I not only want to refrain from smoking but also want to have the first-order desire not to smoke to be effective in my actions, then, Frankfurt says, I have a "second-order volition." Its content is that I should refrain from smoking because I have a first-order desire not to smoke. Frankfurt calls a person who has no second-order volitions a "wanton": a wanton does not care about why he acts. And so he says: "When a *person* acts, the desire by which he is moved is either the will he wants or a will he wants to be without. When a *wanton* acts, it is neither."[13] Frankfurt has gone on to suggest that a person's second-order volitions reflect the fact that he cares about certain things.

A person who cares about something is, as it were, invested in it. He *identifies* himself with what he cares about in the sense that he makes himself vulnerable to losses and susceptible to benefits depending upon whether what he cares about is diminished or enhanced.[14]

And a further reflection of what one cares about is that one has second-order volitions that derive from one's caring: "The formation of a person's will is most fundamentally a matter of his coming to care about certain things, and of his coming to care about some of them more than about others."[15]

A conflict between one's second-order volitions and one's first-order desires requires a form of resolution that is different from the resolution

[13] Harry Frankfurt, "Freedom of the Will and the Concept of a Person," in *The Importance of What We Care About: Philosophical Essays* (New York: Cambridge University Press, 1988), p. 19.

[14] From "The Importance of What We Care About," in Frankfurt, *The Importance of What We Care About,* p. 83.

[15] Ibid., p. 91.

of inconsistencies among one's first-order preferences. It involves, as Frankfurt says, identification, taking one's volitions to be one's real self and one's first-order desire to be inauthentic; and it requires, too (as he elsewhere adds), the capacity for decision, for making up one's mind.[16] To the extent, once more, that government action limits one's ability to act on one's desires in ways that reflect and endorse the second-order volitions that one has identified with, it is, once more, possible to say that it is helping one to make one's life.

The fundamental arguments here are two. First, if the ground of autonomy is that it is required to shape one's own life, then we should distinguish, in using the power of the state to limit people's actions, between constraints that substantially interfere with their making of their lives and ones that don't. The latter do not threaten life-making and cannot be ruled out, therefore, on the basis of such considerations. Second, given our actual irrationality, which itself interferes with our life-making, it will be fine—sometimes, at least—to constrain people to do what is reasonable, where this is a matter of shaping the execution of their will rather than their will itself.

This very rough and preliminary exploration of some of the connections between our notions of reason and our entitlement to political freedom has brought us back, once more, to questions of identification. For, if Frankfurt is right, we need a notion of identifying with what one cares about if we are to resolve some of the many internal contradictions that threaten our claims to be reasonable people. It is, I hope, obvious enough that one reason for caring about things is that one thinks of oneself as being a person of a certain kind: so that what Frankfurt calls "identifying with what one cares about" can be structured by what I called, in the first lecture, one's identifications.

I want in a moment to begin to draw some conclusions for the political project of shaping the identities (and thus the lives) of citizens, the project I shall call "soul-making." But before turning, finally, to that project I should like to point out a different connection between our cognitive limitations and our identities, one that shows up clearly in political life.[17] We cannot gather and process the information it takes to develop reasonably based views on all of the complex questions of policy

[16] See "Identification and Wholeheartedness," in Frankfurt, *The Importance of What We Care About,* pp. 159–76.

[17] See *Elements of Reason: Cognition, Choice, and the Bounds of Rationality,* ed. Arthur Lupia, Mathew D. McCubbins, and Samuel L. Popkin (Cambridge and New York: Cambridge University Press, 2000).

that face a modern society, even if that project is the one to which we dedicate our entire life. Yet, surprisingly, most of us in fact have opinions on many public questions: we are "for" or "against" globalization; pro– or anti–labor unions; supporters or enemies of the Kyoto treaty. Part of what makes this possible, of course, is the existence of political parties that provide us with total packages of views on all the major questions; and we side with one of them by way of an affiliation that depends, quite often, on their positions on topics that we *have* investigated, or because they are defended by people whose general moral judgment we trust. It is almost true, in a society where there are two parties, that, as W. S. Gilbert had it:

> Every boy and every gal
> Who's born into the world alive
> Is either a little Liberal
> Or else a little Conservative.

(Or is so, at any rate, by the time he or she grows up.)

In other words, what parties do in politics is reduce a plentitude of possible *prises de position* to a few more manageable monoliths: and that is something that identities do for us more generally. They produce packages of life-building elements that have this to be said for them: that they have worked to some degree for a variety of human beings in one tradition or another. If we had the time, cognitive capacity, and imaginations to work out every human possibility for ourselves, we might be tempted by the thought of complete novelty: by the idea that we should be totally original. But, of course, without any recognizable elements our individualities would then impose impossible cognitive burdens on others: there would be nothing they could infer from our dress about our gender and sexuality, for example. And, as a result, our lives would not be responsive to other lives in the Hegelian manner.

Let me now say a little more exactly what I mean by "soul-making," beginning by way of a return to the question of the ethical evaluation of one's single human life.[18] Living a life means filling the time between

---

[18] There are, of course, traditions that suppose that we may have, in some sense, more than one life. It would be an interesting question to explore for such traditions what difference it makes that one is supposed to have a sequence of lives. Since in some such traditions—those of Hinduism, for example—the shape of later lives reflects facts about earlier ones, there is a clear sense in which one has responsibility for happenings in later lives; so that sequences of lives have the sort of ethical connectedness that single lives do in the view I am exploring.

birth (or at any rate adulthood) and death with a pattern of attempts and achievements that may be assessed ethically, in retrospect, as successful or unsuccessful, in whole or in part. And the ethical dimensions of the life include *both* the extent to which a person has created and experienced things—such as relationships, works of art, and institutions—that are objectively significant *and* the degree to which she has lived up to the projects she has set for herself (projects defined in part by way of her identifications). A life has gone well if a person has mostly done for others what she owed them (and is thus morally successful) and has succeeded in creating things of significance and in fulfilling her ambitions (and is thus ethically successful).[19] An individual identity, one's individuality, defines one's ambitions, determines what achievements have significance in one's own particular life. One's individuality makes certain things a significant part of the measure of one's life's success and failure, even though they would not be elements of the measure of success in every life. In my novelist's life—a life that is a novelist's life because I have chosen to make it one—the fact that I have *not* written that witty and intelligent satire of contemporary urban life that I have been struggling toward is a significant failure. My life is diminished by it. In your philosopher's life, the witty and intelligent satire you *have* written is an accidental thing, adding little to your life's value; and its cost was that you failed to complete the thinking-through of metaphysical realism that would have made your life wholly more satisfactory.

To create a life, in other words, is to interpret the materials that history has given you. Your character, your circumstances, your psychological constitution, including the beliefs and preferences generated by the interaction of your innate endowments and your experience: all these need to be taken into account in shaping a life. They are not constraints on that shaping; they are its materials. Faced, as we come to maturity, with a developing identity and a growing understanding of our circumstances, each of us has to interpret those circumstances and construct our identities, so as to make our lives as successful as possible. The identities we make, our individualities, are interpretative responses to our talents and disabilities, and the changing social, semantic, and material contexts we enter at birth; and we develop our identities dialectically with our capacities and circumstances, because the latter are in part the product of what our identities lead us to do.

---

[19] Dworkin defines ambitions in the sense I mean: "Someone's ambitions include all his tastes, preferences, and convictions as well as his overall plan of life: his ambitions furnish his reasons or motives for making one choice rather than another" (*Sovereign Virtue*, p. 322).

By "soul-making" I mean *the political project of intervening in the process of interpretation through which each citizen develops an identity with the aim of increasing her chances of living an ethically successful life.* My interpretation of my circumstances will lead me, as I have said, to have certain ambitions, on the basis of my beliefs and my underlying preferences, which will themselves be shaped by my identifications. Providing me with relevant information—and thus shaping my beliefs—is not soul-making unless it is aimed at reshaping my identity. So governments that inform citizens that smoking and unprotected sex are dangerous are not engaging in soul-making. This is the least controversial kind of government provision of information because our capacity for reason, however limited, is the ground of our right to manage our own lives. That capacity is properly exercised when relevant information is used to shape our decisions.[20] But not all government provision of information is aimed simply at giving citizens bases of decision. The telling of national histories, even when entirely factual, is often motivated by the desire to shape citizens' identifications and, thus, their individualities. It is designed to raise the thought: Now *that* is the kind of country I want to belong to. And if it succeeds in doing that, creating or reinforcing a national identification in order to improve the life of the citizen—rather than the prospects of the *polis*—then such story-telling is a form of soul-making; which is why, I suspect, there are many modern liberals who are, at least, skeptical about this form of nationalist project.[21]

Nor is it soul-making, in my sense, when government aims to alter our identities solely in order to make us do our duty to others; as when a public education system is designed to encourage the sort of civic identity that guides us to respect the rights of our fellow citizens. For this is driven by a concern not for ethical success but, at most, for moral success; and even moral success is not usually the point, because most such moral shaping aims to protect not the person shaped but others upon whom her actions impinge. But a government does seek to shape a young citizen's soul when it insists on sports in state schools in order to develop team spirit, thus shaping her relation to her identities in ways that go beyond what is morally required.

---

[20] The provision of misinformation, on the other hand, interferes with the carrying out of our projects; and where it interferes with the success of those projects that flow from our identities it is especially objectionable on that ground.

[21] Telling me that smoking is dangerous doesn't affect my identity, in this sense, though it *is* aimed to make my life go better.

So, to insist on the point, not everything that government does that forms my identity is soul-making. For soul-making has to be *aimed* at making such changes and so aimed in order to improve the citizen's chances of living an *ethically successful* life. Of course, governments must affect how lives go: for government must enforce contracts and provide the physical security—from assault and the destruction of our property—that is the background to the pursuit of any reasonable life at all. And these acts will certainly affect the circumstances within which I make my life and, thus, the actions I perform, and may well impact my identifications as well. Still, these acts are only soul-making if they aim to improve my ethical prospects by altering the interpretation of my circumstances that guides my life.

It seems to me that there is an understanding of modern liberalism—one particularly prevalent, I think, in the United States and among certain defenders of "free markets" elsewhere—according to which soul-making, thus understood, is wrong. I suspect that it is a resistance to soul-making that underlies much opposition, of the sort expressed by Isaiah Berlin, to positive conceptions of liberty. Let us call this skeptical opposition to soul-making *restrictive liberalism.*[22]

Let me use again the distinction between ethics and morals from the beginning of my first lecture to specify the content of this restrictive view. There is a reasonable place for government in guaranteeing security of life and property and creating the framework of contract because these are matters that have to do with how we treat one another; because they are, in this sense, moral matters. But restrictive liberalism claims that the government should not interfere in ethics, should not be guided by notions as to what lives are good and bad for a person to lead, once he

---

[22] The form of restrictive liberalism I am interested in is a restricted liberalism of principle. It assumes government can be trustworthy and transparent. This is no doubt, to put it gently, a utopian assumption, and there is a tradition of restrictive liberalism that is based not in the arguments I am considering but in that mistrust. It is the liberalism of James Madison, who sought to construct both a constitution of checks and balances in which no power could accumulate too easily anywhere and a rich civil society that would enmesh us in so many networks of interest that no network would ever dominate a majority of us and thus be able to organize the permanent domination of a minority. Madison helped to design a political system that was meant to sustain a wide diversity of thick social identities without government involvement in soul-making. I have some sympathy with these arguments, but I am not going to concern myself with them here. For there are those who would not allow the government to carry out these functions even if it could be trusted, and it is their arguments I am interested in.

or she has met the enforceable demands of moral duty.[23] And so, more specifically, the government should not seek to make me a better person for my own sake. I said something very like this myself in the first lecture. I identified Mill's liberalism with "the view that I should be permitted (in particular, by the state) to make whatever life flows from my choices, provided that I give you what I owe you and do you no harm."

But I have also pointed, from time to time, to ways in which the fact that each of us has a life to make can at least raise the possibility that the state ought to act to help us in that project. And at least some of these possibilities entail a kind of soul-making. Thus, I pointed out that we couldn't respect the autonomy of infants because, not yet having individualities, they begin with no basis for making the choices that will determine how their lives will go. Since parents cannot be guaranteed to prepare children for an autonomous adulthood, the state must, at least sometimes, intervene. As a result, a society *must* engage to some degree in the soul-making of children. It must shape character, preferences, and beliefs; and it should do so with the aim of allowing children to grow into adults whose lives will be successful. Since this shaping will affect the child's conception of her identity and, in particular, will help determine what the adult into whom she grows will take to be her identity, this is soul-making on the grandest scale. It intervenes in a child's interpretation of her situation by forming the tools of that interpretation.

I also argued that the fact that each of us has a life to lead might provide a reason for the state to sustain the materials for making a life, among them the infrastructure that gives sense to our social identities. The free exercise of our identities may require socially provided resources, I said (admitting that I wasn't sure what this might mean in many cases). These socially provided resources, among them the recognition that generates self-respect, go far beyond the provision of objective information or the neutral provision of material resources that will allow the agent to interpret the world and make a life. For each identity that a society sustains in this way is changed by the very fact of government recognition. "Hispanic" in the United States exists as a social identity that includes Mexican-Americans, Puerto Ricans, and immigrants from dozens of Spanish-speaking countries of Latin America and

---

[23] So a restrictive liberal will, of course, take into account people's ethical projects, not least because our duties may include not undermining other people's ethical projects in various ways.

the Caribbean, in part because of the U.S. government's acknowledgment of those people as a collectivity. Many state acts have taken place since the creation of the identity that are aimed at shaping the identities, and thus the ethical prospects, of Hispanics; among them, for example, the provision of bilingual education programs for adults that allow them to maintain a language-based identity while integrating them into American society. So here is a case of soul-making for adults.[24]

And finally, after my discussion of our defection from the rules of reason, I suggested that there were circumstances in which governments might want to mold our environments so that our imperfect cognitive systems will more often settle on the right answer, as understood by applying the rules of reason; and that it might guide us to choices that reflect what our own judgments would have been, if we had applied our rational capacities more effectively. It will not do to say this cannot be soul-making because it can only give effect to our interpretation of our circumstances rather than overruling or altering it. For sometimes, at least, in cases that I am going to consider, the government may seek to intervene directly in making our identities.

These are all instances of soul-making; and if pursued by a government that is guided, at least in part, by a concern to help each of us make a success of our own lives, then they are instances of liberal soul-making. I want now to say a little more about each of these three forms of liberal soul-making: in the education of the young, in sustaining social identities, and in saving us from our own rational incapacities. I shall begin with the last of these; and to do so I would like to borrow some ideas from Ronald Dworkin.

In *Sovereign Virtue* Dworkin argues for a political morality that is governed by two central principles. According to the *principle of equal importance,* "it is important, from an objective point of view, that human lives be successful rather than wasted, and this is equally important, from the objective point of view, for each human life." The *principle of special responsibility* declares that each of us has special responsibility for the

---

[24] This does not cease to be soul-making just because the social identity in question was not itself wholly the product of intentional state action. Even where it is the fact that the identity already exists that leads to government support for it, that support provides a resource for individuals who have access to the identity, because they may require it for ethical success. But, as I say, in so doing it helps to give meaning to the identity and thus helps form the identities of those who take it up.

success of our own life. "Though we must all recognize the equal objective importance of the success of a human life, one person has a special and final responsibility for that success—the person whose life it is."[25]

But Dworkin has an especially helpful discussion—one that appeared first as a Tanner Lecture, in fact—of how each of us should be permitted to take special and final responsibility for the success or failure of our own life. In an essay on "Equality and the Good Life," Dworkin answers the question, "By what standard should we test a life's success or failure?" What is the metric by which our fundamental ethical choices are evaluated?

The question, he rightly insists, is not whether we get more or less of what we want (more or less of what he calls our "volitional well-being") but whether we get more or less of what is worth having; more or less, in his formulation, of our "critical well-being." Given his commitment to special responsibility, you will predict that he takes it that what is in our critical interest depends, in part, on what our plan of life is, what projects we have selected for ourselves. His metric is provided by what he calls the "model of challenge." That model, he writes,

> adopts Aristotle's view that a good life has the inherent value of a skillful performance.... The model of challenge holds that life is itself a performance that demands skill, that it is the most comprehensive and important challenge we face, and that our critical interests consist in the achievements, events and experiences that mean that we have met the challenge well.[26]

Now the notion I want to borrow from Dworkin is a useful distinction between three ways in which our circumstances figure in the evaluation of how well we have met the challenge. Some of our circumstances act as parameters, he says, defining what it is for us to have lived a successful life. They are, so to speak, part of the challenge that we must meet. Others are limits—obstacles that get in the way of our making the ideal life that the parameters help define. And the rest are resources. In thinking about her own life, each person must decide how to allocate her circumstances between these categories, just as an artist must decide which aspects of the tradition she inherits define what her art is and which are barriers to or instruments for her creativity.

[25] Dworkin, *Sovereign Virtue*, p. 5.

[26] Ibid., p. 253. On the challenge model, as he says later, living well is "responding in the right way to one's situation" (p. 260).

We have no settled template for that decision, in art or in ethics, and no philosophical model can provide one, for the circumstances in which each of us lives are enormously complex.... Anyone who reflects seriously on the question which of the various lives he might lead is right for him will consciously or unconsciously discriminate among these, treating some as limits and others as parameters.[27]

Among the circumstances Dworkin regards as his own parameters is his being American. His American-ness is, he says, "a condition of the good life for" him.[28] So, for example, even though he has long taught jurisprudence in England and has no doubt influenced the development of English legal thinking, there surely is, for him, a special significance to his contributions to American constitutional jurisprudence, a significance that derives from the fact that America—and not England—is *his* country.[29] Clearly Dworkin's talk of parameters here recalls much of what I have said about identification: to identify as an L is to treat one's being an L as a parameter.

Here, once more, social identities seem absolutely central to ethical life. Consider, to give another example, homosexuality. For some people, their homosexuality is a parameter: they are gay, and, happy or unhappy, rich or poor, the life they seek to make will be a life in which erotic relationships with members of their own sex will be central. Others think of their sexuality as a limitation: they want desperately to be rid of homosexual desires, and, if they cannot be rid of them, they would at least like to succeed in not acting on them. (When I was a student here there were some people who apparently regarded their *hetero*sexuality in this way.)[30]

I think the distinction between parameters and limits is indeed crucial and that making it is central to ethical life. Furthermore, it seems to me absolutely right to insist that many aspects of the allocation between

[27] Ibid.

[28] Ibid., p. 261.

[29] Among the limits Dworkin admits to is that he is not as good a sailor of recreational boats as he would like to be. Ibid., p. 243.

[30] It is an important part of Dworkin's view that you can be wrong about whether something is a parameter of your life: it is not simply up to you. So he might say that it is ordinarily just a *mistake* in our society to think this way: or, at any rate, that it is a mistake to think it under pressure from the irrational homophobia of our culture. But he could also say that for such people their sexuality just is a limitation; which is what he says about those who have, but wish they did not have, a "generous appetite for sex" (ibid., p. 82).

parameter and limit must be up to me. This is part of my special responsibility: not only must I meet my challenge, I must also define it.

Here is another place where our understanding of social identities helps us: for it allows us to see that though this act of definition must be mine, the resources I have to draw on in defining my challenge are provided as much as anything by my society. You will recall that I discussed in the first lecture the ways in which the narrative patterns associated with identities help people shape their lives. Because these stories are socially transmitted and produced, they are different in different places. And so because I draw on narrative resources provided by a particular set of social groups, the way I define my challenge will reflect things that are particular to those groups as well.

Dworkin's mobilization of these ideas generates an activist state, because the equal importance of our lives means that each of us is entitled to an equal share of our society's resources in making a life, and some of his most original proposals have to do with how we should measure and equalize resources.[31] But nothing in here yet requires that governments take a view about the relative merits of the different challenges entailed by different possible assignments of our characteristics to the status of parameters and limitations: so far, for all we have said, legitimate governments will intervene to provide us with an equal share of the resources we need to make our lives; but beyond the demand that we do our duty to others, they will not take a view about what lives we make. That is, for each of us, our own special responsibility.

I have been suggesting, on the other hand, that our limited rationality raises the possibility that the state may have to evaluate at least *some* challenges and engage in soul-making based on those evaluations. I shall explore that possibility and some other kinds of soul-making in my final lecture.[32]

---

[31] Among other things he takes seriously the notion that the equality of resources to which we are entitled covers some of our natural endowments as well, so that the disabled are entitled to compensation for their disabilities and the untalented are entitled to a guaranteed base-line income if the market does not provide one. For a brief summary of (my understanding of) Dworkin's position, see my "Equality of What?" in the *New York Review of Books,* May 2001.

[32] I want to remind you again that even the restrictive liberal distinguishes ethical from moral interventions in our lives and permits the latter. So, in particular, if some element of your identity is associated with an immoral project, if part of your self-defined challenge is doing injustice, the restrictive liberal will have a perfectly principled reason for rejecting your challenge and intervening in your shaping of your life. There is no paradox in saying that we will not let a couple force their adult daughter into a marriage that does not meet with her approval in the name of autonomy: their autonomy is a right to shape their own

## III. SOUL-MAKING

At the end of the last lecture, I promised to defend a form of soul-making motivated by a recognition of our defections from the rules of ideal reason. But I want to do this in the context of a clear understanding that restrictive liberalism is not the requirement that the state ignore our identities; that it be color-blind or gender-blind, as it is common now to express that idea. Soul-making is deliberately shaping identities, and, as Dworkin's challenge model proposes—rightly in my view—each person has the central place in determining the parameters of her life. But providing you with resources, as Dworkin's picture also makes clear, is perfectly consistent with taking no view at all about how you have evaluated your challenge. This is as true of identity-supporting resources, such as civic celebrations of ethnically significant holidays, as it is of handouts of money. Restrictive liberals do not oppose providing you with resources; rather they are against, roughly, both telling you what to do with them (beyond not using them in ways that are unjust) and trying to make you want to use them in any particular one of the many morally permissible ways. So if you need certain resources because of your identity that others do not, there is no reason why a restrictive liberal should ignore this fact in designing social arrangements. The provision of public lavatories marked for gender is a reflection of the fact that people's gender identities often entail a sense of bodily privacy that makes the presence of the other sex an embarrassment in that context. That provision need not be an endorsement of that norm of gender identity, and need not be seen as an attempt to force us to interpret our genders in a way that entails this conception of privacy: it could be supported by a restrictive liberal as a mere reflection of the fact that this is how we feel.

It is important, I think, that restrictive liberalism is actually somewhat less limited in its potential interventions than is sometimes assumed, for another reason: a restrictive liberal, too, can acknowledge the need to do something about our pervasive irrationalities. So before considering modes of soul-making that go beyond restrictive liberalism, I would like first to propose, as a thought experiment, a mechanism that

---

with her approval in the name of autonomy: their autonomy is a right to shape their own lives, not to shape their daughter's, and respect for the autonomy of others, properly understood, is a moral obligation. (It does not follow, of course, that any intervention to change a person's character that will lead them to do their duty more often is *eo ipso* justified.)

should be congenial to restrictive liberalism by which the state could provide us with a tool for dealing with one form of irrationality: namely, a certain sort of weakness of will.

I am not going to provide an account of what weakness of the will consists in, or even of what is irrational about it. (Though I shall say that some of Frankfurt's ideas are helpful in answering these questions.) Saint Paul confessed to the Romans: "For the good that I would I do not: but the evil which I would not, that I do."[1] I shall take it for granted only that (a) sometimes, like Saint Paul, we find ourselves not doing what we judge to be all-things-considered best for us to do, even when no one else's interests are at stake, and that (b) this is to breach the rules of reason. All of us have fallen off diets, or bought frivolous things when we had resolved to save, or left tasks to the last minute that we knew we would have done better if we had undertaken them steadily over a longer time.

Recognizing this, and understanding that every life would go better if we had mechanisms for controlling our akratic tendencies, the government might step in to propose one helpful solution. Each of us will be given a government-authorized Self-Management card. With modern technology it would be relatively easy to set it up so that each of us could manage our appetites (whether for calories, for nicotine, for alcohol, or for heroin) in the following way. We could sign in, on the web, to the relevant government website and list those things that we did not wish to be able to buy. One would be free to bind oneself for a certain period in this way, so that a change of mind would be given effect only after due deliberation. By law, all goods would be classified according to categorizations relevant for this purpose, and all stores would require the presentation of the Self-Management card before selling anything. The card would be swiped and read before any sale. A person who sought to buy anything that was listed as among the items proscribed on the website would be told that the store was not able to sell it to her, unless, of course, she went back to the website and altered the list. Here we adopt Ulysses' response to the temptations of the sirens, with the government providing the infrastructure.

Notice that this is something that could not be privately arranged. If there were any shops that did not insist on the card, then the device would not work for me. When I am dieting, I should not consume

---

[1] King James Bible, Romans, chapter 7, verse 19.

liquor or chocolates or a whole list of other high-calorie foods. I know this. I remove them from my house when I am dieting; I tell my friends not to offer them to me. But if I arrive at the supermarket, tired from work at the end of a long day, I know I will succumb and buy myself a Kit-Kat. So, when I go on the diet, I simply enter chocolates onto my Self-Management account as proscribed for the period of the diet and only a criminal will sell them to me. Since, as it happens, I am fairly law-abiding and my friends are responsible, the fact that it would be a criminal transaction to acquire some actually means that, once the entry on the website is done, I will not get chocolates.[2]

Perhaps it is the case that all of us could take heroin once without being addicted. In that case, I might be interested in having the experience. So I might sign myself up for one dose of heroin and go out and buy it, knowing that the temptation to do so again would require my reflectively signing on and that I could resist the temptation to do that, even though, faced in the store with a second chance at heroin, I might not resist it. The whimsicality of our akratic desires is thus made manageable; and lives that might have failed utterly if heroin had been freely available are in fact lived successfully.

Here, then, is a state-enforced scheme that gives each of us a tool for the management of our lives; nevertheless, it is entirely up to us to decide how to make use of it. You are free to have your Self-Management card declare all goods available to you. So the state here takes no view about the first-order question of how we wish to define the challenge of our lives—if you opt for the struggle with heroin addiction (or even drift into it irrationally), this system permits it. But it does express a second-order commitment to helping us make lives successful by whatever standards we ourselves have defined.

The Self-Management card makes clear that the state can respond to our irrationalities without soul-making. This is important because some people seem to think that there is a direct argument from restrictive liberal premises to the conclusion that there is no role for the state beyond the equalization of resources or as the guarantor of basic moral obligations. Here, however, is a role for the state in enabling our ethical

---

[2] Such a system might obviously be extended to deal with narcotics. The government might say that everyone was presumptively signed off from acquiring heroin, but that one could sign on for its use for a fixed amount and period if one chose. Because of the psychology of addiction, it might seem best with an actual proposal to say that, with heroin and such drugs, one would have to sign up a day in advance to make sure that one had time to reflect on what one was doing; but that might offend the restrictive liberal.

success that is consistent with restrictive liberalism and derives from our shared recognition of our incapacity to live by the rules of reason.

But I want, now, to go further and argue that our irrationalities can provide grounds for state soul-making in defense of our ethical projects: sometimes it will be right for the state to help people by shaping their individualities because their unshaped identities are the result of a limited capacity to follow the rules of reason.

Social identities are, as I have insisted all along, among the elements of our individualities. To the extent that social identities are incoherent (in a sense I shall be exploring soon), their incoherence can be an obstacle to the coherence of individual identities that include them. If our irrationality leads us to fail to see or respond to the incoherence of certain social identities, then someone might seek to reshape those social identities, thus reforming those whose individual identities are partially defined by them, in the name of the success of their individual lives. And sometimes, so it seems to me, that someone might be the state.

By the incoherence of a social identity, I mean this: that it has a set of norms associated with it, such that, in the actual world, attempting to conform to some subset of those norms undermines one's capacity to conform to others. (The more substantially this undermining of norms by each other damages the prospects of success of the lives of those who bear the identities, the more incoherent I shall say they are.) The incoherence of a social identity can lead to incoherence in individual identities: to someone's having an identity that generates projects and ambitions that undermine one another. Clearly this will lead to problems for those who identify with an incoherent social identity; their lives will go worse than they might have if they had access to a (more) coherent social identity. A project of reform of the identity to make its norms more coherent would therefore be in the interest of those people. If we could achieve this reform by informing people of the facts of incoherence, then government might choose to do so; and it would be engaging in soul-making to do this, as I observed when I mentioned certain forms of nationalist identity building projects earlier. But if irrationalities of some sort lead citizens not to respond to the facts in this reasonable way, we might then consider other mechanisms of reform, if any were available.

I think that there are many ethnic and racial identities in the modern world that fit exactly this abstract characterization. They are incoherent; their incoherence has been regularly announced to no obvious effect; and there are available mechanisms of reform that could be carried out by governments that would lead people to new, more coherent identities. Furthermore, while these reforms would also sometimes lead people to treat others better (and so have a moral dimension to them that is important as well) they would certainly also increase the chances of the ethical success of the lives of those whose identities they are.

To establish that I am right in any particular case I should need, then, to argue three things: that the identity was incoherent; that being informed of the incoherence had little effect; and that there were mechanisms of reform, other than the provision of that information. I do not have the time to do this in any great detail for even a single case. But let me sketch in the argument for one case: that of one American racial identity.

An identity is incoherent, I said, if some of the norms associated with it are mutually undermining. And by "norm," here, I did not mean anything especially grand. Identities afford reasons for action to those who identify with them, of the sorts I suggested in the first lecture; and, as a result, they will say to themselves sometimes, "Because I am an L, I should do X." Any such appeal (if it is, indeed, reasonable) is, in the terms I am proposing, an appeal to a norm associated with that identity.

Most social identities, especially of historically subordinated groups, have norms of solidarity: "Because I am an L," an L will say, "I should do this thing for that other L." One way in which an identity can be incoherent, then, is if what I called in the first lecture the *social conception* that in part defines the identity pulls, so to speak, in different directions, because it has criteria for ascribing the identity that are inconsistent with the facts. Racial identities in the United States have exactly this feature. Many Americans believe that a person with one African-American and one European-American parent is an African-American, following the so-called one-drop rule that prevailed in some legal conceptions of black identity in the period before slavery and the legal institutions of "Jim Crow," America's system of apartheid, were abolished. While most Americans understand that this means that some African-Americans will "look white," they mostly suppose that this phenomenon is rare in relation to the African-American population as a whole. So, while they acknowledge that there are African-Americans who can "pass for white," they believe it to be a general truth that African-Americans in general are very likely to have been subject to the sort of racial discrimination that manifests itself in the sort of everyday discourtesy from public officials that remains a regrettably common feature of American social life.

The set of beliefs I have just described is not logically incoherent; there are certainly what philosophers call "possible worlds" in which they are all true together. But in the actual world these beliefs are not correct, because they are inconsistent with the fact that very many— perhaps even a majority—of the Americans who are descended from African slaves "look white," are treated as white, and identify as such.[3] To put the matter as paradoxically as possible: most people who are African-American by the one-drop rule are, are regarded as, and regard themselves as white. Most people in the United States have a social conception of the African-American identity that entails that this is not so. So they have a social conception that is inconsistent with the facts. Of course, most people do not know this. And as a result it is also part of the social conception of African-American identity that there are some people of African-American ancestry who were raised as white people, not knowing of their African ancestry; who look like other white people and thus have the skin-privilege associated with whiteness; and are, as a result, not really African-American. People who have thought about the matter a little will know that this means that the one-drop rule is not to be taken too absolutely and that, as a result, their notion of what it means to be an African-American has fuzzy boundaries. But, because they do not realize the inconsistency that I have just identified, they regard this as a minor anomaly that makes little practical difference.

The result is that the norm of solidarity for African-Americans entails that African-Americans very often have, in the one-drop rule, a reason for identity-based generosity to people they believe, on the basis of another part of their social conception, to be white. If they acted on the one-drop rule–based norms, their identity-based generosity would be directed more often than not toward people they regard as whites.

This would be only a mild incoherence that posed no substantial

---

[3] This fact was drawn to my attention by Brent Staples in a Du Bois lecture in early April 2001 and will, no doubt, be discussed in the book that will be based on them. He was kind enough to refer me to Robert P. Stuckert, "African Ancestry of the White American Population," *Ohio Journal of Science* 58, no. 3 (May 1958): 155. This article describes its statistical model and the sorts of data against which it was tested and concludes: "The data presented in this study indicate that the popular belief in the non African background of white persons is invalid. Over twenty-eight million white persons are descendants of persons of African origin."

threat to the critical interests of the lives of most African-Americans, if acts of individual identity-based generosity were the only norm associated with American blackness. But, of course, it is not. And among the other norms strongly and centrally associated with that identity is support for policies of affirmative action in employment, government contracting, and education. Very many Americans are inclined to say, "As a black person, I support affirmative action." Now, by affirmative action they mean something like this: that various social goods, among them jobs and places in colleges and universities, should be allocated in a way that gives weight to making the average chance of getting these social goods about the same for blacks and for whites. If blacks are between twelve and thirteen percent of the U.S. population, they think that, *ceteris paribus,* they should be represented as about that percentage of those receiving those goods.

Support for affirmative action, thus understood, derives from many considerations. That black people generally have received less than their fair share of these social goods historically and continue to do so, in part as a consequence of historical racial injustice, in part as a result of persisting racial prejudice, and so are entitled to compensation for that wrong; that the presence of a significant number of black people in positions of social authority and respect—as lawyers, public officials, doctors, teachers at prestigious institutions—will reduce the extent of negative stereotyping of black people in general; that the presence of significant numbers of black people in all major social positions will guarantee that black interests will be taken into account in decision-making and that anti-black prejudice will less often be expressed in contexts of decision and thus be less determinative of the outcome; and so on. These arguments are not usually individually self-regarding; they are driven by the desire that things should go better generally for black people in the United States. Many African-Americans, that is, are what black people in America call "race men" and "race women." It is important to them that black people should do well; and making a contribution to that end is one of the aims by which they define the success of their lives.

Now, all decent people will wish that black people in America should not do worse than others because they are treated by state and society as black. We should all wish that the United States, like all other states, not be a racially discriminatory society. As a result, all decent people want African-Americans to do better, on average, than, on average, they currently do. But while the race men and women certainly think this, this is not the full content of their thought. They take pleasure in the successes and failures of other black people not just to the extent that this reflects an increase in justice, but as a reflection of their identification as black. Central to their identifications is a form of partiality: the success of black people generally matters to them more than the successes of others.

It is the similarity of this sentiment to the sentiment that underlies much patriotism that leads people to call such dispositions "nationalist." Like other nationalists, these people have the thought that they would like their people to do well, *because they are their people.* It may well be that if African-Americans ceased to be (or, at any rate, to think of themselves as being) the victims of unrecompensed injustice, they might mostly cease to identify as African-Americans, so that this form of nationalism would cease. But while it exists, the success of many African-American lives is thus tied up with the coherence of the project of racial uplift.

The inconsistency of a race man or woman's social conception of African-American identity with the facts thus poses more than a minor threat of incoherence. For without a clarification of the issue of who is black, the content of policies that meet their aim cannot be identified and the state cannot even consider whether it can, in justice, undertake policies that help to make the lives of African-Americans go well by helping to achieve one of the identity-related aims of African-American nationalists.

I said I needed to establish three things, of which the first was that racial identity in the United States was, in my sense, incoherent. I hope that I have begun to discharge that obligation.

My second charge is to show that information would not by itself solve the problem. That is evident in this case. There has been a great circulation of exactly the sort of information that I have been providing among educated Americans in the last few decades and, more particularly, among African-Americans. During this same period, however, the sort of black nationalism I have identified has become stronger, *especially among the very middle-class black people who are most likely to have gotten this information.* But the incoherence it entails has not evaporated. There is little discussion and certainly no consensus as to how to reconcile the standard social conception of African-American identity with the facts.

When I first found myself in the United States, some twenty-odd years ago, I assumed that the fact that racial classifications were biologically incoherent—a fact that lies at the heart of the intellectual difficulties in the social conception of race that I have been discussing—was widely known at least among the educated. I can report, after speaking to thousands of educated Americans since, that it continues to be a surprise. Talk of the "social construction of race" has become standard in the last few years, but this is a slogan, not the expression of a coherent understanding. And this could not be so if Americans applied the rules of reason to their thinking about their racial identities, because it is an inconsistency between one set of beliefs—about the prevalence of passing—and another—about how to ascribe African-American identity—that lies, as I said, at its heart.

One reason, I believe, why Americans are less troubled than the rules of reason suggest they should be by these facts is a consequence of a practice that Hilary Putnam, I believe, dubbed *semantic deference,* a practice that is a central feature of languages that are the shared possession of very large numbers of people, with very different experiences and large variations in the extent and the subject matter of their knowledge. Under this practice all of us use words whose precise applications are determined finally by experts. Whether or not we are lawyers, we speak of having contracts, even though most of us would not be in a position to begin to explain what the conditions are in English or American law that must subsist for a contract to exist between two parties. Whether or not we are theoretical physicists we use the word "string" (as I did once in the first lecture), which has a technical meaning that it is beyond my competence (and arguably beyond any current person's competence!) fully to elucidate. We use these terms believing that there are experts somewhere—and, if no current experts, then procedures that could be learned or applied—that would in fact settle such questions. There is no harm (and, indeed, much benefit) in this practice of what Hilary Putnam was also, I think, the first to call "linguistic division of labor." As a result of it, I can refer to things that I could not specify procedures for finding, and then pass on knowledge about them to others. But because we are so used to assuming deference to experts elsewhere, we do not standardly inquire into whether the experts actually exist or into whether their procedures are sensible, reliable, or coherent. I do not know whether, after sufficient legal training, I would be inclined to suppose that the concept of a contract was determinate enough to guarantee that the arrangements I have with my publisher are, in fact, contracts. I do assume that they are and that the relevantly empowered legal officials would decide that this was so if writer's push ever came to publisher's shove.

Now, in the case of race it is widely supposed that there is such a category of experts; that they are biologists or physical anthropologists or medical people of some sort; and that their judgments would mostly confirm widespread commonsense beliefs about races. But, as I have argued often elsewhere, this is not, in fact, the case. Many of these experts do not use the concept; those that do, employ it in ways that do not conform to much racial commonsense; and many of the experts that employ it are not life scientists but social scientists. Not knowing this is, I think, part of the reason that many people have not bothered to do their own conceptual housekeeping. They assume it is being done elsewhere.

Notice that this assumption is itself, in a certain sense, an adjustment to our own knowledge of our own cognitive limitations. We do not have the time or the competence, we suppose, to tidy up all our own concepts and so we accept a practice that divides the task with others. If we all had all the time and intellectual tools, we think, we could do the job for ourselves.

So, while many people use the word "race" in ways that reflect defections from the rules of reason, that they do so is not itself entirely unreasonable. It is a reflection of one of the many adjustments to our cognitive weaknesses that it is sensible for us to make; exactly the sort of practice that we can use reflection on our cognitive limitations, which I recommended in the last lecture, to defend.

Now, given semantic deference, the mere fact that the government makes announcements of these incoherences in a society already somewhat suspicious of government pronouncements on race is unlikely to be very effective. Many people would continue in their current ways (as they already have, despite the widespread diffusion of the notion of the "social construction" of race), supposing that there were experts or forms of expertise somewhere that could settle the difficulties, even after government racial propaganda had sought to draw those difficulties to their attention. In particular, therefore, many African-Americans would continue to have identities whose success was tied up with mutually undermining reasons.

That, I hope, discharges my second burden: I take it that I have shown that the incoherence of American racial identities will not be solved merely by the further dissemination of the already extremely widely disseminated facts about that incoherence. Part of my evidence is that black nationalism of the sort I identified just now is, as I pointed out a while ago, especially common among those who are best informed about these matters.

My final task, then, is to suggest that there are government actions that would be helpful here; helpful, particularly, in reshaping the social identity *African-American* in ways that, in reducing this incoherence, would increase the possibilities of success, the critical interests, in Dworkin's formulation, of African-Americans. Part of the difficulty here is that much government action in the domain of race is rightly guided not by ethical but by moral concerns. You do not need ethical reasons—in the narrow sense—for government action in this sphere, because there are moral reasons for ending racial injustice.

Nevertheless, my aim is to suggest that there may be ethical reasons for adopting state policies that respond to the incoherence of American racial identity, beyond the mere circulation of the facts through state-funded education of both young people and adults.

What sort of policies could these be? Let me offer, by way of example, just one possibility.

Current American state practice presupposes, by and large, that there is a fact of the matter about everyone as to whether or not she is African-American. One is required to fill in forms for all sorts of purposes that fix one's race, and other people—arresting police officers, for example—may also be required to do so as well. As a result, many people, who think of themselves as clearly and obviously black or white or something other than either of these in the racial system, are encouraged by this practice in the belief that the racial system is in fact relatively straightforward. Were the government to modify these practices it would remove at least one of the major struts that gives support to the idea that social conceptions of race are consistent with reality: the fact that the state appears to be able to construct successful practices that assume that social conception. Such a modification could be motivated in many ways (not the least by the recognition that the relevant social conceptions *are* rationally defective). But it might, surely, also be motivated by the thought that government action here could help to reshape racial identities in ways that would diminish their incoherence.

It will be correctly observed by many, at this point, that the policy I am speaking of here is necessary only because the state already collects racial "data." Why not simply say that the state should stay away from all racial classifications? This would, in fact, be fine for my present purposes: for it would be an instance of a state policy in shaping identity motivated in part by a concern for the ethical coherence of the lives of those with racial identities and based on a recognition of the role of defections from the rules of reason in their current incoherence.

But there is a reason not to go this far. For the United States government has reasons to collect some racial "data" in order to enforce its antidiscrimination laws. After all, antidiscrimination law presupposes that it is wrong to deprive people of certain socially available opportunities in virtue of their racial identities. One of the best forms of evidence for such practices consists in statistical discrepancies in employment, housing, lending, and the like. The wrongs underlying these statistics are moral wrongs; but they are wrongs because of the principle of equal importance, because such treatment denies that people of one racial identity are entitled to the same chances of success in their lives as people of others. So it is a moral wrong that we bar for ethical reasons.

Antidiscrimination law does not have to be motivated as soul-making, nor, in particular, as soul-making in response to a recognition of our defections from the rules of reason, which is my current topic.

But it is worth insisting that much antidiscrimination law is, in fact, soul-making, though not of the kind motivated by recognition of our irrationality. For when everyday social practices—such as the provision of racially segregated public accommodations or the proscription of interracial relations—project "an inferior or demeaning image on another" and "that image is internalized" then, as Charles Taylor insisted in a passage I quoted in my first lecture, that "projection of an inferior or demeaning image on another can actually distort and oppress."[4] The result is that changing these everyday social practices—not just by ceasing to enforce them legally but by beginning to proscribe them by law—can be one way of reforming the social conception of the racial identity *black* with the aim of improving the success of the lives of black people through the reform of their identities. That is soul-making *par excellence;* and I share with Charles Taylor and other multicultural liberals the conviction that for wrongly historically derogated identities such soul-

---

[4] Taylor, *Multiculturalism and the Politics of Recognition.*

making is more than helpful; it can be one of the duties of a state that cares equally for the lives of all its citizens.

I have been considering arguments for soul-making that result from an acknowledgment of our pervasive irrationality. But liberal soul-making may aim, as I have argued regularly in the course of these lectures, at the sustaining of social identities in ways that derive directly from the recognition of their ethical importance. This is the core of the argument for multicultural liberalism I have just summarized. Restrictive liberalism is going to be skeptical of this view, of course, just because it entails soul-making in the sorts of ways I have suggested for the case of American racial identities.

Now I said in the last lecture that the ethical evaluation of a life depended, first, on whether one had achieved one's ambitions and, second, on whether one had made or experienced anything of significance. We could call the first dimension the subjective dimension of success—not because it is not an objective question whether one has achieved one's ambitions, but because each subject determines what her ambitions are. In creating a self—shaping one's identity—one determines the parameters of one's life and thus defines one's ambitions. Let us call the second dimension of ethical success—the creation and experience of significant things—the objective dimension. If restrictive liberalism is the view that government should not engage in soul-making, does that entail that government should never take a view about *either* the subjective *or* the objective dimensions of a citizen's ethical life?

Suppose that the state has granted us each the equal share of material resources to which we are entitled. Suppose that it has guaranteed us the liberties—including the protection of life, person, and property— that we deserve. Suppose that there is in place a democratic politics, and that each citizen has a vote and the right to stand for office. Then we can consider our question in two stages.

First, is it plausible that it is wrong for that democratic state to propose identity-shaping legislation that is governed by a concern for the subjective success of the lives of citizens? Here the multicultural liberals might say that, once people have identities and the ambitions they generate, a concern for the success of citizens' lives would lead governments to create or support social institutions that allow those ambitions to succeed. People have sexualities. These lead them to have ambitions for family life in couples. An institution of marriage, which provides supports for and recognition of those couples and the families they create, is a natural consequence of a concern for the subjective ethical success of those who have a family as one of their ambitions. What it means to be a husband or wife is shaped in part by legal rules and meanings. So laws that interpret the significance of marriage, like the race-regarding laws I mentioned a little while ago, are soul-making enterprises. Equality may require that the resources for supporting marriage not detract from the lives of those who have no ambition to be coupled. But it seems consistent with respect for the equal importance of each citizen's life to provide support for those whose subjective ambitions include coupling. Nor does it seem to detract from a citizen's special responsibility, her central place in taking responsibility for her own life: for the success or failure of the marriage will still largely be the doing of its principals.

It might be objected that successful relationships are an element of objective success in life, as well. Perhaps the judgment that sustains marriage (suitably configured) as a liberal institution derives from this fact. So consider another case: that of government regulations designed to guarantee that meat labeled as *halal* or kosher is in fact prepared in the ways required by Muslim or Jewish traditions. Here it seems plausible that conformity to religious dietary codes is valuable only to those who have a commitment to those codes. (This view would be agreed to by Jewish and Muslim traditions: though they might hold that whether you have such commitments is a matter of birth, not of choice.) It is because some people have being Muslim as a parameter that eating only *halal* meat (which contributes to being a good Muslim) is among the conditions of success of their lives. Others, born and raised Muslim, may regard themselves as Muslim in certain contexts, but not see the dietary code as an important part of Muslim tradition. For them, keeping the code is not important, because they do not take it to be important.

Once again, equality does not seem *eo ipso* to rule out government provision of this service. No non-Muslim or Gentile is obliged to take any notice of the labeling; and provided the government would not refuse similar service for other dietary codes on religious grounds, there seems no sense in which this establishes religion or privileges one religious view among others. And special responsibility is respected, too, because citizens retain prime responsibility for the subjective success of their lives, both in defining whether or not dietary codes are parametric for them and in living (or not living) up to them.

Turn now to the question of objective success; and consider, for example, the question of subsidies for the arts. One possible justification
for these is that a flourishing culture provides a context in which people
can create and experience significant things. For various reasons some
such significant things—opera, say—will not be produced by the mar-
ket.⁵ There seem to be two regular lines of objection to government provision of subsidies on this basis. One is that the question whether opera
is valuable is, at best, controversial, at worst, a mere matter of opinion.
Opera matters, on this view, to the extent that people care about it and
so there is no objective basis for supporting it. If that were true, then
this would be another instance of government sustaining subjective
success. But I do not think that it is a sensible view that the arts matter
only because and to the extent that people care about them. If that were
so, then the disappearance of poetry would have no more significance
than the disappearance of pushpin.⁶ Suppose, for the moment, that I am
right.

A second line of objection is that, even if experiencing opera is an objectively valuable element of success, sustaining it because it enriches
lives involves the state in exactly the sort of evaluation of a person's interpretation and definition of her own life that the restrictive liberal
seeks to protect. We can hear echoes here of Mill's ringing defense of individuality in chapter three of *On Liberty:* "If a person possesses any tol-
erable amount of common sense and experience, his own mode of laying
out his existence is best, not because it is the best in itself, but because it
is his own mode."⁷

I am considering the view that making opera and the arts more generally available at government expense—even when no adult is forced to
attend to them—is justified because the arts can contribute to the critical well-being of citizens, whether or not this fact is one that they recognize, and whether or not they have adopted identities—as aesthetes
or connoisseurs, say—that give the experience of the arts a subjective
importance for them. But on any plausible view of the value of the arts,
this value can be realized in our lives only if we experience and attend to
them with a certain degree of commitment. And that sort of investment

⁵ These thoughts about opera grew out of a conversation with Paul Boghossian.

⁶ Though I confess to having said this (if only in passing) in the past. See my "Cos-
mopolitan Patriots," *Critical Inquiry* 23 (Spring 1997): 617–39. Reprinted in *Cosmopolitics:
Thinking and Feeling beyond the Nation,* ed. Pheng Cheah and Bruce Robbins, pp. 91–114.

⁷ John Stuart Mill, *On Liberty* (Amherst, N.Y.: Prometheus Books, 1986), pp. 77–78.

in the arts amounts to an identification with them; it entails the sort of entanglements with one's ambitions and projects that are the stuff of identity. I am not speaking of anything especially grand here: the person who sets aside time during a holiday for reading novels, or who slips in and out of art museums during her lunch break, or who commits some time each week to listening to music is making a life in which the arts matter. In a society without state subsidy of the arts, it must be other lesser arts that shape her soul. But if the state does become entangled in such subsidy it is bound to make decisions that affect what arts are actually available, what effects it has in people's lives; and so it will be in the business of soul-making.

So far as I can see restrictive liberals will be against it for this reason, even though they can acknowledge that many lives go better with these subsidies than they would without. But if the point of government is, at least in part, to create a social world in which our lives can go well, as well as possible, then I think this is enough reason to support the arts through government as intelligently as we can. And this is a project that can be argued for and supported democratically, because, in our reflective moments, we acknowledge that there may be arts whose value we have not yet learned.

I can think of many reasons for skepticism about this project. Government-supported art can be pompous or vacuous; the apparatus of subsidy is ripe for corruption; the energy of an art world may be sapped by bureaucracy; the resources of the state can be unequally directed to the support of the arts favored by the powerful or to the sustenance of the symbolic capital that sustains their power. All this is true; but I do not think that the mere fact that it entails soul-making is an argument against it.

My final brief remarks about soul-making have to do with the education of the young. And here the case for soul-making is simply overwhelming. If you accept any of the central ideas I have been defending, you will agree that children need to be prepared for a life with an identity; that social identities will be among their tools in self-making, as will many other socially provided resources. Because people are entitled to the resources for self-construction, because their lives matter and identity matters to their lives, the state must secure these resources for them, if nobody else will. And it is just an empirical fact that we cannot rely on parents to do this unaided: especially given the richness of resources needed to prepare a person for a modern life. Even if there are parents who could do this ably on their own, there are many who cannot, and some, alas, who do not care about their children sufficiently to guarantee them what they need, or whose views about what they need are demonstrably and dangerously mistaken.

This fact by itself does not give us the materials we need to decide how government should play its part. Neither the thought that some identities are obstacles to individuality nor the thought that they are instruments of self-creation seems much help: for it seems preposterous to suppose that children could be aided—and equally unattractive to suppose that they *should* be aided—to reach adulthood with no social identities at all; but, on the other hand, that they will need some identity or other seems to under-constrain what we may do in shaping them in childhood. And this matters because it is empirically clear that how we shape them will help determine what lives they will choose to make. We may not, as liberals, want to impose a life upon someone against her will; but what may we do before she has a will at all?

I have left these questions to the end in part because I find them deeply perplexing. How are we to decide what must be taught to children? Surely what—of all the limitless learning in our libraries—they need to know will depend on many things, including their identities. And, equally surely, what identities they develop will depend on what they know. How should a liberal state decide curricular controversy?[8]

Let me end with a suggestion of one way in which the concept of identity can be mobilized in addressing this issue. Some of the greatest controversies about education in democracies occur when people feel that their own children are being taught things that are inconsistent with claims that are crucial marks of their own collective identities. I shall call a claim—whether moral or not—that is, in this sort of way, implicated with a certain collective identity, an *identity-related claim.*

The currency of controversy about the teaching of identity-related claims is not particularly surprising in this age of what Charles Taylor has dubbed the "politics of recognition." The development, which I have already insisted on, of the liberal idea of an identity has meant that

---

[8] My discussion here draws pretty directly on an essay of my own entitled "Preliminary Thoughts on Liberal Education," *New Political Science* 39/39 (Winter/Spring 1997): 41–62. Reprinted in *The Promise of Multiculturalism: Education and Autonomy in the Twenty-first Century,* ed. George Katsiaficas and Teodros Kiros (New York and London: Routledge, 1998), pp. 34–55.

a great deal of politics—especially nationalist and ethnic politics, but also, for example, a lesbian and gay politics that is somewhat modeled on ethno-national politics—turns on the state's acknowledging a person's identity and protecting each person's ability to flourish while publicly expressing that identity. Much debate about what shall be taught in the schools about identity-related claims is thus centrally concerned with insisting on the state's recognition of some identities (Christian, say) or its nonrecognition of others (lesbian and gay).

Now it will be immediately clear why the notion of raising children to autonomy—with its corollary that we should equip them with the truths they need—does not help much in deciding what should be taught about these particular questions. It does not help because there is substantial social disagreement as to what the truth *is;* and such disagreements, we can predict, will not be settled by the appointment of commissions of experts to resolve them, in the cases where the claims in dispute are identity-related.

You might think the answer should be to stress the democracy in liberal democracy. Let us have public debate among equals and then vote for what should be taught. This seems to me how we *must* decide these questions, in one sense. But among the options in that public debate will be one that says that on some topics we may require the state to step back and leave the matter to the parents. It is not the case that the only option is to teach what the majority believes to be true. And I should like to argue against majority rule in cases where certain identity-related beliefs are in dispute.

I start with the assumption that the role parents play in the raising of children gives them rights in respect of the shaping of their children's identities that are a necessary corollary of parental obligations. We do not believe that social reproduction should be carried out as it is in *Brave New World.* We believe that children should be raised primarily in families and that those families should be able to shape their children into the culture, identity, and traditions that the adult members of the family take as their own. One liberal reason for believing this is that families help to guarantee the rich plurality of identities whose availability is, as I have said, one of the resources for self-construction.

But once we have left the raising of children to families, we are bound to acknowledge that parental love includes the desire to shape children into identities one cares about, and to teach them identity-related values, in particular, along with the other ethical truths that the child will need to live her life well. A state that actively undermined parental choices in this regard in the name of the child's future autonomy would be a state constantly at odds with the parents: and that would be unlikely to be good for the children. A compromise is therefore necessary. Here is what I propose: where identity-related propositions are at stake, parents are permitted to insist that their children not be taught what is contrary to their beliefs; and, in return, the state will be able to insist that the children be told what other citizens believe, in the name of a desire for the sort of mutual knowledge across identities that is a condition for living productively together.

Thus, it seems reasonable to teach children about the range of religious traditions in the communities within which they live (indeed, in the world), without requiring them to assent to any of them, so that, to begin with, at least, they will assent only to the religion they have learned at home. This allows the children the knowledge to make identity choices as they themselves grow to autonomy; but it gives parents a special, primary, place in shaping those choices. Only where a parent's choice seems to compromise the possibility of an autonomous adulthood—as would be the case with a refusal, on religious grounds, to allow one's children to learn to read—must the liberal state step in.

This proposal has as a consequence that if intolerance of other identities is built into an identity, or if learning the views of others except as shameful error is one of its norms, we will be seeking, in public education, to reshape that identity so as to exclude this feature. This is liberal soul-making, again. And that makes it plain that liberalism is, of course, more than a procedural value: it places a substantive weight on creating a social world in which each of us can live a life of our own.

I have avoided, the attentive will have observed, one obvious alternative approach to these questions of religion and curricular controversy. That would be to regard the very existence of religious identities as a reflection of our defections from the rule of reason. Fully reasonable people, many philosophers, at least, think, could not believe what most religious people claim to believe; and, to the extent that those beliefs are central, as I have argued, to their identities, their identities are incoherent in the sort of way racial identities, which presume falsehoods, are. A state that cared for us would set about the project of soul-making entailed by reforming our metaphysical convictions.

This argument is certainly too quick. First, because contemporary (and historical) religious traditions in many places do not share the concern for doctrinal correctness that characterizes much Christianity, for example, or some modern streams of Islam. It is arguable that many forms of modern Judaism, while committed to certain practices, are theologically quite noncommittal; and I do not have to remind this audience that there was once a bishop of Woolwich—and former dean of Trinity College—who confessed that being "honest to God" led to atheism.

But the argument is also too quick because the notion of the incoherence of an identity has to do with threats to the success of a life deriving from the ways in which its norms pull in different directions. It is not clear to me that this condition is met by many religious identities. False beliefs by themselves about one's identity do not make it incoherent: otherwise, given our defections from reason, all of us would be likely to have substantially incoherent identities.

It may be that the best reasons for religious toleration are not identity-related. Liberal religious tolerance began in Europe after a period of devastating religious wars. Attempts to convert others to what various states took to be the correct view turned out to lead to vast amounts of human suffering. I have only been concerned to deny that the arguments from incoherence that I offered about American racial identities can obviously be carried over to religion.

I have explored in this lecture some issues raised by the practice I dubbed "soul-making," which I defined as *the political project of intervening in the process of interpretation through which each citizen develops an identity with the aim of increasing her chances of living an ethically successful life.* I have defended the view that the state *can* intervene legitimately in soul-making because of our irrationality and *must* sometimes so intervene because our individual identities are in part the product of shared identities that are socially produced.

Our individualities are not simply the products of what is within us. What social psychology teaches us is that what we are and what we do is shaped as much by the social contexts that frame our decisions as by our own inner dispositions.[9] Since the state is one of the main forces in cre-

[9] L. Ross and R. Nisbett, *The Person and the Situation: Perspectives of Social Psychology* (New York: McGraw-Hill, 1991).

ating that context, which is so central to shaping our choices and identifications, it cannot but be involved in shaping our identities. In a sense I have been drawing out the consequences of a thought that is sometimes termed "communitarian": the idea that who we are is profoundly dependent on the thoughts, aims, and actions of others. I agree that a respect for individuality that ignores this fact is doomed to human irrelevance.

But I have not drawn the conclusion that because the state is bound to shape our identities, it should simply do so purposefully and with the good of each of us in mind, engaging freely in soul-making. Rather I have suggested three particular grounds for shaping souls: that children, not having individualities, must be helped to develop them; that our own defections from reason provide some basis for democratically grounded interventions in the social meanings of the identities from which our individualities are constructed; and that those of our moral obligations to each other that the state must enforce may best be sustained by the shaping of our characters.

I want to end by underlining something I said in the first lecture about the relevance of philosophy for politics. If I may rephrase what I said there, I suggested that philosophy is more helpful in framing questions than in providing policies. My hope has been to argue that a philosophical appreciation of the resources of the concepts of "identity" and "reason" is useful in framing many questions that face modern societies. I do not care too much whether you like my answers. But I do hope that I have helped in the reformulation of some of those pressing questions.

*Lecture I. Mean Stories and Stubborn Girls*

*Lecture II. What It Means to Be Free*

DOROTHY ALLISON

THE TANNER LECTURES ON HUMAN VALUES

Delivered at

Stanford University
May 14 and 15, 2001

DOROTHY ALLISON has been called "one of the finest writers of her generation" by the *Boston Globe* and "simply stunning" by the *New York Times*. She was born in Greenville, South Carolina, graduated from Florida Presbyterian College, and did graduate work in urban anthropology at the New School for Social Research in New York. She serves on the board of PEN International, and has lectured or taught master classes in writing programs at universities around the country, including Yale, Stanford, Wesleyan, the University of California at Los Angeles, Columbia, Rutgers, Dartmouth, Vassar, Emory, and Hamilton College. Her books include a memoir, *Two or Three Things I Know for Sure* (1995); a collection of essays, *Skin: Talking about Sex, Class, and Literature* (1994), a *New York Times* Notable Book of 1995 which won the American Library Association Gay and Lesbian Book Award and the Lambda Literary Award in Lesbian Studies; a volume of poetry, *The Women Who Hate Me: Poetry 1980–1990* (1991); the short-story collection *Trash* (1988), which won the Lambda Literary Award for Fiction and for Best Small Press Book; and her award-winning novels, *Bastard Out of Carolina* (1992), which was a finalist for the National Book Award, won the Bay Area Book Reviewers Award for Fiction, and was a *New York Times* Notable Book of 1992; and *Cavedweller* (1998), which won the Lambda Literary Award for Fiction and was a finalist for the Lillian Smith Prize.

## I. MEAN STORIES AND STUBBORN GIRLS

She said to me, "The stuff you write—such mean stories."

It was 1989. The woman was a college professor at Columbia University, and what I remember most clearly was the gorgeous mohair suit she was wearing as she spoke. I had been admiring that suit, watching the way the nap of the fabric caught the light. It was not something I would have worn, but I appreciated it. It was evidence that the professor knew exactly who she was and what she had to be confident about. I had no such certainty. I had just finished my stint as a guest in her class, and though I had enjoyed myself, it had been hard work. Few of her students seemed to have read my stories, but those who had were passionate, and the discussion had gone deeper than I had expected. There had been a few awkward moments when one or another stumbled over the word "lesbian," but on the whole the students had been sharp and revealing about their family lives, the stories they wanted to write.

I had known, though, that there was something more the professor wanted, some reason she had walked out with me. I listened as she said it again, said "such mean stories." I stared at her face—the eyes glinting bright as she looked slightly past me. I stepped forward but could not get her to look me in the eye. When she spoke the word "mean" she emphasized it, the intonation precise at the edge of her chin. Did she mean the phrase the way I had meant it? I could not be sure. I knew little about her family background, nothing about how she saw her own life in relation to the stories she chose to discuss in her classes.

Meaner than what, I wanted to ask her. Meaner than who?

"My sister," she said suddenly. "You remind me of my sister. She always wanted to write." I wanted her to say more, but she only reached up to finger the lapel of her suit.

"Your sister?" I prompted.

"Yeah, my sister." And that was all she gave me.

My life would be so much easier if everyone I met had published a memoir. It would explain all the things that get left unspoken. Best of all would be if people wore those patches Samuel Delaney invented for one of his novels—little panels that bluntly detailed genetic and social background in easily readable lines of code. Instead, I have to figure people out by close observation and dogged patience. All too often I get it wrong. It took me years to get the mean story behind that college professor's suit, to learn just how much like me she was, and how it was she had lost her younger sister.

When I was growing up, people would start to tell a story. They'd begin by saying something like, "She was so funny. And after she had that third child, she would tell you things would just make you sick laughing." But then they would stop. Their faces would go blank. They would change the subject and never go back to that funny, passionate cousin. What happened to her, I wondered. What happened to the child? When I asked, no one would answer. It was something I had to figure out for myself. I puzzled it out piece by piece, one story building on another, until I gradually realized that cousin was one of those that went off the bridge.

I heard the bridge story hundreds of times when I was a girl—in fragments, in short one-note references, or sometimes in lists that did not get finished, and, most often, in sudden awful curses. My aunt would say, "Before the bridge." It was plain I was supposed to know what she meant. Before the car went over the side rail, before the family was lost in the flood, before the baby drowned under her mother's body, and before the cousins washed up downriver—before all that. All time was before the bridge or after. Many of us grow up with such mysteries. It was the stories my mother and aunts would not tell that were the defining events of my family.

What car? Which child? Which cousin? Did it really happen? I could not know for certain. The stories changed over time and were never fully revealed. I knew there had to be a larger story behind the ones that were told.

When I sat down to write my memoir, *Two or Three Things I Know for Sure,* I went looking for newspaper clippings—something to prove or disprove the legends. No one in my family could be trusted. They loved good stories too much, and they liked to make them better. I told myself that fragments that had been repeated so often had to have a core of truth. Some fraction of the real could be traced, I was sure, if I could find the evidence that predated what the family made of it.

It took a friendly newspaperman in Columbia, South Carolina, to track down the bridge story. There was a car wreck. It did go off the side of a bridge. There were three children who died, and one was a newborn baby. The woman driving was one of my cousins, but no, she was not running from her husband. The car had been headed toward Augusta, and a cousin there on leave from the army. There was no runaway flight from a violent man. There was only a senseless accident.

No one was left alive to question, so I had to rethink everything for myself. All the drama that I had pieced out over time from hints and fractions of story had to be examined again. *He beat her up and she run with them babies.* The legend had shaped what I thought I knew. *She always swore she'd steal those children and leave his ass.* The woman I had imagined looked back at me from the stories I had written, another creature in new skin. *She was a piece of work, that girl, nothing stopped her once she made up her mind.* The heroine I had imagined grinned back at me and shrugged.

She had been trying to get discount cigarettes bought cheap at a PX. No drama in that. She had just had the bad luck to try to cross that bridge the one day in South Carolina history when it froze. The drama that had her steering over the edge blinded by tears and rage was only that—a drama, not fact. Oh, yes, there had been times she had run. There had been half a dozen times my cousin had stormed out, had raged and cried and packed up the children. She had moved back in with her mother once, gone to stay with a sister another time, slept in her car at least twice, and had her and the baby's picture made over at Sears Roebuck, with her uncombed hair still sticking straight up in back. "Oh, she was something," my aunt Grace had said about her.

Do you understand what I am saying? I am like everyone else in my family. I want a good story, I want it to mean something. I want the bridge to be the climax, not another moment of despair. I want to make sense of loss. I want glory. Oh, I want my cousin to go off the side in a flash of wild glory, not drop into the dark like a stone.

I keep boxes of clippings. I don't know many writers who don't— newspaper articles, magazine scraps, copies of letters, and even Associated Press stories I download off the net. They are my compost, my research bins. I have whole drawers devoted to men who kill their entire families. I have them sorted by the number of children. I have other drawers for women who kill. I have sorted those by whether they tried to kill their children, with subsets of those who did or did not kill themselves.

All those clippings strike me as deeply familiar. I measure my fiction against them, always wondering if my stories are as mean as the world that shaped them. Maybe my fictions are not mean enough. Is my purpose equal to the people I portray? Do I steal the heat out of my aunt in the moment when the car headed for the side of the bridge? Does it all assume a different dimension when I make it over and tell you she had not fled her husband? There is a problem in drawing lessons of life from fiction, just as there is a problem in drawing fiction from the events of our lives. There is always a disjunction, and what I mean by my stories may not be what you take from them.

What I try to make is what I think my cousin deserved. What I try to bring to the lives I steal is significance and respect. What I demand is for attention to be paid to those who are mostly not seen, not acknowledged. In this, I am no different than any other American writer. I speak for my own. I try to be something of a voice for those I treasure. In doing that I make a connection to others who would speak for their own. The more specific and revealing we become, the greater chance we have for impact and connection. That is the great power of literature. Some days I fear that my stories are not up to the demands of the people who made me a storyteller. Other days, I simply make what I can.

Can you think about your life as a story? Think for a moment about your life as if it were a story that someone else was writing, someone like me. Do you believe you are safe? Do you believe that your life will vindicate your education, that your successes will validate the times you acted out of fear rather than reason, that your best impulses will offset your worst? I call that a sense of entitlement. It is characterized most often by a feeling that you belong wherever you are, or that you will with a little effort. I used to believe this was a sense that characterized only the rich and upper middle classes, that it was never found among my kind—the poor or the marginal or the queer. I have learned the hard way that I was wrong, that a sense of entitlement sometimes appears among those for whom there is no reason to expect it. But as a measure for the embattled, I still find it useful. I watch for it, and its absence.

I went to a very small private college on full scholarship, a national merit scholarship. I remember my terror at the freshman introductory symposium. It did not matter if we were going to study French, or math, or anthropology. For a moment we were to think about what a liberal education could mean. I remember sliding down in my seat and looking around me uncertainly. The people who looked back at me might have been as uncertain as I, but I did not believe that. I believed they all knew what was coming, what they were doing. I thought they were nothing like me.

"You are special people," the president of the college began. "You are the cream of your generation." In our seats we all shifted and looked around, pleased and fearful, wanting to believe him. "You can do anything," he said. "There are no barriers that will stop you if you only hold to your purpose. The world is wide open."

Does that sound familiar? Are you one of those who have heard such a speech? I wonder if you heard it the way I heard it. That man said wonderful, proud things to us. He was followed by professors who smiled and nodded and greeted us by name. Their words filled me up, lifted my head, and made me think beyond what seemed my heretofore-small ambitions. The president talked about God. The professors talked about social responsibility. In our folding chairs we sat up straighter and looked around.

It was 1968, an interesting time in American history for the discussion of ethics. It was the time of the antiwar movement, the still vibrant civil rights movement, the early stages of the women's movement. The headline on the magazines asked: Was God dead? Troops were moving into South Vietnam in record numbers. The world outside was full of upheaval, but we were safe on our little campus.

Behind everything we were to argue and discuss was that first sentence they spoke to us. "You are special people. Special."

I did not believe them for a minute.

Oh, I did believe that I was extraordinary. But what I meant by that phrase was not what the president of the college meant. It seemed to me that my success in getting into college was tempered by my shame at how much of a struggle the attempt had been. All around me the other members of my generation were questioning what education meant, whether they should be there at all. For me there was no such question. I had seen only one chance to get out of our mildew-stained tract house and to get free of my stepfather's storming rages and knotted fists. My roommate told me she feared she would become just like her mother, driving the station wagon to the mall and cooking the same meals over and over, going on the same vacations and laughing at the same tired old jokes at the dinner table. What I feared most was my mother's pushed-in features and loose mouth, the gray exhausted face I would wear soon enough if I found no way to escape it. I had worked three summers as a waitress. I had taken a second job pulling greasy mop-heads off cold steel frames to pay my way onto that campus, and I was terrified that I might not be allowed to stay. I feared being revealed as an impostor, no scholar, just another desperate waitress's daughter. I feared being sent back to my stepfather's house, and I had a very real sense of the people who would do that—the gatekeepers who would turn out over-ambitious girls like me.

I sat in those early lectures with my mouth shut tight, and my hands in fists, never realizing I was exactly the person for whom scholarships are designed—smart, determined, hard working, and ready to change my life. I believed that I was passing, and I was ashamed of myself for doing so.

Who could have interrupted that process? Who could have rewritten my story and saved me two decades of self-hatred? What would have made me know myself just like those with whom I found myself studying? Is it not exactly what a democracy wants—the lifting up of the children of the working class? Is that not the goal of a just society—welcoming to full participation those who have always felt themselves marginal and denied?

I had told the scholarship people that my mama was a waitress and my daddy a truck driver, but it was the *way* I portrayed them that was a fiction—too noble to be genuinely related to me, too fantastic to be believable. I kept my mama a waitress, but such a waitress! I made her the kind of woman who, if you left a dime more than what she expected by the plate, would run after you to make sure you meant to give it to her. The myth is ragged but clean. I made my mama so clean, she became a mirror to my own despair.

And my stepfather? That violent, contemptuous monster who had darkened my nights from the day my mama married him? I erased my stepfather, replacing him with a good father who worked two jobs to pay the bills cancer had run up on my mama's accounts. I erased the fact that he beat my sisters and raped me, that he humiliated and cursed us until we thought we deserved the names he called us. I left out the stories of all the times he stopped working and sat on the couch in his underwear, staring into space and muttering how he was going to kill us. I left out the fact that I was completely terrified of him, that it was, in fact, terror that dominated my teenage years, not the dream of an education.

I left out, edited, and rewrote our lives. Most of all I edited out the fact that when I met my fellow scholars—all those other freshman students—I hated them. I hated each and every one of them. They made me ashamed of myself—or rather I made myself ashamed just by looking at them.

What does it feel like to hate people for no real reason that you can justify, simply because their lives are not yours? I felt as if they made me hate my own life. But did they? Was it their joy that made my misery, their happiness that compounded my grief and shame? Was it their security that triggered my terror? They were not criminals, those boys and girls I so feared. They were simply living their own lives, going about what their mothers and fathers wanted for them.

For the past few years I have been living inside the story of a young woman who is about to graduate from a small, exclusive private college when she is the victim of a terrible accident that robs her of everything—language, history, talent, and skill. To write out of her, I have had to live inside her, and I have had to find ways to love her. I wonder some days at my own impulses, why I chose this story. I know that I based her on students I have had, but I know also that much of her I took from the girls I met my freshman year in college.

The year I started college was a different time, and the world was smaller than it is now for girls. But I think of the girls of my freshman class with great admiration. Those girls are the ones who went off and joined the Peace Corps or became missionaries, got married and made babies while trying to rewrite what it meant to be a wife and a mother. They did in fact become friends of mine. They were generous and kind—and it seems to me that I have spent much of my adult life trying to understand and not hate them. My ethical challenge has been not to dismiss them or sin against them as I felt I had been sinned against.

To write a good story you have to completely inhabit the people of your story. You cannot fake it. You have to climb inside and fully be someone else, all of them, even those parts you have despised or feared. You have to dream what they dream. It has been easier for me to imagine a child full of rage, a stubborn girl who fights not to be poor and held in contempt. But now I place myself in a young woman whose shames would strike my stubborn girls as minor, whose sins would not even measure on her scale. The girl I am imagining is the kind of young woman I see whenever I go to small colleges to speak or read.

Let me stop and explain something to you.

From my earliest youth, I believed two things that could not mesh. I believed my family were exactly what we were said to be—criminal, lazy, damned, and horrid. At the same time I believed us beyond any such labels. I believed us favored, blessed, strong, stubborn, and courageous. I believed we were beloved of god for what we suffered and endured—which curiously enough is a message I picked up from literature, song, and sermon. I watched the aunt for whom I was named give birth to eleven children with little help from a husband who drank too much and lost job after job, living up to the worst of the stories told about people like us. I was contemptuous of my uncle, and my aunt, but in awe of them at the same time. I believed we—my aunt, my uncle, and all of us—were stronger and better people than those who did not drink or have more than one or two children, children they pampered and adored. Somehow I believed us stronger than those for whom the way was smoothed and clear.

Is this an idea you have entertained? Is this a myth you too have believed? It is the split in convictions that runs like a seam right down the center of all my hopes and aspirations. I always felt that we were better than those who had more than us. I always believed that though we might be treated with contempt, we were tougher and stronger and more worthy than those who named us less. Most importantly, I always believed that if there were a genuinely just scale on which the human heart could be weighed, then my people would weigh out greater than those blessed with money and power and position. Has this life not given us greater, meaner challenges? Who told me this was better? Who turned these curses to blessings? Was it in my mother's words that I began to believe that we had something the rich didn't have? Or was it in the novels of John Steinbeck, the stories of Flannery O'Connor, the essays of James Baldwin, and the poems of Walt Whitman? American working-class art sustains and nourishes the children of the poor by holding up a mirror that enlarges us even as it shows us our misery.

To this day, these two ideas haunt me. I know the awful impact of poverty, the damage of despair and the self-fulfilling nature of stunted aspirations. But knowing all that, I developed the conviction that those of us born poor, or queer, or people of color, or simply different in any of the many ways this culture holds the different in contempt—that we were intrinsically better than those who had never been tested by adversity. It is no advantage to realize that as a culture we have this same schizophrenic notion—that Americans fear and hate the poor even as we drape over them an idealized veil of awe and sentimental fantasy.

Perhaps I could ignore this conflict if I had not chosen to become a mother, but raising what I acknowledge is a frankly middle-class child, I can not afford the gloss that much of our culture puts over these issues. I want to give my boy exactly what every other mother wants to give her son—love and security and every advantage. I read him books and teach him the names of all the dinosaurs. I am buying him music lessons and showing him where on the map of the world his ancestors originated. I have given him photos of my mother and all the family to whom he is related—his dad and his other mother's family. I never lie, but there is much I do not tell him. I have not told him the bridge story, though I came close a time or two. I feel the familial urge, the interrupted story I could so easily take up and pass on.

What stops me is this: I fear to raise a child of despair. I dread to raise a boy who will hate and fear the world into which he was born.

Let me be unsparing about what I believe.

In a meritocracy, people would actually get what they earn. In a just society there would be no tricks, no lies, no compromises that favor the few over the many, no misrepresentation, no theft of the soul. In a just society, we would trust each other instead of battling always for the little chance of doing better than the one next to us.

We do not live in a just society. There are tricks and lies and misrepresentations and compromises. Sometimes the guilty go free. Sometimes the innocent are convicted. Prejudice is more common than compassion. Fear and hatred still dominate who and what people will accept as part of their lives. Not all children get the opportunity for education, or even for basic medical care. For all his innocence and talent and passion, my son may be hated by people who will never know his true worth.

How do I arm my son against that hatred, against injustice and shame and despair? How do I raise a strong, principled man in a society with so much confusion about just what that would mean? I want for my son the life lived by the young people I met in my freshman class in college—those children of the middle class who I was sure had grown up with no omnipresent sense of fear, with no secret suspicion of their own worthlessness. What I have always called a sense of entitlement is what I want for my boy.

But I wonder, I can not help but wonder, if that sense of entitlement is an advantage or a secret flaw in the psyche. I was raised on reassuring promises that as a working-class girl I had strengths and powers denied to the gently born and carefully raised. Looking at my own child, I find myself faced with new and terrible fears. What do I risk in trying to make my son more like the children with whom I went to college? What do I risk in the same efforts I am directing at my nieces and nephews and cousins, my constant encouragement that they go to college or try for better jobs? Will I steal the strength out of their stubborn pride if I keep insisting they adopt the behavior of those they have always held in contempt?

I give my son what I give you, I give him stories—large complicated stories, multilayered and sometimes difficult to understand. Sometimes I give him pieces of the story, the way my aunts gave me the story of the bridge. I know it may take a long time for him to be mature enough for the full story. No matter, I lay the groundwork for the full story.

Sometimes it seems my family has lived on resentment, survived on a diet of liquid bile and outrage. We have turned it to milk. Mostly we have done that through humor, a self-depreciating, bitter recitation of our own worst impulses. We have practiced a deliberate distillation that turns misery to vindication. We have made our worst experiences over into art.

Let me tell you the story of how I got through my last year of college, that year when the scholarships had been cut back so far I did not know how I would manage. That summer before, I worked every hour I could and tried not to spend a dime of what I earned. It was a time when you could, if you were desperate, buy frozen pot pies six for a dollar. I bought them—turkey, chicken, spaghetti pot pies. I got through workdays on three or four such little pies, spending less than a dollar on nutrition. I went off to my last year of college with watery eyes and a greenish tinge to my skin. I stepped into my first class and promptly passed out on the floor. Diagnosed with a severe vitamin deficiency, I boasted I was that rarity, a twentieth-century American walking around with an eighteenth-century syndrome—scurvy.

Who gets such diseases? A twenty-one-year-old college student can—a girl who knew even then how to tell a good story. This is how you learn to look at your own life from the outside, making misery over into story, wedding stubbornness to need. I lived off the story of my bout with scurvy for years. I told it over and over until I had refined it to parable.

"Did you ever hear what happened to all those sailors who crossed the oceans in the eighteenth century, those who went months without fresh fruit or vegetables? They got scurvy, beriberi, or pellagra." I would grin and nod and watch my audience. I knew how to do this, turn round the story in my own mouth. I would deliver the punch line with awful intent, say, "I replicated the experience on a college campus in 1972, went into full scale vitamin deficiency and fell over in statistics class! Oh! Talk about special! I am proof we are special."

It is 2001. What is the lesson I want you to take from a story I have been telling for thirty years? I want you to think again about that word "special." I want you to join me in the task I have set myself for my son and my nieces and nephews and for all the children I claim as my own.

We are special, yes, all of us. When I sit down to write out of my fictional middle-class girl, I ask myself all over again what makes a human being special. I ask what is worthy of being loved. I ask what is worthy of being admired. I ask what it is we should honor and what it is we should discard. I do so in the full knowledge of how I used my own experiences against those who were not responsible for them. I remember telling my scurvy story over and over. I acknowledge that I deliberately set out to horrify those who cared about me, that I told that story so that it would haunt them and make them uncomfortable—all the more so because I made them laugh at it.

This is one of the things a storyteller does, one of the responsibilities of story-telling, and it is not simple in any sense. The impulses that guide story-telling and the uses to which stories are put are infinitely complex—some of them not at all benign. Some of the impulses of story-telling are defensive or even destructive. I want to make it plain that I have never been comfortable with the emphasis on moral constructs in the art of fiction. I stand more with Oscar Wilde than with John Gardner. I know that is complicated by the fact that I am completely forthright about my own feminist convictions and my understanding of how my life has been shaped by growing up poor in a society that fears and hates the poor even as it mythologizes them.

I believe in moral responsibility. I believe in holding people to account for what they do. I believe that a man who beats a child is a criminal. I believe a man who breaks his marriage and terrifies his wife is responsible for everything that comes back on him because of those acts. I believe that a woman who fails to protect her children will be haunted by her own failures. I believe that a lesbian who lies to her lover about her family because she is ashamed of them will most likely lose that lover. I have in mind a moral and ethical code, which I do not always manage to uphold in my own life, but in my writing I hold the world to the standard of that code. I put my characters to measure against it. Still, it is always my desire that it be impossible to reduce any of my work to political slogan or easy categories. And I have never found a standard—political, moral, or religious—by which I would easily condemn any single individual.

As the daughter of a family in which many of the men went to jail and most of the women were pregnant before they married, I know what it feels like to be treated with contempt for those facts. I knew what it felt like to know myself a lesbian and that I was hated for that—while feeling myself in no way hateful. Always it has seemed I have lived in communities in which we shared an ethical system by which we were able to honor and trust each other—outside the ethical system of the larger society, the one that held people like me, my family, and my lovers in contempt.

As a junior in college I read *The Pedagogy of the Oppressed.* I don't know if that book is still read, but it resonated powerfully with the novels I was finding, the ones that seemed to offer hope to people like me. It was the discovery of the notion that the privileged might have a responsibility to the poor that began to ease my fear and shame. Was it the novels of John O'Hara that told me that or the social studies of C. Wright Mills? Where did I develop my notions of a just society? Was it my anthropology classes or the novels of John Steinbeck? Where in fact did I begin to construct a notion of justice? Was it in reading the Bible or the essays of James Baldwin?

What does it mean if our youth embrace the small in fear of what they might have to pay for wanting large? Is a nation damned when it keeps shaping its children to the small and the fearful? What is loss if our children believe the best they can hope for is the life of the walking wounded?

Can we truly imagine a world in which the children of the upper classes are raised to acknowledge their responsibilities to those less fortunate? Is that not how a democracy should work? If a country were just, and if merit were genuinely the way in which people's worth was measured, then would it not be reasonable that the rich would give back to those who have not had their advantages? If justice were the rule, would we not treasure our most despised, nurture our less fortunate, and honor our stubborn, hard-working poor?

I do not believe this is a just society. I do believe that we are a people who yearn for justice. I believe that our institutions and laws and systems at their best move us toward greater justice. I believe in this country, in its best impulses, its most fervent reach toward justice and equality. I keep in mind all the ways our nation fails its own, but I remain hopeful. It is too tempting to dismiss those that are different from us, for me just as for those I have imagined my adversaries—the rich and privileged who always seemed to be looking down on my family from a great cruel distance. It is tempting to reduce the complicated nature of our culture to a simple system of good guys and bad guys. It is far more difficult to inhabit the shadowy territory in which nothing is so simple or so certain, and where mostly people act out of fear or misunderstanding rather than prejudice or hatred.

The things I have learned as a writer are exactly what has most changed what I believe as a citizen. The complexity that I know makes a good story is what has broadened my political convictions and opened my imagination to people who, as a girl, I feared with my whole soul. But how is a writer shaped to that complexity? How do you learn to tell those kinds of stories?

Maybe you need a bridge story, or its equivalent.

After I graduated from college, I worked for two years for the Social Security Administration—a Kafkaesque position in which my primary responsibility was to administer SSI funds, a job that required me to deny assistance to women who would sit across from my desk shadowed by that yellow-tinged terror I knew too well. Watery eyes and knotted fists defined my days. I had become a gatekeeper. Denying aid, refusing food stamps, signing women and children off of assistance—that was my respectable, middle-class job. My moral and ethical convictions derive in part from the experience of being employed as one of the people this society uses to tell other people they are not deserving of the most basic needs.

Is this what happens to us then—scholarship children invited into the world of the more privileged? Are we always going to come up against such awful moral quandaries? What is there to reassure us of our worth, to save us from hating ourselves? If all your education will mean is that you will find yourself in such a job, hating the work and yourself, how do you survive?

This is what happens all too often to our best and brightest. We are invited into the sanctuary of education, to the citadel of the mind, and the resting place of the human soul. But once there we know no rest, no sense of safety. Having fought so hard to stand against the persistent wind of contempt, we stagger when the wind becomes despair.

These days I go on a regular basis to small colleges and large universities. I go to speak or read my stories, but I go also to look for my kind. I watch for the hesitant girls at the back of the room, the shadow-faced boys at the ends of the rows. I watch for those who flinch when I make my hard-edged jokes about poverty and despair. I watch for the grief and the anger. I look for the expression I saw on my own face that last year I was in college, and I find it. I find it all the time.

These days, I watch for it in my own family—in my cousins, nephews, and nieces, the ones I have tried so desperately to welcome into the middle class, to persuade to try for scholarships. Few of them have been willing to try. Junior college, beauty college, technical school, secretarial school, and mechanics training courses—that is where my family looks for a way out of poverty. But these last few years, I have had a few take me up on my challenges. Now my youngest sister's oldest girl has gone off to a small private college in central Florida.

My niece is gifted, stubborn, and strong. Born with birth defects that could have been a ticket to life-long idleness, she has stubbornly succeeded where others have failed. She has astonished her mother and delighted me. These days she is working her way toward a future almost unimaginable when her mother made the decision *not* to give her up to an institution that would have warehoused her for the length of her life. But she is a junior now, at that place I know so well. She has fought and endured and made funny stories and jokes out of her pain for far too long. Her voice on the phone has flattened. Her signature on her letters has grown wobbly and weak.

This is the moment when we lose them. It is the moment when I almost lost myself. I know how it works. I know the wave and how it sweeps over you, the self-hatred and contempt that almost eat your soul, the moments when you begin to believe the world is right about people like us—that we are not worth the trouble, that we are better off ignorant. I know how being told you are special can turn on you, how it can go sour in your mouth and make you want most of all to just lie down and die.

*Who genuinely believes in education?*

Those of us whose lives have been remade by it believe in it, even as we know the risks.

*Who is most at risk in these wonderful institutions that educate and validate our children?*

Those of us who cannot say the word "special" without feeling the need to spit, to curse, or to laugh—we are at terrible risk. What can we offer our young to get them through intact? How do we nurture them, give them what will feed the soul as well as the mind?

I send my niece stories, just like the ones I offer the shadow-eyed young people who always sit in the back rows when I go to read or talk. I glorify my own, without sentiment or feeble fantasy; I try to document the worth of our lives. I send those messages out.

I tell stories about my aunts. I sing the song of our Aunt Grace, meanest woman in the family and longest lived. I tease the jokes out of our Aunt Dot with her thirteen children and one well-trained husband, who mostly did not speak for the last twenty years of his life. I tell again how the twins, Bobbie and Grace, moved through Greenville High School braced by the shoulders of their brothers, boys so dangerous no one ever dared disrespect those girls, how the boys went off to the county farm for crimes that would never have condemned boys from better families. I tell how they stood up under contempt, better than some boys stand up under honors. I remake, retell, lie a little, and try to vindicate. I am shoring up what I know is in danger. I am cadging a little space for my own in terms that will not shame anyone but those who hate us, and I do it deliberately, with full knowledge of how little it might mean in the long run.

In a world that disdains you the only reasonable response is stubborn disregard of contempt.

In a world that does not nurture you, the only sane response is to value your own—even if some of the stories you tell yourself are not as true as you might like them to be. In a world where you are always at risk, it is only reasonable to try to make within yourself some safe haven, some little space where you are valued for what you know are your strengths—the very stubbornness and bitter humor that a safer world does not value as you do.

I want to believe that there is wisdom, grace, and goodness available to all of us. I am dragging as much of my family as I can into the middle class. I am buying my son music lessons, sending subscriptions to my nieces and nephews, and giving books to second and third cousins who rarely acknowledge the gifts. My intentions are complicated, dangerous, and not certain of success. I want our lives to be easier, more valued and honored, and I do not want to lose any of what I know to be our strengths.

I love this country because of the books that fed me as a girl, the impulse toward justice that sang through them. I love this country because of John Steinbeck and Audre Lord, and Sandra Cisneros and Adrienne Rich, because of a literature that swore in a just society there was no barrier to hope, no obstruction to those willing to struggle, no wall that would block off desire or freedom or love.

In the novels of John Steinbeck mean stories happen. A man starving to death is saved only because a woman is willing to bare her breasts and feed him her milk—his daughter and the milk that will not feed the child she has lost become the promise of life and hope and compassion. What an astonishing tale, what a glorious moment of vindication!

In the poems of Muriel Rukeyser, politics is wedded to poetry and passion is made over into righteousness. In her work it is all right to love the page itself, to love writing, to love the girl, to honor all impulses. My favorite poem of hers is the simplest and in one sense the least political.

"Poem, white space, white space, poem."

I know what I took from those opaque words—the simple insistence that I not fear the unwritten story, the unspoken tale. I know what I felt facing a white sheet of paper in the middle of trying to write the hardest scenes of my first novel, to write out of the mouth of a despairing eleven-year-old girl, raped and abandoned and full of guilt for what she saw as her own responsibility for what had been done to her. I know what that poem told me in my fear and confusion, the comfort and the promise of the words. I know the invitation it offered. I know justice is possible on a blank sheet of paper.

You can make your dreams happen. You do not have to hate yourself—not for your family of origin, nor your sins of omission. You *are* special as we are all special. More still is possible if we open the gates to even more of our brothers and sisters. Greater justice is possible if we acknowledge our common citizenship, tear down the bitter barriers between the few born with a sense of safety and entitlement and all the rest of us.

Join me in that struggle. To remake our society, we must affirm our common condition, our mutual and deeply feared connections. We must honor our most stubborn angry children. We must put our hands out to each other in the conviction that we all share the same hopes, fears, and desires—that we are all special.

## II. WHAT IT MEANS TO BE FREE

When Evann Boland called and asked if I would be willing to discuss ethics and ethical questions I responded first with a joke and then with a laugh. I do not think of myself as the kind of person who is commonly asked to speak on such subjects. I had difficulty thinking I can be trusted with the territory, and that is only partly the product of growing up in a family whose members went to jail the way middle-class boys go off to college. Growing up poor in the American south in the 1950s, I had every reason to develop a conviction that nothing I did would ever be admirable or even acceptable. Growing up knowing myself an un-natural girl, not only a lesbian but rebellious, opinionated, argumenta-tive, and ambitious, I also had a powerful conviction that I was in the deepest, most essential core of myself a dangerous person.

There is a glory in believing yourself dangerous, but it does not de-rive from the same qualities of character that tend to produce a strong sense of ethics or even an ability to make judgments about what is good and honorable. Growing up with a sense of being an outlaw, a member of a despised and violent class, tended to push me in the direction of greater violence, sharper resentments, and angrier expressions of out-rage. How did I not become the thief I expected myself to become, or the liar, the criminal, the woman without family, community, or friends?

I wish I could give a simple straightforward cause and effect expla-nation, but I was raised a Baptist. I fall back on miracles more often than not. I believe there is much in the world that cannot be explained or justified, and the justifications I construct are centered more around story than around cause and effect. Story is more about mystery and people than about explanations or justifications. I believe that more can

The Tanner Lectures on Human Values

be learned from a good story than from a structured essay or a monumental piece of theory. I am a storyteller, not a social scientist.

So let me begin by trying to puzzle out how a working-class, stubborn girl grows up to be asked to speak on ethical issues.

I am suspicious of talent and sanguine on the nature of genius. I have never been comfortable with compliments, even well-meant ones. When people come to me and tell me they loved my books or were awed by a reading I gave, my response is most often a blush and a disclaimer. "You are so wonderful," a woman said to me in Chicago a few weeks ago, "so articulate." "You should have met my mama," I responded. Then a young man asked me to read his stories, telling me he trusted my ear for the false and the self-serving. "Oh, you should have known my Aunt Dot," I told him.

Among the people who shaped me, it was bad manners to preen while being complimented—and that is a difficult ethical posture for an American writer in a time when self-promotion is seen as key to the writer's success. Humility, genuine or feigned, is rare, and everyone seems to long to be named a genius, even without a money prize to accompany the title.

This is the difficulty. I do believe in genius, in the idea that there are people who are special and different from the rest of us. I grew up reading science fiction stories about magical children who could do anything, survive anything. I took such figures as my models, as the standard by which I would judge everything I could accomplish. Magical children can do anything, learn anything, acquire any skill, or simply display talent without benefit of effort. That is the nature of magic and of genius. Genius is dangerous to those raised in a culture that inculcates a sense of inadequacy.

What is the essential difference between the middle class and the working class? Part of it, I am sure, is that those of us born poor and ashamed cannot believe that we are good enough, no matter what evidence of worth we manage. At the same time, we fear and resent those who treat us as if we are not good enough—not valuable in and of ourselves. How do you convince anyone that they are worthwhile? How do you persuade someone that they do not have to constantly manufacture evidence of their worth? How do you convince people that they are free when they have never been made to believe themselves entitled to the full rights of citizenship?

To believe in freedom, in the responsibilities and rights of citizenship, you have to trust that you will not be disenfranchised without cause. For a meritocracy to function, it has to be just—the rewards have to actually come when one puts in the time and effort and hard work. When things are handed over to those who have not genuinely earned them, then the system fails. Why work hard if someone who did not work hard gets put ahead of you?

As a scholarship student at a small, prestigious college, I felt as if I had suddenly become one of the elect. There I was, invited into the preserve of the rich and the entitled. It was also painfully obvious to me, however, that my invitation was conditional. It could be withdrawn at any time. It had riders and limitations. I was a girl, a lesbian, and very nearly an atheist at a small Presbyterian college. There was another thing I realized very quickly. The more I distanced myself from my family, the further inside the preserve I would be invited. If I could, as many before me seemed to have done, erase any echo of my origins, then I might be safer—though never fully without risk. If that was genius territory, it was lined with barbs and stony paths.

Do you know the lifeboat story? I've told it before. I will tell it again. It was one of the essential experiences of my education. It was raised in our freshman orientation class, a seminar in ethical values.

"There are twenty of you in a lifeboat," the lecturer began. Then he gave the list of the twenty—women and children and grown men and almost-grown adolescents, a preacher, a doctor, a nursing mother, an elderly woman, an elderly man. The list quickly became complicated and long. The essential fact was that there were too many for the boat to remain afloat. Worse, a storm was coming. If the load were lightened, then some might survive. If it were not lightened, all would die. This was the dilemma that we were given, an exercise we were to work out together.

As you do the exercise the task set begins to seem rational. But is it? Think about this problem as if it were true and real, as if these were events that you actually must endure or survive. You in your own body must decide if other living beings live or die. You must make moral choices. If you refuse to do anything, then everyone dies. If you select some to live and some to die, then you undertake to say who is worth saving and who is not—and you will have to carry the weight of those decisions.

Of course I understand what they thought the purpose of this exercise to be. In one sense it asks people to think seriously about their role in society, about who makes such judgments and who never gets to decide these things. If we are generous, we can say that such thinking tends toward the moral and the ethical. You define the good society by how you approach this dilemma. Choose or do not choose. Are you capable of deciding who is worth trying to save and who is not?

I understand what might have been meant by the original exercise. It was after all a small liberal arts college with a decidedly religious bent, a Presbyterian college. Back then the dominant liberal theory was situation ethics. This is the situation. Make your decisions. Accept your social responsibility. Making such brutal decisions requires thinking about the implications. Shouldn't we all be thinking about what standards are applied to who survives and who does not? In an ethical society are we not responsible for each other? The lifeboat brings this down to the most immediate and terrifying moment. Look to your left and your right—look at these people you know and those strangers. Some must be tossed over the side to save the rest. Who would you toss over and who would you save?

Is this not how the world works? Is this not, truly, how our lives are constructed? Who gets to go to school and who stays home? Who watches the babies while mama cleans houses and brings home leftover food to supplement the groceries she can buy? Who gets a scholarship? Who does not? Who gets into the drug trial for the new wonder drug that will stop the virus, shrink the tumor, keep that heart beating, those lungs pumping, make conception possible, or relieve the chronic pain? Who can hire a lawyer? Who can not? Who is pretty? Who is ugly? What is pretty? What is ugly? Who got through college on his daddy's money and his mama's ruthless campaign to get that arrest record erased? Who goes to rehab? Who dies of an overdose? Who decides? Who is responsible? Who is inherently valuable? Who can go over the side? Who will chose? I never forget the lifeboat.

These are mean questions, large questions. How we approach them reveals even more about us than how we answer them. But I am a storyteller, not a social scientist. I approach the lifeboat from my own angle.

At the National Book awards in 1992, I got to shake the hand of Ralph Ellison and be introduced to Toni Cade Bambara. They were sitting at the same table. The man nodded at me and the woman took my hand. I can still feel my giddy sense of unreality, my awe and fear.

"That quote from James Baldwin," Toni Cade Bambara said. "I had forgotten it until I saw it in the front of your book. It sent me back to the essays."

I stammered something, hesitant to speak at all. I had read *The Invisible Man* in college, but I had reread *The Salt Eaters* only a few months before. I could not quite get it in my head that I was standing there with people who had done work so wonderful. All I wanted was not to embarrass myself, but how could I say "I love your work" and not sound like a fool? I said it anyway. Ralph Ellison nodded mildly. Toni Cade Bambara smiled a small smile. All I could think was that I should have thought of something else to say.

Later as I was headed out a doorway, Toni Cade Bambara came up to me again and put her hand on my sleeve. "We should talk sometime," she said.

"I would like that," I replied.

The nod she gave me then was welcoming, the smile open and trustworthy. Still, it was two and a half years before we saw each other again—at a small college in New Hampshire for a gathering of women writers that Grace Paley had assembled. We wound up on two panels and did a reading together. She read from a story about some of the characters who had been in *The Salt Eaters.* I read a story pulled out of the first draft of *Cavedweller,* a prose poem about a mother's enormous sense of guilt and shame. After the reading when the conference was winding down, I met up with Toni Cade Bambara walking toward the Dartmouth Inn, and we finally had a minute to talk.

We started out on the subject of faith and the church, an embattled sense of faith on both our parts, a difficult relationship with any church. But we had both grown up to it, and she teased me about my preacher's cadences. I quoted back to her a few lines from the piece she had read earlier. The rhythms of the language were the same.

"We know who we are," she said with a laugh.

We did, I thought. But I can not say now how we got onto the subject of political activism, other than it was so much a part of both our lives. It had been what we had all been talking about over the two days of that gathering. Was there any way to be a woman writer in 1995 and not be an activist? Well, of course, there was. But was there any way we ourselves could write and not be activists? Of course, there was not. It was a select group, one constructed by the very astute Grace Paley. All of us believed that what we wrote challenged every notion this culture had of who and what we were supposed to be. That was inherently political even if we did not use the usual language of rhetoric. Black feminist, lesbian feminist, community activist, cultural warrior—sometimes the language for these categories seems grandiose, but not as large as what is meant by these labels.

Toni Cade Bambara told me she had been editing a videotape, and she didn't know when she was going to finish the book she had been writing for at least a decade. She hadn't been well this winter, she said. I nodded. I knew how that felt. I had been traveling from little college to little college, trying to write on airplanes and in hotels, always exhausted and guilty about not being home with my partner and son. Worse, I was pretty sure that the book I had started out to write was gone, and a completely different one was coming onto the page. I wasn't sure how I felt about that fact, could barely articulate it to myself, much less my editor or agent. I was able to say it to Toni Cade Bambara. We were talking as writers together, and my uncertainties were not so exceptional in that context.

It was storytelling we got onto—the drive toward storytelling, the feeling that there was no one else who would tell the particular stories we had to tell if we didn't. "There isn't," she said at one point. "Not like we do it," I agreed. "Not at all," she said. She did not smile when she said that.

For me the moment was wonderful—coda and completion to all the discussions of the weekend. The women who had read and argued and explained their own work had been passionately engaged in a way I believed writers should be engaged. It had seemed we were united in purpose and conviction, with work to do that pulled us toward the future. There was permission in that context to make mistakes, to be wrong and to go on anyway. I thought about the fragment that Toni Cade Bambara had read earlier that evening, the draft of a story she said she had not yet gotten quite right, the way she said she would get it right. She knew she would. That was a luxurious concept for me, the sense that the work was ongoing and would find its own rhythm. I wanted to believe that more strongly for myself. But it was late, and we were both tired. We would talk again, I said. Toni nodded and went on up the steps. This time I believed it. I looked forward to it.

Months later someone called and told me the news. Toni Cade Bambara was dead, of cancer, in Philadelphia. Most people hadn't even known she had cancer. I had not.

I was, of course, packing to leave for yet another small college. I sat down with the phone in my hand, stunned and grief-stricken. Had she known it was cancer that May evening in New Hampshire? Had she even imagined she might die so soon? I could not believe that was so. She had spoken so passionately about that video, the unfinished book. I looked for my copy of *The Sea Birds Are Still Alive* but could not find it. A few hours later I was on a plane and then, somewhere over Chicago, I started to cry. I had wanted to talk to her again. I had hoped someday to sit down with her for a full afternoon. There was a story I wanted to read to her, some notes I had made on her stories that I had planned to send her. There was a poem I had written when I read that story she called "Ice." There were questions I had not had a chance to ask.

Grief is a comfort when the loss is so great.

That next January I went back to Dartmouth. I wound up sleeping in my friend's basement office on a fold-out couch beneath ten feet of bookshelves. When I could not sleep, I read the titles on the shelves up one side and down the other. One-third down on the right was the spine of a well-worn copy of *This Bridge Called My Back.* I stood up with the quilt still wrapped around me and pulled it down. It had been years since I had last opened that book. This copy fell open to exactly the right page: Toni Cade Bambara's sharp and pointed comments on racism in the women's movement.

"When you leave, take your pictures with you."

I had forgotten that she had written for the anthology, forgotten how short and strong her piece was—as an introduction to the other essays and an invitation to work that needed to be done. What I remembered was the way she had looked when we read together, glowing with eagerness and passion, the way she had looked when we spoke after—exhausted but smiling. I remember the laugh with which she said, "We know who we are."

Grief is not enough when the loss is so great.

I read her short essay again, hearing in it her voice. There was that call to action, those words YOU WORK WITH WHAT YOU HAVE. It was something I might say. It is the legacy of girls raised to make do and make over.

There was the flat statement: "Guilt is not a feeling. It is an intellectual mask to a feeling." I curled up on the futon and nodded. Guilt gets in the way and stops us from acting when we most need to do something. I have a long list of times when guilt has gotten in my way. I read the closing paragraphs.

"Fear is a feeling—fear of losing one's power, fear of being accused, fear of a loss of status, control, knowledge. Fear is real. Possibly this is the emotional, non-theoretical place from which serious anti-racist work among white feminists can begin."

Then there was the demand to "use this knowledge" and the closing two lines.

"For we are all in the same boat. And it is sinking fast."

The lifeboat.

*Jump back.*

Wrapped in that quilt in that basement room, I went right back to being seventeen years old, right back to sitting in a small chapel on the campus of that lovely little college all those years ago. The professor was at the front of the room weaving his body from side to side, laughing, saying, "The wind is rising and the water is coming over the sides. What will you do? What will you do?"

I had been overwhelmingly self-conscious and terrified at seventeen. Fear was not a theoretical concept. It was the sour bile in the back of my throat, the cramping misery in my belly. What was the right choice? Was I supposed to be pragmatic? Should I look those people full in the face? Should I admit what I was really thinking?

I was thinking, "You go over the side, I am staying."

I was thinking, "This is my first damn time in the boat."

I was thinking, "If they knew who I really am, they would toss me right over the side."

There was the lifeboat—Toni Cade Bambara's lifeboat and my own. It was a cauldron of fear and guilt and shame and hope. We don't really have much choice about what we can write, I had said on one of those panels at the women writers' conference. There is always desperation in our lives, more to do than we can manage. There is always more to fight than we have any hope of changing, more contradictions and complications. We are always being asked to choose between one part of our lives and another, our families and our loves, our own lives and our hopes for our lives. It is always urgent, and the water is always pouring in on us.

I had not been thinking then back to when I had first gone off to college, to that place I had won by sheer persistence, luck, and a national merit scholarship. Now I did. I felt myself back in that place, sitting surrounded by the children of the middle and upper classes, girls who had never worked waitress, boys who had never been in a fight. I had hated being asked those questions in that company, hated being asked to pretend this was an exercise. It did not matter that I knew the reason for the exercise, what we were intellectually supposed to understand. I had stumbled into this territory. If I belonged there, then I had to think like a citizen.

Around me, the other students started making lists, determining value, choosing who would go over and who survive. I sat there with the blood pounding in my ears and thought about my mama with her cheap makeup and stubborn features, my sisters already mothers themselves and full of shadowy resentment and fear. It was plain to me how the world worked. There was no imaginary lifeboat. We were already drowning and had been doing so for generations.

I looked up at the professor. He was beaming with enthusiasm and excitement. Surely his enjoyment could not all be intellectual. Surely something else was going on. It had to be a trick question. Maybe we were supposed to refuse to do this. Maybe we were supposed to revolt. A truly moral ethical decision would be to refuse the parameters of the exercise. Maybe we were supposed to refuse to sacrifice some that others might live. I looked around at the other students, white cotton blouses and paisley skirts, blue jeans and plaid shirts—a genuine mix that I could not have predicted if my life depended on it. Who in that room would have spoken on my behalf? Even thirty years after the fact, that is a question I can not answer.

I told myself again that it had to be a trick, but I could not say that out loud. To the left and the right of me, the calculations were going on. Was a pregnant woman one life or two? Was the minister necessary? If he had been a doctor, maybe. An island, someone said. The lifeboat might make it to an island. There might need to be a new society and what would they need there? Women of childbearing age, someone answered.

What if they are lesbians, I wondered. What if the only way you will get children off those women is to rape them? I listened as those students measured out fate, hating them more with every moment. In my head the cadences of a gospel preacher began to boom, all hellfire and high righteousness. Would a just society demand that some die that others might live? Did it?

Curled up on the futon in that New Hampshire basement, I began to chew my nail. I had done the same thing in that chapel all those years ago, chewed my fingernails and refused to look up to meet anyone's eyes. In my head a train was pounding, a roar was booming, a loud angry voice was shouting.

Our fate was our fate. I knew that. No matter that there was a scale that would measure my sisters as more important than the girls sitting all around me. No matter that there had to be some system that would value my boy cousins over those boys—boys who had never been sick with fear or made to hate themselves for the family of their birth. I bit down to the quick, to the welcome taste of blood and outrage.

That is how it works, assigning value and measuring human worth. You choose your lifeboat and you defend your right to your own life. They had given us IQ tests in eighth grade and then had made me do mine again because, as I understood all too well, they did not believe my first score. I lifted my head and fought the urge to scream. If I had let that cry out, what would it have been? Would it have been the voice of a girl in terror or a woman who did not want to die?

Put me on the lifeboat lists. I am smarter than most of the children already in the boat. I am strong and stubborn and used to sacrifice. I am motivated, do not doubt it. Do you need my test scores? Do you need proof I am worthy? What list values my qualities? I had no rich mama or handsome daddy. What list condemns me? Will I be damned for my genetic tendencies toward alcoholism and substance abuse? Let us measure what we mean by worth. Is there such a thing? Do you believe in it? How then do you justify your life? Is that reason enough to barter my salvation? Growing up knowing myself held in contempt and refusing that contempt, does that prove my worth? Does my work buy me space in the boat, passage to the country of the safe? How is it I am to begin to believe that? Why is it only some of us feel driven to justify our lives? Why is it every day of my life I have felt myself back in that chapel with the water rising around me?

I hear the question that remains. What did you do, Dorothy, in answer to the lifeboat quiz? How did you answer the question when it was put to you? Oh, I would love to pretend I was brave and outraged. I would love to tell you how I stopped the exercise, how I rebelled and stormed and cursed people who could make such measurements, professors who could so completely disregard the horror of the dilemma. But that would be a lie, and all I have, as a storyteller, is my sense of truth. So no, I will not lie about this one. I said nothing. I did nothing. When I could, I went and hid in the bathroom. I think I threw up my lunch.

The lifeboat exercise required that I throw my mother and sisters over, and I could not do that—though I believed what was implicit in the lesson, that my own survival would depend on the destruction of others. If I had been strong, I should have stood up and screamed. Throw yourself over, I should have screamed. We will not be thrown over so easily. We will fight you and hate you and haunt your dreams forever. Measure us like stones, and we will fall on your head. Dismiss us like arithmetic, and we will count your days.

There is no lifeboat, and of course there is. The world is the lifeboat and some of us are already in the water. And yet we are in this thing together. Our world is not so small or embattled that we must become monsters just to keep a few afloat. This is what I should have said. Throw no one over. Leave no one behind. Earn your humanity. Behave as if each of us mattered—until you understand how true that is.

If I were free, if I believed myself fully a citizen of this country, perhaps I might have spoken those words. But at seventeen, I believed none of that. I was sure I was not free. I knew I was not welcome in the boat. That seemed to me to excuse me from thinking like everyone else in that room. I had the luxury of not feeling myself part of the decisions. I could hate those who would decide, and pretend that I was nothing like them, that I had no responsibility in the brutal equations going on all around me.

Freedom is the right and the responsibility to change the rules. Believing yourself a full partner in the society gives you the right to stand up and argue how that society will function. You might suggest we all take turns in the water, that we build bigger lifeboats or put more on board, or that we simply behave as if all of us must be saved or none. We could see how that changes the equations. We are free to make our world reflect our best convictions, not our most base pragmatism.

In the world as I choose to speak of it now, none of us is going down alone. We will all hold fast to each other—as I wish now I had held fast to Toni Cade Bambara that night in New Hampshire, followed her up the steps and said to her all the things I thought I would say some other time.

## THE TANNER LECTURERS

### 1976–77

OXFORD     Bernard Williams, Cambridge University

MICHIGAN     Joel Feinberg, University of Arizona
*"Voluntary Euthanasia and the Inalienable Right to Life"*

STANFORD     Joel Feinberg, University of Arizona
*"Voluntary Euthanasia and the Inalienable Right to Life"*

### 1977–78

OXFORD     John Rawls, Harvard University

MICHIGAN     Sir Karl Popper, University of London
*"Three Worlds"*

STANFORD     Thomas Nagel, Princeton University

### 1978–79

OXFORD     Thomas Nagel, Princeton University
*"The Limits of Objectivity"*

CAMBRIDGE     C. C. O'Brien, London

MICHIGAN     Edward O. Wilson, Harvard University
*"Comparative Social Theory"*

STANFORD     Amartya Sen, Oxford University
*"Equality of What?"*

UTAH     Lord Ashby, Cambridge University
*"The Search for an Environmental Ethic"*

UTAH STATE     R. M. Hare, Oxford University
*"Moral Conflicts"*

### 1979–80

OXFORD     Jonathan Bennett, University of British Columbia
*"Morality and Consequences"*

CAMBRIDGE     Raymond Aron, Collège de France
*"Arms Control and Peace Research"*

HARVARD     George Stigler, University of Chicago
*"Economics or Ethics?"*

MICHIGAN     Robert Coles, Harvard University
*"Children as Moral Observers"*

STANFORD    Michel Foucault, Collège de France
*"Omnes et Singulatim: Towards a Criticism of 'Political Reason' "*

UTAH    Wallace Stegner, Los Altos Hills, California
*"The Twilight of Self-Reliance: Frontier Values and Contemporary America"*

## 1980–81

OXFORD    Saul Bellow, University of Chicago
*"A Writer from Chicago"*

CAMBRIDGE    John Passmore, Australian National University
*"The Representative Arts as a Source of Truth"*

HARVARD    Brian M. Barry, University of Chicago
*"Do Countries Have Moral Obligations? The Case of World Poverty"*

MICHIGAN    John Rawls, Harvard University
*"The Basic Liberties and Their Priority"*

STANFORD    Charles Fried, Harvard University
*"Is Liberty Possible?"*

UTAH    Joan Robinson, Cambridge University
*"The Arms Race"*

HEBREW UNIV.    Solomon H. Snyder, Johns Hopkins University
*"Drugs and the Brain and Society"*

## 1981–82

OXFORD    Freeman Dyson, Princeton University
*"Bombs and Poetry"*

CAMBRIDGE    Kingman Brewster, President Emeritus, Yale University
*"The Voluntary Society"*

HARVARD    Murray Gell-Mann, California Institute of Technology
*"The Head and the Heart in Policy Studies"*

MICHIGAN    Thomas C. Schelling, Harvard University
*"Ethics, Law, and the Exercise of Self-Command"*

STANFORD    Alan A. Stone, Harvard University
*"Psychiatry and Morality"*

UTAH    R. C. Lewontin, Harvard University
*"Biological Determinism"*

AUSTRALIAN NATL. UNIV.    Leszek Kolakowski, Oxford University
*"The Death of Utopia Reconsidered"*

## 1982–83

OXFORD    Kenneth J. Arrow, Stanford University
*"The Welfare-Relevant Boundaries of the Individual"*

| CAMBRIDGE | H. C. Robbins Landon, University College, Cardiff<br>*"Haydn and Eighteenth-Century Patronage in Austria and Hungary"* |
|---|---|
| HARVARD | Bernard Williams, Cambridge University<br>*"Morality and Social Justice"* |
| STANFORD | David Gauthier, University of Pittsburgh<br>*"The Incompleat Egoist"* |
| UTAH | Carlos Fuentes, Princeton University<br>*"A Writer from Mexico"* |
| JAWAHARLAL NEHRU UNIV. | Ilya Prigogine, Université Libre de Bruxelles<br>*"Only an Illusion"* |

## 1983–84

| OXFORD | Donald D. Brown, Johns Hopkins University<br>*"The Impact of Modern Genetics"* |
|---|---|
| CAMBRIDGE | Stephen J. Gould, Harvard University<br>*"Evolutionary Hopes and Realities"* |
| MICHIGAN | Herbert A. Simon, Carnegie-Mellon University<br>*"Scientific Literacy as a Goal in a High-Technology Society"* |
| STANFORD | Leonard B. Meyer, University of Pennsylvania<br>*"Music and Ideology in the Nineteenth Century"* |
| UTAH | Helmut Schmidt, former Chancellor, West Germany<br>*"The Future of the Atlantic Alliance"* |
| HELSINKI | Georg Henrik von Wright, Helsinki<br>*"Of Human Freedom"* |

## 1984–85

| OXFORD | Barrington Moore, Jr., Harvard University<br>*"Authority and Inequality under Capitalism and Socialism"* |
|---|---|
| CAMBRIDGE | Amartya Sen, Oxford University<br>*"The Standard of Living"* |
| HARVARD | Quentin Skinner, Cambridge University<br>*"The Paradoxes of Political Liberty"* |
| | Kenneth J. Arrow, Stanford University<br>*"The Unknown Other"* |
| MICHIGAN | Nadine Gordimer, South Africa<br>*"The Essential Gesture: Writers and Responsibility"* |
| STANFORD | Michael Slote, University of Maryland<br>*"Moderation, Rationality, and Virtue"* |

## 1985–86

| OXFORD | Thomas M. Scanlon, Jr., Harvard Univesity<br>*"The Significance of Choice"* |
|---|---|

CAMBRIDGE       Aldo Van Eyck, The Netherlands
                *"Architecture and Human Values"*

HARVARD         Michael Walzer, Institute for Advanced Study
                *"Interpretation and Social Criticism"*

MICHIGAN        Clifford Geertz, Institute for Advanced Study
                *"The Uses of Diversity"*

STANFORD        Stanley Cavell, Harvard University
                *"The Uncanniness of the Ordinary"*

UTAH            Arnold S. Relman, Editor, *New England Journal of Medicine*
                *"Medicine as a Profession and a Business"*

## 1986–87

OXFORD          Jon Elster, Oslo University and the University of Chicago
                *"Taming Chance: Randomization in Individual and Social
                Decisions"*

CAMBRIDGE       Roger Bulger, University of Texas Health Sciences Center,
                Houston
                *"On Hippocrates, Thomas Jefferson, and Max Weber: The
                Bureaucratic, Technologic Imperatives and the Future of the
                Healing Tradition in a Voluntary Society"*

HARVARD         Jürgen Habermas, University of Frankfurt
                *"Law and Morality"*

MICHIGAN        Daniel C. Dennett, Tufts University
                *"The Moral First Aid Manual"*

STANFORD        Gisela Striker, Columbia University
                *"Greek Ethics and Moral Theory"*

UTAH            Laurence H. Tribe, Harvard University
                *"On Reading the Constitution"*

## 1987–88

OXFORD          F. Van Zyl Slabbert, University of the Witwatersrand, South
                Africa
                *"The Dynamics of Reform and Revolt in Current South Africa"*

CAMBRIDGE       Louis Blom-Cooper, Q.C., London
                *"The Penalty of Imprisonment"*

HARVARD         Robert A. Dahl, Yale University
                *"The Pseudodemocratization of the American Presidency"*

MICHIGAN        Albert O. Hirschman, Institute for Advanced Study
                *"Two Hundred Years of Reactionary Rhetoric: The Case of the
                Perverse Effect"*

STANFORD        Ronald Dworkin, New York University and University
                College, Oxford
                *"Foundations of Liberal Equality"*

UTAH    Joseph Brodsky, Russian poet, Mount Holyoke College
*"A Place as Good as Any"*

CALIFORNIA    Wm. Theodore de Bary, Columbia University
*"The Trouble with Confucianism"*

BUENOS AIRES  Barry Stroud, University of California, Berkeley
*"The Study of Human Nature and the Subjectivity of Value"*

MADRID    Javier Muguerza, Universidad Nacional de Educación a
        Distancia, Madrid
*"The Alternative of Dissent"*

WARSAW    Anthony Quinton, British Library, London
*"The Varieties of Value"*

## 1988–89

OXFORD    Michael Walzer, Institute for Advanced Study
*"Nation and Universe"*

CAMBRIDGE    Albert Hourani, Emeritus Fellow, St. Antony's College, and
        Magdalen College, Oxford
*"Islam in European Thought"*

MICHIGAN    Toni Morrison, State University of New York at Albany
*"Unspeakable Things Unspoken: The Afro-American Presence in
    American Literature"*

STANFORD    Stephen Jay Gould, Harvard University
*"Unpredictability in the History of Life"*
*"The Quest for Human Nature: Fortuitous Side, Consequences, and
    Contingent History"*

UTAH    Judith Shklar, Harvard University
*"Amerian Citizenship: The Quest for Inclusion"*

CALIFORNIA    S. N. Eisenstadt, The Hebrew University of Jerusalem
*"Cultural Tradition, Historical Experience, and Social Change:
    The Limits of Convergence"*

YALE    J. G. A. Pocock, Johns Hopkins University
*"Edward Gibbon in History: Aspects of the Text in* The History
    of the Decline and Fall of the Roman Empire"

CHINESE
UNIVERSITY OF
HONG KONG  Fei Xiaotong, Peking University
*"Plurality and Unity in the Configuration of the Chinese People"*

## 1989–90

OXFORD    Bernard Lewis, Princeton University
*"Europe and Islam"*

CAMBRIDGE    Umberto Eco, University of Bologna
*"Interpretation and Overinterpretation: World, History, Texts"*

HARVARD       Ernest Gellner, Kings College, Cambridge
              *"The Civil and the Sacred"*

MICHIGAN      Carol Gilligan, Harvard University
              *"Joining the Resistance: Psychology, Politics, Girls, and Women"*

UTAH          Octavio Paz, Mexico City
              *"Poetry and Modernity"*

YALE          Edward N. Luttwak, Center for Strategic and International
                 Studies
              *"Strategy: A New Era?"*

PRINCETON     Irving Howe, writer and critic
              *"The Self and the State"*

## 1990–91

OXFORD        David Montgomery, Yale University
              *"Citizenship and Justice in the Lives and Thoughts of Nineteenth-
                 Century American Workers"*

CAMBRIDGE     Gro Harlem Brundtland, Prime Minister of Norway
              *"Environmental Challenges of the 1990s: Our Responsibility
                 toward Future Generations"*

HARVARD       William Gass, Washington University
              *"Eye and Idea"*

MICHIGAN      Richard Rorty, University of Virginia
              *"Feminism and Pragmatism"*

STANFORD      G. A. Cohen, All Souls College, Oxford
              *"Incentives, Inequality, and Community"*

              János Kornai, University of Budapest and Harvard
                 University
              *"Market Socialism Revisited"*

UTAH          Marcel Ophuls, international film maker
              *"Resistance and Collaboration in Peacetime"*

YALE          Robertson Davies, novelist
              *"Reading and Writing"*

PRINCETON     Annette C. Baier, Pittsburgh University
              *"Trust"*

LENINGRAD     János Kornai, University of Budapest and Harvard
                 University
              *"Transition from Marxism to a Free Economy"*

## 1991–92

OXFORD        R. Z. Sagdeev, University of Maryland
              *"Science and Revolutions"*

CALIFORNIA
  LOS ANGELES Václav Havel, former President, Republic of Czechoslovakia
              (Untitled lecture)

| | |
|---|---|
| BERKELEY | Helmut Kohl, Chancellor of Germany<br>(Untitled lecture) |
| CAMBRIDGE | David Baltimore, former President of Rockefeller University<br>*"On Doing Science in the Modern World"* |
| MICHIGAN | Christopher Hill, seventeenth-century historian, Oxford<br>*"The Bible in Seventeenth-Century English Politics"* |
| STANFORD | Charles Taylor, Professor of Philosophy and Political Science,<br>    McGill University<br>*"Modernity and the Rise of the Public Sphere"* |
| UTAH | Jared Diamond, University of California, Los Angeles<br>*"The Broadest Pattern of Human History"* |
| PRINCETON | Robert Nozick, Professor of Philosophy, Harvard University<br>*"Decisions of Principle, Principles of Decision"* |

## 1992–93

| | |
|---|---|
| MICHIGAN | Amos Oz, Israel<br>*"The Israeli-Palestinian Conflict: Tragedy, Comedy, and Cognitive<br>    Block—A Storyteller's Point of View"* |
| CAMBRIDGE | Christine M. Korsgaard, Harvard University<br>*"The Sources of Normativity"* |
| UTAH | Evelyn Fox Keller, Massachusetts Institute of Technology<br>*"Rethinking the Meaning of Genetic Determinism"* |
| YALE | Fritz Stern, Columbia University<br>*"Mendacity Enforced: Europe, 1914–1989"*<br>*"Freedom and Its Discontents: Postunification Germany"* |
| PRINCETON | Stanley Hoffmann, Harvard University<br>*"The Nation, Nationalism, and After: The Case of France"* |
| STANFORD | Colin Renfrew, Cambridge University<br>*"The Archaeology of Identity"* |

## 1993–94

| | |
|---|---|
| MICHIGAN | William Julius Wilson, University of Chicago<br>*"The New Urban Poverty and the Problem of Race"* |
| OXFORD | Lord Slynn of Hadley, London<br>*"Law and Culture—A European Setting"* |
| HARVARD | Lawrence Stone, Princeton University<br>*"Family Values in a Historical Perspective"* |
| CAMBRIDGE | Peter Brown, Princeton University<br>*"Aspects of the Christianisation of the Roman World"* |
| UTAH | A. E. Dick Howard, University of Virginia<br>*"Toward the Open Society in Central and Eastern Europe"* |
| | Jeffrey Sachs, Harvard University<br>*"Shock Therapy in Poland: Perspectives of Five Years"* |

| UTAH | Adam Zagajewski, Paris<br>*"A Bus Full of Prophets: Adventures of the Eastern-European Intelligentsia"* |
| PRINCETON | Alasdair MacIntyre, Duke University<br>*"Truthfulness, Lies, and Moral Philosophers: What Can We Learn from Mill and Kant?"* |
| CALIFORNIA | Oscar Arias, Costa Rica<br>*"Poverty: The New International Enemy"* |
| STANFORD | Thomas Hill, University of North Carolina at Chapel Hill<br>*"Basic Respect and Cultural Diversity"*<br>*"Must Respect Be Earned?"* |
| UC SAN DIEGO | K. Anthony Appiah, Harvard University<br>*"Race, Culture, Identity: Misunderstood Connections"* |

## 1994–95

| YALE | Richard Posner, United States Court of Appeals<br>*"Euthanasia and Health Care: Two Essays on the Policy Dilemmas of Aging and Old Age"* |
| MICHIGAN | Daniel Kahneman, University of California, Berkeley<br>*"Cognitive Psychology of Consequences and Moral Intuition"* |
| HARVARD | Cass R. Sunstein, University of Chicago<br>*"Political Conflict and Legal Agreement"* |
| CAMBRIDGE | Roger Penrose, Oxford Mathematics Institute<br>*"Space-time and Cosmology"* |
| PRINCETON | Antonin Scalia, United States Supreme Court<br>*"Common-Law Courts in a Civil-Law System: The Role of the United States Federal Courts in Interpreting the Constitution and Laws"* |
| UC SANTA CRUZ | Nancy Wexler, Columbia University<br>*"Genetic Prediction and Precaution Confront Human Social Values"* |
| OXFORD | Janet Suzman, South Africa<br>*"Who Needs Parables?"* |
| STANFORD | Amy Gutmann, Princeton University<br>*"Responding to Racial Injustice"* |
| UTAH | Edward Said, Columbia University<br>*"On Lost Causes"* |

## 1995–96

| PRINCETON | Harold Bloom, Yale University<br>I. *"Shakespeare and the Value of Personality,"* and<br>II. *"Shakespeare and the Value of Love"* |

| OXFORD | Simon Schama, Columbia University<br>*"Rembrandt and Rubens: Humanism, History, and the Peculiarity*<br>    *of Painting"* |
|---|---|
| CAMBRIDGE | Gunther Schuller, Newton Center, Massachusetts<br>I. *"Jazz: A Historical Perspective,"* II. *"Duke Ellington,"* and<br>    III. *"Charles Mingus"* |
| UC<br>RIVERSIDE | Mairead Corrigan Maguire, Belfast, Northern Ireland<br>*"Peacemaking from the Grassroots in a World of Ethnic Conflict"* |
| HARVARD | Onora O'Neill, Newham College, Cambridge<br>*"Kant on Reason and Religion"* |
| STANFORD | Nancy Fraser, New School for Social Research<br>*"Social Justice in the Age of Identity Politics: Redistribution,*<br>    *Recognition, and Participation"* |
| UTAH | Cornell West, Harvard University<br>*"A Genealogy of the Public Intellectual"* |
| YALE | Peter Brown, Princeton University<br>*"The End of the Ancient Other World: Death and Afterlife between*<br>    *Late Antiquity and the Early Middle Ages"* |

## 1996–97

| TORONTO | Peter Gay, Emeritus, Yale University<br>*"The Living Enlightenment"* |
|---|---|
| MICHIGAN | Thomas M. Scanlon, Harvard University<br>*"The Status of Well-Being"* |
| HARVARD | Stuart Hampshire, Emeritus, Stanford University<br>*"Justice Is Conflict: The Soul and the City"* |
| CAMBRIDGE | Dorothy L. Cheney, University of Pennsylvania<br>*"Why Animals Don't Have Language"* |
| PRINCETON | Robert M. Solow, Massachusetts Institute of Technology<br>*"Welfare and Work"* |
| CALIFORNIA | Marian Wright Edelman, Children's Defense Fund<br>*"Standing for Children"* |
| YALE | Liam Hudson, Balas Copartnership<br>*"The Life of the Mind"* |
| STANFORD | Barbara Herman, University of California, Los Angeles<br>*"Moral Literacy"* |
| OXFORD | Francis Fukuyama, George Mason University<br>*"Social Capital"* |
| UTAH | Elaine Pagels, Princeton University<br>*"The Origin of Satan in Christian Traditions"* |

## 1997–98

UTAH            Jonathan D. Spence, Yale University
                *"Ideas of Power: China's Empire in the Eighteenth Century and To-
                day"*

PRINCETON       J. M. Coetzee, University of Cape Town
                *"The Lives of Animals"*

MICHIGAN        Antonio R. Damasio, University of Iowa
                *"Exploring the Minded Brain"*

CHARLES
UNIVERSITY      Timothy Garton Ash, Oxford University
                *"The Direction of European History"*

HARVARD         M. F. Burnyeat, Oxford University
                *"Culture and Society in Plato's* Republic*"*

CAMBRIDGE       Stephen Toulmin, University of Southern California
                *"The Idol of Stability"*

UC IRVINE       David Kessler, Yale University
                *"Tobacco Wars: Risks and Rewards of a Major Challenge"*

YALE            Elaine Scarry, Harvard University
                *"On Beauty and Being Just"*

STANFORD        Arthur Kleinman, Harvard University
                *"Experience and Its Moral Modes: Culture, Human Conditions,
                and Disorder"*

## 1998–99

MICHIGAN        Walter Burkert, University of Zurich
                *"Revealing Nature Amidst Multiple Cultures: A Discourse with
                Ancient Greeks"*

UTAH            Geoffrey Hartman, Yale University
                *"Text and Spirit"*

YALE            Steven Pinker, Massachusetts Institute of Technology
                *"The Blank Slate, the Noble Savage, and the Ghost in the
                Machine"*

STANFORD        Randall Kennedy, Harvard University
                *"Who Can Say 'Nigger'? . . . and Other Related Questions"*

UC DAVIS        Richard White, Stanford University
                *"The Problem with Purity"*

OXFORD          Sidney Verba, Harvard University
                *"Representative Democracy and Democratic Citizens: Philosophical
                and Empirical Understandings"*

PRINCETON       Judith Jarvis Thomson, Massachusetts Institute of
                Technology
                *"Goodness and Advice"*

HARVARD         Lani Guinier, Harvard University
                *"Rethinking Powers"*

## 1999–2000

YALE
Marina Warner, London
*"Spirit Visions"*

MICHIGAN
Helen Vendler, Harvard University
*"Poetry and the Mediation of Value: Whitman on Lincoln"*

HARVARD
Wolf Lepenies, Free University, Berlin
*"The End of 'German Culture'"*

CAMBRIDGE
Jonathan Lear, University of Chicago
*"Happiness"*

OXFORD
Geoffrey Hill, Boston University
*"Rhetorics of Value"*

PRINCETON
Michael Ignatieff, London
*"Human Rights as Politics"* and *"Human Rights as Idolatry"*

UNIVERSITY
OF UTAH
Charles Rosen, New York
*"Tradition without Convention: The Impossible Nineteenth-
　　Century Project"*

STANFORD
Jared Diamond, UCLA Medical School
*"Ecological Collapses of Pre-industrial Societies"*

## 2000–2001

MICHIGAN
Partha Dasgupta, Cambridge University
*"Valuing Objects and Evaluating Policies in Imperfect Economies"*

HARVARD
Simon Schama, Columbia University
*"Random Access Memory"*

UC SANTA
BARBARA
William C. Richardson, The Kellogg Foundation
*"Reconceiving Health Care to Improve Quality"*

OXFORD
Sir Sydney Kentridge Q.C., London
*"Human Rights: A Sense of Proportion"*

UTAH
Sarah Blaffer Hrdy, University of California at Davis
*"The Past and Present of the Human Family"*

UC BERKELEY
Joseph Raz, Columbia University
*"The Practice of Value"*

PRINCETON
Robert Pinsky, poet, Boston University
*"American Culture and the Voice of Poetry"*

YALE
Alexander Nehamas, Princeton University
*"A Promise of Happiness: The Place of Beauty in a World of Art"*

CAMBRIDGE
Kwame Anthony Appiah, Harvard University
*"Individuality and Identity"*

STANFORD
Dorothy Allison, novelist
*"Mean Stories and Stubborn Girls"* and
　　*"What It Means to Be Free"*